Frederic May Holland

The rise of Intellectual Liberty from Thales to Copernicus

Frederic May Holland

The rise of Intellectual Liberty from Thales to Copernicus

ISBN/EAN: 9783337365783

Printed in Europe, USA, Canada, Australia, Japan

Cover: Foto ©Thomas Meinert / pixelio.de

More available books at **www.hansebooks.com**

THE RISE

OF

INTELLECTUAL LIBERTY

FROM THALES TO COPERNICUS

BY

FREDERIC MAY HOLLAND

AUTHOR OF "THE REIGN OF THE STOICS," "STORIES FROM ROBERT BROWNING," ETC.

NEW YORK
HENRY HOLT AND COMPANY
1885

PREFACE.

Wishing to show how thought was set free and new truth brought to light, during the twenty-two hundred years from the age of Thales to that of Copernicus and Servetus, I have tried to collect the important facts, especially such as had not been stated in English, to arrange them in their historic relations, not yet fully delineated in any language, and then to let them tell their own story, without needless comment. I did not start with the intention of proving any thing; and it was only when I was ready to write the last chapter, that I found myself justified in drawing the conclusions set forth. Authorities differ widely, especially about medieval history, and dates of publication are often given incorrectly—that, for instance of the *Involuntary Servitude* by La Boëtie being put in half-a-dozen different years by as many of the standard books of reference. Oversights are almost unavoidable in any comprehensive work, and I shall be grateful for help in correcting my own, but I trust I shall not be hastily charged with inaccuracy on account of not having followed a popular guide. I hope ere long to publish a continuation extending as far as the French Revolution.

F. M. H.

Concord, Mass., Nov., 1884.

TABLE OF CONTENTS.

CHAPTER I. EARLY PHILOSOPHY.

		PAGE
Introduction		1
I.	The Buddha and other Prophets...	1
II.	The Ionians	3
III.	Persecution at Athens	7
IV.	Socrates	16
V.	Plato	24
VI.	Other Disciples of Socrates	28
VII.	Aristotle	32
VIII.	Conclusion	35

CHAPTER II. THE CONQUEST OF PAGANISM DURING THE LAST THREE CENTURIES, B. C.

Introduction		36
I.	Pyrrho and the New Academy	36
II.	The Stoics	38
III.	Epicurus	41
IV.	Lucretius	51
V.	Science	57
VI.	Victory	59

CHAPTER III. PARTIALLY SUCCESSFUL ATTEMPTS AT REACTION DURING THE FIRST TWO HUNDRED YEARS OF THE ROMAN EMPIRE.

I.	The Policy of Augustus	61
II.	Jesus	65
III.	The Stoic Martyrs	70
IV.	The Emancipation of Women	76
V.	The New Testament	78
VI.	The Early Christians	82

		PAGE
VII.	Reign of Liberal Paganism	85
VIII.	Lucian	91
IX.	Conclusion	95

CHAPTER IV. THE SUPPRESSION OF FREE THOUGHT AND ESTABLISHMENT OF CHRISTIANITY.

I.	Tertullian	97
II.	The Alexandrians and their Pupils, including Zenobia	101
III.	The Decline of the Empire, the Result of Despotism	106
IV.	The Establishment of Christianity	109
V.	Triumph of Bigotry	119
VI.	General Survey of Classical Thought	122

CHAPTER V. EARLY MEDIEVAL HERESY.

I.	Rationalists before A. D. 1,000	126
II.	Berengar, Roscellin and the Catharists	131
III.	Other Early Agitators	140
IV.	Abelard and Heloise	144
V.	Averroes and Maimonides	153
VI.	Waldenses and Mystics	154
VII.	Conclusion	158

CHAPTER VI. SUPPRESSION OF HERESY, DUALISM AND PERSECUTION OF MYSTICISM AND SCHOLARSHIP IN THE THIRTEENTH CENTURY.

I.	The Situation	162
II.	The Crusade against Tolerance	164
III.	The Destruction of Catharism by the Inquisition	169
IV.	The Persecution of Mysticism	174
V.	Satirists and Rationalists	178
VI.	Royal and Popular Resistance to Oppression	185
VII.	Summary	196

CHAPTER VII. THE REVOLT OF FRANCE AND GERMANY IN THE FOURTEENTH CENTURY.

I.	The Situation	200
II.	Philip and Boniface	201
III.	The Templars	208
IV.	Dolcino	211
V.	Dante	213
VI.	The Mystics	220
VII.	Louis of Bavaria	230
VIII.	Other Opponents of the Papacy before 1360	233
IX.	Summary	238

CONTENTS.

	PAGE.
CHAPTER VIII. OPPOSITION IN NAME OF BIBLE AND COUNCILS, 1360 TO 1450.	
I. Introduction	241
II. Wycliffe and his followers	241
III. The Bohemians	251
IV. The Great Councils	257
V. Joan of Arc and other Mystics	261
VI. Retrospect over Medieval History	268

CHAPTER IX. THE REVIVAL OF LEARNING, LITERATURE, AND ART, 1450 TO 1517.

I. The Revival of Letters	275
II. Leonardo da Vinci, Machiavelli, and Pomponatius	283
III. Art and other Secular Influences in Italy	292
IV. The Northern Renaissance	298
V. Satirists	305
VI. Savonarola and the German Mystics	319
VII. Summary	325

CHAPTER X. THE REFORMATION.

I. The Situation	327
II. The Establishment of Protestantism	328
III. Erasmus and other Liberal Catholics	336
IV. Copernicus and other Practical Reformers	342
V. Rabelais and other Nominal Catholics	352
VI. Servetus and other Liberal Protestants	362
VII. Unbelievers in Christianity	376
VIII. Summary	380

CHAPTER XI. CONCLUSION.

Harmonious Movements	385
Growth of Tolerance	387
Emancipation of Women	389
Political Liberty	391
Book Men	393
Causes of Conservatism	397
Morality of Unbelievers	399
Happiness	401

CHAPTER I.

EARLY PHILOSOPHY.

Five and twenty centuries ago, scarcely any man rose above the station in which he was born. Few could choose even what to do, much less what to think. There were no teachers but the priests. Urgent business was constantly delayed, and atrocious crimes instigated, by dread of signs and omens. All the keys of knowledge were in hands busy with slaying sacrifices, pointing out auguries, and collecting fees. Rulers, priests, and people worked together to keep things as they were, and make every one think and act alike. The establishment of order had been necessary for social existence, but there was constant danger of the stagnation that always breeds corruption.

That the earth is brighter and richer to-day than it was then is largely due to men and women who toiled and died to stir up mental activity and encourage individuality. Widely different beliefs and unbeliefs have worked together in the rise of Intellectual Liberty! What its early champions wrote and suffered, and how their exertions are connected with other forces, is here told up to the time when its worst enemy was crippled by the Reformation, when Copernicus made possible a rational view of the Universe, and when the murder of Servetus called out a mighty protest against intolerance.

I.

The oldest denunciations of despotism and conventionalism which have come down to us, are those of the Hebrew prophets. History can show few grander figures than those of Moses before Pharaoh and Elijah on Mount Carmel; nor has the superior holiness of morality above ceremony, a truth incompatible with the authority of priests, ever been set forth more fearlessly than by Amos,

Hosea, Isaiah, Micah, and Jeremiah. These great men, however, were too intolerant, as well as too desirous of supernatural inspiration to be classed among rationalists, though these latter have often been aided by their example.

So also it was in the name of special revelation, rather than of reason, that the great emancipation from Brahmin despotism was achieved by that glorious liberator who called himself the Buddha, or Enlightened, and whose existence is beyond all question, though his biography is full of fables, and his death is put at various dates from 2422 to 400 B. C. His adherents were probably those mendicant monks and nuns whose opposition to Brahminism in Western India was noticed about 300 B. C. by the Greek ambassador, Megasthenes. Buddhism appears also to have prevailed in Bactria, while this country was under Grecian Kings. There is plainly mention of the Buddha and his mother by Clement of Alexandria, who shows that Hindoo thought was known to Alexander Polyhistor, an Ephesian or Phrygian scholar who lived nearly a century earlier than Jesus. That the author of the *Sermon on the Mount* was under the influence of the *Dhammapada*, or *Path of Virtue*, is not improbable, since these two works agree in holding such views of poverty and non-resistance as are not at all Hebraic. And Buddhism is certainly to be honored for that fearless opposition to priestly tyranny which has caused it, despite its recognizing no book as infallible, to be called the Protestantism of the East, for that emancipation of morality from theology which has enabled thousands of millions to live in virtue and happiness, and finally for that unexampled tolerance, which makes this the only religion not known to have stained itself with systematic persecution for differences in belief, and which led the great monarch of all India, Asoka, who first made this a state-religion, about 250 B. C., to practice such toleration as was scarcely known in Christendom before the present century. The more men have thought they knew about the Incomprehensible, the less they have hesitated about murdering any one who would not accept their creed.

Modern Buddhism has its superstitions, and its monks, nuns, and priests; but they are kept from much temptation by their freedom to leave their order at pleasure; and while in it, they teach the people so faithfully, that Mrs. Leonowens says, there is scarcely a man or woman in Siam who cannot read and write. (*The English Governess*, p. 78). Still this hierarchy, like all others, has little sympathy with science or advanced thought. Buddhism has been a great help to Ceylon, Burmah, Siam, China, Thibet, and Japan; but, as these countries advance, it must be left behind and pass away. It has done the world inestimable service by preaching and practicing self-control, but it has done very little in comparison to promote self-culture.

Neither the Buddha nor the Hebrew prophets appealed so directly to the authority of reason as Kapila is said to have done in founding the Sankhya philosophy in India; but we know little of this last system, except that it has had scarcely any influence on Western thought.

II.

Europe did receive its first light from Asia, but it was not from the valley of the Ganges. On the shores of the Ægean, the birthplace of Homer, Æsop, Herodotus, and Apelles, the cradle of liberty, the center of art and commerce, in a land still noted for its climate and its scenery, dwelt the first men who are known to have loved truth for its own sake, and to have sought to explain natural phenomena rationally. There, about 600 B. C., was founded the Ionic school of philosophy, by Thales, one of the seven wise men, and father of Grecian astronomy. He left nothing in writing, and it is doubtful how much truth there is in the reports that he traveled in search of knowledge to Egypt, and there measured the height of a pyramid, that he found out the number of days in the solar year, that he suspected the rotundity of our earth, that he foretold an eclipse, and that he knew that moonlight comes from the sun. He seems, at all events, to have taught that the earth with all her forms of life developed herself out of water which he called the source of all things, and to have maintained that the sun, moon, and stars, which the Greeks worshiped as deities, were only masses of matter like our earth. The same love of liberty, which led him to place himself in this opposition to the prevalent theology, is also shown in his defending the independence of Ionia against Crœsus, and in such sayings as that, the most dangerous of wild beasts are the tyrants. Nearly as early as Thales and in the same city, Miletus, lived Anaximander, said to have been the first to write about philosophy, to draw maps, to make hydraulic clocks, to introduce sun-dials, and to try to calculate the sizes and distances of the sun, moon, and planets, which, as well as our earth, he said, had formed themselves out of chaos, and would return thither again. He also taught that all land animals had been evolved out of marine ones, and that all creatures, even human beings, would finally resolve themselves into the chaotic mass, out of which they arose. Thus Anaximander may be called the "earliest evolutionist." Similar views of the self-developing powers of matter and the finite nature of man were held soon afterwards by another Milesian, Anaximenes, who distinguished himself by his efforts to overthrow the popular belief, that rain, lightning, earthquakes, etc., are supernatural. Hippo, of Samos, the first Greek who denied the existence of the national gods, is also placed among the Ionic philosophers.

This term is not however applied to a much more famous Samian, Pythagoras, who was so far from being a liberator as to found a despotic and aristocratic secret society, soon broken up by popular indignation, under which he perished. His wife, Theano, was the first woman to write about philosophy. In Ionia was also born Xenophanes, who boasted that he was no man's pupil, and who wandered, chanting his own verses, until he made his way to the Italian city from whose name he and his disciples are called Eleatics. They did not study physical phenomena, like the Ionians, but logical subtleties; and they attached much less value to the testimony of the senses, than to the conclusions of the unaided reason. This way of thinking, which has since prevailed among metaphysicians, soon led to utter uncertainty of opinion, as was particularly the case with Parmenides, hero of one of Plato's dialogues, and as much noted for his virtues as his doubts.

The Zeno, who died bravely in trying to free Elea from the tyranny of Nearchus, also belonged to this school, whose skeptical position he strengthened with some famous paradoxes, for instance that of Achilles and the tortoise. None of the literary productions of the Eleatics, not even the declaration of Melissus, that nothing can be known about the gods, became so famous, however, as the verses of Xenophanes, who thought that all things and beings were joined together, so as to form,

"God, who is One, and the greatest of beings divine, and resembles neither in body us mortals, nor spirit."

And among other fragments of the oldest of philosophic poems are these:

"Not from the first did the gods reveal to us knowledge of all things,
Only in process of time, does research give us truth in her fullness."

* * * * * * *

"Foolishly men have supposed that the gods are born like us mortals,
Having their garments like ours, and with human voices and figures.
Give to the lions, horses, and oxen, fingers and hands like
Ours, then oxen would paint their gods in the likeness of oxen,
Horses too, give their deities, bodies like those of the horses."

* * * * * * *

"Deeds of the gods are narrated by Homer and Hesiod, also,
Which would be shame and abiding disgrace unto any poor mortal,
Theft and deceit and adultery, acts above all most unrighteous."

A generation later than Xenophanes, and in the great Ionic city of Ephesus, lived Heraclitus the Obscure, who long afterwards was erroneously termed "The Weeping Philosopher." He seems to have been the first to teach that all natural phenomena take place necessarily, that is according to fixed laws, independent of supernatural control, and to denounce the current belief in lucky and unlucky days, the orgies in honor of Bacchus, the worship of idols, and even the offering of sacrifices, in regard to which he says that a man might as well think he could wash his body with mud, as that blood would purify his soul. He held that all things are in continual motion and development, so that it may with equal truth be said that they are, and that they are not. Thus he may be regarded as the forerunner of Hegel, but he differed from this German in teaching that not only the sun, moon, and stars, the plants, animals, and various parts of our earth, but even the souls of men, are only the changing forms of the all-animating and all-composing vital heat. Here he resembled the Ionic philosophers, among whom he is ranked by some high authorities; but he should rather be placed midway between this school and the Elean, for while giving more authority than these latter did to the senses he yet attributed the power of reaching the highset truth to the reason acting independently of sensation. Among his extant sayings are these: "No man can bathe twice in the same stream," "War is the father of all things," "A man's character is his destiny," "The world was not created by any God or man, but has always existed, and always will exist, an ever-living fire."

Our list of early philosophers, outside of Athens, must close with two Sicilian poets of the fifth century B. C., Empedocles and Epicharmus. The former was noted for his devotion to popular liberty, his generous philanthropy, his opposition to anthropomorphism, and his knowledge of medicine, meteorology and other sciences, in studying which he seems to have perished by an eruption of Ætna. He is also famous for his theory of the origin of all things out of the spontaneous attraction and repulsion of the four elements, earth, air, water, and fire, which at first produced only ephemeral monsters, but gradually developed forms more and more fitted for survival, and finally created man. Epicharmus, who like Empedocles had studied among the Pythagoreans, was one of the earliest writers of comedy, and took particular pains to make the gods and sacred heroes ridiculous, as well as to represent religion arising out of the deification of natural forces.

These primitive philosophers had not the scientific apparatus, the society of fellow-students, and the light of past experience necessary for sure knowledge of truth, but their crude fancies had such originality and independence as opened the way for better work. That there was no persecution in Ionia may be attributed to the early date at which this country passed under the sway of the Persians, who hated idolatry, polytheism, and anthropomorphism, and who worshiped nothing but fire, a position curiously resembling that of Heraclitus. Xenophanes taught among Ionian colonists whose mental habits were so similar to his own that he founded a school of disciples; and Empedocles was deservedly popular on account of his great services to liberty and his generous use of his rare medical skill and vast wealth.

III.

The first city within the present limits of Greece to welcome the new views was Athens, where Æschylus was allowed to represent the supreme Deity as the oppressor of mankind in his *Prometheus*, a drama whose effect may have been lessened by that of a continuation which has not come down to us. But here the philosophers soon suffered a series of persecutions, at first mainly instigated by political opposition to their patron, Pericles, but kept up in that fear of the wrath of the gods which was called forth by the Peloponnesian war.

The earliest martyr was Anaxagoras, who came from Ionia during the war with Xerxes, to Athens, where he taught Euripides, Thucydides, Aspasia, and Pericles. His chief peculiarity is the introduction of intelligence as the source of life and motion. He did not give this power self-consciousness or personality, but he made it play so prominent a part that he was nicknamed "Intelligence." Partly under this guidance, and partly under that of the laws of matter, he supposed all things to be formed out of an infinite number of little particles, which resemble their products in nature, and originally existed as chaos. From the union and separation of these seeds of life come birth and death. The soul is part of the universal intelligence and thus able to judge the correctness of the information which the senses furnish, though not to produce knowledge independently. It is to our possession of hands that he ascribes our superiority over the lower animals. His own favorite study was astronomy, and he was wont to say that it was for this end that he was born. When charged with lack of patriotism, he pointed up into the sky and said, "Behold my country." He seems to have been the first to explain the causes of eclipses, as well as of the rising of the Nile. He is also said to have predicted the fall of a meteorite, which he might easily have done by noticing when such phenomena are most frequent annually. Like other Ionian philosophers, he taught that the sun is a ball of burning matter, and this so offended the Athenians, who worshiped it as Apollo, that he was accused of a capital crime, according to a decree, proposed by a priest named Diopeithes, and providing that any denial of the national religion, or philosophizing about the gods, should be punished as treason. Pericles tried in vain to defend his teacher, who was banished, or according to other accounts, fled before the trial, and at all events died in exile.

Similar charges were actually presented against his beautiful and brilliant pupil, Aspasia, the friend of Socrates and mistress and counselor of Pericles, who succeeded in having her acquitted. The banishment of his music teacher, Damon, seems also to have been due in part at least to bigotry. And this was certainly the cause of the temporary rejection of the more accurate system of measuring the year, proposed with the sanction of Pericles by Meton the astronomer, whose cycle of nineteen years exceeded the real period by less than ten hours, whereas there was a loss during this time of more than three days according to the eight-year method in use. In 432, while Meton, Damon, Aspasia, and Anaxagoras were being treated thus, Phidias, who had but just finished his famous Jupiter at Olympus, was prosecuted for the impiety of introducing figures of himself and Pericles on the shield of his Minerva, and died in prison. And the banishment a few years later of a general who was greatly needed, Thucydides, seems partly due to his having held the views of Anaxagoras, as is plain from his language, in his history, about an event which soon showed how much Athens lost in holding fast to theology and rejecting science.

Forty thousand of her soldiers, among them many of her best citizens, had failed in an attack on Syracuse, and were about to save themselves from destruction by retreating in the night of August 27, 413, when the moon became eclipsed. The prophets declared that this was a sign of the wrath of Diana, and that she could not be appeased, unless the army remained quiet for the next twenty-seven days. So the retreat was given up, and the Athenians waited a whole week, watching their enemies hem them in more and more securely. At last fear got the better of superstition, and they undertook a retreat, which resulted in immediate rout and general massacre. The few survivors were sold into slavery, and the generals killed themselves in prison to avoid execution. An irreparable injury was thus inflicted on the city which represented popular liberty and high culture, as no other did for many centuries. This ruinous defeat under Nicias, as well as that of the Thebans under Pelopidas in 364, might have been prevented, and both these generals saved from death, if they had been able to assure their soldiers, as Pericles and Dion did under similar circumstances, that eclipses are not signs of divine wrath.

And that the failure in Sicily, which brought on the fall of Athens and a pause in political and intellectual progress, was largely the result of religious bigotry is plain from the fact that the sending to Syracuse of the irresistible Spartan commander was due to the persuasions of Alcibiades, who had abandoned his country because, while gallantly leading the very army whose fate has just been recorded, he had been put on trial for his life, on a charge of having mutilated statues of Mercury, and having parodied the Eleusinian mysteries, spectacular illustrations of future rewards and punishments. On his refusal to appear before the judges, he was condemned to death, his property was confiscated, and the priests cursed him in the name of all the gods.

It was the news of this sentence that provoked him to go to Sparta, reveal the plans and weaknesses of Athens, and urge her enemies to send aid to Syracuse and to take permanent possession of Deceleia, the key to Attica. These terrible blows he followed up by persuading Chios and other Ionian allies of Athens to revolt, and Persia to give large sums to Sparta. He soon deserted the Peloponnesians, however, was invited by the Athenian soldiers and sailors to their camp during a revolution instigated by himself, gained at their head great victories, ending with the conquest of Byzantium, made truce with Persia, and returned in triumph to Athens. Her people welcomed him with great rejoicing, revoked his sentence, and gave him supreme command. Unfortunately he landed on the day when the statue of Minerva was taken to the sea to be bathed and clothed in new garments, and when the city was supposed to be in such affliction at the absence of her favorite deity, that no public business could be performed. The priests renewed the charge of impiety, and took advantage of a disaster, caused by the disobedience of a subordinate, to deprive Athens of the only man who could have averted her fall.

Great as were the faults of Alcibiades, it must not be forgotten, that the charge which was most urged against him, was that of mutilation of the Mercuries, in which there is no evidence that he took part, and also that after his second condemnation he did his best to save his country from that crushing defeat at Ægospotami which closed the war. The whole intellectual and political history of Europe would have been much brighter, if Athens could have been more tolerant towards Alcibiades and Anaxagoras.

Among the latter's pupils was the great poet whom Mrs. Browning calls,

" Our Euripides the human,
  With his droppings of warm tears,
And his touching of things common
  Till they rose to touch the spheres."

Her husband, who has enabled us to see, not only the depth of pathos, but the full scenic beauty of the *Alcestis*, has told us how its author was driven from Athens by the bitter satire of Aristophanes, who defended the old order of faith. The Syracusans are said to have showed mercy to every Athenian who could quote Euripides ; but his ninety tragedies won only five prizes, while those of Sophocles received twenty ; and the philosophic dramatist narrowly escaped prosecution for making Hippolytus deny the obligation of an oath to conceal a guilty secret. We can still read in his *Ion*, and in fragments of *Sisyphus, Bellerophon*, etc., how he invoked air as the real Jupiter ; how he suffered Ion to censure Apollo for his violence to Creusa, and to declare that if this deity and the other gods should make proper atonement to the victims of their guilty loves, it would strip their temples ; how he ascribed all belief in religion to a benevolent fraud, designed to frighten people into good behavior, and how he even ventured to say :

"Doth any man assert that there are gods
   In Heaven ? I answer there are none : let him
Who contradicts me, like a fool, no longer
   Quote ancient fables ; but observe the fact,
Nor to my words give credence. Kings, I say,
   Kill many, but rob more of their possessions,
And violating every sacred oath,
   Lay waste whole cities ; yet, tho' they act thus,
Are more successful far than they who lead
   In constant piety a tranquil life.
And I have known small cities who revere
   The gods made subject to unrighteous power,
Vanquished by spears more numerous. But I deem
   Should any sluggard 'mong you pray to Heaven,
Nor earn by his own labor a subsistence,
   He soon would learn whether the gods are able
To shield him from calamitous events."

[Woodhull's Translation vol. III. p. 343. See also pp. 114, and 388].

Similar language was used by Diagoras, a poet from Melos, who could not reconcile the massacre and enslavement of his innocent fellow citizens, with the existence of any gods. Besides open atheism, he ventured to disclose the Eleusinian secrets, and also to fling a wooden statue of Hercules into the fire, with the words: "There is a thirteenth labor for you!" He was accused at Athens in 411, but took flight before the trial; on which a reward of about a thousand dollars was offered to any one who should kill him, and twice as much for his capture alive. He is said to have perished in a storm during his flight, but some relate that he saved himself from being treated like Jonah, by pointing to various other ships, which were in danger, and saying " Do you suppose that each of them has a Diagoras on board?" One of the last of the Ionic philosophers, Diogenes of Apollonia, is said to have been in similar danger at Athens, but perhaps he has been confounded with Diagoras.

The Melian atheist is said to have been much influenced by Democritus, who belongs in this period chronologically, though he did not stay long enough in Athens to suffer any persecution, except the attempt of Plato to destroy his books. These amounted to sixty treatises on music, physiology, morality, metaphysics, astronomy, geography, physiology, mathematics, optics, painting, agriculture, botany, medicine, diet, tactics, etc., but only fragments are extant. His most noted doctrine is the atomic theory, derived from Leucippus, of whom little else is known, and presenting as the basis of all existence, an infinite number of infinitesimal and indivisible particles, differing only in size, shape, and position, keeping up an incessant motion according to mechanical laws, and thus forming all things, even the soul iself, which is subject to dissolution like the body. Besides these atoms and the vacuum, or space in which they move, nothing can be certainly known to exist according to Democritus, who, however, does not deny the existence of the gods, though he attributes to them but slight power, and supposes belief in them to be mainly an inference from dreams. Our ideas of Deity, as well as of the atoms and the vacuum, are so dim that absolute truth is sunk in a bottomless pit, the knowledge derived from the senses being only relative. This system took a great step towards making morality independent of theology by teaching that pleasure and pain are the tests of what is useful or injurious, and thus the natural guides of man towards his chief end, happiness; a theory elaborately expounded afterwards by the Epicureans, utilitarians, and evolutionists. Such was the wisdom won by Democritus through study of all previous philosophies, and travel through Greece, Italy, Egypt, Arabia, and Persia; and thus did he show that he was sprung from Ionians who had fled across the sea to Thrace in search of liberty. Among his maxims which have come down to us are the following:

"Not every pleasure is to be chosen, but only that which is noble." "Only they who hate injustice are dear to the gods." "More people become good by effort than by nature." "We should not abstain from crime out of fear, but out of regard for duty." "It is good, not only to do no wrong, but to wish to do none." "Speech is the shadow of action." "To conquer self is the noblest victory." "The wrong-doer is more unhappy than the wronged." "Reverence should be shown openly, and truth spoken bravely." "It is the sign of a great soul to be able to bear with others." "Delay spoils a gift." "Agreement nourishes friendship." "He who has no friend is not worthy to live." "Give even a little, rather than promise much." "They who blame readily are not fitted for friendship." "He who praises the foolish harms them greatly." "It is the fool who despises what he has and longs for what he has not." "The sign of liberty is freedom of speech."

The title of "Laughing Philosopher" was not given him until three hundred years after his death. More in harmony with the known facts, is the story that he was the first to dissect animals. It is not he, but his contemporary Hippocrates, however, who seems entitled to the honor of having been the first to teach that diseases are of natural not supernatural origin, and are to be cured, not by prayers and sacrifices, but by diet and medicine. He was of priestly birth, but generously gave up the claims of his own order, from whose sway Grecian science now began to rescue medicine, as had been already attempted with meteorology and astronomy, and as was essayed in regard to ethics by Democritus.

And the same city, Abdera in Thrace, which was the birthplace of the great Atomist, was also that of Protagoras, who, in the year that Diagoras was persecuted, 411, was banished from Athens for commencing a book with the confession: "As to the gods I do not know whether they exist or not; since such knowledge is impossible for many reasons, especially the difficulty of the subject and the shortness of the life of man." The forerunner of agnosticism was drowned in his voyage from Athens. His books were taken away from the owners and burned in the market-place, the earliest instance of this sin against knowledge. He went so far in asserting the rights of free thought, as to teach that whatever appears true to any one is true for him, so that each man is the measure of all things. He also held that all our knowledge is relative, that matter is the substance beneath all phenomena, and that pleasure is the sole motive for action. The theory, that virtuous means simply pleasurable on the whole and with reference to ultimate as well as immediate results, while vicious means painful, is fully stated by Plato, though only as one to which Socrates compels assent from Protagoras, who is further represented as enjoying great honor throughout Greece, a fact shown in his title of "The Wisdom," Sophia. It was his claim to teach this that led him to call himself a Sophist. This name, which he was the first to take, meant originally a teacher of useful knowledge, especially the arts of eloquence and argument, which were particularly important in Athens, where litigation was frequent, and every man had to be his own lawyer. Protagoras was born in poverty, and had first earned his living as a porter, so that he was obliged to ask pay from his pupils, a custom followed by the other Sophists, who thus are said by Plato to sell food for the mind, a practice of which this wealthy aristocrat speaks with undeserved contempt. Pericles and Euripides were among the pupils and friends of Protagoras, who charged some two thousand dollars for a course of lessons, but permitted any pupil who was dissatisfied to pay whatever sum he should declare on oath in a temple, to be all that was due.

Among other noted Sophists were Hippias and Gorgias, both of whom won much fame, not only as teachers and orators, but as ambassadors, and the latter of whom is said to have been honored with a statue of gold erected at Delphi by the contributions of all Greece. Most of these teachers were great travelers, but Prodicus, the friend of Socrates, who borrowed from him the lofty allegory of *The Choice of Hercules*, or as Lowell calls it, *The Parting of the Ways*, spent most of his life in Athens, where he is said to have narrowly escaped having to drink hemlock, for attempting to explain the nature of the gods. That the Sophists generally and habitually attacked religion and morality, as has been asserted, is utterly incompatible with the fact that they depended on their popularity for a livelihood; but that Protagoras and Prodicus did expose themselves to martyrdom shows that these Sophists at least were not merely mercenary. That Gorgias, Hippias, and Protagoras, were teachers of exalted morality, like Prodicus, is plain from the language attributed to them by Plato, and this writer places his most reprehensible theory in the mouth of Callicles, who considers the Sophists good for nothing. Some of them seem certainly to have given altogether too much time to merely verbal quibbles, but their main offense in Plato's eyes appears to have been that they made light of his philosophical views. Gorgias, for instance, argued that if any thing not accredited by the senses is to be believed in, every thing should be which may be conceived of by the intellect. The conservative Athenians, like some of the church-fathers, were in general opposed to the Sophists, for reasons which held good against Plato and Socrates also, namely, that it seemed dangerous to teach young men to argue on all subjects, and defend any opinion or action for which they might be attacked. Little as he who gave such weapons might wish to have them used against religion and the laws, he could not prevent it. That the Sophists were not as a class, free-thinkers, is stated by Plato, *Republic*, p. 143, but they became necessarily though unintentionally the first professional teachers of free thought. They may have sought for popularity and pay rather than for truth; but yet they did a great work for the mental development of Greece, as has been gratefully acknowledged by Grote, Hegel, Lewes, Denis, and even Plato, who in the dialogue called *The Sophist*, pp. 230–1, describes him as the minister of the art of intellectual purification, the teacher who cross-examines and refutes his pupils until he has freed them from self-conceit, and forced them to think for themselves.

IV.

And what the Sophists did as part of their trade now became the sacred mission, the life-work of a man who followed it so successfully and disinterestedly and died for it so bravely that Socrates still stands before us, the grandest figure in all the history of thought. His birth at Athens 469 B. C., made him the contemporary of Æschylus, Sophocles, Euripides, Aristophanes, Phidias, Pericles, Cymon, Thucydides, Cleon, Alcibiades, Critias, Thrasybulus, Xenophon, Plato, Protagoras, Anaxagoras, and other great men who were leaders in such intellectual activity as has never been witnessed since. None of them had so much influence as he on mental progress, despite his humble birth, lifelong poverty, unconventional habits, and ridiculous ugliness. He had gained what he could from every book and teacher within his reach, but all he learned only increased his mighty originality. In developing his powers he relied mainly on conversation, which he gradually came to use as a regular means of giving instruction and mental stimulus. It is by no means certain that he ever followed his father's trade of sculptor. All accounts represent him as spending his whole time in his friends' houses or in the streets and other public places, arguing with everybody who would answer him, while he was supported by the voluntary offerings of his pupils, prominent among whom were Crito and Alcibiades. The latter's life and honor he saved at the battle of Potidæa, a few years after which, 423, he is represented by Aristophanes as well-known for his skill in argument. His own safety in the retreat at Delium was due to his calm courage and presence of mind. Only once did he hold office, in 405, when he was president of the assembly, at which it was proposed to put to death without legal trial six admirals who had won a great victory but had failed, in consequence, as they pleaded, of a storm, to pick up the dead and wounded. Against the fury of popular indignation Socrates stood alone and steadfast, so that the fatal decree had to be postponed until a more pliant official came into power. So during the reign of terror in which fifteen hundred citizens were murdered by the thirty tyrants, he blamed their cruelties openly, went on teaching in spite of their prohibition, and when they commanded him to bring Leon of Salamis to Athens to be put to death, paid no attention to the order, a disobedience which would probably have cost his life, if the tyranny had not soon been overthrown.

He was as exemplary in private as in public life. Plato called him the best and wisest and most just of all men whom he had ever known, and Xenophon is never weary of praising his patience, temperance, chastity, simplicity of life, honesty, and especially his thoughtfulness for his friends. His freedom from the worst form of self-indulgence then prevalent is attested by the silence of Aristophanes as well as by the statements of both Plato, (*Banquet*, p. 219), and Xenophon, (*Memorabilia*, I., 2, 29 and 30). The latter disciple represents his master as always ready to give information and instruction to whoever will take it. Thus Xenophon's Socrates urges Aristodemus to believe in the gods, Aristippus to care less for self-indulgence, Chærephon to make friends with his brother, Aristarchus to set his free-born poor relations to work for their support, Crito to employ a friend for protection against litigation, Pericles the younger to fortify the mountains between Attica and Bœotia, Charmides to engage in politics, Epigenes to take care of his health, and his own son Lamprocles to have patience with Zanthippe, whose ill temper did not attract the notice of either Plato or Aristophanes, and is not without excuse in her husband's neglect to labor for his family's support. It was in keeping with the moral standard of the times for Socrates to tell Theodota how to gain and keep the lovers on whom she lived, but far above it for him to praise the husband who treats his wife as his equal, and the master and mistress who are kind and just towards their slaves.

Xenophon appears so sure of his master's conformity to the established ideas of religion and morality that, if we had no other source of information, we should find it difficult to understand either why Socrates was put to death or how he became so famous. There is nothing heretical in the *Memorabilia*, except the theory that right and wrong are not made so by the will of the gods, but by innate tendency to increase or diminish happiness. Socrates makes utility the test, not only of goodness but even of beauty, according to Xenophon, who was so anxious to make his master appear orthodox, and so free from any desire to set forth a philosophical system of his own that his testimony on this point must be accepted, especially as it is confirmed by Cicero, who declares that Socrates was wont to curse those who separated the ideas of the useful and the virtuous, which, by their nature, are in harmony. Plato also places decidedly utilitarian language in the mouth of the hero of the *Protagoras, Crito, Republic, Charmides, Theatetus, First Alcibiades, Greater Hippias,* and *Hipparchus*. The last three dialogues are of doubtful authenticity, but if they are not Plato's, we have so many more witnesses to the utilitarian tendency of the teachings of Socrates, who cannot indeed be said to have founded a regular system of ethics, but who certainly seems to have been one of the first to teach that goodness consists in promoting not merely one's own happiness, but the welfare of the community, and that general expediency is the true aim of legislation, propositions stated in the *Memorabilia, Crito, Theatetus,* and *Republic,* but not in the *Protagoras,* which is simply self-regarding. Such were the views of the first philosopher who made morality his main study in place of the physical inquiries hitherto predominant. Thus it was that Socrates brought philosophy down from the skies to dwell among mankind.

To this purpose was due a habit which Xenophon incidentally mentions, and which Aristophanes and Plato make very prominent, namely the fondness of Socrates for cross-questioning people and making them contradict themselves. In the *Memorabilia* this is said to be done only in order to open a way for positive instruction, but in Plato's dialogues any such aim is repeatedly disavowed and all such instruction is frequently refused to those who ask for it. There is no doubt of the authenticity of the *Eutyphro, Charmides, Laches, Meno, Lysis, Theatetus, Theages, Ion, Euthydemus, Gorgias,* and *Apology,* all which represent Socrates as deliberately upsetting the received definitions of piety, temperance, courage, friendship, and truth, without seeking to establish any new ones, and as even professing again and again that he is unable to teach any thing, and that all he knows is that he knows nothing. The judges who condemned him to death had but just been told by him, according to Plato, that he had nothing positive to teach, that he was wiser than his neighbors only because he knew his own ignorance as they did not, and that, deeply as he was wont to offend people by convicting them of error, he considered this such a sacred duty that he should never give it up, however he might be threatened with punishment. As he made virtue depend on knowledge, it is particularly remarkable to find him holding that neither could be taught. The same preference for negative over positive teaching appears in several dialogues of rather uncertain authorship, namely, the *First* and *Second Alcibiades,* the *Greater* and *Lesser Hippias, Hipparchus,* the *Rivals,* and *Cleitophon.* In the last the pupil declares that he must leave his master, because he can get nothing but exposures of error, which he has long heard with great pleasure and profit, but which he now wishes to supplement with some definite statement of what is really true and good. The utilitarianism attributed by Plato to Socrates seems most useful as a weapon of attack, and where the master is made to propound any other positive teachings, there is good reason, as we shall see, to suppose that here we have mainly the views of the disciple. Thus Plato's Socrates gave his life to overturning the established ideas of truth and goodness, and forcing people to confess their ignorance.

Aristophanes gives a somewhat similar view of the work of Socrates, but differs from Plato in making it include an attack on the existence of the gods, and also systematic instruction in the art of escaping moral duties and legal liabilities, which skill was secretly imparted to any one who would pay for it. Both Plato and Xenophon, however, agree in declaring that Socrates had great respect for the national deities as well as for the laws of the land, that he taught nothing in private, that he asked no pay from his pupils, but often shrank from accepting presents, and, finally, that his only aim was to make people wiser and better.

In fact, Socrates spent his time and finally laid down his life in carrying out a theory of the value of free inquiry so advanced that but few rationalists really hold it even now. He lived and died for a method of instruction which would close our churches and revolutionize our schools. Men who are trying to prove that skepticism is not very dangerous morally, may well remember the confidence with which the best and wisest of the Greeks declared that the state of mind which most promotes morality is that of constant search for truth. Nothing favors virtue so much as vigor of thought, and this can come only by thinking for ourselves. The good teacher is not he who tells us what is true, but he who sets us to work to find it out. The true friend of virtue is not he who confirms us in our inherited ideas, but he who forces us to improve them. Such, at least, was the opinion of Socrates. His real successors are Pyrrho, Lucian, Abelard, Hume, Voltaire, Lessing, Buckle, Mill and Renan.

Reverence for the laws of Athens seems to have kept Socrates from applying his own methods of inquiry to theology; and this reserve, together with respect for his character and fear of his power to make opponents ridiculous, enabled him to teach for many years in safety; but in 399 he was tried for his life, on the charge of denying the national divinities, introducing new gods, and making the young men immoral. He was able to assure his judges that he believed in all his nation's deities, and especially in the divinity of the sun and moon. The views about these bodies held by Anaxagoras he rejected indignantly. But the effect of this speech, still preserved by Plato, must have been much impaired by the fact that he had never been initiated at Eleusis; that he had been the friend of Euripides and Prodicus, and that among his favorite pupils were Alcibiades, who had profaned the Eleusinian mysteries, and Critias, who had said that it was only the wish to rule others which had led men to pretend that there were any gods. More serious was the charge of introducing new divinities, for it was well known that he claimed to be under special divine guidance. This indeed he did not ascribe to any particular person, nor did he pretend to have seen visions, or heard voices, or received any revelation of duty or truth. He tells his judges that he was never thus commanded to do any thing, but often restrained from action, especially from taking part in politics. Among other results of this secret oracle were his refusing to take unfit persons as disciples, his choosing at Delium the path by which he escaped from the enemy, and his avoiding a street in Athens where he would have been run over by a herd of swine. It is simply a mistake in gender to talk of the Demon of Socrates; what he really called it was something divine; and, in fact, it was simply such a presentiment of danger as no able thinker would now consider supernatural.

The fatal point of the indictment was the charge of corrupting the youth. Every judge knew that gross immorality had been practiced by both Alcibiades and Critias, that the former had not only committed sacrilege, but had joined his country's enemies, secured the failure of the expedition to Syracuse, caused Deceleia to be fortified, negotiated the alliance of Sparta with Persia, and instigated the revolt of the Ionians. It was also well known that Critias had been the leader of the thirty tyrants, who had but just been overthrown. Among their champions had fallen Charmides, the uncle of Plato, and the only man whom Socrates is said to have advised to take part in politics. Prominent among the liberators of Athens was Anytus, one of the prosecutors, and he complained that his son had been led by Socrates to despise his father's business, that of a tanner, and thus left open to the temptations which finally carried the young man into a drunkard's grave. Another disciple, Xenophon, was then absent without leave as a soldier of fortune in Persia, and was afterwards banished for fighting against his native city. Socrates had also, owing possibly to the fact that his own friends were mostly in the upper class, while the great body of the people were still swayed by that superstitious bigotry which had recently persecuted Alcibiades and Anaxagoras, frequently spoken with contempt of the system of popular government which had but just been restored.

What really insured his condemnation seems, however, to have been his refusing to ask any favors of his judges, and addressing to them that grand vindication of himself which should not be called an apology. He appeals to the Delphic Oracle, which had pronounced him the wisest of all men, as a proof that the gods had commanded him to cross-examine all pretenders to wisdom, and stir up every one to activity as a gad-fly does a horse. This philosophic mission of searching into himself and other men is thus a divine charge, which he will not desert, even to save his life. He warns his judges that it would be useless for them to offer to forgive him and spare him as long as he should cease to cross-question and puzzle people. His words, as recorded by Plato and translated by Professor Jowett, are these: "Men of Athens, I honor and love you; but I shall obey God rather than you, and while I have life and strength I shall never cease from the practice and teaching of philosophy, exhorting any one whom I meet after my manner and convincing him." "For this is the command of God, as I would have you know; and I believe that to this day no greater good has ever come to the state than my service to the God. Wherefore, O men of Athens, either acquit me or not; but whatever you do, know that I shall never alter my ways, not even if I have to die many times."

That such a speech was followed by his conviction is not surprising. Indeed it is a strong proof of the liberality and intelligence of the Athenians, that out of five or six hundred judges the majority against him was at first but six, according to some manuscripts of Plato. He could probably have saved his life even then, if he had chosen to take advantage of a law providing that any culprit found guilty of a capital crime might propose some minor penalty, which he was willing to suffer instead of death, and let the judges take their choice. Socrates, however, told the men who had just voted him guilty, that what he really deserved was to be supported for life by the state, as a public benefactor. He did offer to pay a fine of about fifteen dollars, a sum which he finally increased, at the entreaty of Crito and Plato, to five hundred. It was too late for this, however. Such was the indignation of the judges that they refused to hear Plato speak, and eighty of those who had voted for acquittal, now took part in sentencing Socrates to drink hemlock.

He would have been executed at once, but the sacred ship was about to carry the yearly offering of Athens to Delos, and so he was suffered to live thirty days longer, until its return. His legs were fettered, but he was allowed to write poetry and talk freely with his family and friends. Crito bribed the jailer and urged Socrates to escape, but he refused to violate the laws, which seemed to stand before him, reminding him how much they had done for him, and how often he had shown his regard for them, and warning him that flight from prison would make him the enemy of justice, and prevent his finding welcome among the virtuous, so that he had better be a sufferer than a doer of evil. Such at least is the account given by Plato, who also tells us how his master met his friends for the last time, and argued with them in favor of immortality, taking care to say : "I wish you to think of the truth and not of Socrates ; agree with me if I seem to speak the truth, but if not, withstand me might and main, that I may not deceive you in my enthusiasm, and, like the bee, leave my sting in you as I die." He closes by reminding them that all he really wishes them to do is to look to themselves, and walk according to his precepts.

As sunset drew near he bathed himself, in order to save his wife the trouble of washing a dead body, and then bade his family farewell. Now the jailer came to say: "Socrates, you have shown yourself the noblest and gentlest and best of all who ever came to this place, and I am sure you will not be angry with me. Fare you well, and try to bear lightly what must needs be. You know my errand." Bursting into tears he went out to prepare the poison. Crito urged his friend to delay drinking it until the sun had fully set, but Socrates was ready to go. When the cup was brought, he asked if there were enough for a libation to the gods. There was not, so he prayed them to prosper his journey to the world below, and drank off the poison cheerfully. His friends burst into tears, but he alone remained calm, and begged them to suffer him to die in peace. After walking to and fro, as was directed, he lay down, and the chill of death mounted up from his feet towards his heart. His last words were to beg Crito to pay the cock due to Æsculapius in gratitude for a happy death.

v.

Fortunate are we in having so much of his free and ennobling spirit preserved in those matchless dialogues, full of such lofty imagery, keen satire, touching pathos, life-like sketches, and spirited conversation that Plato may be justly called the Shakespeare of philosophers. Peculiar to the great Athenian, however, is the galaxy of precepts like these:

"Neither retaliation nor the warding off of evil by evil is ever right." "May I, being of sound mind, do unto others as I would that they should do unto me." "Truth is the beginning of every good, both to the gods and also to men." "Justice is the excellence of the soul." "The right treatment of slaves is to do them, if possible, even more justice than those who are our equals." "In his relations to strangers, a man should consider that a contract is a most holy thing, and that all the concerns and wrongs of strangers are more directly dependent on the protection of God than the wrongs done to citizens." "You are created for the sake of the whole, and not the whole for the sake of you." "The temperate man is the friend of God, for he is like Him." "Without the sense of honor and dishonor, neither states nor individuals ever do any good or great work." "The greatest penalty of evil-doing is to grow into the likeness of bad men." "Knowledge is the food of the soul." "To do wrong is only second in the scale of evils; but to do wrong and not be punished is first and greatest of all." "No pleasure except that of the wise is quite true and pure; all others are a shadow only." "Faint heart never raised a trophy." "Beloved Pan and all ye other gods who haunt this place, give me beauty in my soul and may the outward and inward man be at one!"

Plato's chief service to mental liberty was by preserving and illustrating the lofty theory of Socrates, that truth is not to be reached either through blind reliance on other men's opinions, or through jumping at conclusions, but through a daring and careful re-examination which leaves no objection unanswered, but rejects no legitimate deduction as too dangerous, and that the knowledge so gained is the firmest of moral safeguards. Modern Platonists have given much less attention to this theory than to another, more plainly favorable to independence than to correctness of thought, which was probably developed under Pythagorean influence after the death of Socrates, and which teaches that the highest objects of knowledge are abstract ideas to be reached by intuition, without the aid of the senses.

Such ideas of Justice, Beauty and Truth, the *Phædrus* pictures the gods as beholding constantly, while the disembodied soul gains more or less lasting vision according to her power to control the lower passions harnessed to her chariot, and thus becomes prepared to re-enter life in a form corresponding to the fullness of her contemplations. This knowledge of abstract ideas in a pre-existent state is appealed to in the *Phædo*, as an argument for immortality. In the seventh book of the *Republic*, the philosopher is said to have risen to truth so far transcending that possessed by other men, that they are like prisoners in a cave where nothing can be seen but shadows. The *Timæus* and *Cratylus* teach the existence of ideal prototypes corresponding to all general names; for instance, an eternal man who is the pattern by which all other men have been created. Plato had so much more than some of his own followers of the spirit of Socrates, and was so anxious to have his theory rest on that firmest of foundations which is made up of vanquished objections, that he actually devoted two of his ablest dialogues, the *Sophist* and *Parmenides*, to urging the strongest reasons for believing that those ideas he reverenced so much were merely the creations of his own thoughts. Plato has not left any answer to many of his arguments against his own theory, as we may justly call it, since we know, from the testimony of Aristotle, that it was not held by Socrates. Idealism in this form has since made few converts, but it has done much to lead people to rely for knowledge on their intuitions rather than on observation and experience.

Plato's vigor of imagination led him to suggest some new truths of great value, like the rotundity of our earth, but it often tempted him to prefer his own fancies to the facts discovered by others, as he did when he assigned ten thousand years as the period during which all the heavenly bodies come round again to their former position. Thus he utterly ignored the great work which Meton had done, and which his own disciple, Eudoxus, was doing, in calculating the real cycle of changes through which the sun and moon pass. Equally characteristic was his thinking, that our drink passes through the wind-pipe into the lungs, that fire is composed of pyramids and earth of cubes, that the first animals created were men, the vicious among whom degenerated into women and then to fishes, while those who sought knowledge mainly through the senses turned to birds, and those who cared nothing for even such philosophy sank into quadrupeds and reptiles—fancies not without influence on modern thought. Plato's own indifference to scientific methods, as well as to practical discoveries, seems to have done much to prevent later philosophers from imitating Thales, Empedocles, and Anaxagoras.

As a moralist, he sometimes tries to measure right and wrong by degree of conformity to the ideal standard, as is attempted in the *Timæus*, *Philebus*, *Gorgias*, *Theatetus*, and

Republic. In other parts of the last two dialogues, as well as in the *Crito* and *Protagoras*, and especially in his latest and most practical composition, the *Laws*, he has to make use, as a convenient instrument for demonstration, of the utilitarianism which he learned from Socrates.

The theory of politics, which occupies the two longest dialogues, though sustained by appeals to utilitarianism, is not however derived either from this system or from idealism, but from the usages of Sparta and Crete. From these countries he borrowed the disfranchisement of the working classes, the turning of all the citizens into a standing army living in barracks, inhospitality toward foreigners and restriction of travel, the gymnastic training of girls and boys together, the practice of infanticide, bringing up of the survivors by the state, neglect of the sick, exclusion of commerce, and prohibition of gold and silver, measures most strongly urged in the *Republic*, which work is also marked by the attempt to abolish private property and marriage among the soldiers and rulers, both which classes were to consist of women as well as men, the supreme power being held by a highly educated, hereditary aristocracy. In the *Laws*, the magistrates are elected, and are obliged to make all the children follow the same studies for the same length of time, and to punish with imprisonment or death all who believe, either that the gods do not exist and take care of mortals, or that they may be moved by prayers and sacrifices. That he was one of the first to denounce this prevalent superstition, as well as to proclaim the right of women to be as highly educated as men and to take an equal part in the government, is certainly to be remembered gratefully, but we must regret his intolerance and still more his advice, in both *Laws* and *Republic*, to the rulers to keep themselves in power by deliberately deceiving their subjects. A third dialogue, the *Statesman*, recommends the rule of a philosophic monarch unrestricted by laws. Thus Plato's writings are a curious result of Spartan, Pythagorean and Socratic influences over a brilliant but eccentric intellect.

He was but twenty-eight at the death of Socrates, after which he traveled to Egypt, Italy, and finally Sicily, where his reproof of the despotism of Dionysius the Elder caused him to be sold as a slave. He was soon liberated, and returned to Athens, where he collected a costly library and founded a school, called the Academy, from the name of the grove, consecrated to a mythical hero, where it was situated. Among his many disciples was Aristotle. When Syracuse passed into the hands of the younger Dionysius, Plato was invited to help him and his uncle reform the government. The customary prayer for the continuance of the tyranny was abolished by Dionysius, who asked his guests what were the first steps to take in order to set Sicily free. Plato, however, according to a letter written by one of his disciples, if not by himself, replied that it was too early to think of that, and what the young king had, first of all, to do was to free himself from ignorance, and then he would know how to liberate others. Dionysius, who fancied himself already a philosopher, was much offended by this rebuke, and ere long gave up his plans of reform, banished Dion, and placed Plato in honorable captivity. The philosopher was soon released and afterward made a third visit to Sicily, where he tried in vain to reconcile Dionysius with Dion. The latter had the sympathy of the Academy in overthrowing the tyranny, but perished in trying to become such a philosophic despot as is described in the *Statesman.* No wonder that Plato's last years were gloomy. His successors at the head of this school, Speusippus and Xenocrates, did not fully accept his doctrine of ideas, and skepticism ultimately triumphed even in the Academy. Thus he seems to have succeeded much better in pulling down than in building up.

VI.

Plato disliked the Sophists, but their influence did much to enable other disciples of Socrates to found three schools, which preserved respectively so much of his disputatiousness, his utilitarianism, and his unconventionality, as to become the forerunners of the Skeptics, Epicureans, and Stoics. After the death of the master, all the disciples were sheltered for a while by Euclid of Megara, who, during the war, had often gone to Athens by night and in a woman's dress, in order to argue with the great dialectician, from whom he learned the *reductio ad absurdum*, which he employed with peculiar success in defending the theory of Parmenides that the Absolute is indivisible against Plato's separation of it into different ideas. Among his followers was Eubulides, who did much to force people to think and speak accurately, by insisting on puzzles like this: " You say you lie. Now if you speak the truth, you are a liar. But if you lie, then you tell the truth." Still later in this Megaric school came Stilpo, who taught Zeno the Stoic that pain is no evil and that wisdom is sufficient for happiness, and who was banished from Athens by the Areopagus, for saying that the great statue of Minerva was the child of Phidias, not of Jupiter, and therefore no god. Similar fondness for argument marked the Eretrian and Eliac philosophers, the latter of whom followed Phædo, the narrator, according to Plato, of the death of Socrates, and who are not to be confounded with the Elean school established during the previous century by Xenophanes, in Italy.

Little heed was taken of logical subtleties by Aristippus of Cyrene, who traveled about, teaching his pupils to enjoy themselves, and receiving great sums of money, which he spent with Lais and her frail sisters. He valued pleasure even more highly than Socrates did, but differed from his master mainly in prizing sensual and momentary delights. " The present alone is ours," said the Cyrenaic, who, however, took some pains to keep himself and his pupils from being enslaved by sensuality. Both pleasure and pain were positive realities to him, and the only tests of right and wrong ; which words when used otherwise he thought had merely a conventional meaning, a view already presented by Archelaus, a disciple of Anaxagoras. Aristippus is further noted for rejecting the Platonic ideas, and holding that all knowledge is relative, as well as for many sayings like his answer to the question, what advantage the philosopher had over other men : " If all laws were repealed we should still live as we do now." So when Dionysius, at whose court he spent much time, bade him take the lowest seat at table, he remarked : " Doubtless you wish to make this place honorable." His most faithful pupil was his daughter Arete, who made a philosopher of her own son, named after his father, but nicknamed "Mother-taught." Other disciples were Anniceris, who thought more than his master did of friendship and patriotism, and who ransomed Plato from slavery ; Hegesias, who is called "The Orator of Death," because he spoke of life with such dissatisfaction as to tempt his hearers to suicide ; and Theodore the Atheist, who wrote a book about the gods which, as Diogenes Laertius says, is not to be despised, who carried the scorn of conventional morality even further than Aristippus, and who narrowly escaped being forced to drink hemlock by the Areopagus. His pupil Evemerus wrote a Sacred History, in which he asserted, on the basis of inscriptions he professed to have found in his travels, that Saturn, Jupiter, etc., were only deified chieftains, an opinion which kept gaining popularity afterward.

Similar hostility to idealism and very different views of pleasure were held by Antisthenes, the first philosopher who devoted himself to the moral training of the poor. He held that virtue alone is sufficient for happiness, and that pleasure is morally dangerous, so that he was wont to say, he had rather be mad than glad. He imitated his master's plainness of dress and speech, which habit as well as the name of the place where he lectured, caused him and his disciples to be called Cynics. These currish philosophers went about in no garments but their mantles, bareheaded and barefoot, carying great sticks and wallets, living by beggary, freely reviling whatever they thought immoral or artificial, and openly rejecting all refinements, and even decencies. The founder, Antisthenes, taught that the moral law is the same for both sexes, that virtue is the only acceptable worship, and that no knowledge of God can come from graven images. Among his sayings are : " Men have many gods, Nature but one." " If I could catch Venus, I would shoot her ; for she has led many good and beautiful women astray." Once he interrupted a priest who praised the other world and blamed this, with : " Why don't you die ? " When he heard bad people praise him, he asked : " What ill deed have I done?" To those who inquired what he had learned from philosophy, he answered: "To be company for myself." Before he knew Socrates, he was a Sophist, or professional teacher of rhetoric, and no man could be more persuasive, but in his old age he was wont to threaten to strike those who offered themselves as pupils. Once he tried thus to drive away a young Paphlagonian, who said, "Hit as hard as you please, but I shall never leave you until you cease to speak."

This was Diogenes, who when he was subsequently captured by pirates and sold as a slave, declared that he should never be one, for Antisthenes had made him free. He was offered for sale in Crete, and answered to those who asked what he could do, "Govern men." A rich Corinthian bought him as tutor for his children, whom he brought up so successfully that he was then permitted to live as he pleased. He seems to have spent most of his time at Corinth, where he lived for a while in a tub, and where he answered to Alexander's question, "What can I do for you?" "Stand out of my sunshine." It was to light a fire for his master that he once crossed the market-place with a lantern, and thus provoked questions which he parried by saying, that he was looking for an honest man. To a profligate fellow who wrote up over his door, "May no evil enter here," he said, "Where are you going to live yourself?" When he saw a temple hung with the votive gifts of those who had been saved, he exclaimed: "How much more space would be needed for the offerings of the worshipers who perished!" So he was wont to mock those who sacrificed to the gods for health, and then made themselves sick in feasting on such portions of the flesh as were not burned upon the altars. Such was his coarseness of speech and action that he was nicknamed, "The Crazy Socrates."

His most noted disciple was Crates, called, "The Door Opener," on account of his habit of calling, without knocking, on any one who needed counsel or rebuke. He gave up his large property to follow Diogenes, but afterwards, despite his poverty, rudeness of behavior, and ugliness, won the heart of the high-born, young, and wealthy Hipparchia, whose brother he had saved from suicide. Crates advised her not to marry him, but she insisted on doing so, adopted his way of life, and went about in male attire.

This sect was the only one mentioned in this section, that survived the century. Indeed, it lasted until it was supplanted by the Christian monks. Epictetus declares that the true Cynic is the father of mankind, looks on all men as his sons, and all women as daughters, keeps himself pure from sin, and free from desire of self-indulgence, bears the worst treatment patiently, and labors continually for every body's good. It is Christian injustice to Paganism that has caused *cynical* to mean *misanthropic*.

VII.

Meantime a more important system than any we have mentioned, except Plato's, was founded by one of the latter's disciples, who, though greatly his inferior in literary skill, was fully his equal in ability, and immensely his superior in knowledge; so that Aristotle's influence on philosophy, has been greater than any other Greek, as is shown by his having given us many words like energy, category, and metaphysics. For twenty years he was a pupil of Plato, and much of his subsequent life was spent in criticising his master's views, especially the theories that knowledge is reminiscence, and that universal terms, like the general idea of man, exist eternally and independently, so as to furnish the patterns after which individuals are created. Aristotle taught that these universals exist only in the individuals, and are simply common properties in which members of the same race or class agree to form it. Knowledge he ascribed primarily to individual experience and to sensations felt during the present life. Again and again he says: "It is in facts that we must seek general principles, and these must always accord with the facts." "More reliance must be placed on facts than on reasoning, for this should agree with facts." His works on natural history describe many curious habits of animals, like the cuckoo's making other birds rear her young, the cuttle-fish's escaping in a cloud of its own ink, and the building of nests by fishes; and Aristotle is especially memorable for discovering a great law of development, much contested even by modern naturalists, but now generally admitted, namely, that of epigenesis, according to which the parts of the embryo do not pre-exist in the germ, but originate by successive differentiations. Many of his statements, however, must have proceeded from hasty observation or mere conjecture, and his lack of skill in classification is marked. He professed to follow the inductive method, to proceed from particular facts to general principles, but his desire to solve all possible problems often made him jump at conclusions, and his belief that the divine purpose is everywhere to be discerned, sometimes led him to assert the real occurrence of what he thought such a purpose would effect. Thus he has been regarded as an opponent of the very method which he did more than any one else to found.

More generally acknowledged is his claim to be honored as the father of logic. And this science he carried so far that both Kant and Hegel acknowledged that no further progress had been made up to their own day. Thus he did so much, not only to point out the real source of knowledge, but to teach the art of reasoning, that he may be said to have been the first to give proper weapons to free thought. Politically he favored monarchy, but he insisted on the right of the citizen to the protection of just laws. Slavery of barbarians to Greeks seemed to him necessary and right; but he thought that slaves should receive instruction in virtue and be emancipated if they behaved properly, and his own servants gained their liberty as his bequest. So, while admitting that wives should be in subjection, he insisted that they should not be treated as slaves. His influence on his own age must have been that of a practical but very moderate reformer. His ethical system recognized the fact that all men seek for happiness, but defined this object as virtuous activity. Thus Aristotle made happiness a form of virtue, whereas utilitarians make virtue a form of happiness; and he further differed from them in defining right as placed between two wrong extremes where it may best promote the individual's highest good. The claims of the universal welfare are acknowledged in his description of justice, but not so fully as is required by utilitarianism. The great value of his treatise on morals is in its practical precepts and distinctions, which make it still one of the most useful and interesting of books. His theology was free from anthropomorphism, gave no room for special providences or prophetic dreams, and allowed little activity or personality to the nation's gods. Immortality, as we understand it, he rejected, though he ascribed power of existing eternally and impersonally to the highest part of the soul. These views, together with his having honored the memory of his wife and his benefactor in a way alleged to be impious, caused him, after the death of his pupil and patron, Alexander the Great, to be prosecuted by the high priest of Ceres, and exposed to such danger of perishing like Socrates, that he fled from Athens, declaring that he did not wish to have this city make a second error in philosophy.

Aristotle has had fewer readers than Plato, but more students; and his opinions have had far greater authority over all whom they have reached. Plato's attempts to solve the great problems of thought have stimulated fresh endeavor, but Aristotle's solutions were accepted as finalities for many centuries, and their authority has not yet wholly passed away. One philosopher did more to force men to think independently, and the other to teach them to reason correctly. Plato is a good example of the brilliant originality to be gained by disregarding all authority, even that of actual facts; but Aristotle shows us that truth can not be reached unless we take heed, not only of all circumstances and phenomena, but of the results attained by other thinkers. No one has paid more close attention than he to the opinions of other authors, and to the institutions established around him; and hence no one has been able to add more to the world's stock of knowledge. This treasure, however, he would have been able to increase much more considerably if he had not wasted part of his strength on problems which either cannot be solved, or are not worthy of elaborate solutions. Much unprofitable work was done, not only by him, but by his followers. His school was called, from his habit of walking to and fro while lecturing, the Peripatetic, and is also known as the Lyceum, a name given from its location in the shady promenades near a temple of the Lycian Apollo. Among the early members were Strato, surnamed " The Naturalist," because he was the first to assert that there is no God but nature, and no divinity but that of sun, moon, stars and earth ; Dicæarchus, who opposed not only the theory that the soul is immaterial and immortal, but the practice of relying on dreams and oracles ; and Theophrast, who ridicules superstition in his book on traits of character, and is also noted for opposing the sacrifice of animals to the gods. He was lecturing to 2,000 hearers, in 307, when all the philosophers left Athens because her citizens took advantage of the partial revival of democratic government to pass a decree, provoked by the favor shown both by the Peripatetics and the Platonists to oligarchy and foreign rule, prohibiting the teaching of philosophy without permission of the state, and threatening death for disobedience. The exiles were invited to return the next year, however, by the repeal of the edict, and freedom of speech was not again restricted while Athens was under pagan rule.

VIII.

Thus, after glancing at Judaism and Buddhism, we have seen how innovators from Ionia taught with little opposition, until Anaxagoras and Alcibiades were driven from Athens ; how this persecution brought ruin on the State ; how Socrates died a martyr for liberty of speech ; how Plato kept alive his master's spirit while teaching a new system ; how the Megarians, Cynics, and Cyrenaics went still further in imitating the great Athenian ; how Aristotle placed philosophy on a firmer foundation than before; and how he and his disciples were banished for political rather than religious heresies. The next chapter will show how philosophy changed from a victim to the victor of paganism.

CHAPTER II.

THE CONQUEST OF PAGANISM DURING THE LAST THREE CENTURIES B.C.

The incorporation of the Greek cities into the Macedonian empire caused great loss of power to their priests, whose position was now little better than that of state functionaries. And as Alexander and his successors brought Athens into close political and commercial relations with Egypt, Palestine, Persia, India, and Scythia, thinking men were enabled to compare different forms of worship, and perceive that no one was intrinsically superior to the rest. At the same time the munificent patronage of the Ptolemies gave great currency to scientific methods of thought, and thus room was made for new systems of philosophy to save educated people from fear that errors in belief might call down the wrath of the gods, as well as from subjection to the authority of prophets, priests, and oracles. Now arose kingdoms whose subjects differed so widely in religion, that errors in opinion could no longer be punished by law. A peculiarly tolerant policy was necessarily adopted towards the provinces conquered by the Roman republic, whose citizens learned to respect the religions, not only of the Jews, Parsees, and worshipers of Isis and Cybele, but of the believers in Druidism and the Norse mythology, as equal in sanctity to the rites established in Italy, while the increased knowledge thus gained of the dangerous tendencies of superstition caused the irreligious forms of philosophy to grow rapidly in favor.

I.

The most original of these new systems was founded by Aristotle's contemporary, Pyrrho, who had followed Alexander through Persia to India, and thus found how much men vary in opinions, customs, and laws. This experience, with knowledge of the differences between philosophers, and of the illusions of the senses, led him to maintain that no one has ever reached absolute truth, or found out any thing about the Infinite, and that true wisdom consists in not taking sides with any religion or philosophy, but looking at all theological and metaphysical disputes as a disinterested and curious spectator. This position, which Pyrrho found peculiarly agreeable, is expressed in Greek by a word from which he and his followers are called Skeptics. In conduct they were in the habit of following the usages prevalent around them, but their main efforts were directed toward holding their judgments in suspense, welcoming any ideas that seemed useful, and carefully avoiding such zeal for any opinion as seemed hostile to peace of thought. Of nothing were they more convinced than that skepticism is more favorable than dogmatism to mental tranquillity. Pyrrho himself lived such a pure and peaceful life as nearly to reach the age of ninety, to gain the office of high priest at Elis, his native city, and to be almost the only classic philosopher of any note about whom no scandal has come down to us. It is hard to say whether it is to him or to a follower, contemporary with Cicero, Ænesidemus, that we owe the famous ten arguments, given fully by Sextus Empiricus and briefly by Diogenes Laertius. These are designed to show that we have no right to be confident in any opinion, because, first, the senses often deceive us; second, men differ in their natural needs and tastes; third, our senses often differ from each other in the impressions they give us of the same object; fourth, the same man varies in opinion according as he is well or sick, sane or insane, drunk or sober, hungry, frightened, in joy, or in sorrow; fifth, different nations differ utterly in morals and theology; sixth, we do not know substances in themselves but only by their properties; seventh, objects appear differently on account of their position; eighth, many things affect us very differently in small and in large quantities; ninth, what is rare is more valued and noticed than what is common; and tenth, nothing can be known by itself, but only in its relations to something else.

Such arguments forced even the Platonists to admit that truth is utterly beyond our reach, and that the Infinite or Absolute is incomprehensible ; so that it is useless to inquire after any thing more than mere probability, and even this is unattainable in regard to God or immortality. Thus the rejection of the authority of observation and experience by Plato naturally led his followers into an extreme type of skepticism now obsolete. Such was the logical process which produced the Middle Academy, the credit of founding which is contested between Arcesilaus and a later Platonist, Carneades, who came to Rome as an ambassador, B.C. 156, and publicly argued, first in favor of the necessity of justice and then against its possibility, with such skill that Cato the Censor persuaded the senate to banish all philosophers. The new views could not be expelled permanently, but soon made many converts, among whom, in the last century B. C., were Messala; Cotta, who plainly denies the existence of the gods in Cicero's *De Natura Deorum* ; Lutatius, the first Roman who wrote history in the secular tone already taken by Thucydides and Polybius ; and Varro, who argued in favor of public worship, merely on the ground of its utility to the state. But the most famous of these skeptical Platonists are Brutus and Cicero. A full exhibition of the state of thought just before the appearance of Christianity is given in the famous dialogues in which the great orator and his friends talk about God, immortality, providence, and divination, as questions where there is much to say on each side, and no certainty to be ever reached.

II.

Both the great patriots just mentioned owed much to those more conservative philosophers, the Stoics, so called after the frescoed porch in which were held the lectures of their founder. Zeno was born in Citium, a Greek colony in Phœnicia, and studied in Athens under Platonist, Peripatetic, and Cynic teachers, by whose aid and that of the writings of Heraclitus he was able to bring forward his own system about 300 B.C. His fundamental doctrine is that whatever exists, even the human mind and that all-pervading, all-animating Soul of the World which holds the highest place in the Stoic faith, has material substance. Our senses are trustworthy, and it is by using them and reasoning logically about what they give us that all knowledge comes. Ideas are merely our own thoughts. Thus the human mind is like a sheet of paper on which the senses write. The same comparison has since been made by Locke, but seems to have originated with Aristotle, who gave less authority and authorship to the senses than did the Stoics. These latter have suffered under Cicero's charge, that they stole all Aristotle's teachings and merely altered the terms, as thieves do the ear-marks of stolen cattle. The best defense that can be made for the Stoics is that they went much further in materialism than did the Stagirite. Some of them seem even to have been forced to admit that the virtues, being realities, must be animals.

Their materialism did not hinder their teaching and practicing the loftiest morality, as is manifest in the writings of Seneca, Epictetus, and Marcus Aurelius, as well as in such lives as that of their great founder, whose integrity caused the keys of Athens to be placed in his charge when the city was in civil war; that of King Cleomenes, the worthiest successor of Leonidas, the champion of the poor, oppressed Spartans, and the last defender of Grecian liberty against Macedon; that of Tiberius Gracchus, who fell a martyr to his attempt to give the plebeians their share of the public lands; that of Cato, whose name is still the watchword of liberty and justice; and that of his heroic daughter who sat in council with the other would-be liberators. How bravely later pupils of this school opposed Tiberius, Caligula, Claudius, Nero, and Vespasian, will be related in the next chapter, as well as how grandly and beneficially the five Stoic emperors reigned.

This moral teaching, though not systematically and formally utilitarian, was brought into practical agreement with that of J. S. Mill by the assumption that the law of nature which the Stoics accepted as the supreme rule of virtue, commands us to seek the universal welfare and promote the happiness of all men.

(See *Plutarch's Morals*, Goodwin's Edition, vol. 11, pp. 399 and 443, and the *Reign of the Stoics*, pp. 195 and 211.

All their teaching was inspired by faith in the perfect goodness of God and the universal brotherhood of man, of which latter doctrine Zeno was the earliest teacher west of India. Their proverbially strict morality forced them to reject many of the fables current about the gods ; but they zealously urged that these deities kept constant watch over the welfare of mortals, and gave frequent intimations of their will through dreams, oracles, etc. Panætius stood almost alone in denying that auguries could be drawn from the flights of birds, or the entrails of victims offered in sacrifice. It was his pupil Sulpicius, who, while Supreme Pontiff, declared that there are three kinds of religion—that of the priests, which gives the gods human form, feelings, etc., and is false; that of the philosophers, which disputes about every thing so as to be unsatisfactory; and that of the politicians, which asserts whatever the people need to believe for their own good, but only that.

The best part of the Stoic theology is their denial that the gods are ever angry with any one, or do any harm, or that they ought to be feared by man. The *Hymn of Cleanthes*, written two hundred and fifty years before the birth of Jesus, tells how Jove will end all discords, and bring all things to unity, the good with the evil. This lofty poem, like all the utterances of Stoicism, is full of trust in the Order of Nature, and confidence that every thing is done according to law. The current superstitions about punishments after death the Stoics rejected unanimously, though admitting the immortality of the soul, except, however, that she would ultimately share the universal dissolution in which this world seemed destined to pass away. Destiny played as prominent a part in their creed as in those of other Greeks and Romans, but a much more wise and philanthropic one. They held that no man could escape his fate, and that any attempt to modify it was sinful and ruinous, while to accept it cheerfully and bravely would insure holiness and happiness. Special providences and miracles they were consistent enough to reject, as they did the fables of future torments. Thus they sought to purify the national religion, so that all the good in it might be preserved.

III.

The time was now come for more radical treatment of the popular beliefs, especially that in Fate, whose darkness is shown by the legend of Œdipus. He is born doomed to slay his father and marry his mother. They and he do all they can to prevent such sin; but these efforts only lead him blindly on to his own ruin and that of all his race. Thus destiny works itself out with no regard for human virtue or happiness, no heed to prayers or sacrifices, and no possibility of resistance even by the gods. These deities have power enough, however, to punish those who neglect them. King Agamemnon has to slay his own daughter that he may appease Diana's wrath, and Phædra and Hippolytus perish because chastity displeases Venus. Favor with one god is sure to bring down the wrath of some other one, as it did on Hercules, Æneas, and Ulysses. Unusual prosperity calls forth general hatred, such as destroyed Polycrates. Even the greatest and best of the gods is represented by Æschylus as so hostile to human happiness, that our race is saved from ruin only by the might of Fate and the self-devotion of Prometheus. Hundreds of foul legends show that the hate of the gods was thought less cruel than their accursed love. And the religion of the Greeks, like those of all ancient nations, was darkened by fear, not only of these jealous, cruel, and capricious lords, but also of numberless mischievous and malignant ghosts, who were provoked by the neglect of their relatives to cause all sorts of calamities; for instance, tempests and diseases, especially insanity and epilepsy. The word *demon*, though not so dark in meaning as it became later under Hebrew and Persian influence, often assumed somewhat of its present terror. Thus the faith of the Greeks and Romans was made hostile to happiness by fear at once of the fates, the gods, and the demons. The efforts a man might make to shake off belief in any one of these powers were likely to increase his dread of the others. Suppose that the gods were only deified mortals, then they were to be feared like other demons. Suppose that gods and demons were ruled by Fate, then all the more absolute must be the tyranny of this pitiless despot. Suppose the gods to rule even Destiny, then all the more awful must be their jealousy, anger, and caprice. In Greece and Rome there also reigned fears that after death the soul would suffer at the body's being tossed about on the waves, eaten by wild beasts and vermin, burned by fire, or buried in the earth, and that it might either be doomed by arbitrary Fate or some angry god to reappear in a loathsome reptile or predestined criminal, or be confined forever in a universal subterranean prison-house, so gloomy that the high-minded Achilles had rather be a poor man's servant than reign king of the dead. And those who had escaped these primitive fancies went no further, before the advent of Stoicism, than to suppose that, while a few highly favored souls entered Elysium, many others were consigned to endless torments in Tartarus.

The greatest of the Roman poets tells us how foully life was crushed to earth by the weight of Religion, when Epicurus, the glory of the Greeks, dared to be the first to raise his eyes against her hydra-headed shape, and to withstand her face to face. No fear had he of the thunders of the gods, but stories about their wrath only inflamed his courage, till he taught his followers to tread on their enemy as she had trodden on them. Thus he revealed the worth of human life and made earth equal heaven. So writes Lucretius about the great liberator of thought.

Epicurus was born, early in the year 341, on the island of Samos, to which his father, who was a schoolmaster, had come, among other Athenian colonists. That he gained his first experience of the evils of superstition by assisting his mother to practice witchcraft, may be merely a slander. At eighteen he went to Athens for a year or two, but had seen little of other philosophers and read few books except those of Democritus, when, at the age of thirty-two, he began to teach in Mitylene and Lampsacus. There his disciples were few, though enthusiastic, but they became very numerous at Athens. Thither he came in 306, one year after the unsuccessful attempt to limit free speech described at the close of the last chapter. Epicurus taught without molestation, as he was all the better enabled to do by his taking part in public worship, and keeping clear of politics, in which there was then but little to be accomplished.

He bought a house in the city, and laid out there the garden which became the home of his disciples, whose frugal wants he supplied freely, so that they did not suffer when Athens was besieged and distressed by famine. Epicurus was wont to boast that his own food cost him less than a penny a day, and that he needed only bread and water to be able to equal Jupiter in happiness. To one friend he wrote, "Send me a little Cythnian cheese, so that if I choose, I may fare sumptuously." The feasts, which were held every month to bring all the friends together, and every year, apparently on the 2d of February, to celebrate the founder's birthday, were rich in nothing but the wit and cheerfulness of the guests. Among them was a slave and several women, one of whom, Leontium, wrote a book of some ability against Theophrast. Her reputation, like that of her sisters, is not spotless, for public opinion at Athens did not favor the attainment of high culture by ladies of good character. But it is certain that Epicurus never practiced or favored sensuality, but took much pains to repress it among his friends. One of the most zealous modern opponents of Epicureanism, Lecky, justly pronounces its founder "a man of the most blameless character," and similar testimony is given by early antagonists like Cicero, Seneca, and Chrysippus, the last being almost contemporary with Epicurus. The chief fault now charged by competent critics is vanity, but this cannot have been excessive in a man who said to his friend : "Among the infinite blessings which wisdom has given us, O Metrodorus, I have never thought it an evil that this famous Greece has not known us, nor even heard our names."

Such a speech would scarcely have been made after the school was fairly established at Athens ; for there Epicurus soon won many followers, not so much through the power of his formal teachings, as through that of his personal society. Such a large and harmonious company of friends has never since been known. Before the close of the thirty-five years which he spent tranquilly in his garden, his disciples became numerous enough to fill whole cities. The Macedonian and other conquerors were destroying the political institutions on which the religion of the Greeks was founded, and hence, Epicureanism, though bitterly attacked by the Stoics, Peripatetics, and Platonists, encountered but little actual persecution, except in Crete and Messene, during the second century B.C.

The three hundred books which Epicurus wrote have almost entirely perished, but Diogenes Laertius has preserved three letters in which the great rationalist gives a summary of his philosophy. Besides these, we have the enthusiastic poem of Lucretius, already quoted, and also many criticisms and extracts in Cicero, Seneca, Plutarch, Epictetus, and Marcus Aurelius, as well as some supposed traces of Epicureanism in *Ecclesiastes*. So soundly were the fundamental principles laid down by Epicurus, that no changes were made by any of the disciples. One of the system's chief peculiarities is that its adherents cannot be divided into schools. The senses are taken as the sole and sufficient source of knowledge, and all errors ascribed either to misinterpreting or to discarding them. Nothing can be created out of nothing, and whatever exists has done so from all eternity. There is no reality but that of matter. The ultimate elements of all bodies must be indivisible, for infinite and endless divisibility is inconceivable. These atoms vary in size, weight, and form, but not in substance ; and these differences, with others in their number and arrangement, enable them, in their continual motion through boundless space, to produce all things and beings, even the soul and the gods. Dreams and visions prove the existence of deities, but there is no proof that they take any notice of our conduct.

They must be supposed to be perfectly good, and if so they can have no jealousy or anger. They must also be thought perfectly happy, but this requires that they should not trouble themselves about human actions, or any other natural phenomena. Whatever takes place is the result of physical causes, acting themselves out in innate and natural laws. All life and thought proceed from the constant motion of the atoms; and these have power to change their direction spontaneously. This variability, which is the most important addition made by Epicurus to the atomic theory laid down by Democritus, enables the mind to develop itself independently, and thus each man can become the author of his own destiny, and defy the Fates. To the independence of the soul, the only limit is her connection with the body. Both come into existence together, both grow, flourish and decay together, and both dissolve together into the original atoms out of which they were compounded naturally. Demons can therefore have no existence, and there is no reason to fear them, or any evils after death. Nor need we dread either fate or the gods. In public worship Epicurus himself joined gladly, as he might well do, since his philosophy did the gods much more honor than was then paid by any of the reigning theologies. Some of his disciples, however, were less reverential, and one of them, named Danæ, as she was led to execution for having saved her lover from being put to death by a tyrant, exclaimed: "Men do right to despise those gods who suffer me to die for this!" The general attitude of the Epicureans toward the national religion was simply that of good-natured indifference. Great pains are taken by Lucretius, as well as by his master, to guard the reader against admitting the agency of the gods, the demons, or the Fates. For this purpose several explanations, often puerile, are given of every natural phenomenon, with the assurance that after all it makes little difference which supposition we take, provided that we keep clear of supernaturalism. Scientific accuracy was never much valued in the Garden, and its master refused to admit that the sun has any considerable size, that the earth is round, or that there are human beings on the other side.

In fact, the Epicureans did not value any kind of culture for its own sake. Their object was happiness; and learning, virtue, and pleasure were all measured by the same standard, that of tendency to produce felicity. In recognizing this as the true aim of man, Epicurus agreed with Aristotle, Zeno, and most other classic philosophers ; but he went much further than they did in identifying pleasure with happiness. He takes care, however, to tell us that : " When we call pleasure the end of life, we do not speak of the pleasures of the debauchee, or the sensualist, as some think who are ignorant of our opinions or who misrepresent them in malignity ; but we mean freedom of the body from pain and of the soul from anxiety. For it is not continued drinkings and revels, nor the society of women, nor rare and costly viands that make life pleasant, but it is such sober contemplation as searches out the grounds of choice and avoidance, and puts to flight those vain fancies which harass the soul." Health of body and tranquillity of soul are the main elements of happiness according to Epicurus ; and he considers the state of the mind more important than that of the body, since mental pains and pleasures affect all our future existence, but bodily ones touch us only for the moment. He who is truly wise would be happy even while he is being roasted alive, says Epicurus ; and he has himself left us a letter, sadly misrepresented by Plutarch, telling us that, though he was dying of the most excruciating pangs, yet memory of what he had taught gave him such bliss, that this day which would be his last was the happiest of all his life.

Especially necessary for true happiness is the protection of the soul against superstitious fears and useless longings. All our desires are divided by Epicurus into three classes · First come the natural and necessary ones, like those for food and drink, wishes which it is easy to gratify and injurious to leave unsatisfied ; and these should be indulged moderately. But when these desires go beyond what is necessary to avoid pain, they become unnecessary though they remain natural, and then they enter the class of wishes which can be either repressed or gratified without danger, and may be indulged in or refrained from, according as the tendency in that particular instance is to increase or diminish happiness. Then, lastly, come those desires which are not only unnecessary, but also unnatural, since they arise solely out of errors in opinion, and which are not only hard to gratify, but injurious to those who indulge them; of such desires ambition is a good instance, and all these evil passions the wise man will repress as completely as possible. A similar classification is made of our pains and pleasures under four canons. First, such pleasures as do not lead to equal pains are to be sought. Second, such pleasures as do this are to be shunned. Third, such pains as produce greater pleasures are to be endured. Fourth, such as do not are to be avoided. In making these classifications of pleasures, pains, and desires, Epicurus goes far beyond Aristippus, and also in laying stress on tranquil, rational, and permanent happiness, rather than on momentary gratification. Indeed, the preference of repose over excitement is one of the essential features of Epicureanism. Its disciples were commanded to scorn the pleasures of luxury on account of the pains they bring.

Its wise man will not fall in love, nor will he marry unless under exceptional circumstances. Nor will he become a politician, and especially not a tyrant; while he will not suffer himself to be a Cynic, a beggar, or a drunkard. Tranquil happiness will be his aim and this he may if he chooses attain here on earth. Hereafter there is nothing to fear or hope. Our happiness depends not on how long, but on how wisely and virtuously we live. Out of the natural distinctions, just described, between such pains and pleasures as increase our happiness and such as diminish it, arise the moral laws.

Thus Epicurus declares, with perfect consistency and accuracy that, "We cannot live pleasantly unless we live prudently, nobly, and justly, nor can we live prudently, nobly, and justly without living pleasantly." Prudence in rightly choosing and avoiding pains and pleasures he found so important as to say, "Better is the misfortune of the man who has planned his way wisely, than the prosperity of him who has aimed foolishly." Among other virtues, meekness and gratitude seem to him especially sacred.

All we really need to be happy according to Epicurus, is virtue; but there is much else that is valuable, though not essential. Especially important is friendship. It is so much for our happiness to have friends that the wise man will gradually come to love them for their own sake, and will even be willing to die for them. He who can do this is happier than he who is friendless. The Epicurean was not, however, taught to give the interests of others, or the welfare of the State, the value which these objects had for the Stoics, and now have for modern utilitarians. Nor was this theory as well provided with sanctions as it might have been on its own ground, or as well qualified as some of its rivals for calling out exceptionally high virtue. Still it has the great advantages, that it may be adopted by any one, whatever his opinions about theology or metaphysics, that it can be easily understood, and that it is not likely to tempt any one to sacrifice his own happiness intentionally. Perhaps it has made no saints, but it has certainly not made any hermits, persecutors, or hypocrites. But the real character of Epicureanism is best to be understood from these sayings of its founder, preserved partly by his disciples, and partly by his critics and adversaries:

"It is both more noble and more delightful to give than to receive a kindness." "If you would gain true liberty, serve philosophy." "It is misery to be continually beginning to live." "He enjoys wealth most who needs it least." "Great pains are short, and those that last long are but slight." "Seldom does fortune find the wise man unprepared." "Cheerful poverty is noble." "He who does not find his own possessions ample, would be miserable, though he were lord of all the earth." "Live according to nature, and you will never be poor; follow public opinion and you will never be rich." "If you would make Pythocles rich you should not add to his possessions, but take away some of his desires." "Consider with whom you eat, rather than what you eat; for feeding apart from your friends is living like a wolf." "The beginning of safety is knowledge of our faults." "Laws are made for wise men, to keep them not from doing but from suffering wrong." "Thanks to nature that what is necessary is most easy to get, and what is most hard is not needed." "Only the wise man knows how to be grateful." "He will treat his slaves mercifully, and call them his friends." "Even though he lose his eyesight, he will still endure life." "It is not he who renounces the gods believed in by the people that is impious, but he who believes what others do about them." "It is possible for the wicked man to hide himself, but never will he feel confident that he can do so." "The law which is not useful to society is unjust." "In my sickness I did not make speeches about my sufferings, nor talk about them with those who visited me; but I continued to discourse as before on the nature of things, taking care above all to show how the mind, while sharing in the movement of this poor little body, may remain tranquil and look after its own true interests. Thus I gave the doctors no reason for boasting that they were doing something important for me, but my life went on nobly and happily."

Thus Epicurus lived and taught, until the day came, when he wrote the letter already quoted, begged his friends to remember his doctrines, and passed tranquilly away. This was in 271 and apparently on January 31st. His will directed that four of his slaves should be emancipated, that his own memory and also that of his parents and brothers should be duly followed, that the children of two friends should be provided for, and that the bulk of his property, including his library and his garden, should be devoted to the support of his school. This continued to flourish for five or six centuries at Athens, and to exert a mighty influence over all ancient thought.

Epicureanism, though well known throughout Greece at the time of its founder's death, did not show itself in Italy until a century later, when the religion of the Romans had life enough left to persecute, though that of the Greeks had not. Two teachers from the Garden, Alcæus and Philiscus, were banished in 173, B. C.; and twelve years later a decree was passed threatening with the same punishment all philosophers and rhetoricians who introduced new ways of thinking. In 156 similar measures were taken against Carneades and his followers, as already mentioned. Less than a century later the political revolutions had so weakened religious institutions that the most famous of Epicureans seems to have excited no opposition by publicly declaring in the senate, while head of the Roman hierarchy, that death is merely an eternal sleep, or by neglecting during the thirty years of his pontificate to do any thing to check the decay of faith in the gods, or by openly and constantly disregarding all omens and auguries, for instance those which threatened his army before he won his last victory at Munda, and those appealed to by his wife and friends when they sought to keep him away from the senate-house on the fatal Ides of March. Cæsar's generous toleration of the utmost freedom of speech compatible with his own supremacy, won the applause of all Rome, and should still be remembered in his favor, as should the disorders and oppressions fostered by the aristocracy which he overthrew. Still his establishing an absolute monarchy certainly did no credit to his school of philosophy. This had now become the most popular of all at Rome, according to Cicero, who tells us that its adherents were among the best of men, a statement to be expected from the friend of Atticus. Cassius, too, was a staunch Epicurean, except in committing suicide.

Especially remarkable is the influence over Roman literature of the genial sect. Besides Greeks like Philodemus, whose library was found at Herculaneum, and several early Latin authors of little importance like Amafinius, Rabirius, and Catius, it inspired those great poets, Ennius, Lucretius, Catullus, Virgil and Horace. The first of these five was at Rome while the Epicureans were persecuted, but he boldly declared, that though the gods exist they pay no heed to our doings, for if they did it would go well with the good and ill with the wicked, as is plainly not the fact. Great applause was won by the actor in one of his plays, who uttered this doctrine as follows:

"Ego deum genus esse dixi, et dicam semper cœlitum,
Sed eos non curare opinor quid agat humanum genus,
Nam si curent, bene bonis sit, male malis, quod nunc abest."

Still extant are, also, the lines in which he ridicules those starving prophets and astrologers who pry into the skies, but cannot see what lies before their feet, and who beg a trifle from the people to whom they promise wealth.

"Quod est ante pedes nemo spectat, cœli scrutantur plagas."

* * * * * * * * * *

"Quibus divitias pollicentur, ab eis drachmam ipsi petunt."

And the Roman Homer further distinguished himself by translating the fictitious history in which Evemerus spoke of Saturn, Jupiter, etc., as mere men who reigned and passed away, and also by versifying the comedies in which Epicharmus had ridiculed the gods, and shown that they are nothing more than names given by superstition to the all-potent forces of nature. Thus Rome received the most advanced results of Grecian thought.

Pacuvius, the nephew of Ennius, is noted for saying that it is the sky which is really the father of all things, which gives them birth, form, motion and nourishment, and finally takes them back into itself, that there is no goddess Fortune, though chance rules all things, and that those men who understand the language of birds, and learn more from the hearts of other animals than from their own, must be heard but need not be listened to. For thus freely may be rendered the lines :

"Nam isti qui linguam avium intelligunt,
Plusque ex alieno jecore sapiunt quam ex suo
Magis audiendum quam auscultandum censeo."

No translation can easily be given of the pun made by Attius, the contemporary of Pacuvius, on the rapacity of the augurs :

"Nil credo auguribus, qui aures verbis divitant
Alienas, suas ut auro locupletent domos."

And I need only mention another minor poet who advocated Epicureanism between the time of Ennius and that of Lucretius, namely Lucilius the satirist.

IV.

That only fragments of these poems have come down to us is not so much to be regretted as it would be if we did not possess a masterpiece of philosophic poetry written by the "chief poet on the Tiber-side," as Mrs. Browning rightly calls Lucretius. In all classic literature there is no author who is more worthy of our attention. And this not merely on account of the zeal with which he shows what great crimes religion has persuaded man to commit, and how dark our life has been made by fear of the gods, but also on account of his sunny faith that earth would be a paradise if it were free from these terrors, his generous sympathy with all suffering and sorrow, his hearty delight in the beauties of nature, his high morality, his deep reverence for Epicurus, and his constant pleasure in his own great work. Easily can we picture him and his friends, when

"On soft grass beside a stream and under some tall tree they lie,
  Making merry at slight cost, while brightly smiles the tranquil sky,
  And kind Spring the greensward sprinkles with her flowers of richest dye."   —II. 29-33.

All he writes is inspired by firm conviction that the one thing needed for living happily is a pure heart. "At bene non potuit sine puro pectore vivi." Indeed it is because Epicurus is found to help his disciples gain this that the Athenian sage is said to be a greater benefactor than Ceres, Bacchus, or Hercules. Living wisely and virtuously is so important to Lucretius that he does his utmost to make us rise out of the theological stage of thought into the scientific. Many of the arguments by which he would work out this great deliverance have become antiquated, but modern thought has not yet fully mastered his central idea, namely, that all events take place according to fixed laws, so that all phenomena are fully accounted for by natural properties and forces, without the necessity of referring to any supernatural agency or intention.

The poem opens with a dedication to the productive power of nature, personified as Venus. Then follows a glowing tribute to him who freed Greece from bondage to religion, that mother of wicked deeds like the murder of Iphigenia. Liberty from torturing fears can be maintained only by keeping ourselves fully aware of the uninterrupted reign of those physical laws which make spring give us roses, summer wheat, and autumn grapes. Every-where we see the order of nature ; and all experience forbids us to suppose that any thing can be created out of nothing or can return again into nothingness. We see the various forms of matter constantly changing one into another, while matter itself endures eternally. Some of these forms, like those fine particles which are smelled but not seen, must be extremely small. All visible things may be divided into such invisible corpuscles ; but the smallest of these are indivisible ; for if matter were infinitely divisible, it would not have its known permanence and solidity. Flint and iron must be formed out of solid elements. Softer substances can also arise out of similar elements, when these are separated by sufficient portions of space; and that space exists is certain, for if it did not, motion would be impossible. Space exists, and the atoms also ; of these elements all things are composed. This view, as Lucretius shows, is much superior to those of Heraclitus, Empedocles, and Anaxagoras. That the second of these three daring innovators, for instance, was mistaken in calling earth, air, water, and fire the four elements is shown by the fact that these are only transitory forms, behind which we must find the eternal principles. One of these latter, space, is further shown to be infinite in extent, and the atoms are declared to be infinite in number. Space and atoms have kept continually meeting together and separating spontaneously from all eternity, and after trying motions and unions of every sort which were soon given up, have at last happened to fall into forms which were naturally fitted to endure and have accordingly done so as the component parts of our earth.

Then the second book describes the processes by which all forms of life have been produced out of the accidental union of differently formed atoms, more or less separated by portions of space. Much labor is given to showing how these corpuscles vary greatly but not infinitely in form ; how they are colorless, odorless and without sensation, and how they owe their power of union to that spontaneous tendency to change of motion which is the cause of free will in man. One of the most important propositions here advanced is that of the probability of the existence of other worlds like this.

Strongest of all the six books in argument is the third, designed to show that we have nothing to fear after death from the gods, and no reason to dread being haunted by ghosts and demons. We see the mind oppressed by the body's diseases, and we know how the overpowering violence of wine disorders the soul. Mind and body grow up and become old together. Children go about with feeble limbs and slender sagacity. The body matures and power of mind develops also. Then, finally, when all our frame is shattered by the mastering might of time the intellect gives way. It naturally follows that the soul is dissolved, like the body, into its original elements, some of which Lucretius considers indescribable, though not supernatural. Again, if the soul is immortal and makes its way into our body at the time of birth, why is it that we are unable to remember the period before we were born? But if the nature of the mind can be so completely changed that all memory of past actions is lost, that, methinks, does not differ greatly from its death. If souls transmigrate so that a man is born again as a child, why is it that the latter is childish and not manly in intellect? It may be answered, that the soul grows weak in a tender body; but those who admit this must acknowledge also that the soul shares the body's weakness so far as to partake of its mortality. Such arguments prove that death is nothing to us, for it is merely our ceasing to exist. We felt no distress on account of aught that happened before we were born, and so we shall feel none, whatever may take place after we die. All the stories of Tantalus, Sisyphus, and the daughters of Danaus have no meaning except as images of the mental tortures, which in this life punish the superstitious, the lascivious, the ambitious, and the discontented.

The fourth book, and the most fanciful, attempts to account for our sensations by explanations which modern psychology has rendered valueless, but the closing pictures of the folly and danger of sensuality must always have keen interest for the moralist.

Nearly one half of the next book is given to astronomical speculations, in weaving which Lucretius seems to have been but little benefited by such progress as had even then been made in science. We must, however, admire the boldness with which he incidentally denies that the sun and moon are divinities, or that the earth is so well adapted to the wants of man that there is sufficient reason to believe in special creation and providence. The last six hundred lines of this fifth book are more closely in harmony with our most advanced views of the history of man than is any other portion of classic literature. This passage begins with pointing out the great fact of the survival of the fittest. Then comes a description of those early men who could not till the ground, and who had no knowledge of fire or of metals, and no clothing, not even the skins of wild beasts. By and by they got themselves huts, furs, and fire; the man united himself with one woman in marriage, and then the race began to soften, and neighbors came together in friendship. Various sounds were uttered naturally, as is done by all animals in expressing different emotions, and thus the advantage of giving names to things became manifest, so that language arose spontaneously. Then the sun taught men how to cook food, as they saw the ripe vegetables soften in its heat. Cities now were built and kings enthroned. Temples and altars, too, were reared to the gods, whose shapes were seen in dreams, whose power was supposed to guide the regular succession of the seasons, and whose home was fancied to be the sky, out of which snow, rain, hail and lightning seem to be sent down. "O wretched generation, how many tears and terrors have ye prepared for us! True piety is not prostrating ourselves before statues and sprinkling blood on altars, but it is keeping our mind in perfect peace." Meantime forest fires melted metals for men, who found that tools could thus be fashioned. Copper first came into general use, and slowly it gave place to iron. Weaving was invented and the ground was cultivated. Music and dancing began to make life happy. Ships, walls, and roads, poems, pictures, and statues, men learned to make by slow degrees as they advanced step by step. "Thus time and reason gradually bring forth all things. One by one and in due order come to light all the different arts, and advance towards complete development."

Thus ends the finest part of the poem. The remaining book tries with poor success to give the causes of various phenomena, especially thunder and lightning, magnetism, and pestilence, and ends with a powerful picture of the horrors of a great plague.

That this horrible scene is that in which Lucretius meant to leave his readers seems incredible. Nor can he have intended to say so little about the most attractive part of Epicureanism. Fully to carry out his purpose of freeing man from subjection to religion it would have been necessary for him to devote at least one more book to showing how morality arose spontaneously, not supernaturally, and thus encouraging us to believe that we are able to live divinely without assistance from the gods. That the poem was really left unfinished by its author is manifest on every page. Of the circumstances of his death at the age of forty-four we know nothing; but Virgil was in all probability right in saying that he who found out the causes of all things, and trod under foot every fear, and inexorable fate and the roar of greedy Hades, lived and died happily.

> "Felix qui potuit rerum cognoscere causas;
> Atque metus omnes et inexorabile fatum
> Subjecit pedibus strepitumque Acherontis avari."
> —*Georgics II.* 490-2.

The poem just quoted deals a sharp blow to the fancies still current, that birds and beasts have supernatural knowledge, by showing how their movements are naturally influenced by the same meteorological causes which produce storms.—II. 415-22.

The sixth Eclogue also gives such an account of the origin of all things from those seeds or elements, out of which are formed earth air, fire, and water as would have satisfied Lucretius. Virgil's greatest work, however, was produced under a reactionary conservatism, as was that of Horace.

One of the most significant facts about the great poem of Lucretius against religion is that no answer appeared for seventy-five years, and then only an insufficient one, by Manilius.

Little notice was taken by contemporaries, and this may be due to the fact, that it came to light at the same time as the union of Cæsar, Pompey and Crassus, in the first triumvirate B. C. 55, and but a few years after the fatal weakness of the Roman system of government was made manifest by the conspiracy of Catiline. It was during the trial of the conspirators, that the head of the national hierarchy declared his disbelief in all future rewards and punishments, and the whole senate listened without protest. The unwillingness to resist these attacks on religion made by Cæsar and Lucretius, was largely due to the prevalence of the views of Epicurus, Pyrrho, and Carneades. But it was also owing to the fact that Rome was now invaded by superstitions of a peculiarly immoral character. Thus in 186 the senate had attempted to suppress the secret worship of Bacchus, on account of resulting murders and adulteries, for which several thousand guilty fanatics were brought to justice ; in 139 the Chaldæan astrologers had to be expelled from Italy ; and in 50 the consul was obliged to deal the first blow in destroying the temple of Isis, zealous worship at which was one of the surest signs of unchastity. But the most important help to intellectual liberty came from studies whose importance few philosophers appreciated.

V.

The year 306, when Epicurus began to teach at Athens, is also memorable as that in which the title of king of Egypt was formally assumed by the first Ptolemy, rightly surnamed Saviour, since he founded such libraries, menageries and museums, and brought together so many scientific and literary workers that he did more than any of the philosophers to deliver nis age from ignorance. Under him and his successors, Alexandria became the center of science. Such exactness of speech and thought as was unknown even to the Peripatetics was now introduced by Euclid, still a well known author, by Archimedes who founded hydrostatics, by Apollonius of Perga who discovered the laws of conic sections, and by other great mathematicians. Thus astronomy was enabled to speak with authority, and to make new revelations. Before 250 B. C., Aristarchus of Samos announced that the sun is the center and ruler of our system, and thus dealt a fatal blow to the fancy that sun, moon, and stars are all under the dominions of gods enthroned on Mount Olympus or in the clouds around our earth. This great discovery I attribute to Aristarchus, and not to an earlier Samian, Pythagoras. The latter did indeed teach that the earth moves, but he seems to have thought that the sun moved also, and that the real center of the system was merely a luminary created by his own imagination. At all events his views were kept secret by his disciples, but Aristarchus taught the truth so plainly that he was charged with impiety towards the earth by Cleanthes the Stoic. Soon afterwards the size of the earth was calculated with approximate success by Eratosthenes, who first suggested the method of locating places according to latitude and longitude which was afterwards brought to such perfection by Hipparchus of Rhodes, that both terrestrial and celestial geography were almost established scientifically. This success, together with his enrolling the visible stars to the number of 1080, his thereby discovering the precession of the equinoxes, his detection of the eccentricities of the solar and lunar orbits, his calculation of the solar year but 12 seconds more than its real length, his tables of the apparent motions of the sun and moon, his directions for the systematic prediction of eclipses and for the study of plane and spherical triangles, and his construction of a map of the starry firmament as well as of accurate tables of the apparent motions of the sun and moon, are such achievements as place the name of Hipparchus above that of any observer in Alexandria. It is doubtful whether any one else in all antiquity showed as much scientific ability. It was on the basis of his observations, and with the aid of an astronomer from Egypt, that Julius Cæsar was able to accomplish his famous reform of the calendar, and take this important means of regulating human life forever out of ecclesiastical control. The Roman year then varied from 355 to 378 days according to the caprices of the priests, who had managed to get the seasons three months out of the way. The great

Epicurean established the period still in use, of three years of 365 days followed by a fourth of 366; and no change has since been found necessary except that adopted in 1581 of not taking the close of a century as a leap year, unless divisible by 400.

This achievement greatly promoted the ascendency at Rome of scientific views, which must have been regarded with favor ever since it was found out in 168 that a great battle could be won by showing the soldiers that there was no need to dread an eclipse. Thus the Romans were enabled to conquer the terrified Macedonians in a war into which their king, Perseus, had been inveigled by an oracle, running somewhat thus: "You the Romans shall conquer." No martial defeat is more significant than that of this monarch who followed oracles by a republic whose soldiers had respect for astronomy.

VI.

Thus the religion of Rome was simultaneously attacked by philosophy, science, foreign superstition, and civil war. No wonder that Lucretius and Cæsar met with no resistance from its adherents; that the augur, Marcellus, was able to write against augury and yet retain his place; that Cicero, while saying all he could against the Epicureans, did not think it best to find much fault with their views about theology; that this great orator said even the old women had given up believing in punishment after death, and that he represented a priest as arguing that there are no gods. Such a denial could not, as he admits, (*De Nat. Deorum*, I. 22) be safely made in a public oration, and there was still a general belief that, whatever the gods might be, it was for the welfare of the state to worship them, a view of which Varro, the antiquarian, is the best known representative.

During the twenty-five years between the publication of the great poem by Lucretius, B. C. 55, and the opening of the first public library at Rome in the Temple of Liberty, B. C. 30, free thinking was less opposed in the metropolis, and free speech less restricted, than was the case any where else before the present century, except in Athens, where tolerance flourished for about seven hundred years after the Garden was opened by Epicurus. The temples at Rome were deserted and dilapidated, lucrative places in the priesthoods remained vacant, and sacred festivals had become nearly obsolete, when Octavius returned, in B. C. 29, from his conquest of Anthony and Cleopatra. The notorious irreverence of Julius Cæsar, as well as his good-natured indifference to personal criticism, exerted a deep influence in the metropolis. From Rome and Athens, as well as from Rhodes and Alexandria, rays of light shot out over the empire and fought against various forms of darkness. Thus, after many martyrdoms, were liberty of speech and scientific views established in opposition to Greek and Roman Polytheism. This is the first and still one of the greatest victories achieved by free thought.

CHAPTER III.

PARTIALLY SUCCESSFUL ATTEMPTS AT REACTION DURING THE
FIRST TWO HUNDRED YEARS OF THE ROMAN EMPIRE.

We have seen how freedom of thought was attained in Athens under the successors of Alexander, and finally in Rome during those civil wars which ended with the defeat of Antony and Cleopatra at Actium. On the return to Rome of the victor, who soon took the title of Augustus, he found the temples deserted and in ruins, vacancies among Flamens and in other priesthoods waiting for candidates, and the games of the Lupercal given up. Men of sense had found out the falsity of the national religion, but philosophic and scientific culture was so rare that there was still a general longing, especially among women, for something to worship. Jehovah, Isis, Cybele, Bacchus, and other foreign deities had great popularity ; as was the case with the Chaldæan astrologers and other fortune tellers. In order to check these dangerous superstitions, and at the same time promote such a slavish state of mind as was necessary to the permanence of the empire, Augustus made steady efforts during all his reign to revive the national religion. In the first year after his return he built or repaired ninety-two temples in the metropolis, where he also soon erected three hundred shrines, called trivial from their location at the street corners, where they were dedicated to the deified ancestors and other petty divinities whom the common people loved. In honor of these little gods a new festival was founded in the month henceforth called August. So numerous did festivals and holidays now become that they occupied one third of the Roman year. This was in keeping with the wish of the emperor to amuse the citizens, for whose wicked pleasure he had 8,000 men and 3,500 wild beasts killed in the arena. Theaters and bath-houses were kept in constant activity, while food and money were distributed lavishly. Building of temples continued during the forty-five years of this reign; and the example of the emperor was followed by his crafty wife and by his leading adherents; to one of whom, the mighty warrior, Agrippa, we owe the majestic Pantheon, reared in gratitude for Actium. Well might Augustus say that he found Rome built of brick, and left it of marble.

One of the most important religious events of this period was the celebration of the Secular Games, so-called because they originally took place at intervals of 110 years, a period made long enough to prevent any one from witnessing two such solemnities.

The stately ode to Apollo and Diana, sung by noble youths and maidens, may still be read among the works of Horace; for this "Pig of the Epicurean herd," as he jestingly calls himself, stooped, despite his boast that he was too free to follow any master, to become the poet-laureate of the reign of despotism and superstition. He even professed some faith in special providences, and praised people who offer sacrifices. Still his prevalent opinion was that the gods dwell in unbroken idleness; his ridicule of dreams, witches, goblins, astrologers, and miracles was unsparing, and his pleasures were not troubled by any scruples.

Horace, like Mæcenas and Virgil, was too fond of the favor of Augustus to be a consistent disciple of the Garden. Nor did this school of philosophy gain much credit from Nero's friend and victim, despite the freedom with which Petronius ridiculed superstition and exposed his master's vices after his own doom was sealed. Greater praise belongs to the pains taken by Seneca's correspondent, Lucilius, to place the eruptions of Ætna among natural phenomena, the boldness in attacking the priesthood which caused Veiento's banishment, and the frankness with which Pliny the Elder, whose philosophical affiliations, like those of the author just named, are rather uncertain, declares, at the beginning of his Natural History, that it is a sign of human weakness to inquire about the figure and form of God, that it is ridiculous to suppose that the ruling power, whatever this may be, gives any heed to our affairs, and that it is a comfort to know that the Deity cannot do every thing—for instance, raise the dead. Later in this work he exposes the falsity of magic and astrology, utterly denies the possibility of immortality, and calls the practice of deifying the emperor, an attempt to make a kind of God of him who has but just ceased to be a man. Still Epicureanism found no champion of much prowess during the two centuries from Lucretius to Lucian.

The year of the Secular Games, B. C. 17, is also memorable for the publication of a powerful presentation of the grandeur and terror of classic polytheism, by a poet whose private character is good enough to permit the hope that there was some sincerity in his conversion from the Epicureanism manifest in the Georgics. The praise given in this latter poem to Lucretius is not repeated in the Æneid, where Virgil writes as if he and his readers really believed, not only in Jupiter and Tartarus, but in omens from the flight of birds, spectral visitations, prophetic dreams, and other miracles. That the only action of which all his gods and goddesses approve unanimously is the seduction and desertion of Dido, shows the moral value of the religion which Augustus and his poets loved.

How cruelly these deities had punished those who despised them had been related, with great animation and elegance, in the Metamorphoses by Ovid, who was hard at work versifying the national calendar, and incidentally praising the recent law against libel, when he was sent into life-long banishment, partly because he had written too licentiously, even for his emperor, and partly because he knew too much about the abominations in the palace. The same penalty fell upon Cassius Severus, who had attacked the emperor's friends with excessive severity, and spoken freely for liberty before his pupils as well as in his history, which latter was burned by the senate. So was that of Labienus, whose zeal against tyranny had caused him to be nicknamed Rabienus by the courtiers, and whose indignation now led him to starve himself to death in the tomb of his ancestors. These outrages took place during the last six years of the reign of Augustus, but he had begun by suppressing the publication, commenced by Julius Cæsar, of the proceedings of the senate, the last refuge of free speech, while soon after the Secular Games he had searched through Greece and Italy after Sibylline books, and burned all those whose predictions were obnoxious, to the number of two thousand. Worship of Jehovah, Isis, Cybele, and Hesus was checked by this emperor, and his successors. No wonder that Pollio, whose public library has been mentioned, and Messala, who had fought beside Brutus at Philippi, thought it best to give up writing history and speaking in public, or that Tiberius, though he was son-in-law of the emperor and own son of the empress, was driven by his fears into voluntary exile. That Livy was permitted mildly to censure Julius Cæsar is due to the devout tone of his history; as the solitary independence which Tibullus was allowed to hold among the Augustan poets may be attributed to his early death. One result of the reactionary and repressive system, thus established by Augustus, and maintained with terrible cruelty by his successors, is that no great author appeared for nearly forty years after his death, and even then Rome had to look for her literature to the provinces, where this tyranny had been but little felt. Seneca, Columella, Quintilian, and Martial came from Spain, both Plinies from Como, Apuleius and Fronto from Africa; Phædrus, Plutarch, Epictetus, and Galen from the shores of the Ægean, and Lucian from the banks of the Euphrates. Most of the few and obscure writers in the generation after Livy and Ovid perished under Tiberius, Caligula, and Claudius, for such trivial offenses as speaking disrespectfully of Agamemnon, or writing an obituary poem in anticipation of the death of the emperor's son. Schoolmasters were banished for praising tyrannicide: a lawyer, named Julius Gallicus, was drowned in the Tiber for defending a client obnoxious to the emperor. When a similar case was offered to the noted orator, Domitius Afer, he replied, "Who told you that I can swim better than Gallicus?" The only safe field for eloquence was in carrying on prosecutions for treason; and success here was rewarded not only with enormous wealth, but with consulships and priesthoods. Spies and informers were in high favor during nearly all this century, and so were executioners and assassins.

II.

It is to the hatred of Tiberius against every appearance of political independence, as well as to that pitiless intolerance of all differences about belief or worship in which ancient Judaism outstripped all contemporary religions, that we must attribute the crucifixion, probably on March 25, A. D. 29, of the most famous of martyrs. His words are so well known, and his life still so little understood, that I shall only attempt, as I have already done in the *Index*, a Boston newspaper, for September 6, 1883, to say whether he was strictly a rationalist.

No one should speak positively about the opinions of Jesus, for the records of his words are uncertain as well as unreliable. The Greek of the New Testament is only at best a translation from the language he really spoke, and there are strong reasons for believing that none of the Gospels was written until long after his death. In fact, we have no right to be confident that any particular saying is really his, especially as we often find contradictory and inconsistent assertions put into his mouth. Still, there are some general opinions which occur so often and are expressed so earnestly that they have been generally and reverently accepted as his, and have done much to determine his place in history.

There can be little doubt that Jesus showed a noble freedom from prevailing superstitions and formalisms as well as a daring courage in disobeying despotic mandates. In predicting that the temple would be destroyed, he ran much greater risk than any one would now in declaring that Christianity will pass away. Calling himself greater than the temple was claiming to stand above the national religion; and such phrases in the first three Gospels agree with his prophecy in the fourth, that worship would soon cease to be held at Jerusalem. All the narratives say that he drove by force from the temple the sellers of the birds and animals used in sacrifice; and it has been inferred from the statement that he "would not suffer that any man should carry any vessel through the temple," as well as from his desire to have the building called "the house of prayer," that he wished to put down the whole system of burnt offerings supposed to have been ordained by Jehovah through Moses. Perhaps he was only trying to suppress unseemly noises in a place used mainly for devotion; but even this was rebellion against the priests. The charge that he threatened to destroy the temple shows that he was not considered friendly to the national worship. We never read of his making any offering there; but we find him bidding those who would do so put it off, in order to do their duty toward their brethren. Evidently, he thought that love to God and man was holier than the whole Jewish ritual. Two ceremonies which he found already in use, baptism and the paschal supper, he seems to have regarded with some favor; but the former rite was never administered by him, and the passage to the effect that he declared it necessary to salvation is spurious. That he meant to turn the Jewish passover into the Christian communion is particularly unlikely from the fact that he invited no one but the twelve Apostles, not even his own mother, to participate. His wish was evidently to found religion on morality rather than ceremony; and thus he worked directly, though unconsciously, in favor of free thought. Ceremonial religion means subjection to priests. Put morality above ceremony, and you make conscience free.

Among the precepts of Moses most hostile to individual liberty were the command to keep the Sabbath and the prohibition to eat certain kinds of food. But Jesus declared that no man can be defiled by what he eats. Still plainer was his assertion of his right to heal the sick on the Sabbath as well as that of his disciples to gather grain in the fields. That he wished to have Sunday observed instead of Saturday is merely an unauthorized fancy. His words and acts show plainly that he did not wish to have observance of the Sabbath enforced. The same disregard of the authority of Moses was shown in the declaration of a new law about divorce. And, in commanding non-resistance, Jesus condemned not only Moses, but Joshua, Samuel, David, and Elijah. Indeed, he passed a daring censure on the conduct which had most been praised in the past, and which the men around him were most eager to imitate, as the nation soon did, to its destruction. What he said against fasting, swearing, and washing of hands, is less important, but not to be overlooked. Here, he did not come so directly in conflict with Moses as with the scribes and Pharisees; and the severity with which he denounced these religious rulers is rather to be wondered at than imitated: for Paul, who had been brought up among them, never speaks of them but with praise. Jesus called them whited sepulchers and vipers, and in the same spirit sent a defiance to his sovereign beginning with, "Go and tell that fox." Similar independence appears in his behavior when on trial by Herod, the high priest, and Pontius Pilate. It seems to be the come-outers, iconoclasts, and non-conformists who imitate Jesus best.

There is, however, reason to believe that some of the passages just referred to express not so much the sentiments of Jesus as those of the Church of the second century, which had then separated much more widely from Judaism than was attempted previously. Paul, the most independent of the Apostles, is shown by *Acts* xxi, 24, as well as by his own Epistles (I. *Cor.* vii., 18), to have kept the law himself and to have directed all Jews to continue to do so, in spite of their becoming Christians. His view that Judaism was about to give place to Christianity, and was not obligatory on heathens who became Christians, met with so much opposition from the eleven Apostles that they can scarcely be supposed to have heard such ideas from Jesus. The *Revelation*, undoubtedly a Christian utterance of the first century, is full of reverence for the temple and the law; and this feeling reigned in the early Church according to *Acts*. Other ancient documents might also be cited to justify the opinion that nearly a century elapsed before Christianity reached the position to which it would have been elevated at once, if Jesus had really treated the temple, the Sabbath, and the law as he is said to have done. It is probable that Judaism had much the same hold on him as Catholicism had in the fourteenth century on Tauler and other mystics, who honored its creeds and its ceremonies, but only as helps to morality, and with full knowledge that duty has an intrinsic importance, in comparison with which forms and dogmas are worthless. What Jesus was historically is of little importance compared with the fact that the Four Gospels represent him as a rebel against the religion in which he was brought up, and thus give the strongest encouragement they can to heretics, come-outers, and free-thinkers.

But it must be remembered that Jesus justified his independence, not by declaring the right of all men to follow reason and conscience, but by claiming that he had a supernatural authority, greater than ever had been given to any other man, or ever would be. Nothing less was involved in his calling himself Christ or Messiah, and it was for making this claim that he was condemned to death. Again and again, he asserts his right to be called Lord and Master, to forgive sins, to rule the winds and waves, and to command angels and evil spirits. All who have taught before him are thieves and robbers, but his words are never to pass away. He is the bread of life, the true vine, the way, the truth, and the life. No free-thinker ever spoke of himself thus. I would not insist on single phrases, but all that is said of his relations with his fellow-men shows his desire for unreasoning agreement and unhesitating obedience. Those who would enter his kingdom must become like little children. Those whom he called to follow him must forsake business and property, father, mother, children, brother, sister, and wife. Even waiting to bury a dead father was not allowable. Keeping all the moral law blameless was not sufficient for him who would not give up all his property and devote himself to propagandism. The work of the disciples after his death, unto the end of the world, among all nations, was to be "teaching them to observe all things whatsoever I have commanded you." Denial of his inspiration was the only sin which could never be forgiven; and refusal to listen to him or the apostles or any of the seventy disciples was a greater sin than that of Sodom.

Here, the foundation was laid for that exaltation of theology above morality which has since done so much harm. To the same effect are such texts as, "He that believeth not shall be damned;" "He that believeth not the Son shall not see life, but the wrath of God abideth on him;" "He that heareth my word and believeth on him that sent me hath everlasting life, and shall not come into condemnation;" "No man cometh unto the Father but by me." Perhaps none of these speeches were spoken literally by Jesus; but they are all closely connected with him, as are the passages about becoming childlike, committing the unpardonable sin, and incurring greater guilt than that of Sodom. Thus, Jesus has been continually appealed to as an authority for such reliance on faith as has greatly hindered the growth not only of morality, but of her best protector, liberty. Especially unfortunate for the progress of freedom have been these two sayings: "Blessed are they that have not seen and yet have believed," and "Compel them to come in, that my house may be filled." The fundamental law of liberty is that no one should be constrained to enter even the house of God, or urged to believe any thing to which he is not led by his own experience. How far Jesus is to be held responsible for the despotism exerted in his name by the Christian Church, it is hard to say. We hear of his promising the Apostle thrones, giving them the keys of heaven or hell, with power to settle what should be considered right and wrong, and declaring that he who will not obey the Church shall be considered outside of it, like the heathen. But, on the other hand, we often find him check the bigotry of his disciples; and it may be judged from some passages in Matthew, as well as in Acts, that he wished to have all the brethren take part in church government. Whether his personal preferences would have been for Episcopalianism or Congregationalism can never be known. What is certain is that he did not wish to have individuals think and act for themselves. He cannot be charged with striving to check liberty of thought, for he probably did not know what it was, though he might have learned something about it from the Sadducees if he had not treated them as teachers of error. What independence he showed was as a mystic, not as a rationalist; and the great work of his life was in laying the foundation for a religion which gave a much higher place to ceremony than he would himself have wished, but which has not shown any more regard for faith and belief than was fully warranted by his words and acts.

III.

So the repression of free thought was carried on, sometimes with cool craft and sometimes with bloody fury, during a century and a quarter after the battle of Actium; but no opposition of importance was made except by the Stoics. Augustus sought their friendship and suffered them to dissuade him from many cruelties. But Tiberius had nothing to do with them, except to murder Cremutius Cordus for calling Brutus and Cassius the last of the Romans, in a history which the senate promptly suppressed. Julius Kanus, when Caligula closed a controversy by saying that he should be put to death, answered, as if this was the greatest favor the tyrant could bestow; and when his friends expressed regret, said: "Why are you sad? You are anxious to know whether the soul is immortal. I shall find out at once." (Seneca, *Dial.* ix., sec. xiv.)

Among the conspirators against Claudius was Pœtus, whose wife, Arria, strove in vain to save his life. When he was compelled by law either to suffer his memory to be disgraced and his property confiscated in consequence of his execution, or else to inflict capital punishment with his own hands, his courage gave way, and she offered to die with him. Her son-in-law, the famous Thrasea, said: "Would you have your daughter kill herself with me, when my turn comes?" "If she has lived as long and happily with you as I with Pœtus, I am willing," answered Arria. At last she was suffered to arouse her husband's courage by plunging his dagger into her own breast, and then giving it back with the words: "My Pœtus, it does not pain me." (Pœte, non dolet.)

Thrasea lived to assist his fellow-stoic, Seneca, in giving the empire five years of such good government that the *quinquen-*

nium Neronis became proverbial, as should be remembered in excuse for the brilliant free-thinker's connivance at the tyrant's crimes. Nor should we forget Seneca's constant activity in doing good, or the purity of his private life. So, while regretting the favor he shows to augury and astrology, we must admire his independence, not only in censuring two abuses which long found defenders among less original moralists, namely the gladiatorial games and the practice of giving to every one that asketh, but also in zealously urging the duty of mental culture, in neither recognizing undue authority in others nor claiming it for himself, in denying that the gods are angry with those who do not worship correctly, and in asserting the equality of slaves with their masters, as well as the right of women to the highest education. Among the many passages which show his advanced position are these: "I know of nothing more destructive of virtue than witnessing the games in the arena." (*Epistle* 7, sec. 2.)

"The wise man will never give without sufficient reason; for unwise gifts must be reckoned among base extravagances." "He errs who thinks it easy to give alms." "Prodigality is never noble, especially not in charity." (*De Vita Beata*, Dial. 7, ch. xxiii., sec. 5, and ch. xxiv., sec. 1. *De. Ben.*, book i., ch. ii., sec. 1.)

"No one drives away vice until in her place he accepts wisdom." "Ease without books is a living death." "In the perfection of our reason lies the happiness of life." (*Epistle* 75, sec. 10; 82, sec. 3; 92, sec. 2.)

"The mind can reach nothing grand unless it rushes out of the beaten track into regions where it has feared to mount." "Knowing any thing consists in making it our own, and not thinking of masters." "If we are satisfied with what is already found out, we shall find nothing more." "Those who have gone before us are not masters, but guides." "Truth is open to all, and has not yet been taken possession of, but much will be left to be discovered by future ages." (*De Tranq.*, ch. xvii., sec. 11; *Epistle* 33, secs. 8, 10, and 11.)

"Read my writings as those not of one who knows the truth, but of one who seeks it and seeks it boldly, coming under subjection to no one, and taking no man's name." (*Epistle* 45, sec. 4.)

"No one has known God; many think ill of him, and he harms them not." "The gods are neither able nor willing to hurt us." "He who is at peace with himself is at peace with them all." "No sane man fears them." "All their power is to do good, and they bear mildly with the errors of wandering souls." (*Epistle* 31, sec. 10; *De Ira*, book ii., ch. xxvii., sec. 1; *Epistle* 110, sec. 1; *De Ben.*, book iv., ch. xix., sec. 1, and book vii., ch. xxxi., sec. 4.)

"Let your slaves laugh, or talk, or keep silence in your presence as in that of the father of the family." "Remember that he whom you call your slave belongs to the same race as yourself. Will you despise a man for circumstances which may become your own?" "We all have one common origin, and no one is nobler than another, unless he is more ready for good deeds." "Who is nobly born? He who is naturally virtuous." (*De Ira*, book iii., ch. xxxv., sec. 2. Epistle 47, sec. 10. *DeBen.* book iii., ch. xxviii., sec. 1. *Epistle* 44, sec 5.)

"It is our mind that makes us rich." "I will lead you to those noble studies which take away sorrow. On all of them you have entered so far as my father's old-fashioned rigor permitted. Oh, if that best of men had cared less for the customs of our ancestors, and been willing to have you master the lessons of philosophy! Yet you have laid the foundations for all studies. Now return to them once more, and they will be your consolation and joy. When they have really entered your soul, you will be safe from trouble." (*Ad Helviam Matrem*, ch. xi., sec. 5, ch. xvii., secs. 3 and 4.)

In exhorting Nero to mercy, he told him that a tyrant is merely a monarch who takes pleasure in shedding blood, and that it is the duty of a king to be the father of his people, to prefer their interests to his own, and to show that the state does not belong to him, but he to the state. (*De Clem.*, book i., ch. xi., sec. 4, ch. xii., sec. 1, ch. xiv., sec. 2, ch. xix., sec. 8.) And nothing can be freer than his frequent blame of the three previous emperors, especially Caligula, whom he stigmatizes as a tyrant. His tragedies, too, which were written to be read to the leading men and women at Rome, declare that he who fears his sovereign will give up justice, and that nobler sacrifice cannot be offered to Jupiter than that of an unjust king. (*Hippolytus*, line 429, *Hercules Furens*, 922.) Seneca was the first to show the full meaning of free thought and assert its rights against both priests and kings, and in favor of women as well as slaves. Much as we may blame his complicity in Nero's earlier crimes, we must not forget that he left the tyrant's service, and was one of his victims.

With him perished his nephew Lucan, who had taken part in a great conspiracy, and whose poem on the battle of Pharsalia is remarkable, not only for being written with his wife's assistance, but for asserting the dignity of the senate, the only institution which could legally check the tyranny of a Roman emperor. The freedom with which he blames the gods for permitting Julius Cæsar to establish monarchy, and ridicules the superstition which placed him and his successors among the gods, is shown in the following extracts, mainly from Rowe's version :

> " Can there be Gods who rule yon azure sky ?
> Can they behold Pharsalia from on high,
> And yet forbear to bid their lightnings fly ?
> Is it the business of a thundering Jove
> To rive the rocks and blast the guiltless grove,
> While Cassius holds the balance in his stead
> And wreaks due vengeance on the tyrant's head ?
> But chance guides all ; the gods their task forego,
> And providence no longer rules below;
> Yet are they just, and some revenge afford,
> While their own heavens are humbled by the sword,
> And the proud victors like themselves adored.
> With rays adorned, with thunders armed they stand.
> And incense, prayers, and sacrifice demand ;
> While trembling, slavish, superstitious Rome
> Swears by a mortal wretch that molders in a tomb."
>
> VII. 445–459.

> "Nor agonies, nor livid death disgrace
> The sacred features of great Pompey's face ;
> There virtue still unchangeable abode
> And scorned the spite of every partial god."
>
> VII. 663–5.

"The gods in Cæsar's triumph took delight;
But Cato knew the conquered cause was right."
—l. 128.

The most formidable opponent of despotism was not Lucan, nor Seneca, but Thrasea, who, however, could do nothing more than leave the senate-house when Seneca's apology for Nero's murder of his mother was read aloud. Three years later, the Stoic patriot persuaded his fellow-senators to spare the life of Antistius, whom the emperor wished them to put to death in revenge for a satire. Such opposition could not be repeated successfully; but Thrasea scorned to visit the senate or take the annual oath of allegiance during the three terrible years in which more than half of Rome was destroyed by fire which Nero was believed to have set; the Christians were cruelly persecuted; Seneca and many other noble Romans perished as traitors; the blood-stained adulteress Poppæa, whom Nero had married and murdered, was raised to a place among the gods; and the insane vanity and indescribable licentiousness of the tyrant was revealed publicly. Nor was any part in the public sacrifices, for the safety of the emperor, and the preservation of the voice in which he showed such pride, or in the religious honors profusely offered to the new goddess, taken by this staunch non-conformist, priest though he was. It soon became known all over the empire, that public worship and politics had become too vile to allow the wisest and most virtuous of the priests and senators to give even his presence. Accordingly, Thrasea was brought to trial for treason and impiety. He scorned to ask mercy or make any defense, knowing that he could not save himself but might harm his friends and family. Arulenus Rusticus, who was a tribune, offered to veto the prosecution, but Thrasea forbade him, saying, "This would be useless to me and fatal to you. My time has come; but you have many years in which you may serve the state." The senate-house was surrounded with soldiers, and the patriot condemned to death. His friends crowded around him, but he bade them depart in silence. His wife, the younger Arria, wished to die like her mother, but he persuaded her to live for the sake of their daughter.

The latter's husband, Helvidius was banished in this session, when was also decreed the death of Soranus and his daughter Servilia, each of whom protested that the other was innocent and begged to be permitted to be the only victim.

Tacitus says that Nero, in killing Soranus and Thrasea, sought to destroy virtue itself. The date of the murder of these great Stoics, A.D. 66, is also that of the banishment of many others. Among them was Cornutus, who told Nero that nobody would read his poetry, and Rufus, who had been the teacher of Epictetus, the champion of the right of women to study philosophy, and the first opponent of infanticide, and who, when set to work in chains on the canal now commenced at Corinth, declared to another exile for free speech, Demetrius the Cynic, that to dig thus for the good of Greece was more honorable than to sing like Nero.

After the tyrant's fall, Helvidius returned with the other Stoics, and tried in vain to persuade his brother senators to assert their independence against Vespasian, who finally commanded him to stay away from the sessions or else keep silence. Refusing to do either, as is described by Epictetus, (*Discourses*, book i., ch. ii.) he was banished, as were many other philosophers, and finally put to death. Free thought was, however, repressed mainly by patronage, until about twenty-one years after Nero's death, when a new reign of terror began, as Domitian "Cleared Rome of what most shamed him," and murdered or banished all the Stoics. Among the exiles was Epictetus, who seems to have been less brilliant and original than Seneca, but much more consistent and earnest. No one has seen more clearly the duty of striving at the same time to secure our own individual happiness and that of our country and friends. (*Discourses*, book ii., chap. xxii., secs. 18 and 19.) Nor has any one ever spoken more powerfully in favor of mental independence. Especially characteristic are the passages in which he urges us not to shrink at being seen to do what we know is right, and declares that no one can be the owner of another's will, and that nothing should be more precious than truth. (*Enchiridion*, xxxv. *Discourses*, book iv., chap. xii. *Fragment* cxxxix.)

His high morality and piety are especially interesting on account of his freedom from any fear of the gods, or any belief in immortality. Worthy of note is also his censure of his emperor and former pupil, Hadrian. (*Discourses*, book iii., chap. i., and xiii.)

Among the fugitives from Domitian was Dion, surnamed Chrysostom or Golden-mouthed, who had advised Vespasian to restore the republic. After long wanderings, in which he sometimes worked as a gardener and sometimes begged his way, he reached the Danube in time to reveal himself to the army, which had revolted at the news of the assassination of Domitian, but was brought back to obedience by Dion's resistless eloquence. Still we have the orations in which he exhorted Trajan to devote himself to the welfare of his subjects and imitate the gods in their philanthropy, as well as those in which he proclaimed to the common people, who were his favorite auditors, the dignity of labor, the sin of slavery, and the folly of turning hermit. Among Domitian's victims was Arulenus Rusticus, who had tried to save the life of Thrasea, and now perished for writing it, as did the biographers of Cato, Brutus, and Helvidius. Even the slaves who published these books by copying them were crucified. It was the assassination of Domitian, in 96 A. D., that put an end to these one hundred and twenty-five years of despotism, and made possible that period of eighty-four glorious years of constitutional government, popular liberty, and literary activity which has been called The Reign of the Stoics.

IV.

Among the philosophers who were banished by Domitian and returned with Nerva were several women, of whom the best known is Fannia, daughter of Thrasea and wife of Helvidius. Twice she had accompanied her husband into exile, before she was herself driven from Rome for having furnished the materials for his memoirs, a copy of which work she carried away safely with her, so that she was able to put it into circulation after her return. It seems to have been in the midst of these persecutions, that Sulpicia wrote the satire in which she blames the tyrant for stripping Rome of wisdom, which is as necessary as valor for national greatness, and prophesies that he will soon perish by the muses' wrath. What we know of her as well as of Fannia, the two Arrias, Servilia, Lucan's wife, and Seneca's mother, shows how much independence their sex enjoyed during a period otherwise reactionary. Portia had sat in council with the other liberators after the death of Cæsar; and the course of Roman politics for the next century was much swayed by female influence, first of Cleopatra, then of Livia, whom Caligula called an Ulysses in petticoats, then of Antonia, who saved Tiberius from being dethroned by Sejanus, then of Messalina, who barely failed in her attempt to uncrown Claudius, and finally of the terrible Agrippina, who succeeded in making Nero emperor, and who wrote memoirs which were used by Tacitus. The wives of governors and generals made themselves so prominent in the halls of justice, and even the camps, as to cause a decree, forbidding women from following their husbands into the provinces, to be proposed during the reign of Tiberius to the senate, which rejected it by a large majority. Epictetus, who came to Rome under Nero, found the ladies reading Plato's *Republic*, which asserts their rights to be educated like men and take equal part in the government. Octavia, the sister of Augustus, was the patron, not only of Virgil but of the philosopher, Athenodorus, who dedicated a book to her. At the close of the century Plutarch exhorts a young bride to study the works of wise and learned men. All the Roman ladies now spoke Greek, according to Juvenal, who tells us how Mævia slew wild boars in the arena, Lauronia put to silence the counterfeit Stoic who reproached her sex, Manilia drew up documents as skillfully as any lawyer, and other women discoursed about Homer at their dinner-parties, went into training to fight as gladiators, and kept informed about whatever happened in all parts of the world. Meantime the old forms of marriage, which gave the husband absolute power over the wife, had given place to simple contracts, which made both parties equal before the law, suffered women to manage their property as they chose, and enabled them to protect themselves from ill-usage by the effectual, though morally dangerous remedy of easy divorce. Ortolan tells us in his *History of Roman Law*, (section 448) that marital power was now almost extinct, while the lifelong tutelage of women under their kinsmen had passed away. Lecky says that women " arrived during the empire at a point of freedom and dignity which they subsequently lost, and have never wholly regained." (*History of European Morals*, Vol. ii., p. 322, Am. Ed.) Maine thinks that, " no society which preserves any tincture of Christian institutions is likely to restore to married women the personal liberty conferred on women by the middle Roman law." (*Ancient Law*, p. 152. Am. Ed. See also Friedländer *Sittengeschichte*, Vol. i., p. 379, 3rd Ed.)

v.

This recent emancipation of the Roman women, together with the honored place in Hebrew history of Deborah, the ruler of Israel, Huldah, who told her king and people their doom, Abigail, who disobeyed her husband openly, and Esther, who persuaded hers to change his royal decrees, as well as the omission of obedience from the character of the good wife in *Proverbs*, must be kept in mind when we read the *Epistles* in which Peter and Paul command women to keep silence in the churches, and wives to obey their husbands in every thing and submit as unto Christ, the same words being used here as in enjoining subjection on slaves. The Apostle to the Gentiles, who had himself seen Queen Berenice sit among his judges, went so far as expressly to sanction that most disgusting of barbarisms and revolting abuse of power, as J. S. Mill justly calls it, by which one human being is suffered to consider himself as having a right to the person of another. (See Mill's *Political Economy*. Book ii., ch. xi., xiii., Vol. i., pp. 425 and 451. Boston, 1848. 1 *Cor.*, vii., 4, xiv., 34, 35. *Eph.* v., 22, 24, 33, vi., 5. 1 *Tim.* ii., 11, 12. 1 *Peter*, ii., 18 ; iii., 1.) The denial of the protection of divorce to women for any cause, (*Mark*, X., 12), and the prohibition of baptism by females in the early church are also not to be overlooked. Nor is the fact that precisely the same words are used, not only in the Greek text of the *Epistles* but in our English versions, to command the obedience and subjection of wives to husbands, as of slaves to masters, and of all men to God. (Compare 1 *Peter* iii., 1, ii., 18-25. *Hebrews* xii., 9. *Eph.* v., 22, 24. *Col.* iii., 18. *Eph.* vi., 5. *Heb.* xi., 8. 1 *Peter* iii., 6.)

The abject obedience enjoined towards husbands and slaveholders was also commanded in favor of tyrants. Thrasea had but just begun his constitutional opposition to Nero, when Paul said to the Romans: "Let every soul be subject unto the higher powers: the powers that be are ordained of God. Whosoever therefore resisteth the power, resisteth the ordinance of God." And Peter declared, while the great struggle to sustain the rights of the senate was at its crisis: "Submit yourselves to the king as supreme, for so is the will of God." It was after this was written, that Nero was condemned to be scourged to death by the senate, whose support was much relied on by Otho in the conflict with Vitellius, and whose authority stood high with Trajan, Antoninus Pius, and Marcus Aurelius, when all the books of the New Testament had been composed. But no Apostle or Evangelist favors setting any legal limits to monarchical power; three of the *Gospels* make Jesus approve of paying tribute to Tiberius, for the reason that his face was stamped on the current coin, an argument which would condemn the American, English, and French revolutions; and nowhere in the New Testament is there any sympathy with the last struggle of the Jewish nation against such tyranny as justified rebellion, according to *Judges* and *Maccabees*. So great has been the authority of the Apostles and Evangelists for eighteen centuries, that their sanction of despotism cannot be left unnoticed in a history of liberty.

Neither can we overlook their upholding the worst error in the Old Testament, and insisting that theological and ceremonial mistakes are sinful and hateful unto God. Paul at least knew enough about Greek literature to be aware that the philosophers had taught for centuries, that "The gods are never angry, and do nobody any harm." Such language as has just been quoted from Seneca was very common, when the *Epistles* were written. Yet the Apostle to the Gentiles declares, that the form of worship which was universal among them and which fed such holy souls as those of Socrates, Plato, Cornelia, Portia, Cato, Epictetus, and Marcus Aurelius, was so displeasing to the heavenly Father, as to make him give all these erring children up to be tempted by the vilest of passions, and even send them strong delusions so that they should believe a lie, and all be judged accordingly; that idolators shall not inherit the kingdom of God; and that the Lord Jesus shall come in flaming fire to take vengeance on those who do not know God or obey the Gospel, and who shall be punished with everlasting destruction. (*Romans* i., 18–22. 2 *Thess.* ii., 11, 12. *Gal.* v., 20, 21. 2 *Thess.* i., 7–8.)

Many such declarations of the divine wrath against the heathen are to be found in the *Revelation* which was probably written shortly after the death of Nero, the letters of whose name and title have a numerical valuation in Hebrew amounting to six hundred and sixty-six, and whose place as the sixth Cæsar is referred to in chapter xvii., verse 10. An author, who knew of the great fire which nearly destroyed Rome, of the horrible persecutions of the Christians afterwards, and of the simultaneous revolt in Spain, Palestine, Gaul, Germany and Africa, of generals each of whom sought to make himself emperor, may be pardoned for thinking that the Roman empire would come to an end at once, and be succeeded by the promised millennium. Nor is his indignation against the persecutors unnatural; but his denunciation of them, as well as his prophecy of national ruin, must have done much to provoke further cruelties. Peculiar intolerance appears in the introductory warning against the only person, who at that time made claims to apostleship which could be called in question, the author of that permission to eat meats offered to idols, and to live with an unbelieving husband or wife, which had but just been given to the church at Corinth. (See 1 *Cor.* vii., 12, 14, viii., 4, x., 23–27. *Rev.* ii., 2, 14, 20, xxi., 14.)

But even the most liberal of the Apostles warned the Corinthians and Colossians against philosophy, (1 *Cor.* iii., 19. *Col.* ii., 8.) and put heresy in the same black list as murder and adultery. (*Gal.* v., 19-21.) Paul apparently knew of nothing worse than thinking for one's self. Those who ventured to do so were rejected from fellowship by the earliest Christians and forbidden hospitality, (*Titus* iii., 10. 2 *John* 10. 2 *Peter*, ii., 1.) while those who spoke against the clergy were regarded as: "Wandering stars unto whom is reserved the blackness of darkness forever." (*Jude* 8-13.) Matthew makes Jesus say, that he who will not yield to the church is to be treated as one of the heathen, who were under the divine wrath, according to the *Apocalypse* and the *Epistles*. All the *Gospels* represent failure to agree with the Apostles and their master as sinful, and unreasoning obedience as highly meritorious. Even the unutterable guilt of Sodom is said to be less than that of not listening to the disciples; while charging Jesus with insanity is called an unpardonable sin. We are also told: "He that believeth and is baptized shall be saved." "He that believeth not the Son shall not see life but the wrath of God abideth on him." "Whosoever shall not receive the kingdom of God as a little child shall in no wise enter therein." "Blessed are they that have not seen and yet have believed."

These words, as well as the apostolic teaching of justification by faith, show how necessary is acceptance of the authority of Jesus for salvation, according to the New Testament. Morality, of course, is insisted on also, and very strictly, but it is nowhere acknowledged that salvation can be attained by those who have no faith. Much as this doctrine of salvation through belief rather than ceremony aided the assailants of papal tyranny, the general current of free thought before and after that struggle has been greatly checked by the support thus given to the idea that mental independence may imperil eternal happiness, as well as by the sanction of absolute monarchy and conjugal tyranny, and the failure to favor intellectual culture. This is all the more to be regretted, because the New Testament has obtained more power in Europe and this country than any other book, an influence easily to be accounted for—partly by the unrivaled eloquence with which it proclaims the universal brotherhood of all Christians, promises that earthly distinctions will be abolished at entrance into heaven, ascribes all phenomena to the agency of supernatural persons, teaches the great virtues of purity and love, through the most impressive, not only of teachers, but examples, and offers eternal salvation to all who will believe and be obedient —and partly by the consummate skill with which the Church has been organized into an army of champions for a common cause. Thus the early Christians, while contending for beliefs and ceremonies which were deadly rivals to those insisted on by the emperors, were yet working even more mightily than they to carry out the great reaction in which political freedom, mental independence, and literary culture were swept away.

VI.

This success was mainly due to a fact already referred to, but more prominent in the Church Fathers than in the New Testament. The Jewish, Greek, and Roman priests merely performed ceremonies, and left the work of preaching and teaching to be done by any one who might choose to take it up; but among Christians there has been until recent times very little preaching or writing about theology except by ecclesiastics. Some distinction between clergy and laity, seems to be recognized in *Philippians*, *James*, and *First Peter*. Paul, according to *Acts*, took great pains to ordain pastors over every church he organized, but from the lack of reference to episcopal authority in those *Epistles* which are undoubtedly his, it is probable that it was the other Apostles, who established the hierarchy of deacons, priests or elders, and bishops. The last two titles were nearly synonymous until the end of the first century, however, and such is the usage in the *Epistles* to *Timothy* and *Titus*, which should not be put later than this time, and which zealously assert the divine authority of ecclesiastics and the sinfulness of disobedience. So does the *Epistle* of *Jude*, which has been already quoted, and which may be ascribed to the beginning of the second century, as may the strongly hierarchical *Second Epistle General of Peter*. Still more favorable to clerical rule are the epistles attributed to Clemens Romanus, Ignatius, and Polycarp and apparently written in part at least about 150 A. D. A command to be subject to priests and deacons, as to God and Christ, is found in the *Epistle of Polycarp to the Philippians*, which is probably authentic, as are passages in the letters of Ignatius declaring that the bishop sits in the place of God, and that nothing is to be done without him. To find the superiority of bishops to priests plainly asserted, however, we must go on to the middle of the third century, and look in the writings of Cyprian, as well as in the so-called *Apostolic Constitutions*, which forbid rebellion against the clergy. Thus their domination was gradually developed as a logical result of the doctrine of justification by faith. No book can foresee the future well enough to decide all controversies. Uniformity of belief can be maintained only by the authority of living rulers. The appearance of heresies, even in the first century, favored the supremacy of the bishops, and it was but one step further in logic, though a long stride in history, to assert that purity of faith could not be kept up without a pope.

Even the most rudimentary form of such an organization naturally placed free thought under restrictions never felt before.

The Jews had never decided the rival claims of Essene, Pharisee, and Sadducee. Even while the pagans punished those who worshiped none of the gods, there was no objection to a man's placing any one of the national deities as high as he pleased. Such fierce controversies as soon arose about the rank and offices of Father, Son, and Holy Ghost, were impossible outside of the Christian Church. No heathen or Jewish books had made such a distinction between orthodox and heretical as is seen in the New Testament; and the early Fathers are much worse than the Apostles. Ignatius is charged with telling the church at Antioch that: "Whosoever declares that there is but one God, so as to take away the divinity of Jesus Christ, is a devil and the enemy of all righteousness." Similar language was used during the latter part of the second century by Tertullian, as will be seen at the beginning of the next chapter. An inevitable result of this subjection to church authority was a dislike to classic literature, towards which none of the early Fathers show much respect, except Justin Martyr, who also distinguished himself by placing not only Abraham, but Socrates and all others who had lived divinely, among Christians, as well as by strongly condemning gladiatorial games, the guilt of which is not noticed in the New Testament.

Nothing shows better the narrowness of the Church in the second century than the readiness with which she cast out as heretics the most scholarly and liberal of her children, namely the Gnostics, so-called because they expected to be saved through knowledge. Bigotry has destroyed their writings so thoroughly, that we know little of them except from hostile sources. They called themselves Christians, but cared little for the authority of bishops or apostles, and borrowed freely from cabalists, Parsees, astrologers, and Greek philosophers, in building up their fantastic systems. Most of them agreed in asserting the eternity, potency, and innate depravity of matter, as well as in ascribing the creation to a Demiurge, who was the God of the Jews, and who had a nature sadly limited in power and intelligence, as is shown by the many defects, not only in nature but in the Old Testament. Some of the earliest of these visionaries were called Ophites, and charged with worshiping the serpent as the emblem of wisdom, as well as with honoring Cain, Esau, and other rebels against the Demiurge, and with circulating a *Gospel according to Judas Iscariot*. The Gnostics generally believed that it was to free man from the tyranny of Jehovah that Christ came, and that he had no real flesh and blood, which latter heresy was condemned as Docetism. The resurrection of the body, as well as the outward second coming and material millennium, they rejected utterly. Among their many and wholly independent teachers are Cerinthus, whom the Apostle John is said to have refused to meet in a bath-house for fear the roof should fall on them; Valentine, a Pythagorean, who formed a powerful sect of believers in his doctrine of a great hierarchy of Æons or emanations from God, Basilides, a Platonist, who gained many followers to his teaching, that it is by man's innate strength that the race rose from Paganism through Judaism into Christianity, and that the individual must raise himself from the earthly life to the heavenly; Marcellina, who is said to have "led multitudes astray in Rome," during the reign of Marcus Aurelius; and Carpocrates, who gave Zoroaster, Homer, Pythagoras, Plato, Aristotle, and Paul equal honors with Jesus, and taught that all men must finally be saved, though most would have to be purified by transmigration. Especially noted are Marcion, the Stoic, and his followers, among whom was the learned virgin, Philumene, for the boldness with which they rejected several of the *Gospels* and *Epistles*, as well as the entire Old Testament. They were especially shocked by the commands given to the Hebrews to rob the Egyptians, and to massacre the wives and children of the Canaanites. Much as we may fear that the Gnostic literature was more remarkable for boldness in speculation, than for clearness of reasoning or respect for facts, it is a great pity that it should have been almost entirely destroyed by ecclesiastical bigotry.

VII.

Most of the Gnostics just mentioned belong to that period of constitutional rule and mental freedom which lasted from A. D. 96 to A. D. 180; and which also gave us the works of Plutarch, Quintillian, Suetonius, Juvenal, Pliny, Tacitus, Dion Chrysostom, Arrian, Ptolemy, Apuleius, Fronto, Marcus Aurelius, Galen, Pausanias, Celsus, Gaius the jurist, and Lucian. To these happy years also belongs the delivery of those discourses taken down by Arrian from the lips of Epictetus.

First in time, as well as in popularity, is Plutarch, whose extant works fill a much larger space than those of any other classic author, and whose biographies of Solon, Aristides, Demosthenes, Cicero, Brutus, Dion, Cato the younger, Agis, Cleomenes, and the Gracchi, did much to educate the leaders of the French revolution. Some of the treatises known as *Plutarch's Morals* do great injustice to both Stoicism and Epicureanism, and others show that he is far too credulous to be much of an authority about either history or science ; but the general tendency of these miscellanies is hostile to superstition, and favorable to female independence and mental culture. Particularly valuable are the *Conjugal Precepts*, the *Discourse to a Prince*, and the essays on *Bashfulness, Superstition, Those whom God is Slow to Punish*, and the *Virtues of Women*.

Passing for a moment from Greek to Latin, we meet the four contemporaries, Tacitus, Juvenal, Pliny, and Suetonius. The great historian's real views about theology are probably to be found in such declarations, as that the gods do not try to protect us, but rather to avenge themselves ; that they care as little for the most virtuous as for the vicious; and that their permitting Nero to go on so long in iniquity shows that they had nothing to do with the prodigies supposed to have taken place after his murder of his mother (*History*, i., 3, *Annals*, xvi., 33, and xiv., 12). There can be no doubt of his hatred of tyranny, his sympathy with the champions of constitutional freedom, and his deep conviction that, as he makes one of these martyrs, Cremutius Cordus, declare during his trial in the senate, errors in speech should be punished by words only (*Annals*, iv., 35).

His own earliest work, showing how necessary it is that eloquence should decline under a monarchy, seems to have been written during the reign of Vespasian. But it was not until after the fall of Domitian that he could record the doom pronounced by history upon tyrants. Similar censures were also made by the superstitious and scandal-loving Suetonius, and involved no risk in the reigns of Nerva and Trajan, who, like their successors Hadrian, Antoninus Pius, and Marcus Aurelius, ruled constitutionally. Trajan even permitted senators to coin money in their own names and thus exercise what

Jesus considered a decisive privilege of sovereignty. These liberty-loving emperors allowed great freedom of speech, and Hadrian used only his influence against Favorinus for attacking astrology; but a law was enacted against secret assemblages, and Ignatius, with another bishop, was put to death by Trajan, who sanctioned the torture of deaconesses and execution of men steadfast in Christianity, carried on by Pliny, nephew of the naturalist, and who gave orders that all known to believe thus should be punished, but no attempt made to find them out. This persecution was discontinued by Hadrian, who was too skeptical to be intolerant, as well as by Antoninus Pius, who honored freedom of speech and was too practical to be superstitious; but it was renewed by Marcus Aurelius under exceptional circumstances which we shall soon have to consider fully.

Juvenal drew on himself no hatred, except from the worshipers of Isis, Cybele, and Jehovah, as he blamed the Roman matron for breaking the ice to plunge herself into the Tiber, crawling on bare and bloody knees around the Campus Martius or going on pilgrimages to Nubia, the Egyptians for carrying their quarrel, whether the crocodile ought to be slaughtered or worshiped, into murder and cannibalism, and the Hebrews for making every seventh day one of idleness. Much more courage appears in his lashing the follies and vices of the wealthy nobles, and declaring:

"No merit see I in a pedigree;
Virtue alone is true nobility."

His eighth *satire* is inspired by this sentiment, which is not consistent with his scorn of newly emancipated slaves. His ridicule of them, as well of the women who were asserting their rights, seems to have met with little protest from contemporary authors, but, nevertheless, these reforms went on, and were much assisted by such laws as that of Hadrian permitting females to bequeath property, that of Antoninus Pius allowing them to inherit it, and that of Marcus Aurelius facilitating emancipation.

How worthy the Roman women really were of independence may be judged from the letters of the Pliny just mentioned. He shows that he had many friends whose virtue came up fully to his own standard, which was that of a Stoic. Among the most interesting epistles are nine relating trials which he prosecuted before the senate, whose members voted by secret ballot, and acted with such great freedom as proves that the monarchy really was a constitutional one under Nerva and Trajan. The latter, as he gave to the prætorian prefect, who commanded the guards stationed at Rome, the dagger that marked the office, said : "Take this and use it for me if I rule justly; if otherwise, against me." Hadrian was capriciously despotic, but Antoninus Pius treated his subjects like his fellow-citizens ; as we know from the testimony of Marcus Aurelius Antoninus, who himself delighted to honor Thrasea, Helvidius, Cato, Dion, and Brutus, and who was always faithful to his own ideal of a kingdom which maintains equal rights and equal freedom of speech, and holds nothing so sacred as the liberty of the people. Under him, indeed, the empire differed but little from a republic ; as may be judged from the difficulty he had in persuading the senate to pardon the adherents of Avidius Cassius, who rebelled A.D. 175, but was killed by his own soldiers. The senators refused to proclaim universal amnesty until their emperor's second letter, in which he begged for it as a consolation for the death of his wife.

That sublime and touching book which he wrote for his own support amid the greatest trials, is full of passages like these :

"If any one can show me that I am wrong in word or action I will gladly change, for I seek the truth by which no one was ever harmed." "It is not right that I should give myself pain, for I have never given any willingly to others." "The immortal gods are not angry with the wicked ; and why should I be, who am destined to end so soon, and who am myself a sinner?" "The best way to revenge myself is not to become like him who wrongs me. Remember that men exist for each other, and that they do wrong unwillingly." "It is peculiarly human to love those who do wrong." "Do not make yourself either a tyrant or a slave to any man." "Take heed not to become like the Cæsars, but keep yourself the friend of justice and the enemy of pomp." "Do not be ashamed of being helped, for you are like a soldier storming a wall, and what if you can not climb the battlement except with a comrade's aid?" "To change your mind and follow him who sets you right does not lessen your independence." "If you are able, teach others what is right; if you are not, remember that meekness was given you for this." "Find all your joy in passing from one philanthropic action to another." "My nature is patriotic, and my country is Rome as far as I am an Antonine, but as I am a man, it is all the world. Only what is useful to these countries is useful to me." "Have I done any thing for the common good? Well then, I have had my reward."

Thus spoke the last great Stoic as he battled against the Northern barbarians, who already threatened to overrun the empire, at that time much weakened by a terrible invasion of the Parthians, by the revolt of Egypt which was the granary of Rome, and by the pestilence which is said to have destroyed half of the population despite Galen's utmost efforts.

With this reign begins a long period of defeats, persecutions, rebellions, and civil wars. Sad is the contrast with the internal peace and prosperity which the empire had enjoyed for nearly two centuries after the battle of Actium, with little interruption, except that terrible year which succeeded the death of Nero, and which led the Apostle John to prophesy the speedy destruction of the nation and end of the world. New calamities naturally drew increased attention to these predictions, as well as to the similar ones forged about this time in the dreaded name of the Sibyls, by some Christian, who declared that Marcus Aurelius would be the last of the emperors. Unfortunately this monarch was so superstitious as to think that the gods could be seen bodily, and had shown him remedies against giddiness and spitting of blood in dreams. (*Meditations*, xii., 28, and i., 17.) He was led by a shameless impostor named Alexander, who had passed off a tame serpent for an incarnation of Æsculapius, and was then selling oracles in Paphlagonia at the rate of seventy or eighty thousand a year, to throw living lions into the Danube in hope of regaining the favor of the gods. (See Lucian's *Alexander, the False Prophet.*) He offered so many costly sacrifices that the white oxen are said to have exclaimed: "If you conquer, we are lost!"

This excessive zeal led one of the most kind-hearted of men to suffer Justin Martyr to be beheaded, and Polycarp, Blandina, and other men and women to be tortured to death in the arena, though he did not himself witness any of these horrors, most of which took place in Gaul and Asia Minor, while he was fighting on the Danube. If he had done nothing more than enforce his own law, banishing people who stirred up superstitious fears, we might consider him excused by the dangers that threatened his empire. That he permitted men and women to be murdered cruelly, merely for speaking what they believed to be the truth, and abstaining from ceremonies they thought impious, is a memorable instance of the wickedness into which religion may lead even the best of men. This, indeed, is all the more remarkable from the fact that Marcus Aurelius, although one of the staunchest of Stoics, made an impartial division of the salaries, now paid by the State to philosophers, among the advocates of the four great schools, so that the followers of Plato, Aristotle, and Epicurus were as liberally treated as those of his own beloved master, Zeno. That he patronized the Epicureans, while persecuting the Christians, may be due to the fact that the former, though believing as little in the national deities as the latter, made no predictions of the coming ruin of the empire, and had no scruples about fighting in its defense.

We, like Celsus, author at this time of a book against Christianity, known only through the portions preserved in the answer made by Origen, may blame the early Christians for lack of patriotism, dislike of mental culture, willingness to believe without examination, readiness to admit people of disreputable antecedents into their communion, scorn of business interests, and excessive humility. But we must regret that they were attacked by any weapons but argument and ridicule. Only one man in that age seems to have been able, while rejecting all their peculiar beliefs, to do full justice to their unrivaled purity, generosity to the poor, and moral courage. This was Galen, the great physician, and the first real Agnostic; for careful study of the various schools of philosophy had taught him that all such questions as those about Deity and immortality lay wholly beyond the reach of human thought, while his scientific researches taught him to prize such practical knowledge as has actually become the most valuable possession of man.

VIII.

How little even Marcus Aurelius could do to preserve the old faith is shown in the great popularity obtained by his contemporary Lucian, who satirized paganism and Christianity with equal boldness, and described the ease with which the unprincipled Peregrinus Proteus took advantage of the credulity, generosity, and scorn of worldly riches in the early church to make himself wealthy, no more keenly than he did the arts by which an oracle in the name of Æsculapius was established by Alexander. Hearing that this prophet gave oracular answers to questions delivered, sealed and returned apparently unopened, the witty free-thinker sent him scroll after scroll, which he had sealed up so securely that the seer was unable to open them clandestinely, and had to get what knowledge he could out of the servants who brought them. Thus, on being asked in writing whether his long hair was false, and informed that the inquirer was studying local history, Alexander said: "King Attis was not Sarbaldalachus!" So when the question was, where Homer was born, the oracle replied: "Go not by sea, but take thy way on foot!" Then Lucian sent eight times the usual fee, with a scroll, asking when that rascal of an Alexander would be found out, and received eight answers which had nothing to do with anything in heaven or on earth. After boasting of these victories over the oracle, and trying to prevent a Roman senator who held a high office in Paphlagonia from marrying a girl who Alexander pretended was his daughter by Luna, the skeptic visited the prophet,

and bit severely the hand held out to be kissed. Lucian
was attacked by the attendants, but they were called off by
Alexander who saw that his enemy was protected by an escort
of Roman soldiers. The servant of Æsculapius now announced that he would show how potent the god was in reconciling strifes, and then privately persuaded the skeptic,
that it would be for his own interest to conduct himself rev-
erentially. Soon after, Lucian left for Greece in a ship lent
him by Alexander, but narrowly escaped being thrown into
the sea by the sailors, the captain fortunately taking his part.
After this he set about accusing the impostor publicly, but
was prevented by the entreaties of the king of Pontus and
Bythinia. On the death of Alexander, and the failure of his
accomplices to agree who should take his place, Lucian did
however, publish, A. D. 182, his narrative, which was partly
designed, " to vindicate the honor of Epicurus, that truly good
and pious man, endowed with most divine knowledge, who
alone was acquainted with the beauty of truth, and taught it
to others, blessing all those with freedom and happiness who
attended to him." (*Francklin's Lucian*, vol. ii., pp. 451-497).
So numerous were the Epicureans at this time on the northern
coast of Asia Minor, especially at Amastris, now Amasserah,
a sea-port about eighty miles to the westward of Ionopolis,
the residence of Alexander, and so active were they in exposing his impostures, that he publicly burned a book by Epicurus,
and commanded all Epicureans to depart before he celebrated
his mysteries, which represented the birth of Apollo and
Æsculapius, the recent discovery of the latter in the form of
a serpent, and the loves of the moon and the prophet. The
Christians were also sent away, but there was profound peace
between Alexander and the Stoics, Platonists, and Pythagoreans.

Lucian's own preferences are plain, not only in this narra-
tive but in the dialogue called, *The Double Indictment*, where
Stoicism, personified as the Portico, brings a lawsuit against
Epicureanism, here termed Pleasure, for stealing away Diony-
sius, who was nicknamed the Deserter. The "Lady of the
Pictures," as Zeno's school is called after the pictures in the

porch where he taught, blames her adversary for teaching men to wallow in the mire, for denying the providence of the gods, and for poisoning the mind of Dionysius. Epicurus answers that no unfair means were used to gain over this free man in a free city, who left the Portico, because he was disgusted at its secret profligacy, and convinced that the happiness it promised was a mere sham and that his own health required him to live like a man, not a statue, and to make no sacrifice of present happiness in hope of future bliss. It is plain from this dialogue, as well as from those called *Hermotimus*, the *Banquet*, the *Fisherman*, etc., and also from the letters and *Meditations* of Marcus Aurelius, that such excessive self-denial and asceticism had now become a part of Stoicism, that the sect was full of hypocrites, whose numbers had been greatly increased by the patronage given by Antoninus Pius and his successor. The other schools were no purer, and that of Epicurus seems to have at last sunk much lower than would have been permitted by its founder, though his original error, of giving the disciple no higher object than his own happiness, was largely to blame for the more serious mistake of neglecting the dependence of happiness on fidelity to the moral laws. Before the close of the fourth century the sect had become extinct, and it produced no original author after Lucian.

There was nothing new in his attacking the popular theology, but no one had been able to make it so ridiculous as he does in the well known series of short dialogues about the amours of the gods, which point he saw to be the weakest in the whole ancient mythology. A longer and extremely powerful composition of the same nature represents Jupiter as utterly baffled by a philosopher, who forces him to confess himself merely the tool of fate. Peculiarly strong in its opposition to every form of theism is the dialogue called *Jupiter the Tragedian*, because it opens with the theatrical lamentations of that deity over the prospect that all faith and worship will be destroyed by the arguments which Damis the Epicurean is urging against Timocles the Stoic. The frightened deities assemble in a council, at which Momus tells them that they ought not to be angry with any philosopher who is led to question their existence by seeing how the virtuous are suffered to perish in poverty, disease, and slavery, while the wicked gain wealth and sovereignty, and how the robbers of temples and other criminals remain unpunished, but the innocent are condemned. Neptune wishes to have Damis struck by thunder, and Hercules offers to pull down the house where the dispute is held, but Jupiter decides that no such acts can be permitted by the Fates, and that all he and the other gods can do is to listen to their champion, and pray for his success. The Stoic describes the order and harmony of all things, but is told that he has no right to ascribe to Providence what may be only the result of necessity or of chance. His appeal to Homer and Euripides is met by the argument, that the former's gods have many weaknesses, and that the latter was really an unbeliever. Timocles next urges that all nations worship, but Damis thanks him for reminding him that there are so many and wide variations in religion, as show that it is all confusion and error. After vainly referring to the oracles, then much in discredit on account of their ambiguity, the Stoic asks if the universe can go on without a ruler any more than a ship can without a pilot; but the Epicurean says there is little reason to praise the pilot who made Sardanapalus a king and Socrates a criminal, and who is constantly running the great ship against rocks. Finally, Timocles declares that the existence of altars proves that of the gods, but Damis only laughs at him, and compares him to a malefactor who takes refuge in the temple as in a sanctuary; and Jupiter admits that, so far as thinking men are concerned, his cause is lost. In the *Icaro-Menippus,* Jove is represented as pulling up a trap-door in the floor of his palace and listening to the prayers, two of which are from different men asking incompatible favors at the same time, and promising the same sacrifice, so that the deity cannot tell what to do. Faith in immortality is derided in the *True History of the Necromancer* and the *Dialogues of the Dead,* though these, like the *Tyrant,* are mainly designed to show the vanity of all earthly pomp. To politics Lucian paid little attention, and the picture of Nero at the Isthmus of Corinth, is probably by some other hand, as is the *Philopatris*, an accusation of Christians for lack of patriotism. That our author was right in calling himself not only a hater of pride, imposture, falsehood, and ostentation, but the friend of truth, honor, beauty, simplicity, and every thing that is amiable and good, appears in his eulogy of his friend Demonax, the philosopher, who, when the Athenians were talking about building an amphitheater to exhibit gladiators, told them : "Before you do this you should destroy the altar to Pity," and, when they were going to stone him because he would not offer sacrifices, nor let himself be initiated into the Eleusinian mysteries, disarmed all their rage by saying : "Wonder not, O Athenians, that I have not sacrificed to Minerva, for she standeth not in need of my offerings. And as to the mysteries, the reason that I have kept away from them is that if I should find them to be bad, I should not be able to conceal this from the uninitiated ; but if they are good, I fear that philanthropy would compel me to reveal them to every body," an argument against all secret societies which are not needed to protect their members against tyrants. So unsparing is Lucian in his sarcasms, even against his own master, Epicurus, that we must take care to give him the full benefit of his own maxim : "Nothing truly good and valuable is ever the worse for the ridicule thrown upon it, but comes out only the brighter and more splendid, like gold from under the hammer."

IX.

These dialogues did not prevent Lucian's becoming governor of Egypt, and so shrewd and selfish a man would not have gone on writing them if they had in the least interfered with his comfort, his reputation, or his ambition. They show, too, as does the history written but a little later by Diogenes Laertius, that Epicureanism was very flourishing during the second century. From these facts, as well as from the steady growth of Christianity, we see that the efforts of the emperors, from Augustus to Marcus Aurelius, to protect the national religion against foreign faiths and domestic unbeliefs, had met with but little success. Literary activity was sadly checked by Tiberius, Caligula, Nero, and Domitian; but even in the midst of this century of tyranny the rights of free thought had been brilliantly vindicated by Seneca, Tacitus, Juvenal, Dion Chrysostom, Epictetus, Lucian, and the Gnostics enjoyed the protection of rulers who loved liberty. Meantime that last refuge of free speech and political independence, the senate, was heroically defended against Nero and Vespasian by those great Stoic martyrs, Thrasea and Helvidius, and was restored by Nerva to an authority which it retained for nearly a century, no influence having yet been exerted on politics by the strong preference for absolute monarchy shown in the New Testament. Nor did the opposition there offered to the emancipation of women prevent the rapid progress of this movement, which was powerfully encouraged by Seneca and Plutarch. Thus the second century left rationalism in such popularity that its prospects would not have been worse in the days of Lucian than in those of Lucretius, if the diminution of mental activity had not opened the way for the triumph of a new form of superstition and intolerance, while the decline of martial vigor, under the pressure of tyranny, threatened the empire with ultimate conquest by barbarians, whose ignorance made it certain that they would support religion against philosophy.

CHAPTER IV.

THE SUPPRESSION OF FREE THOUGHT AND ESTABLISHMENT OF CHRISTIANITY.

How closely these two events are connected may be seen in the works which Tertullian, the first Christian to attract notice as a Latin author, published about 200 A.D. He declares that the resurrection of Jesus ought to be believed in because it is impossible; that heresy causes eternal death; that heretics are not to be disputed with or permitted to appeal to Scripture; that the Christian's authority is not the Bible but the Church; that nothing can be learned from any heretic; that those who possess Christ have no need to be curious about further knowledge; and that investigation is unnecessary for those who have the Gospel. "Nobis curiositate opus non est post Christum Jesum, nec inquisitione post evangelium."

This language, as well as the forbidding of Christians to become schoolmasters or professors of literature, is in full harmony with the dislike of mental culture already pointed out in the New Testament, (see p. 81); with the general condemnation of those primitive Unitarians contemporary with Tertullian, the Artemonites, for studying Euclid, Galen, and Aristotle, and with the charge laid by the so-called *Apostolic Constitutions* on the disciples of the third century to abstain from heathen books. (I., VI.) So strict were the limits of orthodoxy, however, as to bring even this hater of heretics under the charge of being himself one of them, though this is due mainly to his insisting on the speedy coming of the millennium, favoring the strictest asceticism, condemning second marriages, forbidding women to wear ornaments, and yet asserting their right to prophesy. Such were the views that had but just been taught in Phrygia by Montanus, Priscilla, and

Maximilla, the last of whom said: "After me there is nothing but the end of the world." The existence of female bishops was characteristic of this sect, which soon spread to Africa, where two of its members, Perpetua and Felicitas, gained the crown of martyrdom. It was only the excessive desire of the Montanists to maintain the purity of the Church, and carry out the teaching of her founders, that caused them to be condemned as heretics. Maximilla, after devoting her vast wealth to spread what she thought the true faith, and journeying with bare feet over snow-clad mountains to do good to the sick and ignorant, had to exclaim: "They chase me like a wolf from the fold; yet I am not a wolf!"

There was no heresy in Tertullian's vivid pictures of the activity of demons, which had been admitted by Matthew, Mark, Luke, and Paul, nor in his placing the emperor second to God, nor in his insisting, as Justin Martyr and Athenagoros had done, on the literal resurrection of the body, a doctrine afterward embodied in the creed falsely attributed to the apostles. It was an advance on the New Testament for the African controversialist to condemn infanticide and the gladiatorial games, which latter had been justly said by Minutius Felix to teach murder. Here the apostles would, no doubt, have agreed with Tertullian; but they would certainly not have approved of his making God and the soul material; and it is probable that they would not have sanctioned his asserting that each individual has a right to choose his own religion; that no one is injured by another's choice; that there is nothing religious in compelling people to follow any religion, and that no one, not even a man, can wish to have worship paid him unwillingly. How such noble sentiments came to be uttered by so fierce a hater of heresy is a problem, easily solved by the fact that the Christians were then being persecuted by the pagans. When the Church grew strong enough to persecute, she did so with little hesitation.

Thought was still free enough at the beginning of the third century to permit Diogenes Laertius to compile the best record extant of the opinions of Epicurus and his predecessors for the benefit of some lady supposed to be either Julia

Domna, the empress, or else a Platonist named after the Stoic heroines Arria. Alexander of Aphrodisias was able to gain great fame as an expositor of Aristotle, whose system he considers incompatible with belief in personal immortality. The latter, at least, of these champions of philosophies soon to pass into oblivion, belongs to Alexandria. And it was in the capitol of Egypt, and during the first half of the third century, that Sextus Empiricus wrote an elaborate statement of Pyrrhonism, of which a translation is given in Stanley's *History of Philosophy*, and in which the Skeptics, who hold that knowledge about theology and metaphysics is too far out of reach for us to need to feel any anxiety on such subjects, are contrasted with the Dogmatists, who talk of Truth as if it were their own private property, an error charged not only on the Peripatetics and Stoics ; but also on the Epicureans. The authority of the established rules of morality is admitted by Sextus, but he insists that we ought neither to believe nor disbelieve any thing so firmly as to make us uncomfortable or unable to receive further light ; and he gives most of his first book to the ten illustrations of human liability to error already stated on page 37. The second book discusses the nature of deductive and inductive proof, and lays great stress on the fact that all our knowledge is relative. The third and last exposes the groundlessness, inconsistency and mutual contradictions of the current beliefs in motion, time, space, virtue, and deity. "Let the dogmatists first agree among themselves as to whether God hath any body, or a form like man's, or any special residence ; and then we can tell whether we should agree with them. Surely if He were self-evident there would not be such disputes as to who, or what, or where He is. Moreover, those who say that there is a God can not be excused from impiety, for if they say that He takes care of all things, they make Him the author of evil, and if they say that He takes care of some but not of others, they make Him weak or else partial."

A new school of liberal thought had already arisen in this learned city, under the lead of Pantænus, who retained his Stoic respect for knowledge when he became a Christian, and who taught Clement of Alexandria to do such ample justice to heathen philosophy as seemed heretical to popes and patriarchs. We can have only praise for the scholar who dared to say: "Plato, Antisthenes, and Cleanthes spoke by divine inspiration." "Each soul has its own proper nutriment, some feeding on the Hellenic philosophy, the whole of which, like nuts, is not eatable." "Those can not condemn the Greeks who have only a mere hearsay knowledge of their opinions, and have not entered into a minute investigation." "Before the advent of the Lord, philosophy was necessary to the Greeks for righteousness, and now it is conducive to piety. For this was a schoolmaster to bring the Hellenic mind, as the law the Hebrew, to Christ." "It is impossible for a man without learning to comprehend the things which are declared in the faith." "The multitude are frightened at the Hellenic philosophy, lest it lead them astray. But if the faith (for I can not call it knowledge) which they possess be such as is dissolved by plausible speech, by all means let it be dissolved. For truth is immovable." (*Clement of Alexandria, Ante-Nicene Library*, vol. i., 71–2, 353, 360, 366, 372; ii., 350.) At the same time he says to the heathen, who declined to give up the customs handed down by their fathers, "And why do we not use our first nourishment? Why do we increase our patrimony? Do we still do the things for which, when infants, we were laughed at? Then why do we not abandon the usage which is evil, even should our fathers feel hurt, and betake ourselves to the truth, and seek Him who is truly Our Father, rejecting custom?" "Let us then avoid custom as we would the mythic sirens. It chokes man, turns him away from truth, leads him away from life. It is a wicked island, heaped with bones and corpses, and in it sings a fair courtesan, Pleasure. Leave her to prey on the dead." (Vol. i., pp. 85, 106.)

We are also indebted to this truly liberal Christian for saying that women have as much right as men to study philosophy, for filling a whole chapter of his *Miscellanies*, the 19th in book iv., with praises of Miriam, Theano, Aspasia, Leontium, and Sappho, for asserting that Peter kept his wife until her martyrdom, for recommending matrimony, as well as manual labor and the use of the bath and the gymnasium, for acknowledging that much might be learned from heretics, and for placing the authority of the Bible above that of the Church. (*Writings*, vol. ii., p. 167, 193-5, 451-2, 135-7 ; i., 310-12 ; ii., 376, 476.)

II.

Thus Alexandria became the teacher of Christendom ; and her influence increased under Clement's great pupil Origen, who is said to have written 6,000 books, and is known to have opposed the still lingering expectation of a speedy end of the world, denied literal resurrection of the body, and proclaimed that the divine goodness will ultimately raise all sinners, even the devil and his angels, through stages of purification into final blessedness. (*De Principiis*, book i., ch. vi. ; *Writings* in *Ante-Nicene Library*, pp. 53, 59.) He kept open what in that day was the safest refuge from the yoke of biblical and ecclesiastical infallibility, namely, the theory that only spiritual truth is to be sought in what seems incredible, as did the account of the creation to this early rationalist, or immoral, as did the story of Jesus driving out of the temple the sellers of the birds and animals needed for sacrifice, and overturning the tables of the money-changers, so that the coin was poured out on the ground. Even Origen's confessing Christ, under the tortures which finally caused his death during the terrible series of persecutions commenced by Decius in the middle of the third century, did not prevent his condemnation as a heretic by Jerome and Pope Anastasius in the next century, as well as still later by the emperor Justinian and his servile council at Constantinople. Still the new school found many champions, among whom was Origen's pupil Dionysius, bishop of Alexandria, who met the local Second Adventists with such tolerance and ability as to persuade them to confess and renounce their delusion, which soon became extinct in the Eastern Church, though, unfortunately, it still survives in the Western, and who openly asserted his right to study all the writings of the heretics, declaring that he had heard a divine voice saying: "Read whatever falls into thy hands, for thou art capable of judging and proving all things; and from the first, this has been to thee the occasion of faith." (Neander, *General History*, vol. i., pp. 652, 712.)

Among the teachers of Origen, at Alexandria, was the founder of a new school of heathen philosophy, which soon took the place of all the rest, and which greatly strengthened the tendencies of Christianity toward mysticism, asceticism, allegorizing, and Trinitarianism. This system, usually termed Neo-Platonism, but more correctly called Alexandrinism, was first taught about 200 A.D. by Ammonius, surnamed Saccas, because he had been a porter. He committed nothing to writing, but is known to have asserted that Plato and Aristotle are really in harmony, and also to have taken many ideas from Pythagoreanism as well as from Christianity, to which latter he was for a time a convert. It is either to him or to his great pupil, Plotinus, that we owe the introduction into Western philosophy of an Oriental dogma, which still holds a place among us, namely that the highest knowledge comes in a way transcending observation and experience, and baffling all logic, so that truth is to be discovered, not through laborious investigation, but by sudden intuition, and is most fully known in moments of exalted ecstasy. My readers are too familiar with Emerson, Lowell, Whittier, Shelley, Wordsworth, Coleridge, Parker, and Miss Cobbe, to make it necessary to say more about the fundamental dogma of Transcendentalism. Its earliest votaries fell into as strange vagaries as its latest. Thus, Plotinus was so thoroughly ashamed of his body, that he would never say when or where he was born, or allow his picture to be taken; for he said it was bad enough to have to drag about a shadow, without having to leave a shadow of that shadow behind. It was his refusal to take any pains to relieve this shadow's sufferings that caused his death. Similar dislike of the body was the cause of the suicide of Jamblichus, who made himself conspicuous in the beginning of the fourth century as a defender of magic, demonology, and the mystical might of sacred numbers. A later champion of this system,

Proclus, wished to destroy all books except the oracles and Plato's *Timæus*. Belief in the infallibility of Plato, aversion to logical argument, and fondness for superstition are so common in this sect that it is pleasant to find it produce at least one free-thinker.

Porphyry, a Tyrian, whose name is a Greek synonym for Malchus, or the king, had been a Peripatetic, and kept at work cross-questioning, first Plotinus, and then, when the master became tired of replying, his fellow-pupil, the Amelius mentioned in Robert Browning's *Colombe's Birthday*, until he managed to bring the Alexandrine system of philosophy into logical consistency. A similar service was performed for the writings of Plotinus, which have come down to us in Porphyry's edition. One of this keen thinker's own books did much to awaken mental activity from the torpor of the Dark Ages, by starting the great Realist and Nominalist controversy, as we shall see in the next chapter. And while Porphyry did his utmost to have men honor whatever he found good in religions, he pointed out their defects with great skill and courage. Thus he protested against the growing fondness of his own school of philosophers for trying to gain knowledge and power by approaching the gods through magic, or, as they called it, theurgy, so vigorously as to call forth vehement opposition from the superstitious Jamblichus. He also wrote a voluminous and elaborate work against the Christians, who paid it the compliment of destroying it with a thoroughness which did not even spare the apologies of Eusebius, Apollinaris, Methodius, and Philostorgius, who had quoted Porphyry in attempting to answer him. "The Old Man of Tyre," as he was nicknamed, is known to have put these three puzzling questions: 1. If Jesus is the only way of salvation what has become of the people who have not heard of him? 2. If the Old Testament is inspired why do not the Christians offer sacrifices? 3. If it is measured to us according to the measure with which we mete to others, how can any one of us be punished everlastingly? Among other biblical defects he pointed out the inconsistency of the quarrel between Peter and Paul, described in *Galatians*, chapter ii., with their infallibility, and the culpability, not only of Peter in denouncing the fatal curse on Ananias, and then on Sapphira, but even of Jesus in telling his brothers he should not attend the Feast of Tabernacles, and then going up to it in secret. (*John* vii., 8, 14. The former of these verses inserts " yet " without sufficient authority.) Not until the present century did students of the Bible see the great value of the discovery made by Porphyry, when in view of such facts as the improbability of King Nebuchadnezzar's falling on his face and worshiping a Jew, or of any prophet's predicting a long series of unimportant events in pagan history, closing arbitrarily with the year 167, B.C., he suggested that what is still called the *Book of Daniel* was not written by this author, nor in his time, but about four hundred years later, and at the date just given, by some zealous plotter against Antiochus Epiphanes. This monarch's ferocious attempt to root out the religion of the Hebrews, provoked one of them to forge a picturesque romance, describing the vengeance of the Lord upon idolatrous tyrants in the past, and announcing the speedy restoration of the Hebrew monarchy. This fiction was published under the honored name of Daniel ; and thus was ushered in that great rebellion of the Maccabees, which saved Judaism from perishing before the birth of Christianity. It is for making this discovery that Jerome calls Porphyry a mad dog, but all impartial scholars now acknowledge its value.

Among the instructors of this great critic was Longinus, who adhered more closely to Plato's real meaning than did the other members of this school, and who wrote the famous treatise *On the Sublime*, in which he declared that genius can not develop itself properly, except in an age of freedom. " Whence it follows that we who can not drink of Liberty, the source of all that is beautiful and noble, can be nothing better than pompous flatterers." But this philosopher is best known as the teacher and prime-minister of Zenobia, who was by birth an Arab, in education a Greek, in ambition a Roman, in morality a saint, and by nature, as well as fortune, an empress. Her wisdom and energy helped her husband, Odenathus, to become king of Palmyra, wage war successfully with the Persians, and force the Roman emperor to acknowledge him as a colleague. She was left a widow in A.D. 267, but maintained herself as an independent sovereign for seven years, during which she conquered Egypt and Armenia, so that her kingdom extended from the Euphrates to the Sahara, and from the Red Sea to the Euxine. Under her sway pagans, Jews, and Christians of every sect enjoyed such equality before the law as they found nowhere else, and Palmyra became the center of Asiatic commerce, as well as the home of literature, philosophy, and art. Zenobia is said to have compiled a history of Egypt, Syria, and Arabia for her own use. Her favorite amusement was hunting lions, and she usually traveled on horseback, though she sometimes walked mile after mile at the head of her troops. Then she wore a helmet, but her state dress was a diadem and a purple robe trimmed with jewels. Her voice was clear and manly, her complexion dark, her eyes of uncommon luster, her teeth so white as to be like pearls, and her beauty of form and feature as faultless as her reputation. It was only after two fierce battles and a stubborn siege, that she was overcome by the emperor Aurelian, who saved her from the fury of his soldiers in reward for her protecting the empire against the Persians, as he declares in a letter to the senate, where he praises her generosity, timely severity, prudence, courage and constancy. This letter is preserved by a contemporary, Trebellius Pollio, and is a sufficient answer to the charge, made nearly two centuries after her capture by Zosimus, and repeated by Gibbon, to the effect that she threw the blame of resisting Rome on Longinus and other counselors, who were beheaded accordingly. No such cowardice is consistent with the statements either of Trebellius or of his literary partner, Vopiscus. Both relate that Aurelian led her through Rome in triumph, loaded with golden chains, but spared her life, contrary to almost universal usage. So little is recorded of her in history, that those who would have a full idea of her greatness must be referred to William Ware's romance, called *Zenobia, or Letters from Palmyra.*

III.

Her life, like those of Porphyry and Origen, was passed in the dark days of the Roman empire, which never recovered from the ravages of war and pestilence under Marcus Aurelius. The Northern barbarians, against whom he battled until his death, continued to make invasions into Gaul, Italy, Spain, Africa and Greece during the next three centuries, and in the year 476 put a violent end to the Western empire. Their ravages were assisted by a disastrous succession of civil wars and bloody revolutions. Of twenty-nine emperors who reigned during the century preceding the accession of Diocletian, 284, twenty-four were murdered by their own subjects, a twenty-fifth was slain in a battle won by the Goths, still another sovereign perished wretchedly in Persian captivity, and some fifty pretenders to the throne met with violent deaths, mostly through assassination, as was the case with many of the comparatively legitimate sovereigns. The frequency of this crime arose from the fact that an absolute monarchy is the only government in which a revolution can be caused by one man's death, as it is also the one in which such a change can usually be effected in no other way. Thus nothing is more unstable in politics than a despotism, as nothing is now found to be firmer than a republic. The Roman regicides were peculiarly disastrous because they often involved bloody battles or massacres, and always led to extravagant largesses to the army. Septimius Severus promised $2,000 to every soldier who helped him dethrone the Julian who had bought the empire by paying one-half of that sum to each of the 20,000 prætorian guards. Even a peaceable accession required similar gifts, and this custom with the extravagance of despots suddenly raised out of penury, the destructive Gothic and Parthian inroads, and the excessive taxation carried on under even the best sovereigns, greatly weakened the financial strength of the empire, which, so early as the reign of Marcus Aurelius, was scarcely equal to carrying on a long war, despite the full treasury left by Antoninus Pius, and the forty-four years of peaceful prosperity enjoyed under him and Hadrian.

This pecuniary weakness must have been greatly increased by the general incapacity of pagan and early Christian authors to understand the real value of the arts of peace, or of what may be called the business virtues, such as industry, economy, prudence, foresight, and enterprise. Plato's *Republic* was based on the degradation of farmers and mechanics as men of brass and iron, while soldiers and politicians were formed out of silver and gold ; and the almost forgotten assertion of Posidonius, that some of the great philosophers had been mechanical inventors, provoked Seneca to devote his 90th *Epistle* to protesting indignantly that philosophy was far above anything of the sort. It was particularly unfortunate that the *Gospels* forbade taking thought for the morrow, commanded the virtuous rich man, who would be perfect, to give away all his property, placed the enthusiastic Mary above the industrious Martha, sent Lazarus to heaven because he was poor, and Dives, who evidently loved his brothers, to hell because he had been rich, and represented Jesus as saying : " Blessed be ye poor ; for yours is the kingdom of God." " But woe unto you that are rich ; for ye have received your consolation." " It is easier for a camel to go through the eye of a needle than for a rich man to enter into the kingdom of God ! " These precepts were accepted as literally as possible by the early church ; and even Clement of Alexandria appears void of comprehension of the moral value of wealth and civilization. Lactantius condemns traveling in order to carry on business ; and the loan of money on interest is absolutely prohibited by him, as well as by Cyprian, Ambrose, Chrysostom, Jerome, Augustine, and other Fathers, who thought themselves fully justified by many passages in the Old Testament. (See *Levit.* xxv., 36 ; *Deut.* xxiii., 19, 20 ; *Psalms* xv., 5 ; *Prov.* xxviii., 8 ; *Ez.* xviii., 8, 13, 17). This indifference to business interests was a necessary result of the higher honor given to the next world than to this by all the early Christians, whose impractical tendencies were further encouraged by the preference of celibacy to matrimony shown even in *Paul's First*

Epistle to the Corinthians, (vii., 32–5) and very prominent in the writings of Justin Martyr, Athenagoras, Tertullian, Cyprian, Ambrose, Athanasius, Jerome, and Augustine. One of the most unfortunate consequences of this disparagement of social and family ties was the sudden development of the fondness for the life of a hermit to such strength, that it is said to have carried away half of the adults in Egypt before the fourth century, during which it became popular in Italy, Spain, and Gaul. The Christian Fathers, especially Jerome, do their utmost to extol recreants to all duties and decencies, like Simeon Stylites, of whom Tennyson gives far too favorable a picture, the full story being, that the monster's father died of grief at his flight from his family, and that, when his mother came to visit him after twenty-seven years of separation, he kept her weeping and praying for liberty to see him, until she too was murdered by his cruelty. Even as early as 365, a law to prevent the general desertion of civic and military duties, in order to become monks, was issued by a Christian emperor, Valens, who made a vain attempt in 376 to force some of the Egyptian hermits to serve in his army. Nothing did more than monasticism to increase that lack of brave soldiers which was the most fatal weakness of the empire, and which was made much worse, even as early as the third century, by the literal acceptance of the New Testament doctrine of non-resistance by most Christians, in the first three centuries, and by their vigorously condemning all service in the army and use of weapons, even in self-defense.

Rome had ceased, however, to make conquests long before she became Christian, and her victorious career closed soon after the fall of the republic. Carthage, Spain, Greece, Asia Minor, Armenia, Syria, Numidia, and Gaul had all been subdued during the hundred years preceding the crossing of the Rubicon. The first century after the establishment of the empire saw its boundaries nowhere enlarged, except in the tardy subjugation of portions of Britain and Germany by soldiers who won no victory which could offset the shame of the defeat inflicted by Arminius. No rapid conquest of importance was made by any emperor but Trajan; his successor,

Hadrian, thought that more territory had been overrun than could be held securely ; and Antoninus Pius would not even permit a foreign nation to annex itself to the empire voluntarily. Such fears could scarcely have arisen during the republic ; but they were justified by the difficulty which Marcus Aurelius had in defending his territories against enemies who ultimately proved irresistible. That the empire should gradually cease to be formidable in war was inevitable from the nature of its government. Discipline can not long be kept up among troops which have to be coaxed and bribed into fidelity to one despot after another. An army which is managed mainly with a view to suppressing domestic disloyalty, can not meet foreign enemies as vigorously as if conquest were its only purpose. Officers who expect promotion according to their servility to wicked and capricious tyrants, are not likely to develop as much skill and courage, as if these qualities were the chief requisites. And generals will not be so apt to win victory, if it exposes them, like Germanicus, to death under the jealous suspicions of their sovereign, as if it were sure to raise them to the highest honors in a free country. So strong was this tendency to military degeneracy, that the strongest emperors could only check it temporarily, and the weak ones suffered it to increase with terrible rapidity. Thus it was not Christianity, or infidelity, or luxury, that ruined Rome, but simply tyranny, which must always, sooner or later, work out its own doom. Non-resistance and passive obedience might, ere long, have been disregarded as completely by the ancient Christians, as by any modern ones, if imperialism had not favored similar views of politics to its own destruction.

IV.

This necessary weakness of the empire caused the failure of the attempts to suppress Christianity by continuous and simultaneous persecutions in all the large cities, as was first essayed by Decius and his three successors in the middle of the third century, when Origen and Cyprian perished, and many apostasies took place. After more than forty years of toleration, the second and last of these general persecutions began under Diocletian and his colleagues in 303. Churches were pulled down, Bibles destroyed, and leading clergymen burned alive. Nearly a hundred executions took place in Palestine, a fact from which Gibbon estimates the total number of martyrs at this time at about 2,000. Britain, Gaul, and Spain, suffered but little, being under the rule of the father of Constantine. In Northern Africa the persecution was severe enough to produce so many apostates, that the question, how they ought to be treated, brought about the bloody secession of the Donatists. These fanatics, to whom we owe the first attempt to abolish slavery and establish political equality, waged war against their fellow Christians with a ferocity which they tried to justify by the examples of Moses and Elijah, and which continued amid frightful carnage and shameful outrages on women, until Africa passed under the more tolerant rule of Islam. In this region, as well as in Italy, the persecution lasted but two years; but it was kept up for eight in all the Eastern provinces.

Toleration had been for some years practiced in most parts of the empire, when it was legally established in 313 by the Edict of Milan, in which the right of each individual to follow whatever religion he chose was formally guaranteed by Constantine and Licinius. The former now made Christianity the state-religion in the Western provinces, as he did in the Eastern also ten years later, when he became sole emperor. Churches were exempted from taxation, clergymen endowed with special privileges, baptism encouraged by presents from the emperor, the observance of Sunday prescribed, Constantinople dedicated to the Mother of Jesus, the first general council held under the emperor's personal superintendence, and the cross set up as the most sacred standard of the Roman army. This emblem was thus honored, because Constantine declared, as Eusebius says he heard from the royal lips, that he saw it just before the battle which made him emperor, blazing in the noonday sky, and surrounded with the inscription, "Conquer by this." The story is sufficiently discredited by the fact that this crafty and bloody despot cared so little for Christianity, as to hold the office of Pontifex Maximus, or chief-priest of paganism, all his life, to have the ancient auspices consulted whenever government buildings were struck by lightning, to permit the gods to be honored by such sacrifices as had no treasonable or licentious tendencies, to stamp the emblems of Apollo on his coins, to put Sospater to death on a charge of invoking the wrath of Jupiter and Neptune against the state, and to delay his own baptism until he was at the point of death. There is nothing improbable in the story, that his final preference for Christianity was greatly strengthened by finding that this was the only religion which could promise him a free pardon for the wanton murder of his wife, as well as of the gallant son who had but just won the naval victory which gave the father the entire empire.

One of the most remarkable circumstances about these atrocities, is that they took place the year after Constantine's presiding over the great Council of Nicæa; where he had done much to repress the mutual animosity of the bishops. Such was the source from which arose the most ancient of Christian creeds; for that ascribed to the apostles was not drawn up until ten years afterwards, as that attributed to Athanasius was not until five centuries later, some 450 years after the death of its pretended author. Of the original Nicene creed the most important clause is that declaring the Son "of one substance with the Father;" for this is the assertion of what was henceforth called Homoousianism against the heresy of Arius. The efforts to pay Jesus the highest possible honor, had resulted in a dispute whether the Father and Son have the same nature, and are equally eternal. Arius, while anxious to remain a Trinitarian, was yet desirous to make more difference between the incomprehensible persons than seemed orthodox to Athanasius. Both antagonists belonged to Alexandria, from which city the controversy spread all over the Eastern provinces, where the two parties were equally strong. In Italy and other parts of the West there was but little Arianism before these countries were conquered by the barbarians. Such is the general character of a dispute, which it is very difficult to relate accurately, and utterly impossible to decide intelligently, and which derives its importance solely from the bigotry with which various shades of blind belief were advocated by hostile zealots. Constantine's good sense enabled him to condemn the whole controversy for a while as trivial, but being at last obliged to take sides, he did so at Nicæa with the Homoousians, banished Arius and his leading supporters, and had their writings burned. Just before the death of the emperor, however, he changed his party, recalled Arius, banished Athanasius, and took his own baptism from one of the bishops whom he had banished for disbelief in consubstantiality. Neither this lapse, nor his many murders, prevented him from being made a saint by the Greek Church, but there can be scarcely any just praise, despite his ability in war and government, for the tyrant who made persecution a permanent article of the Christian code, and who destroyed the last relics of political liberty by fixing the seat of government at Constantinople, and making appointments to office proceed solely from the crown.

Constantine's example of tyranny and intolerance was followed with increased atrocity by his son, Constantius, who began his reign by slaughtering his relatives, sent many of his subjects to execution on suspicion of treason, never suffered any one so accused to escape, drove Athanasius out of Alexandria by sending soldiers into the cathedral to kill and ravish the worshipers, forced Pope Liberius and other leading supporters of the Nicene creed to recant by his cruelties, ordered churches demolished and many Christian villages depopulated, had the bishop of Constantinople slain in order to install an Arian successor, and for this end carried on a bloody contest, in which 3,000 so-called Christians perished by each other's hands—a larger number than had been put to death by any pagan persecutor. So furiously did other Arians imitate their sovereign and the Athanasians oppose him, that one of the Church Fathers, Gregory of Nazianzen, declared that the kingdom of heaven had already become a hell on earth. Both parties vied in destroying the temples of the gods, and sacrifice had now become a capital crime.

The violent destruction of the old religion was delayed only by the elevation to the throne, in 361, of the brave, learned, virtuous, and zealous Julian, who had already secretly abandoned Christianity, in which he was brought up, and for which he was compelled to feign such attachment as to suffer his name to be appended to one of the sanguinary edicts against the worshipers of his own gods. His efforts while emperor to have the Sun adored as the supreme deity, to which all others should be subordinated, might, perhaps, a century earlier, have united the various forms of European, Asiatic, and Egyptian polytheism into a universal and permanent religion. But the preservation of the old faiths from destruction could not have been accomplished in Julian's day, except during a long and peaceful reign; and the rash attack on Persia, which cost him his life after only eighteen months of rule, made restoring paganism impossible; while his propagandism brought about the failure of his great military scheme by disuniting his subjects, and offending his most valuable ally, Armenia, which had but just made itself Christian through a civil war. Something was done by him for toleration, but much less than he might have accomplished, even in his brief sway, if he had been wiser and more consistent. He recalled all the banished bishops, had the demolished churches, temples, and synagogues rebuilt, commanded that believers in all religions should be accounted equal before the laws, and forbade that any Christians should be compelled to sacrifice. But he gave the heathen priests privileges which, although not greater than those granted by his Christian predecessors to their own favorites, were yet incompatible with religious equality; obliged his soldiers to offer incense to the gods in order to receive the customary gifts, sent Athanasius again into exile, out of jealousy at his influence in Alexandria, forbade the use of classic literature to all school-teachers who despised the faith there taught—a singularly short-sighted and unjust measure, severely condemned by one of his own pagan soldiers, the historian Ammianus—suffered capital punishment and torture to be inflicted for insults to idols, and permitted ecclesiastics to be murdered with impunity by mobs.

This was the fate of the Arian archbishop of Alexandria, who had been guilty of such peculation and persecution as to be entitled to but little sympathy, but who is supposed to have been afterward transformed into the patron saint of England, and one of the Seven Champions of Christendom. Julian's conduct in these respects, as well as his requiring all teachers to obtain permission from the crown, forbidding pagan priests to read Pyrrhonist or Epicurean books, and expressing delight that the gods were destroying all such literature, compel the censure that he did not understand the rights of free thought. How could any one who had been brought up in the Church of the fourth century! He certainly was one of the most kind-hearted, public-spirited, courageous, chaste, just, studious, and conscientious of sovereigns, as well as an able general and author, so far as can be judged from such of his writings as have been spared by ecclesiastical bigotry.

Of his great work in fifteen books against Christianity, we have only such fragments as are contained in the reply attempted by Cyril, the patriarch of Alexandria, who had much to do with the murder of Hypatia. Julian's main point is that the Christians took what was worst in both Judaism and paganism, and left all that was best; for instance, that they united the Hebrew intolerance and belief in a jealous and angry God, who forbade Adam and Eve to acquire knowledge, with such readiness to worship the dead as was found only among the lowest heathens; while they gave up sacrifices which were an essential part of all the old religions, were sanctioned by the preference of Abel's offering to Cain's, and were repeatedly enjoined in that law which Jesus pronounced eternal. He also shows how contrary is the claim that the Jews were a chosen people to the fact of their inferiority to other nations in power, liberty, prosperity, and genius, whether for war, literature, or the arts; blames Paul for sometimes asserting and sometimes denying the superiority of the Hebrews, and changing shape like a polyp on a rock; points out the discrepancy of the Gospel genealogies, calls Peter a phyocrite for the inconsistency condemned by the *Epistle to the Galatians*, extols Plato's account of the creation, in the *Timæus*, as nobler than that in *Genesis ;* asks why, if knowledge of Jesus is necessary for salvation, he did not reveal himself at once to all the nations ; as well as why Jehovah, if he really hated idolatry, took no pains to prevent it outside of Palestine ; declares that the classic literature is morally superior to the Jewish and Christian books ; and blames Paul for asserting, (1 *Cor.* vi., 11), that those of his converts who had been thieves and adulterers were sanctified by baptism. This immoral doctrine, which is taught in *Acts* ii., 38, and xxii., 16, as well as in the less authentic *Mark* xvi., 16, is justly rebuked at the close of Julian's *Cæsars*.

That interesting satire represents the emperors as meeting the gods at a banquet from which Nero and Caligula are hurled into Tartarus, and undergoing a judgment which ends in giving the prize for greatness to Marcus Aurelius, despite the competition of Alexander, Julius Cæsar, Augustus, Trajan, and Constantine, the last of whom claims the protection of the Son, who says : "Let all boldly advance, whether they be libertines or murderers or whatever may be their crimes, for by washing them with water I will immediately make them pure. And if they should relapse they need only smite their breasts and beat their heads and they will become pure again."

Julian's neglect to appoint a successor left the crown to fall to the faint-hearted Jovian, who made a disgraceful peace with Persia, and restored Christianity to supremacy as the state religion, but did not persecute paganism. Neither did the colleagues, Valens and Valentinian, except that their jealousy of treason caused the death of many leading pagans, accused of consulting the gods to find out who should be the next emperor. One youth perished merely for making a copy of a book of incantations ; and many libraries were committed to the flames, because the owners feared that something treasonable might be found therein. Valens, who became emperor of the East in less than a year after Julian's death, was such a zealous Arian that he sent Athanasius for a fifth time into exile ; so he did other leading ecclesiastics of whom he had eighty burned to death in one ship, according to Catholic historians, who blame greatly his violent attempt to force the Egyptian monks to help him fight against the Goths, in resisting which invasion he perished. More efficient protection against these conquerors was found in the conversions now extensively carried on by the Arian missionaries. Among their proselytes was Ulfilas, who has left us the oldest book in any Germanic language, namely, his translation into Gothic of the Bible, from which he omitted the books of *Samuel* and *Kings*, which he knew would only make his countrymen more ferocious.

Theodosius, who reigned from 379 to 395, though with greater power over the Eastern than the Western provinces, gave orthodoxy the supremacy by almost entirely suppressing paganism, as well as Arianism and other heresies. His laws made the sacrifice of animals a capital crime, and even the offering of incense punishable by confiscation of the place so desecrated. All the temples were closed, and many demolished; this destruction, which had been going on with more or less opposition from the government for half a century, being now officially encouraged. Martin, bishop of Tours, took the lead in this work in the West, as in the East did the Alexandrian patriarch, Theophilus, whom we must blame for destroying what remained of his city's famous library. Porphyry's works were burned by Theodosius and his two colleagues, one of whom, Gratian, took away the altar to Victory from the Roman senate, and refused the title borne by all previous sovereigns of Italy, of Pontifex Maximus. The old faith now passed away rapidly in the large cities, though it lingered for centuries in the country regions, a circumstance to which we owe the names, heathenism and paganism.

On February 23, 380, all the subjects of the three emperors were commanded to believe in the sole deity of Father, Son, and Holy Ghost, and to hold the faith taught by the Apostle Peter, and preserved by Pope Damasus, who had won his election at the head of such a furious mob of charioteers and gladiators, that 137 dead bodies were found together in a single church, and whose relations with the Roman ladies were scandalous. Similar bloodshed accompanied the suppression of Arianism in Constantinople and the other Eastern cities, the West being still almost entirely orthodox. To the faith embodied in Damasus, submission was enforced by fifteen edicts, which made nonconformity a disqualification for holding office, and bequeathing or receiving legacies, forbade giving or accepting heretical ordination under penalty of a fine of $2,000, declared all real estate where heterodox worship was offered forfeited to the crown, deprived apostates from orthodoxy of the right to testify, prohibited public disputations about theology, commanded that Arian books be destroyed, ordered the banishment of heretics from the cities, and even threatened capital punishment against some peculiarly obnoxious Quarto-decimans, Eunomians, and Manichæans. The first of the sects menaced by this penalty, which does not appear to have been then actually inflicted, did not celebrate Easter uniformly on Sunday, or the crucifixion on Friday, but kept the Last Supper on the day of the passover, the 14th of the Hebrew month Nisan, as had been done by many of the first Christians, especially the Apostle John, a fact hard to reconcile with his having written the *Fourth Gospel*, which differs from those of Matthew, Mark, and Luke in placing the farewell feast with the disciples on the day before the Jewish festival. The heretics next mentioned were named after Eunomius, an Arian, who taught that no doctrine is true which can not be clearly understood.

The third view was not so much a heresy, as a new religion, which was founded soon after the middle of the third century in Persia, by Manes, who united Zoroastrian, Gnostic, and Buddhist doctrines and practices into a peculiar system of belief and worship, which made its way rapidly in all directions, gaining great popularity through the skill with which it adapted itself to other religions, and the boldness with which it called upon all men to disregard the terrors of authority, and believe nothing until the truth should be sifted out. It was this rationalism which for nine years fascinated Augustine, as it did the Spanish bishop, Priscillian, who in 385 was tortured and beheaded with six of his followers, one of them a woman, at Treves, by the usurper, Maximus, who was urged to persecution by several bishops. This was the first public judicial murder for differences in belief in any Christian country, and the last for several centuries, owing partly to the promptness with which it was condemned by Ambrose, Martin of Tours, and other high authorities, partly to the exemption of the class most interested in theology from secular jurisdiction, partly to the rapid decline of mental activity, and partly to the power soon gained by Moslem and heterodox invaders. Vandal kings, however, joined with orthodox emperors and popes in checking Manichæism, though it was impossible to suppress wholly the influence of its faith in the rights of reason, the equality of the principles of good and evil, the purification through transmigration of souls not fitted for immediate entrance into heaven or hell, the worship of the Sun as the symbol of Christ, the unreality of the great teacher's earthly life and death, the manifestation of the promised Comforter in Manes, and the virtue of abstinence from animal food as well as from marriage.

On the latter point there now arose a great difference between Western and Eastern Christians. Even since the Council of Nicæa the Greek, Russian, Asiatic, Egyptian, and Abyssinian priests have been allowed to retain wives, taken before ordination, though not to marry afterwards, wedding a second wife being prohibited, and complete celibacy exacted of all monks and bishops. There is no better instance of how much good may sometimes be done by one man who knows the time to speak, than is the fact that the utter prohibition of marriage to all the clergy was prevented by the eloquence of Paphnutius, an aged Egyptian bishop, who had never touched a woman, and who had been maimed and blinded in one eye for the constancy with which he confessed Christ under Diocletian. And to the fanatical aversion of Jerome and Ambrose to matrimony was largely due the professed acceptance by the whole Latin Church of the decree in favor of priestly celibacy, issued by Pope Siricius in 385. Little could be done by such measures to keep the priests, bishops, and popes chaste, as we shall see, but much was done to make them work together for supremacy.

V.

The fourth century brought the long war between church and empire to a close, and let those two enemies of liberty reign together. Philosophy was fading away, and Ambrose declared that Christians should have nothing to do with it, while Jerome called it the third plague of Egypt, that of the lice. There were no famous authors except a few partisans of orthodoxy, soon to pass away without leaving able successors. Education had come so fully under state control that the laws of Valentinian prevented any student from coming to Rome, then the chief seat of Western culture, without special permission from the police, or continuing there after he passed the age of twenty. The few secular schools were thinly attended, and little favored by the authorities. Clerical seminaries were ruled by a narrow bigotry which forbade even bishops to read the classics for any purpose, or heretical works except in order to answer them, and which accepted as a divine revelation the dream of Jerome, that he was punished for his fondness for Cicero by being told, before the throne of God, that he was not a Christian but a Ciceronian, and severely scourged by the angels. Science had long ago ceased to make discoveries. Free thought had thus been more completely suppressed than at any time in the previous one thousand years. The results of this suppression may be seen in the failure of Greek literature, during the fifteen centuries which have since elapsed, to produce a single author equal to hundreds who had already become famous. Athens, Alexandria, and Constantinople still had their students and writers, but they have produced nothing of much value or interest. Any single year in the age of Pericles is worth more to us than all these fifteen hundred, so far as Greek literature is concerned. We should not have been able to say any thing more for Western than for Eastern authors, if a new power had not now shown its might first in destroying the ancient civilization, and then in building our modern ones on the eternal foundations of political liberty, industrial prosperity, popular education, and religious tolerance. That English, French, and German thought is worth more than that of modern Greece, or Egypt, is mainly due to the invasion of the Western empire by men of such energy and independence that when their ignorance had been enlightened and their lawlessness duly controlled, they became reformers, teachers, inventors, discoverers, and liberators.

These invaders were at first superstitious and illiterate, and it is as much their fault as that of their Christian contemporaries that the suppression of the ancient religion and philosophy was followed by the Dark Ages. Christianity found no antagonist of any literary ability for centuries after the murder of the eloquent, virtuous, and beautiful Hypatia by a priest-led mob. Neither had this religion any great defenders or expositors for six hundred years after the deaths of Jerome and Augustine, who did much to prevent the birth of saints and sages, by encouraging the monastic system, under which the most virtuous and thoughtful men and women have been forbidden to have children, and confined more closely than modern criminals, as well as in prisons less favorable than ours to bodily health or mental growth. We are too humane to resort, even in checking crime, to such severity as has been employed for many centuries in suppressing morality and learning in the name of religion. Among the last glimmerings of liberal thought in Christendom were the declarations of Jovinian and Vigilantius, that marriage is as holy as virginity, that monks are useless to the world, that relic-worship is idolatrous, and that it is better to use property wisely and beneficially than to give it away hastily. These views were generally condemned as heresies, and Jovinian is said to have been scourged and banished by the emperor Honorius.

Exile was certainly decreed, and at the request of Augustine, against the followers of a British monk, whose name, Pelagius, seems to be a translation of Marigena, the Latinized form of Morgan. This saintly man had traveled from Great Britain to Palestine, teaching such original ideas, as that man is naturally capable of goodness, that no depravity has been inherited from Adam, that children will not be lost because they have not been baptized, and that salvation may be gained outside the church, as well as without any special grace from God. These teachings found much favor in the East, but were finally condemned as Pelagianism ; and in the Latin Church they could gain little hearing, owing to the universal prevalence of a rudimentary form of Calvinism, previously advocated by Tertullian, and at that time powerfully supported by Augustine, who was predisposed, not only by long adherence to the Manichæan belief in the power of Evil, but by remorse for his own wickedness until past thirty, to make the most of such sayings as those ascribed to Jesus, " Without me ye can do nothing." " No man can come to me, except the Father which hath sent me draw him ;" and of Paul's frequent declarations that " In me, that is, in my flesh, dwelleth no good thing." " We were by nature the children of wrath." " By grace are ye saved through faith, and that not of yourselves ; it is the gift of God." " In Adam all die," etc.

Thus was Augustine led to declare, in books which had more influence over our ancestors than any others written for more than a thousand years, that it was the fall of Adam which brought sin and death into the world ; that all other men have inherited such depravity as leads, unless supernaturally checked, to wickedness and damnation ; and that those only can be saved whom God has predestined to receive his grace. These views agreed so well with the claim of the Church to be the only path to heaven, that the British viper, as Pelagius was called by a contemporary bishop, was soon condemned as a heretic throughout the West. Pope Zosimus took his side for a while, but soon yielded to Honorius and Augustine. Eighteen Italian bishops of greater firmness were deposed and banished, and one of them, Julian, wandered through Christendom for thirty years, finding himself every where rejected as an outlaw, but constantly asserting the rights of reason against authority. Augustine maintained that whatever the bishops called heresy should be no longer examined, but be suppressed by the state ; that intolerance is not only a right, but a duty; and that Christian princes ought as much to punish heretics as robbers and murderers. His most elaborate work, the *City of God*, declares that the

Church shows her benevolence by her terrible discipline of the heterodox. (Book xviii., sec. 51, vol. ii., p. 284 in Dod's translation).

So in defending the punishment of the Donatists, now liable to be put to death according to a law which he persuaded the emperor to pass, and which, though he regretted its enforcement, he felt sure was just, he says : "There is a righteous persecution which the Church of Christ inflicts upon the impious." "Does brotherly love, because it fears the shortlived fires of the furnace for a few, therefore abandon all to the eternal fires of hell?" (*De Correctione Donatistarum*, end ch. ii. and ch. iii.) Heretics, he thinks, have no rights of property which Christian princes ought to respect. Priscillian's views he censures, but not his murder. While doing more than any one else to establish belief in biblical infallibility, he showed that persecution is sanctioned, not only by a great array of Old Testament authorities, but by Paul in blinding Elymas, and even by Jesus in saying, "Compel them to come in, that my house may be filled." (*Luke*, xiv., 23, and *Acts*, xiii., 6–11.)

Thus was persecution sanctified, reason fettered, and human capacity discredited by a learned and saintly bishop, whose influence over all the churches and sects has been greater than that of any later theologian. No one has expounded the Bible more devoutly and conscientiously. No one has done more to enslave our race.

VI.

These four chapters have been devoted almost exclusively to classic literature and history. The first thinkers, who freed themselves from bondage to supernatural authority, were the Greek philosophers ; and much good work was done in explaining natural phenomena rationally, before physical inquiries were subordinated to the mentally stimulating, though practically unproductive, study of metaphysics. Athens was the earliest persecutor, and to her own destruction. Memory of the grandeur with which Socrates died, for urging the advantages of such mental activity as takes nothing for granted, joined with the brilliancy of Plato's arguments to give freedom of inquiry a power which soon proved irresistible. Aristotle supplied most effective weapons for the combat against dogmatism, Pyrrho showed how much peace of mind is gained by refusing to be carried away by any form of belief or disbelief, and Epicurus freed his friends from all fear of gods, demons, or fates, by teaching how to account for every thing by natural causes. The religions of Greece and Rome were so much shaken by political changes as to fall an easy prey to the arguments of the Skeptics and Epicureans, who were greatly aided by the rapid development of science under the patronage of the Ptolemies. The great poem of Lucretius against religion expressed the sentiments of intelligent men more generally at the time of its publication, B. C. 55, than could have been the case before, or has ever been since. Similar views were openly expressed by the head of the Roman priesthood, Julius Cæsar; the literature of his age was deeply marked by Epicureanism and Skepticism; and the neglect of temples and festivals showed that the common people had found out how unworthy of reverence were the ancient gods.

The extinction of the national faith was delayed only by the efforts of Augustus and his tyrannical successors to check mental independence and encourage servile sentiments. Horace, Virgil, Ovid, and Livy labored under imperial patronage to make superstition impressive and attractive; but literary activity soon declined under the terror awakened by the punishments frequently inflicted on authors. The appearance of Christianity, during this reactionary age, made the restoration of polytheism impossible, but did very little to encourage intellectual activity, and nothing to save love of political liberty from destruction. It was not freedom, but faith, that Jesus preached. The great martyrs for constitutional liberty were Stoics; and free inquiry is as deeply honored in the *Epistles* of Seneca, as is faith in those of his contemporaries, Paul and Peter, who are also remarkable for opposing female emancipation, then almost complete. The subjection of women to men, citizens to sovereigns, laity to clergy, and reason to faith, was insured by the organization of the Christian hierarchy; and those early champions of liberty in the Church, the Gnostics, were cast forth as heretics, at the very time that constitutional freedom, literary activity, and mental independence were revived by those philosophic emperors who reigned nearly to the close of the second century, and while rationalism still retained a popularity evident in the impunity with which Lucian made the gods ridiculous forever.

This chapter has shown how plainly the illiberal tendencies of Christianity were manifested by Tertullian, who, while protesting against persecution by pagans, denied that heretics have any rights in the Church, or that there is any thing worth learning by the orthodox. All his hatred of heretics did not prevent his being classed among them, for favoring Montanism, an ascetic form of Second Adventism, remarkable mainly for letting women become prophetesses and bishops. Short was the life of a more enlightened form of Christianity, which appeared early in the third century at Alexandria, where Clement did such justice, not only to pagan philosophy but to female capacity, as was wholly new in the Church, and where Origen protested unsuccessfully against literal infallibility, endless misery, and other growing errors. The same school of thought which tried vainly to liberalize Christianity, succeeded in debasing heathen philosophy into Neo-Platonism, which soon became notorious for inability to reason and proneness to superstition, despite the efforts of a few exceptional adherents like Porphyry, who found out the real origin of the book still erroneously ascribed to Daniel. This system is otherwise memorable chiefly for inspiring that most tolerant of sovereigns and bravest of women, Zenobia, that disinterested but inconsistent combatant against Christian bigotry, Julian, wrongly called the Apostate, and that spotless martyr, under the fury of a priest-led mob, Hypatia.

The more rationalistic forms of philosophy vanished before the increase of such mental torpor as resulted necessarily, like financial and military weakness, from the pressure of imperialism, which was now showing its peculiar liability to civil war. The servility and pusillanimity which caused the fall of the empire increased rapidly with the growth of Christianity to such power as soon proved fatal to intellectual activity and liberty of thought. Vainly did the Manichæans profess a rationalism which was considered a capital crime in Bishop Priscillian and his adherents, the first Christians put to death for their opinions under the sentence of Christian judges. Useless were the efforts of Pelagius, Jovinian, and Vigilantius, to teach faith in the natural capacity of man, and to prevent monasticism from checking the transmission of virtue and scholarship by inheritance. Prominent among the champions of this delusive system was Augustine, whose mighty influence made intolerance supreme. Only the conquest of the Western empire by illiterate barbarians was needed to complete the extinction of independent thought.

CHAPTER V.

EARLY MEDIEVAL HERESY.

I.

We pass almost beyond the influence of classic philosophy as we enter the Middle Ages, the period in which free thought appears only as heresy. Western Europe was so much darkened by the ignorance of the barbarians, that nothing more enlightened than their rude and transient Arianism disturbed the Latin Church during the sixth and seventh centuries. The East had still mental activity enough to cause differences in belief; and many heretics had been driven from the Church, when a new sect, whose founder dared to leave her fold of his own accord, arose about 660, and set up against her authority the most liberal standard which could then win followers, that of the New Testament. Its study led a zealous Syrian, named Constantine, to establish in the valleys of the Taurus the great sect of Paulicians, called so on account of the peculiar honor paid to the Apostle to the Gentiles, and noted for disregard of the authority of councils, patriarchs, popes and fathers of the Church as well as for disuse of all ecclesiastical sacraments and titles. They spoke of houses of prayer instead of churches or temples. In place of bishops or priests, they had teachers; though for a while they were ruled by a succession of prophets, who called themselves after Paul's companions, Constantine having set the example by taking the name of Sylvanus. There was little distinction of rank among them; but peculiar honor was given to the preachers, as well as to the scribes, who kept busy in circulating the *Gospels* and Pauline *Epistles*. Those of Peter were rejected, as was the entire Old Testament, which was thought to be inspired by a deity of such limited goodness and wisdom, that the so-called fall of man was really a step toward emancipation. This belief, like the denial of the reality of the birth and death of Jesus, and consequent refusal to honor his mother or his cross, shows that the Paulicians were descendants of the Gnostics, particularly the Marcionites, who had been very numerous in Cappadocia and Pontus, where the new sect continued to flourish until it was transported into Europe. How far its adversaries were justified in calling it by the hated name of Manichæan, it is hard to say. The Paulicians apparently did not give more power to the evil principle than had been conceded by Marcion, or accept the writings of Manes as authorities, or disparage marriage, as had been done by him, as well as by the Church Fathers. But the admission of Manichæans as members could not but have had great influence in a sect which cared more for purity of life than of doctrine. The only charge against them which seems to be sustained, is that of protecting themselves by skillful equivocations from persecution. This, of course, came speedily. The founder was stoned to death in 684, by disciples compelled to apostatize by an imperial official, named Simeon, who was so deeply impressed by the heroism of the leaders, as well as by the truth of their doctrines, that, after striving to forget them in Constantinople, he went back among the Paulicians, became ere long their prophet, under the name of Titus, and was burned to death in 690, with other members of his flock. During the next century the sect had comparative peace, for Leo the Isaurian, who drove all the Montanists into the Church, and most of the Jews out of the empire, was born in the mountain home of Paulicianism, and gave his main strength, as did his two successors, to enforcing its prohibition of consecrated pictures and images. It was not until after a long and bloody contest had ended in the final defeat of iconoclasm that the Paulicians were driven, by a persecution during which 100,000 martyrs perished, into general revolt, in 845, against the emperor. Carbeas, whose father had been impaled, became their leader, formed alliances with the Arabs, fortified Tephrica in the mountains near Armenia, and carried on a ferocious war, which did not end until late in the tenth century, when the Paulicians were permitted to emigrate to Bulgaria, and enjoy their views in peace, on condition of defending the line of the Danube. Some of them seem there to have passed on into a more formidable heresy, which ere long worked its way through Italy and France into England ; but the sect as such makes little further figure in history.

There is no instance of capital punishment for differences of opinion between Christians in Western Europe after 385, when Priscillian was beheaded, until 1000 A. D.; but an Irish bishop, named Clement, was deposed and imprisoned for life in 744, for asserting his right to retain his wife, and rejecting not only the authority of fathers and councils, but also the doctrines of predestination and damnation of unbelievers. Another Irish bishop, named Virgil, was temporarily suspended about this time, for teaching the rotundity of the earth. A century later a Saxon monk, named Gottschalk, who had stated in private conversation that his faith in the foreordination of the righteous to be saved led him to the inference that the wicked were likewise predestined to be damned, was put on trial before the German emperor, and handed over to the archbishop of Rheims, whose synod sentenced him to be whipped severely and imprisoned until he should recant. This he refused to do, and died in his dungeon without the sacraments thought necessary to salvation, so that he was buried in unconsecrated ground.

Such were the circumstances under which the cruel prelate, Hincmar, asked the aid of the ablest Christian writer since Augustine, John Scotus Erigena. This scholar, whose name is supposed to show his Scottish family and Irish birth, was teaching in Paris under the protection of King Charles the Bald, to whom he is said to have replied, on being asked, as they were drinking together, "What is there between a Scot and a sot?" "A table." Among his pupils was the young prince, Alfred, who soon saved England from the Danes, and became the founder of her literature and legislation. Erigena's knowledge of Plato, Aristotle, the Neo-Platonists, and the Greek Fathers, especially Origen, enabled him to show that Gottschalk's view was unphilosophical, and to represent

God as the source of all goodness and of goodness only, evil being merely an imperfect and negative state, destined gradually to disappear, so that even the devils would ultimately be saved, although every soul must suffer the natural consequences so long as it should remain in sin and alienation from heaven. His previous assertion, that the presence of Jesus in the Lord's Supper is purely spiritual, had stirred up little or no opposition, but the eternity and materiality of hell were very dear to the Church. Heresy might also be found in the Erin-born philosopher's saying, that no attributes can properly be given to God, since He is so far above all knowledge, that ignorance is true wisdom, as well as in his attempt to build up a whole system of philosophy and theology on the basis of a definition of the Nameless One as Pure Reason, and in his exaltation of the human reason as a manifestation of the Divine. His great work, *De Divisione Naturæ*, is full of passages like these: "True philosophy and true theology are identical." "Authority is derived from Reason, and not Reason from authority." "All authority not acknowledged by Reason is seen to be weak; but true Reason rests on its own strength and has no need of confirmation by any authority." "We should not fear to declare the truth revealed by Reason, even if it should seem contrary to the Bible" (*De Div.*, i. 66, 69). Nothing bolder was said in Christendom for four centuries. No wonder that local councils were loud in censure, and that the pope asked to have the heretic sent to Rome; but the royal favor, together with the slowness of the medieval Church in finding out much she really had to fear from Pantheism, enabled this forerunner of Bruno, Spinoza, and Emerson to end his days in peace, and leave his works open to the few scholars able to value them aright.

Bishop Claudius of Turin was not interfered with for opposing pilgrimages to Rome, and appeals to the pope, nor Bishop Agobard of Lyons for writing against witchcraft and ordeals. Rationalistic authors had too little influence, and were too few in number, to cause much alarm. Most of what little literary activity there was in Western Europe during the sixth, seventh, eighth, and ninth centuries was employed in checking the lawless violence, and teaching the gross ignorance of the barbarians; and the ablest rulers, like Justinian and Charlemagne, are especially famous for their success in restoring order. This work would have been much better done, if discord had not been kept active by the cruel intolerance with which heretics, pagans and Jews were treated by the medieval prelates and monarchs, who must also be censured for general neglect to educate the people. Charlemagne showed himself far above his contemporaries in this respect, but his plans were not formed with sufficient heed to the wishes of his people to acquire stability. The strong tendency to consolidation of the hierarchy and supremacy of the pope is, to some extent, due to popular need of moral guidance; but this would have been much better given by the Church, if she had been less ready to connive at the cruelty and sensuality of orthodox sovereigns, and to encourage pious frauds. The first half of the ninth century produced two notorious forgeries, that of what is still incorrectly called the *Athanasian Creed*, and that of the *False Decretals*, a collection of documents, either wholly fictitious, like that describing an imaginary grant of territorial sovereignty and royal privileges from Constantine to Pope Sylvester I., the *False Donation*, or else having had the real dates altered to earlier ones, the object being to place the pope above the other bishops, and the clergy above the law. The imposture was protested against as soon as it appeared, and would have been easily detected by examining the papal archives; but more than a hundred popes kept up the fraud, and punished all who tried to expose it. Not until the fifteenth century did truth become as precious to the Church as power.

While Christian history is remarkable mainly for pious frauds and bloody persecutions of Jews and heretics, Moslemism was founding the great universities, observatories, and libraries of the age, and practicing more tolerance than was ever permitted in medieval Christendom. Heretics and Hebrews gladly welcomed the radiance of the crescent in place of the shadow of the cross. Seventy different forms of Islamism were suffered to exist, and the Motazalites had the approval of most of the caliphs at Baghdad, in teaching that there are no books of supernatural origin, that man is the source of his own actions, and that all men are naturally able to know what is true and right ; doctrines as hostile to Christian as to Moslem orthodoxy. Despite occasional persecution, these oriental free-thinkers were permitted to develop, not only a school of philosophy like that of Plato and Erigena at Bassorah, but a more materialistic one at Baghdad. The poet, Abul Allah, was able to say, about 950 : "Moslems, Jews, Christians, and Parsees are all in error." "There are two kinds of men, those with intelligence but no faith, and those with faith but no intelligence." It was during this century that a Bactrian Jew, Chivi of Balkh, published two hundred objections to the truth of the Old Testament ; for instance, the absurdity of making God dwell in temples, or take pleasure in sacrifices, and the probability that the passage of the Red Sea and drowning of Pharaoh was due to the ebb and flow of the tide, as well as that the manna grew wild in the wilderness. Rationalism could not establish itself permanently among Jews or Moslems, but popular education flourished, and knowledge of the Koran and Hebrew Bible became universal, while that of the New Testament was restricted to the priests.

II.

No execution for heresy, except that of Priscillian and his followers in 385, is known to have taken place in Western Christendom before the year 1000, when Bilgard, or Vilgard, and his adherents were burned or beheaded by the bishop of Ravenna for some unknown heresy, said to have been taught to the leaders by the ghosts of Virgil, Juvenal, and Horace. It is not improbable that this story was invented in order to prevent further investigation, and that in origin and nature this heresy resembled that which was soon after common in Italy and France. That very year, a pious peasant of Champaigne, named Leutard, put away his wife, dashed to pieces the crucifix in the village church, and began to preach against matrimony, the Old Testament, and the priests. Many followers joined him, but he, too, was arrested by his bishop, to whom he declared that he had fallen asleep in the fields, and heard a revelation from a swarm of bees. Then Leutard drowned himself, probably to avoid being tortured into confessing who his teacher really was. We shall see that similar doctrines were soon spread over France by proselyters from Italy, and it is probable that these early martyrs held what was afterward known as the Catharist or Albigensian heresy.

Soon after a Norman knight was made suspicious by the praises his chaplain, Heribert, gave to the piety and learning of two canons at Orleans, Stephen and Lisoi. He pretended a wish to be their pupil, and thus found that they were at the head of a secret society, embracing most of the other canons, many nuns, and other religious people, and holding clandestine meetings, at which the authority of the Bible and the Church, the truth of the Gospel history and the value of baptism and the Lord's Supper were denied, and the ordinance of laying on of hands, by unmarried and thoroughly unworldly men, administered as a sign of acceptance with God. These ideas had been brought by an Italian woman, who had also taught what was kept a secret from all but the most advanced, namely that in the Godhead there are two equal and co-eternal principles, Good and Evil, the latter being the God of the Old Testament as well as the Creator of the visible universe. When the knightly spy had wormed out heresy enough, he sent for his king, who had the whole society arrested at a nocturnal gathering. The canons declared on their trial, that they could believe nothing which is not in harmony with nature, and finally exclaimed, "Put an end to us, and do what you will; for we see our King reigning in heaven, and ready to raise us up to joy and triumph at his right hand." As Stephen was led out of the cathedral, Queen Constance, whose confessor he had been, smote him in the face with her cane, and struck out his eye. He, Lisoi, and ten other canons were promptly burned alive, as was Heribert, the chaplain. The others were put in prison, where two or three recanted. Thus in 1022 was the first Catharist congregation in France broken up, and this was the first execution in that country of heretics whose names have been preserved. The same heresy was also discovered, but suppressed for the moment with little violence, at Toulouse, Liege, and Arras, to the last of which cities it is known to have been brought by an Italian. In 1031 a band of Catharists, who had held out for weeks in the castle of Monteforte, near Turin, against Archbishop Heribert, of Milan, were placed with their leader, Gerard, in the market-place of that city to choose between a crucifix and a blazing pyre. A few kneeled to the Christ, but most of them covered their faces and rushed into the flames. Germany, too, had her first martyrdom within the Church in 1052, when some converts to this widely spread heresy were hung at Goslar in Hanover. Such were the first scenes of a persecution which raged during 300 years in Italy, France, Germany, and Belgium, culminating, as we shall see, in the Albigensian war, but not polluting England before the middle of the twelfth century.

The Evil Principle had already been made prominent by the Paulicians and Manichæans; but the new sect cared little for Paul and nothing for Manes, whose most sacred symbol, the Sun, was now classed among the works of Satan. The Catharists may have received members from the Paulicians, but they differed from them and resembled the Manichæans, not only in teaching transmigration and in condemning marriage, meat, property, and resistance to violence, but as a necessary result, in letting those converts who could not break away from the world so thoroughly, form a class distinct from the Perfected, who observed all these prohibitions so strictly, and fasted so rigorously, as often to be detected by their pallor. These most advanced members also called themselves the Pure, from which word in Greek, where it occurs in the Beatitude, came the name of the sect. The same root is found in *Catharine;* and the adoption of this title is said to cause the Germans to call heretic, *Ketzer.* This use of a Greek name, with that of translations of the New Testament made directly from the original, and the ability to quote the Septuagint, favors the supposition that the sect arose in Eastern

Europe; and we shall find its most influential teachers in Bulgaria and Constantinople. Its origin and spread may be ascribed to an ascetic horror at the notorious profligacy of all classes, especially the clergy, which suggested the belief that the Church, as well as the world, must be given up in order to live in purity, and that both had fallen under the control of Satan, then universally considered the author of evil.

Manichæism had loved pompous ceremony, but the Catharists were remarkable, especially in Roman Catholic countries, for the simplicity and intellectuality of their worship. No altar, crucifix, or baptismal font was ever seen in their meetings, where much time was given to the interpretation of the New Testament by preachers educated with great care, for a task which was made all the more difficult by the belief that the narrative of the birth, miracles, death, resurrection, and ascension of Jesus had no literal truth, and must be explained symbolically, as were all passages in favor of a material heaven, or of the resurrection of the body. The Old Testament, with the exception of the Psalms and the Prophets, was rejected summarily. The most characteristic part of their public worship was the joint request of all the less advanced members to the Perfected, to pray for them, and the solemn petition offered up accordingly. The communion was sometimes celebrated, but only with bread, and this was not supposed to be the body of Jesus. Baptism was never used, though that by the Holy Ghost was said to be administered at the most private meetings, when the neophyte, after due pledges of purity and fidelity was received into the number of the Perfected by their laying first their New Testament and then their hands upon his head. Women might receive the *Consolation*, as this was called, but might not administer it, except to the dying; nor might they preach. All bodily contact of believers of different sexes was avoided with the utmost care, especially among the Perfected; but this distinction would be abolished in heaven, according to the Catharists, who were wholly at variance with the Catholics in this view, as they were in such more important ones as that Jesus was simply the highest of the angels; that he saves us by teaching us how to save ourselves, not by making any atonement or propitiation, and that the Good God will finally receive every soul into heaven, except the few which were created by the Evil One. One of these heretics declared on his trial that if he thought God would not save every soul He had made he would spit at Him. Differences in belief were always settled amicably, the great object of the sect being moral purity, for which it is praised by even its persecutors—Bernard of Clairvaux, Hildebrand, and Innocent III. The black-robed and pale-faced Catharist preacher, who never touched a woman, or accepted any gift but the coarsest food, or ate more than enough to support life, or owned any property, had so much more right than the rosy, portly, and gorgeously-dressed bishop, with his guards, his palace, his banquets, and his concubines, to be called a successor of the Apostles, that the heresy spread rapidly through Italy, where its adherents were termed Paterines, after the Milanese priests who labored for sacerdotal celibacy, into France where they were called Weavers, after their most general occupation, and Albigenses, after a city where they were freed by the citizens from the bishop's prison, in 1100.

Before following them beyond the eleventh century we must look at its other rationalists. Perhaps this name does not belong to William the Conqueror, who refused to let Hildebrand raise the Church above the State in England, or to Henry IV., whose struggle against this pope's ambition culminated in the famous humiliation at Canossa. There is no doubt of the rationalism of Berengar, master of the cathedral school at Tours, who was sent to prison unheard, for saying in private letters that he could not believe that the communion flesh and blood are miraculously transformed by the priests into the real body and blood of Jesus. He was set free by Hildebrand, but had to make a formal recantation before a synod at Rome, and burn not only his own writings but those of his chief authority, Erigena. Subsequent expressions of incredulity, for which he was more than once in danger of murder by French mobs, caused him to be forbidden from teaching, except to reclaim those whom he had led into error.

The time of the recantation at Rome, 1050, was that of the

composition by a Spanish Jew, Solomon Ibn Gebirol, of a dialogue in Arabic which insisted on the innate capacity of each man to raise himself to the highest knowledge and happiness, with such boldness that it soon became widely known in a Latin version, as Avicebron's *Fons Vitæ*, and proved a mighty leaven of independent speculation.

Shortly before the end of the century, a Breton logician, named Roscellin, was daring enough to question the doctrine of the reality of abstractions, then held by all Christendom, but already a subject of eager controversy by Moslem philosophers. Thus originated the dispute between Realists and Nominalists, whose importance consists in the fact that all theology is made up of abstractions. The power of the popes and bishops rested on assumptions which must pass away as soon as it could be proved that nothing really exists but individual objects. Nor had the kings and emperors any title to absolute power, which would not share the fate of other products of the imagination. Never did men understand how able they were to think for themselves, until they discovered that all knowledge could not be reached by reasoning from the established definitions of the Absolute and Infinite. How much there is to be learned from the world around us, could never be found out by those whose thoughts were turned mainly to the immaterial and supernatural. Thus the great question has always been, shall we study realities or abstractions? Hence Roscellin's opinion, which may at first seem abstruse and trivial, was really an assertion in behalf, not only of political and religious liberty, but of practical and scientific modes of thought. The question of the real or nominal existence of abstractions became particularly important when it was found that the founder of Nominalism, in denying that general ideas are more than names, and that there is any existence except of individuals, went so far as to assert that each of the three persons in the Trinity is a distinct individuality, a view according to which there are three Gods. He abjured at Soissons, in order to escape lynching, and fled to England, where he wrote under the protection of William Rufus, whose open unbelief joined with his unlimited power, in letting his singularly bad propensities grow unchecked. Even royal favor did not prevent Roscellin from becoming so unpopular in England, especially for censuring the open licentiousness of the priests, that he had to return to France, where he was scourged for heresy by the canons, and where he had to die without the sacraments.

The struggle of Nominalism against Realism could not, however, be put down, though the latter view had the powerful support of Anselm, author of a theory of the atonement which soon became supreme, and is still orthodox. Hitherto Jesus had been thought to have ransomed man by cheating the devil, a fancy singularly appropriate for a Church thriving on pious fraud. The new doctrine, that salvation had been bought by satisfying the wrath of an angry God, marks the age when the Church became mighty enough to massacre heretics, to secure the servility of the priests at the cost of their morality, by making them abandon their wives, and to create those gigantic monsters of intolerance, the crusades, which began with the murder of thousands of Hebrews on the Rhine, and culminated in the slaughter of almost the entire population of Jerusalem, men, women, and children perishing indiscriminately, while the blazing synagogues engulfed their peaceful worshipers. These deeds were rewarded with such liberal promises of heaven, as made the crusaders every where dreaded for their licentiousness, which, with the impoverishment of their wives and daughters, and the celibacy of the clergy, caused professional prostitution to become scandalously common in the twelfth century. How plainly the Church had become the enemy of virtue, as well as of knowlledge, is shown by the number of enemies which now rose up against her.

The twelfth century found Italy so full of Catharists that half the houses in Rome were marked with their secret sign of brotherhood. In Milan they were so popular, that the archbishop could not stir up a persecution, though he preached with a fury which caused him to die in his pulpit. This was in 1173, when they were strong enough at Florence to control the elections. Their activity extended even into Calabria, but was greatest in Lombardy. In 1159 they had spread to England, where a band of thirty fugitives from the Netherlands was brought before Henry II., then struggling against Becket for the supremacy of the law over the clergy, and sentenced at Oxford to be branded in the forehead, scourged, and outlawed. No one dared shelter them, and all soon froze or starved to death. Soon after some Catharists were burned at Cologne, where a girl, who had been spared on account of her youth and beauty, pressed through the crowd, crying, "Show me the master I honor." She saw him expiring in the flames, tore herself from her friends, covered her face, and rushed in to perish with him. A still more characteristic incident took place near Rheims in 1170, when a priest found a young lady walking by herself in the fields, and tried to seduce her. She repelled him so indignantly that he recognized her as a Catharist, and had her burned accordingly. Many women are acknowledged to have perished as heretics, merely because they were too pure for the priests. Members of the sect were also executed at Vezelay, near Sens, for instigating a rebellion of the serfs against their abbot.

Their main strength was in Southern France, especially at Toulouse and Albi. At Lombers, near the latter city, in 1165, as well as at Toulouse in 1178, we see the strange spectacle of Catholic bishops and abbots forced to meet heretic preachers in free discussion, and submit to being publicly denounced as wolves in sheep's clothing, and whited sepulchers, while they could reply only by unheeded excommunications. The Catharists even ventured to hold a public synod of their own, in May 1167, at Saint-Felix de Caraman near Toulouse, the heretic bishop of Albi, two others from Northern Italy and delegates from the Val D'Aran, then without a head, having been invited by leading men in the dioceses of Toulouse and Carcassonne, also bishopless, to meet Bishop Nicetas from Constantinople, and assist in filling these vacancies, in settling the boundary between the two provinces just mentioned, and in deciding the merits of a new view which was as follows :

The Good God is supreme, but his elder son, Satanael, after being expelled with his followers from heaven, where he had reigned as is described in the *Parable of the Unjust Steward*, created the visible universe, including the bodies of Adam and Eve, for whom he had to ask souls from his Father, who sent them down from his own abode, with a charge to abstain from all impurity. Satanael, after becoming the father of Cain by Eve, tempted her and Adam into licentiousness by which their souls remained tainted, as they passed from them into their children. At last the younger son of God had to assume the appearance of humanity, though not real flesh and blood, in order to open the way by which all these souls will ultimately be saved in company with the evil angels.

This view had appeared early in the century in Bulgaria, and one of its prominent advocates, named Basil, was invited to expound it in private to the Greek emperor, Alexius Commenus, who, after persuading him to name his principal adherents, drew aside a curtain, behind which were scribes who had written down Basil's words, and guards who, on his refusing to recant, dragged him to prison, from which he went to the stake in company with many other Bogomiles, as they were called, from the zeal with which they preached the mercy of God in that merciless age.

The deliberations at Caraman were undisturbed, the earlier view, of the equality of the Two Principles, being finally adopted amicably, the new bishops ordained, and the Consolation administered with great solemnity. In 1178 the pope sent his legate, with a whole train of bishops and archbishops, to overawe the heretics; but the people of Albi all turned out on donkeys, and received their visitors by beating tin pans, and ringing hand-bells, and those of Toulouse pointed their fingers at the ecclesiastics, crying, "The hypocrites!" "The real heretics!" Harsher measures were now thought necessary, and in 1181 an army of crusaders, headed by Abbot Henry of Clairvaux, one of the prelates insulted at Toulouse, invaded the territory of Roger, viscount of Beziers, whose predecessor had been assassinated in church for his zeal against heresy, but whose own sympathies are shown by his having thrown the Romish bishop of Albi into prison, and paid great honor to the leading Albigensian preachers. Those bishops who held the sees of Toulouse and Val D'Aran were now captured and forced to recant, as Roger himself did, after a devastating war, soon to be succeeded by one far more terrible.

Council after council had now thundered against the Albigensians, Catharists, and Paterines; all the bishops were exhorted again and again to hunt them down; and Innocent III., greatest of all the popes, partly through his own ability and partly through the weakness of the contemporary monarchs, began his mighty reign in 1198, by sending into Southern France such a special commission as may be called the origin of the Inquisition. Nothing occurred in the twelfth century, however, which prevented the Catharists, at its close, from gaining such an ascendency in Southern France and Northern Italy, that they seemed likely to liberate all Europe from the Church, against whom other assailants had meantime organized themselves.

III.

Knowledge of ecclesiastical corruptions stirred up a pious Belgian layman named Tanchelm, who had journeyed to Rome in order to see how her clergy lived, to declare that the whole hierarchy was under the curse of Christ, that the churches were brothels, and that the sacraments were pollutions. Crowds of armed followers gathered around him and enabled him to take possession of Antwerp, where he reigned for several years in a royal state, under which his brain is said to have been so much affected that he called himself a new Messiah, and celebrated his marriage with the Virgin Mary. At last he was assassinated by a priest in 1125.

It was but a few months earlier that Peter de Bruis, who had been preaching in the Alpine valleys on the Italian frontier against infant baptism, prayers for the dead, and transubstantiation, and had traveled as a missionary into Central France, was burned to death at St. Giles by a mob provoked at his making a fire with crosses in the market-place on Good Friday, and there cooking meat to be eaten by himself and his disciples. This last circumstance shows that he was no

Catharist; nor was Henry of Cluny, who left his cloister in indignation at the sins of the Church, and preached for more than thirty years in Southern France with great success, being especially noted for persuading men and women of bad character to marry. In 1148 he was thrown by Bernard into a prison, where he soon died, leaving the name of Henricians to a sect which was soon merged in the Waldenses.

The same fate now befell Eudo, a nobleman of Brittany, who called himself Eon, the Star, thus claiming to be an æon, or emanation from the Godhead, while he was also enabled by the similarity of his name to the Latin pronoun, *eum*, to pretend to be "He who is to come to judge the quick and the dead." Many churches and monasteries were destroyed by fanatical followers, some of whom perished at the stake.

Open denunciations of the priesthood had already been made in Rome itself by two preachers named Arnold, one of whom was flung into the Tiber and drowned in 1128. His famous namesake of Brescia was one of Abelard's pupils at Paris, where he learned such mental independence that on his return to Italy he proclaimed throughout Lombardy with great eloquence, that the Church had no right to political power, or to any property, except the voluntary contributions needed for her support. His banishment from Italy, in 1139, caused him to return to his master, with whom he was condemned at Sens the next year to have his writings burned and be imprisoned. The latter penalty he avoided by flight, first to a former fellow-pupil, then papal legate, and afterwards Pope Celestine II., then to Constance, and finally to Zurich, where Bernard, who had been doing his best to have him arrested, was obliged to leave him unmolested.

How little sway the Church had over these mountaineers was shown in the strife then at its height between the people of Schwyz and the mighty abbots of Einsiedeln, whose attempts to take possession of their neighbors' lands were met in 1114 by a sturdy resistance which did not quail beneath the ban of the empire or the excommunication of the bishop of Constance. The peasants forced the priests to carry on their functions without regard to this anathema;

Uri, Unterwalden, Lucerne, and Zurich kept up friendly relations with their oppressed sister; and the strife had lasted more than a century before it ended in the partition of the mountain pastures between the abbey and the the villages.

Meantime, Arnold's views had reached Rome and moved the citizens, in 1143, to revolt against Pope Innocent II., who is said to have died of mortification. His successor, Celestine II., had been a pupil of Abelard and a friend to Arnold, so that he was more desirous to reform the Church than to oppose the new Republic, now ruled by a patrician chosen by the people and fifty-six senators appointed annually by ten electors acting under the direction of the citizens. The attempt to deprive the popes of all political power, and thus reduce them to their original and present position, provoked Lucius II. to levy war against the Republic; but he was struck by a stone as he was attacking the Capitol, ax in hand, and died the next day, February 3, 1145. The next pontiff, Eugene III., left Rome at once, and was only able to make two brief visits during his reign of eight years. Meantime the power of the prefect, who had resided there as representative of the emperor was annulled; tribunes of the people were appointed once more; the old Roman law preserved in Justinian's *Pandects* which had been discovered in 1133, was re-enacted, and the falsity of those *Decretals* on which the papal claim to sovereignty rested was pointed out so thoroughly that the forgery was known even to the day-laborers and washerwomen. All this was largely due to Arnold, who entered the city with an army of Swiss and Lombards early in 1146. The brief and friendly reign of Anastasius IV. was followed by the hostile one of Adrian IV., an Englishman who was provoked by the attempt to murder one of his cardinals, into depriving the city of public worship. This interdict drove the populace, who had found themselves impoverished by the cessation of pilgrimages, to expel the leading republicans, and make peace with the pope. Both he and the senate appealed to the Emperor Frederic I. then on his way to coronation at St. Peter's. He took sides with Adrian, and sent Arnold to Rome. There the champion of popular liberty was hung in 1155 at daybreak, to prevent rescue by the people ; his body was burned to ashes which were flung into the Tiber ; and his friends could only show their indignation in a furious attack on the newly-crowned emperor, in which a thousand of them perished. The nineteenth century has heard " Viva Arnoldo da Brescia " resound as a war-cry in Italy ; and Niccolini's great tragedy has done much to accomplish the deliverance for which its hero died.

This struggle of the people of Rome to free themselves from the rule of the popes is merely an instance of the conflicts which took place all over Italy, France and Flanders in the twelfth century between the cities and their feudal lords, who in most cases were bishops or abbots. Brescia broke the yoke of her bishop in 1116 ; but usually the Lombard cities found their most dangerous tyrant in the German emperors, and were therefore forced to ally themselves with the rival despots at Rome, who were ready to build up their own supremacy by assisting rebellion against their competitors. Alessandria owes its name and origin to the aid, given by the very pontiff who supported Becket against England, to the Lombard League of revolted cities, which began its operations in 1167 by rebuilding Milan, recently destroyed after four years of conflict by Frederic I. This emperor, better known as Barbarossa, kept up the war until the great defeat of Lignano, May 29, 1176, forced him to make a truce and finally to guarantee the substantial independence of the Lombard cities by the treaty of Constance, June 25, 1182. This did not end the contest between the papists and imperialists, also called Guelfs and Ghibellines, the longer epithet in each couple belonging to the same party, as may be observed for the reader's benefit. Lombardy in general was against the emperor, as were Venice and Florence, but Ravenna, Pisa, Genoa, Cremona, Pavia, Turin, Ferrara, Arezzo, and other cities gave him almost constant support, and were all the more friendly on this account to the heretical preachers, who suffered as yet little persecution any where in Italy.

The French cities usually found their king ready to help them shake off the rule of the prelates and other princes, but there were a few cases in which he was on the side of despotism. The boldest movement was in Burgundy, where levelers, called Caputiati from the leaden images of the Virgin worn in their caps, proclaimed universal liberty and equality in 1182, but were soon put down by troops led by the bishop of Auxerre.

IV.

The most powerful of rationalistic influences in the twelfth century was the teaching of Abelard. This name is used so naturally and uniformly by himself, Heloise, their friends, and their enemies, that I am inclined to think it was that of his family, though it is commonly thought to have been derived either from *Abeille*, the French for *bee*, or from *bajolare*, a dog-latin verb, said to have been used by his teacher in mathematics, who was so provoked by his pupil's lack of interest as to compare him to a dog too well fed to do more than lick the bacon given him. All the other knowledge of the age, especially about theology and metaphysics, was early mastered by Peter Abelard, whose love for study led him to give up his title and estate, and depart at the age of sixteen from his father's castle in Brittany. Among his early teachers was Roscellin, from whom he learned the unreality of abstractions, a view he began to teach in 1102, when but twenty-three, in a school he had opened at Melun, near Paris. The latter city was already the center of medieval learning, and was especially noted for the lectures which William de Champeaux delivered in support of an extreme form of Realism, according to which such a general name as humanity is the common substance in all individual men, and they do not differ essentially from each other, but merely in properties and attributes. This lecturer was attacked before his pupils by Abelard in 1108, and driven to such a modification of his views that his reputation was at an end, and the young thinker was able to gather a multitude of disciples around him in a new school on Mount St. Geneviève, near where the University now stands, but then outside of Paris.

All the efforts of his enemies could not prevent his being invited in 1114 to the head of the established school in Notre Dame, the highest position attainable by any teacher in Christendom.

Thus Abelard became, at the age of thirty-five, the most famous teacher in Europe. The number of disciples who came to him, during the next six years, from all parts of France, as well as from the Netherlands, England, Spain, Rome, Switzerland, Germany, and Sweden, is estimated at five thousand. Fifty of them, among whom was Peter Lombard, afterward became bishops or archbishops, nineteen cardinals, one of these finally becoming Pope Celestine II., and Arnold of Brescia gained the highest honor that age could give, the crown of martyrdom. To such men Abelard taught the view, intermediate between Nominalism and Realism, which has since been called Conceptualism, and held by Thomas Aquinas, Locke, Reid, and Hamilton. This, at least, appears to have been his position; for he departed from extreme Nominalism in the direction of Realism, so far as to admit that abstract ideas and general terms are not mere words, but are necessary conceptions of the similar qualities and mutual relations of the objects we classify. While asserting the distinct existence of individuals, he showed that they have common qualities in which they form real classes and groups, though these have no existence apart from that of their members. He admitted the existence of collective ideas, so far as that they express actual resemblances, but no further. One of his plainest declarations is to the effect that each individual, while containing much in his own essence which is peculiar to himself and unlike any thing in others, contains also something resembling the corresponding elements in others, but not identical. These similar elements of single men we join together as we form the mental conception which we call humanity, and which is so far, and only so far, real, as that it is composed of realities. Thus while admitting that universals and other abstractions have something more than a nominal existence, he made it depend on human habits of thought. The Realist put his abstract ideas, like the Trinity, the apostolic succession and the divine right of kings, so high as to oppress mankind. Abelard raised men above abstractions.

The mental bondage of the age did not permit him to show the full tendency of his teaching, or even to find it out. Nothing is plainer than his desire to follow Aristotle, whom he says it will not do to blame, because, if he is set aside, there is no other authority left in philosophy. The Stagyrite's independence of priests was not attainable in medieval Paris. Her favorite teacher's aim was not to bring forward innovations, but rather to put them down. Much as Abelard sought mental distinction, it was not that of an heresiarch, but that of a bishop, as William of Champeaux had now become, or rather that of a pope. Marry he did not mean to do, but he had not yet vowed celibacy, though he kept himself above scandal until nearly forty.

Then he met Heloise, who attracted him, not so much by her beauty as by the learning which placed her at seventeen above all women of the age. She had been carefully educated by Fulbert, a canon of the cathedral, who called her his niece, but seems to have been really her father. There was nothing to prevent Abelard's marrying her, except his desire to rise in the Church; but this made him prefer to make her his mistress. Accordingly, after some correspondence, ostensibly on literature, with Heloise, he asked Fulbert to take him as a boarder and her private tutor. The Canon welcomed the proposal, and Heloise soon fell a victim to her lover's brilliant intellect, vast learning, and skill in minstrelsy. He cared for nothing but her society and wrote only lovesongs. These he was vain enough to publish; and they caused such scandal that he had to leave the house.

Soon after she became the mother of a son, whom she called Astrolabe. Fulbert now urged Abelard to marry her, and promised to keep the ceremony a secret. Heloise warned her lover that it would not be concealed, and besought him not to sacrifice his prospects in the Church, ruin his reputation, and expose himself to endless annoyances, which she described in copious quotations from Jerome, Augustine and Seneca. So entirely did she forget her own interests in his that she protested that she would rather be his mistress than his wife, and that she would not change places with an empress. Only at his urgent request did she finally consent to a union, which she insisted would degrade him and ruin them both. The ceremony was performed in private, but Fulbert soon broke his promise of secrecy. Heloise, who had returned to his roof, persisted that she was not married, in spite of cruel treatment which made her elope with Abelard, who placed her in a convent, though not as a nun. This looked as if he wished to get rid of her, and Fulbert had such a mutilation inflicted as made it impossible for him to woo other women, gain a bishopric, or even hold his place in the cathedral school. His pupils would have assembled elsewhere; Heloise and Astrolabe were still left him; but misdirected remorse led him to take the course prescribed by the Church, desert his wife and child and turn monk. Not only did he thus put himself under what soon proved a cruel tyranny, but he insisted that Heloise should precede him; for he felt such a jealousy as she always remembered mournfully. She was not yet twenty, and her fondness for her studies, as well as for her child, made her look at the cloister as a living grave; her friends remonstrated to the last; but her only wish was to please him for whom she says she would have gladly rushed into the fiery pit. All this took place before 1121.

With that year begins a nobler period. Abelard's rebukes of the sensuality of the monks of St. Denis, the abbey he had entered, made them glad to let him resume teaching, as was eagerly desired by his former pupils, who begged him to explain the creed, because they could not believe what they did not understand. So he tried to make the doctrine of the Trinity intelligible, an attempt which always called out the charge of heresy. The position that only individuals exist independently prevented Abelard, who held that the Godhead is an individual, from giving the three persons more than a dependent existence, as attributes of the one God. For this Sabellianism he was tried in 1121, at Soissons, where Roscellin had been found guilty of Tritheism twenty-nine years

before, and where in 1114 the citizens, on finding that their
bishop had arrested two Catharists and was holding a council
to decide what to do with them, had settled the question by
burning them to death. These people threw stones at Abelard
and his disciples, and the prelates refused to let him defend
himself, for the reason that he would do so too skillfully. To
save his life he had to cast his book about the Trinity into a
fire around which all the council gathered. As it burned, and
he wept, one of the accusers complained of its representing
the Father alone as almighty, at which the papal legate, who
was first among the judges, exclaimed: "Every one knows
that there are three Almighties!" A friend of Abelard's,
apparently the teacher who had made the Bajolardus pun, now
quoted from the Athanasian creed: "And yet they are not
three Almighties, but one Almighty." Here the heretic himself asked leave to speak, but was only permitted to read this
creed, which he did, choking with tears. Then he was imprisoned in a neighboring monastery.

Ere long he was permitted to return to St. Denis, where he
ventured to speak of a passage in Bede, the great monkish
historian, opposed to the prevalent belief that the patron saint
of France, who walked two miles with his head in his hands
after it was cut off, was Paul's convert, Dionysius the Areopagite, and also the author of some Mystical books translated
by John Scotus Erigena. The dissolute abbot is said to have
died of grief at this discovery, for which Abelard was scourged
and threatened with capital punishment. Flight saved him;
and the next abbot, Suger, suffered him to become a hermit
on a bit of land, which had been given him in the wilderness
near Troyes. The hut of reeds and straw which he called his
Consolation or Paraclete, a name in ill-repute from the use
made of it by the Catharists, was soon surrounded by thousands
of generous disciples. With them he spent four years, which
would have been happy if he had not been in constant fear of
his persecutors, at whose head now stood Bernard of Clairvaux, the most influential man in the century, through his
zeal, virtue, eloquence, and deadly enmity to progress.

In 1125 the monks of St. Gildas de Rhuys, near Vannes, on

the coast of Brittany, chose Abelard as their abbot, and he gladly took his place among the princes of the Church. The title he held until his death, and the next ten years were passed at his post. Here he probably wrote most of his books, though the *Introduction to Theology* is said to be the work of which a copy was burned at Soissons, but of which others were preserved unaltered by the author and his disciples. Especially daring was the *Sic et Non*, or *Yes and No*, which presents authorities in the affirmative and negative for one hundred and fifty-seven propositions like these : "God is triple." "The Father, and also the Son, may be called Holy Spirit." "The old philosophers believed in the Trinity." " God should not be represented by material images." "Our first parents were created mortal." "The Word did not become flesh." "Christ deceived." "He liberated all He found in hell." "The other Apostles were equal to Peter." "All of them but John were married." "Little children have no sin." "The works of the saints are of no avail to other people." "It is sometimes right to kill one's self." These and other questions which the Church claimed she had settled, Abelard throws open again by quoting on both sides from the Scriptures, as well as from the fathers and the creeds. That ascribed to Athanasius is shown to be at variance with Augustine ; the accepted belief that God's will is done is pitted against the declaration (1 *Tim.*, ii., 4), that He "will have all men to be saved," a wish then thought sure to be disappointed ; such passages as "I form the light and create darkness ; I make peace and create evil" (*Isaiah*, xlv., 7), and "Shall there be evil in a city and the Lord hath not done it ?" (*Amos*, iii., 6), with those about His giving up the heathen to licentiousness and murder (*Romans*, i., 24-29), His hardening Pharaoh's heart, and His sending a lying spirit to make King Ahab lead his army into a fatal battle, are brought up to prove that He is the author of evil ; the proof-text of Romanism, "Thou art Peter, and on this rock I will build my church," is shown to be irreconcilable with Paul's declaration, " Other foundation can no man lay than that is laid, which is Jesus Christ" (1 *Cor.*, iii., 11) ; and it is further argued that the unbaptized will be saved, that unbelievers may be benefited by good actions, and that the *Epistle of James* is not authentic. The *Preface* confesses the difficulty of knowing what books belong in the Bible, and what was the original text, mentions the fact that Matthew (xxvii., 9), attributed to Jeremiah the words of Zechariah about the thirty pieces of silver, and placed the crucifixion at a different hour from that given by Mark ; and even goes so far as to say, "Doubt is not useless, for doubting causes us to seek, and by searching we arrive at truth." This was bold language in an age which said with Ambrose, "If I am convinced by reason, I renounce my faith," with Augustine, "Authority must go before reason," and with Anselm, "Believe and thou shalt understand." The *Sic et Non*, though it has long been known to scholars, could not be printed before the present century, and has never been translated. Abelard's persecutors were not able to lay their hands on it, but hated it merely for its title.

Equally obnoxious was his giving the name of *Scito te Ipsum, Know Thyself*, to an ethical work, whose fundamental principle is that merit consists not so much in the act as in the intention or direction of the will, which he thus sets free from supernatural control, as he did in the *Introduction to Theology*. The same protest against servile reverence is made in his *Commentary on Romans*, a work especially remarkable for the boldness with which the fancy, that Jesus ransomed man from Satan by pious fraud, is set aside, on the ground that the devil had no right to any ransom. If he had gained any power over man it was unjust, and Christ simply annulled it. Anselm's doctrine, that the crucifixion satisfied the Divine justice, and reconciled God to man, Abelard rejected on the ground that so great a sin could not have pleased or satisfied Him, and that He has always loved us too much to need to be reconciled. Jesus saves us by helping us to conquer our sins, according to this Commentary, which also asserts the natural goodness of man, and claims a place in heaven for heathen sages. Among other extant works is a dialogue, where a philosopher declares the natural law of goodness supreme in authority, and a Jew draws a pathetic picture of his nation's wrongs.

Abelard might have been happy at St. Gildas, if he had not been in constant conflict with his monks, who had filled the abbey with their women and children, and met his attempts to reform them by trying to poison him in the sacramental chalice. It was in his own brother's house that a poor monk died of the food prepared for the abbot, who was beset on the highways by hired assassins. His greatest consolation was his success, shortly after leaving his hermitage, in making it the home of Heloise, whose cloister had been suppressed for scandals of which she is wholly clear. The Paraclete was thenceforth a convent, of which she was the head, and to which he seems to have paid occasional visits, but without speaking to her personally.

Just before Abelard finally fled by night from St. Gildas de Rhuys, in 1135, he published the *Story of His Misfortunes*, which is our best authority for his life thus far. This autobiography soon reached Heloise, who wrote him those famous letters in which tender pity and ardent affection are mingled with mild reproaches for his neglect of her who had given herself wholly to him and was still only his. It was solely to please him that she had taken the monastic yoke, and her utmost efforts are too weak to efface the memory of their love. His replies are much less ardent. Her third letter requests him to draw up a new rule for her convent, permitting the nuns to wear linen under their woolen robes, to eat meats more often, and fast less strictly than men, and to exclude visitors more carefully. This petition he granted, though he did not go to the extent desired by Heloise, who asks why any thing not sinful in itself should be forbidden. She also declares, that God cares more for holiness and virtue than for privations, and that Christians ought to think more of giving up their vices than their viands. The most original part of the correspondence is the list of biblical difficulties which she sent him for solution. Among these are the inconsistency of cursing the fig-tree with the moral perfection of Jesus, the improbability that Moses wrote the last chapter of Deuteronomy which relates his own death and burial, the impossibility of any punishment of crime by man, if he who is without sin must cast the first stone, the conclusion, from the words with what judgment ye judge ye shall be judged, that God will deal unjustly with the unjust, and the discrepancy of the prophecy of Jesus, that he should be "three days and three nights" in the grave with the gospel statements that he passed less than two days and two nights there. Alas, that the woman who could ask such questions was not at liberty to give them the only answer which does not violate the sanctity of truth.

In 1136 we find Abelard lecturing once more on Mount St. Geneviève, but soon ceasing to do so, and then passing out of sight, until we hear him offer to defend his orthodoxy against Bernard of Clairvaux, before the king and leading prelates of France at the council of Sens. There our champion appeared on Monday, June 3, 1140, but as soon as he heard what accusations were presented, he appealed to the pope and left the session, thus saving himself and Arnold di Brescia, who was arraigned with him, from immediate arrest. That he had found out how little justice could be hoped for in France was shown by the prompt condemnation of his books. This, according to a statement which a friend published at the time, and afterward lamented as irreverent but not as untrue, took place when the bishops had drunk so freely that the unwonted labor of listening to reading aloud soon put them to sleep. When the reader came to any thing he did not understand, he shouted "Damnatis?" "Do you condemn?" Then the sleepy prelates murmured, "Damnamus," which soon sank into "Namus," "We swim." Thus Abelard was found guilty of fourteen errors, among which were the reduction of the three persons to attributes, the denial of predestination and inheritance of Adam's guilt, the limitation of sin to the intention, and the assertion that Jesus saves us only by his teaching and example. This decision was sent by the council to the pope, who promptly ordered that Abelard and Arnold be imprisoned and their books burned, which latter was actually done at St. Peter's.

Now Heloise hastened to console Abelard; but he soon left her in order to plead his cause at Rome. On the way he stopped to rest at Cluny, where he was persuaded to remain and reconcile himself with Bernard. None of the condemned propositions were recanted, but otherwise he showed such piety and meekness that he was on good terms with the Church when he died, at St. Marcel, near Chateauroux, on April 21, 1142. Heloise reached about the same age, sixty-three, as she survived him until May 16, 1164, when she left behind her a high reputation for piety, goodness and learning. Her knowledge of Greek, which was almost unrivaled in Western Europe, was commemorated for centuries by the annual celebration of public worship in that language at the Paraclete. She is by far the greatest woman who had yet appeared in Christendom, and there was no other like her before the eighteenth century. Her character was much nobler than that of her husband, in regard to whom it should be observed that his licentiousness had passed away before he developed any alarming amount of skepticism, and that the latter was considered much more culpable than the former by ecclesiastics.

v.

Later in the twelfth century appeared two other rationalists who equaled Abelard in ability, and greatly surpassed him in knowledge of their common master, Aristotle. Averroes, or Ibn Roshd, author of what Dante calls the great commentary, strove zealously but vainly to engraft Peripateticism on Islamism, and was not deterred by the banishment inflicted on him in Andalusia from founding a great system of philosophic religion, which was early imported by Jewish adherents into Christendom, where its principle that all souls are alike in nature was developed into such a conception of their unity as proved irreconcilable with the doctrine of individual immortality. Especially beneficial were his recommending the harmonious use of all our faculties as the best way to union with God, representing prophecy as a state natural to man, and protesting against the belief of orthodox Moslems, that right and wrong do not differ in themselves, but only in consequence of the Divine decrees. Singularly in advance of the age are his explaining the frailty and poverty of women by their habit of depending wholly on men, and thus living like plants, and the pauperism in Moslem cities by the indolence of the female population. Bitter personal experience led him to say, "The worst tyranny is that of priests." But the noblest words of Averroes are these: "The religion of philosophers is the study of whatever exists." "The most lofty worship is such knowledge of God's works as leads us to know Him in reality. This in the Divine eyes is the noblest of actions, as the vilest is charging with error and presumption him who carries out this religion, which is nobler than all the others."

A similar attempt to reconcile the Old Testament and Talmud with Greek and Arab philosophy was made at this time by Saladin's court-physician, Moses Maimonides, often called Rambam by the people of whom he is the ablest representative, except Spinoza, and justly entitled the Hebrew Aristotle. His *Guide of the Perplexed* and *Commentary on the Mishna* were burned indignantly in the synagogues; but his fundamental principle that revelation can never contradict reason, and should always be interpreted rationally, had a mighty influence over Christians as well as Jews, though some of the latter paid such blind reverence as to try to keep knowledge within the limits he attained, instead of giving it the free course he wished. How far medieval Judaism, Islamism, and Christianity agreed in their attitude toward rationalism appears in the essentially similar treatment suffered by Maimonides, Averroes and Abelard.

VI.

Heresy was mainly due, as Pierre Vidal, an early troubadour, said in 1194, to the corruption of the Church, which contemporary English satires, attributed to Walter Map, speak of as universal from the priest, who cares more for his harlot than for the Eleven Thousand Virgins, and would sell the whole Trinity for three half-pence, to the pope whose heart is set on marcs of silver, rather than on Mark, the Evangelist.

> "Est Leo pontifex, summus qui devorat;
> Qui libras satiens, libros impignorat;
> Marcam respiciens, Marcum dedecorat;
> In summis navigans, in nummis anchorat."

It was not so much the profligacy of the rulers of the Church, however, as their efforts to suppress rationalism, that called forth a new view peculiarly favorable to individual independence. Abelard, Arnold, Peter of Bruis, Henry of Cluny, and the Catharists were condemned for relying too much on reason and giving too little place to faith. Bernard of Clairvaux sought to save the Church by teaching that truth is not reached by reasoning but by intuition, not by study but by inspiration. Two of Abelard's disciples thought this view better than that for which he was condemned. Gilbert, bishop of Poitiers, went so far in denial of personality as to be forced to a recantation by the Synod of Rheims 1148; while Bernard Sylvester, master of an influential school at Chartres, wrote his *Microkosmos* and *Megakosmos* in such full allegiance to Platonism and utter indifference to the Church and her sacraments, that only his obscurity of style can have saved him from being forced to retract, like his disciple, William of Conches. Hildegard, a German abbess, who wrote a *Materia Medica* and protested against the persecution of Jews and Catharists, had the full approval of Bernard and the pope, as she prophesied that the avarice and ambition which polluted all the hierarchy would soon arouse the nations to cast off its yoke, and seize its wealth. Not until the next century was any attempt made to suppress those yet more dangerous predictions, then known as the *Eternal Gospel*, in which Abbot Joachim, of Floris, in Calabria, announced the speedy establishment of universal liberty in the Reign of the Holy Ghost. Tanchelm and Eon had probably fostered similar expectations.

The Mystic's faith in the soul's capacity for passively receiving direct light from God, and thus becoming independent of the Church, was now widely diffused by perusal of the writings of Erigena and Avicebron. Many such works were translated from Arabic into Latin, under the direction of the archbishop of Toledo, between 1130 and 1150. Among them

was Al Gazali's *Resurrection of Theology*, which had just
been publicly burned in all the Moorish cities on account of the
plainness with which the founder of Sufism, taught its characteristic idea, strikingly set forth in "The Beggar's Courage"
and other poems in Alger's *Poetry of the East*, that the soul
by divesting herself of individuality may become one with
God, when of course she will have no need of mosque or Koran.
Among other importations into Christendom came the *Guide
for the Solitary*, by Ibn Badja, or Avempace, who was put in
prison by the Spanish Moslems for teaching that each soul has
a natural capacity for entering into union with God. This
was not to be done by mental activity but by asceticism,
prayer, and quiet meditation. Ibn Tophail, well known to
Christian Mystics in the thirteenth century, if not in the
twelfth, as Abubacer, describes his *Self-Taught Philosopher* in
a book so-called and afterward much used by the early
Quakers, as shutting himself up in a cavern where full enjoy-
ment of the Inner Light was gained by excluding all the knowledge given by the senses. Similar views were engrafted on
one of their most powerful antagonists, by the Arab translators through whom Aristotle became dimly known to Latin
scholars in the twelfth century. Even that opponent of
Sufism, Averroes, was pressed into the service of Mysticism
because he held that all souls are one in their highest life, and
that the prophetic condition is natural to man, which latter
view was also advocated by Maimonides. And among the
few productions of Greek philosophy then accessible in Latin,
was the *Timæus* in which Plato teaches the natural tendency
of the soul to grow upwards toward her kindred in heaven.

The Christian Mystic found he could agree with Jews,
Moslems, and Pagans, and that a holy soul is above all boundaries between religions. Temple, synagogue, mosque, and
church seemed only converging paths, all leading to unity
with God, but none of them needing to be traversed again by
the soul which had once attained the divine life. What need
of priests or sacraments to those already one with God?
What authority had creeds to those who saw Him face to
face? Nay more, was not every soul drawn toward God so

strongly that all ecclesiastical forms and ordinances could only hinder her upward course?

Thus persecution of rationalism produced Mysticism, which soon claimed complete independence. The results of the new faith were not fully seen until the thirteenth century, but we find Amalric of Bena teaching openly, and with great success at Paris at 1200, that God is every thing, and every thing is God, a proposition tending to obscure all differences between sacred and profane, and even between right and wrong. This form of Mysticism was largely due to dislike of that view of the potency of evil held by the Catharists. These latter, like the Paulicians, had their prophets, and the mystical spirit awakened in the twelfth century was too congenial to heresy, for any sect to resist it easily.

So strong did it soon become over a society originally founded within the Church, and on the basis of Biblical authority, that I may speak here of an event whose importance has, I think, been overestimated. Peter Waldo, a pious merchant at Lyons was led by his reverence for the Bible and the Fathers of the Church to have copious translations made from both sources by two priests, about 1170. Study of the Gospels made him devote himself to a life of poverty, purity, and missionary labor, and give all his property to the poor. Many followers gathered around him, and gradually formed a society under the name of the "Poor Men of Lyons." In 1179 they asked for sanction from the pope, but it was refused after an examination in which the delegates made themselves ridiculous by their excessive reverence for the Virgin. They kept up their labors despite the papal prohibition, and gradually came to discard the doctrine of purgatory, as well as the intercession of the saints, and the efficacy of the sacrament, unless administered by virtuous and holy priests. Forgiveness of sins they sought from God alone, and their own houses seemed as holy places for prayer and the Lord's Supper as the churches. Married life was more honorable, and asceticism in general less strict than among the Albigenses, from whom the Waldenses further differed in having no secret doctrines, or division into castes, and in allowing women to preach.

Their name is derived from that of Waldo, according to
the best authorities, and not from their residence in the valleys. Nor can they be shown to have existed before 1170;
for this theory rested mainly on the passage in the *Noble
Lesson* claiming that this poetic account of their views was
composed about 1100, but it has recently been discovered
that the original date was 1400, and has been altered in the
manuscripts. (See *Revue des Deux Mondes*, August 1,
1868, p. 686–7.) That this new view spread rapidly was largely due to the previous activity of Peter de Bruis, Henry of
Cluny, Arnold of Brescia, and the Catharists. The expulsion
of the Waldenses from Lyons by the archbishop in 1183 only
set them to work making converts through Southern France
and Northern Italy, especially in those Alpine valleys where
they still flourish after cruel persecutions. The first mention
of their presence in Piedmont is in 1198. Their purity of
life and success in teaching even the rudest peasants to read
the Scriptures, are admitted by their enemies. They were
less skeptical than the Albigenses, but they followed the
course best suited in that age for checking the tyranny of
Rome, when they set up the rival authority of the Bible,
avoided weakening their position by belief in Manichæan errors, destined soon to pass away, and yet followed the allegorical system of interpretation so boldly as not only to be
freed from bondage to the letter of Scripture, but to be
brought into close alliance with some daring Mystics. (See
ch. vi., sec. iv., ch. viii., sec v., Herzog, *Romanischen Waldenser*, pp., 19, 131, 133, 178, 188, 190. Schmidt, *Tauler*, p.
194. *Zeitschrift für Historische Theologie*. 1840, i., p.
120–7; iii., p. 54.

VII.

The first five centuries of the seven covered by this chapter,
are remarkable for the small amount of free thought in Europe.
The Paulicians did not leave Asia Minor before the tenth century and the Motazalites never spread beyond the protection
of the crescent, so that the Western Church was even less dis-

turbed by these organized forms of rationalism, than by the isolated speculations of Erigena, and other liberal thinkers who were not considered dangerous enough to be punished capitally. Heretics were first burned in the year 1000, and during the next two hundred years this torture was inflicted on many of the Catharists, who nevertheless continued to increase in consequence of that notorious corruption of the Church, which they sought to explain by preaching that she had been conquered by Satan, and to counteract by practicing an asceticism she could not rival. They became so powerful before the end of the twelfth century, as to hold public synods and disputations with the Romanists in Southern France, where they won the name of Albigenses.

More philosophic opposition to the fundamental theories of ecclesiastical despotism was offered during the second half of the eleventh century, when Berengar attacked the pretensions of priests to work miracles, and Roscellin exposed the unreality of abstractions. The latter work was prosecuted with great success by Abelard, equally famous for the hatred which met his attempts to make theology rational, and for the love of the gifted Heloise. Among his many pupils was Arnold of Brescia, the most famous of those agitators who stirred up revolt against the temporal power of the Church in the twelfth century, without favoring irrational asceticism. The same work was taken up unwillingly by the Waldenses.

All these assailants of the Church of Rome were greatly encouraged by the failure of the crusades against the Turks in the twelfth century. The trial by battle was thought to declare the judgment of God, and was constantly appealed to in order to decide on the title to real estate, the chastity of women, the loyalty of noblemen, the correctness of liturgies, and all other points of controversy. Bernard had predicted a glorious success for the second crusade on the ground that God would not suffer his own cause to be lost. This expedition, headed by the emperor of Germany and the king of France, proved a total failure. The Turks went on reconquering Palestine, and in 1187 Saladin took Jerusalem, which has never been regained except temporarily by the Christians. Then came the third crusade, led by Frederick Barbarossa and Richard Cœur de Lion, but even these mighty warriors could gain no permanent success of importance, and at the close of the century, nearly all Palestine was irrevocably lost. Well might the heretic preacher tell his hearers about Daniel and Belshazzar, remind them of these recent disasters, and then say, "Thus, O Rome, thou hast been weighed in the balance, and found wanting. Behold, thy kingdom shall be taken from thee!"

The great strength of Catharism, Nominalism, and Waldensianism, was in France, where also arose, during the twelfth century, in consequence of the ecclesiastical opposition to rationalism, and under the influence of the works of Grecian, Moslem, and Hebrew visionaries, a tendency to seek wisdom and holiness through such submission to the Inner Light as was equally inconsistent with mental activity and with reliance on outward sacraments. Mysticism had mingled with rationalism in Erigena, and it now became supreme in Tanchelm, Eon, Gilbert, Sylvester, Amalric, and their followers, while it was also represented in Germany by Hildegard, and in Italy by Joachim. Catharism was also penetrated by this spirit which we shall soon find at work among the Waldenses. Meantime the rights of the intellect were maintained against all authority, whether of Intuition, Bible, Church, Koran, or Talmud, by a few isolated scholars, chief among whom are Abelard, Averroes, and Maimonides. Arnold of Brescia, Peter of Bruis, and Henry of Cluny seem also to have preached revolt on rationalistic principles, which were certainly held by Simon of Tournay, who is said to have exclaimed, in closing a lecture at Paris, about the year 1200, "Ah, my little Jesus, how I have set you up to-day! But I shall take you down again to-morrow."

These two currents of rationalism and Mysticism we shall see flowing side by side through medieval history, often influencing the same individual, as they did our own Emerson, and constantly pressing with united force against the barriers with which the Church checked progress. Both were greatly assisted by Jewish, and also by Arab authors. Moslem culture had now become far richer than that of Christendom, and so sunset usually surpasses sunrise, but the glory of the one leads only to darkness, while the other ushers in the day.

CHAPTER VI.

SUPPRESSION OF DUALISM AND PERSECUTION OF MYSTICISM AND SCHOLARSHIP IN THE THIRTEENTH CENTURY.

I.

At the beginning of the thirteenth century, we find Amalric of Bena commencing to teach Pantheism at Paris, where a university has but just been founded. The Waldenses are busy spreading knowledge of the Bible through Southern France, Northern Italy, and the intermediate Alpine valleys, while the surviving followers of Peter of Bruis, Henry of Cluny, and Arnold of Brescia, gladly help the progress of the new and vigorous movement. The forerunners of Protestantism receive full tolerance in Albi, Béziers, Carcassonne, and other cities between the Rhone and the Pyrenees, a region where the Albigensians, or Catharists, openly propagate a darker creed and sterner asceticism than either the Waldensian or the Romish, and find themselves safe in the protection of princes and nobles who hate priesthoods and priestcraft, care little for any doctrines, whether orthodox or heterodox, and live a gay, joyous life, which violates the precepts of the sects as well as of the Church. These patrons of heretics are best represented to us by the troubadours, now in the height of an activity which leads them even further from Catharism than from Catholicism, in their praise of love and mirth.

The Languedocian cities, like many others in France, and all the great towns in Flanders and on the Rhine, are now almost republics; and full independence has been gained by Avignon, Marseilles, Milan, Venice, Florence, Genoa, Pisa, Bologna, and the neighboring seats of commerce, manufactures, and social culture. Italy has not forgotten Arnold of Brescia in her prosperity, and the strife of Catholic with Catharist does much to embitter that between Guelf and

Ghibelline. Abelard's protest against the tyranny of abstractions is exerting ever increasing power over the scholars, not only of France, but of the surrounding nations; and the shorter, though more dangerous path to liberty through mysticism is being brought to light by the writings of Joachim in Italy, as well as by the lectures of Amalric at Paris. These rationalistic and transcendental tendencies are much encouraged by the Jews, now conspicuous as scholars and philosophers, as well as physicians and merchants, all over Europe, and flourishing despite frequent persecutions. Their best friend, the German emperor, has suffered much from the hostility of the popes and the Lombard League, so that the efforts of the German and Italian princes and cities toward independence find little check at this time, especially as a fierce civil war has been excited by the partiality with which Innocent III. is trying to set aside the rightful claimant of the throne. The serfs, too, are seeking to free themselves from a yoke not to be broken except by bloody hands. The shepherds of Schwyz continue at open war with the abbots of Einsiedeln; and the peasants near Bremen are beginning to resent the tyranny of priests and nobles in a way soon to make the Stedingers famous. Germany, England, and the Northern nations are still loyal to Rome, despite her exactions. A few heretics are to be discovered in Paris, as well as in the Rhenish and Flemish cities, but the chief seat of heterodoxy and unbelief is the region extending from Arragon through Languedoc, Provence, and Piedmont into Lombardy and Tuscany. There Catharism has reached its height of power; for its deadliest enemy has already mounted the papal throne. For the moment, however, Innocent III. is fully occupied in fitting out that last great crusade, which even his mighty influence could not prevent the Venetians from diverting to the conquest of Constantinople. A century of struggle for celibacy has not purified the Church, and there are many who look forward with Joachim toward the speedy termination of her reign.

II.

The failure of all attempts, even by the zealous Dominic, to convert the Albigenses, and the steady refusal of the Languedocians to persecute each other, despite the terrible warning of the crusade against Albi and Béziers in 1181, provoked Innocent III., in 1207, to command Raymond VI., count of Toulouse, and mightiest of the princes of Southern France, to permit all that region to be overrun by a great horde of slaughterers of heresy. He refused, and was excommunicated by the papal legate, who was assassinated for it, though not by the order of the count. The latter, in order to escape falling the first victim to the crusade which this murder made inevitable, was obliged to let himself be scourged in church by the bishops before the eyes of his servants and subjects, as well as to promise to aid the attack on his own nephew and vassal, the lord of Albi, Béziers, and Carcassonne. In return, he was guaranteed immunity by the pope, who, however, wrote to his legates, that they should imitate that Apostle who said to the Corinthians, "Being crafty I caught you with guile," and should pretend friendship until the count had helped them conquer his neighbors, after which he too should fall.

The summer of 1209 saw 100,000 French and Burgundian crusaders, wearing the red cross on their breasts, as the invaders of Palestine did on their shoulders, and marching straight against Viscount Raymond Roger, who held Albi and Béziers under his uncle, the count of Toulouse, and Carcassonne under the king of Arragon, and who was then but twenty-four. Vainly had he pleaded for peace, and professed his orthodoxy, on which there was no blemish but tolerance. Béziers, whose citizens boasted that, if God were to choose any city to dwell in it would be theirs, was stormed, and a universal massacre commanded by the papal legate, who, when his soldiers hesitated at slaying Roman Catholics, cried, "Kill all! God will know his own!" No living thing was spared, not a priest, or woman, or child, or animal. Seven thousand dead bodies were found in a single church, and the whole number murdered can not have fallen short of 40,000, as the neighboring peasantry had sought refuge in Béziers. This massacre on July 22, 1209, is one of the bloodiest in religious history.

After setting the city on fire, the pious host rushed against Carcassonne, which had stood a seven years' siege from Charlemagne, and is still strongly fortified. There Raymond Roger defended himself vigorously, until pity for the townspeople, who were dying of thirst and fever, obliged him to let the king of Arragon, who had been brought across the Pyrenees by the news of the Béziers butchery, try to close the war. No better terms could be obtained than leave for the viscount to ride out in armor with twelve companions, and he replied, "I had rather be flayed alive, than abandon the meanest of my subjects." Innocent III. had publicly announced that no faith ought to be kept with any man who was faithless toward God, and his legate now sent an envoy to pretend to be a friend and relative of the viscount and assure him that his only chance of peace was in going to the camp of the crusaders, among whom he would be perfectly safe. Roger's desire to save his people led him to follow this advice, but he was at once made prisoner. Then Carcassonne surrendered unconditionally ; four hundred heretics were burned alive, fifty more were hung, and the rest of the people were obliged to march out so slightly dressed as to show that all their valuables were left for pillage.

The principality was now so far subdued that its rule was offered by the legate to his chief confederate, the duke of Burgundy, who replied, "I have lands enough of my own without taking those of the viscount, who has suffered enough already." No such scruples troubled Simon de Montfort, whose first step was to throw the rightful lord into a dungeon, where, as was acknowledged by Innocent III., he soon died of poison. Albi and other cities now submitted to the usurper, who was able that fall to take away Pamiers, one of the Waldensian cities of refuge, from the count of Foix. This nobleman had permitted his wife, the daughter of Don Pedro, king of Arragon, to join the Catharists. His sister, the beautiful Esclarmonde, or Light of the World, had already been openly received by them as one of the Perfect, and had defended her faith in a dispute with the monks, who could only say, "Go to your spindle, lady; you have nothing to do with things like these." Another sister was known to be a Waldensian.

Many heretics had fled to the castle of Minerva, founded where the Goddess of Wisdom had once been worshiped, and this conquest was the principal event of 1210, when Simon was aided by a fresh army of crusaders, conducted by his wife, Alice. The craft of the legate could not prevent the garrison from coming to terms, which included the promise of mercy to apostates. A crusader exclaimed indignantly, "We have not come to pardon, but to exterminate." He was assured that very few would be willing to recant. In fact, the one hundred and forty Albigensian men and women shut themselves up in separate houses, refused to listen to the bishop who bade them return to the Church, and when told that their pyre was lighted, marched thither joyfully and flung themselves into the flames. This campaign was especially noted for miracles. None of these crusades lasted more than forty days, and it was that of 1211 which stormed Lavaur, the last city of the murdered viscount. The monks chanted their "Te Deum" during the massacre, after which the garrison were executed in cold blood, a noble lady of high virtue buried alive, and four hundred heretics burned at the stake, to the great joy of the "Police-men of God," as they are styled by the pope. Thus closed the first act of this great religious drama.

Raymond of Toulouse had taken no part in the contest, except to supply the invaders with provisions; but he was now told that he must submit to further conditions, so humiliating that the king of Arragon tore in pieces the copy submitted to his decision. Other monarchs would not intercede, and prelates who did so were deposed promptly. The summer of 1212 saw Toulouse and its environs laid waste. The citizens defended themselves with such courage as to keep all their gates open, and make new ones for sorties; the count of Foix and other princes gave aid gallantly, and Montfort met with his first repulse. Monségur, a castle in the Pyrenees, built by Esclarmonde de Foix as a refuge for her sect, was also attacked, but its hour had not yet come. This summer's crusaders had mostly gone to Spain to help the king of Arragon defeat the Moors.

The rescued monarch asked in vain for justice to his brother-in law, the count of Toulouse, and his vassal, the son of the murdered viscount. At last he marched to their relief, and on September 12, 1213, the allied army, 40,000 strong, went into battle at Muret against Montfort, who had but a thousand soldiers, but was enough of a general to bring his whole force against the Spanish knights. Don Pedro exposed himself so rashly as to be soon slain, and then came a general rout, in which some 20,000 perished. This victory was ascribed to the prayers of Dominic, who accompanied Simon the Catholic, as he was now called, and promised his soldiers instant admission to Paradise.

The next year brought such a swarm of crusaders as could not be resisted, and Montfort become lord of nearly all Languedoc from the Rhone to the Pyrenees. The legate tried to keep Narbonne, of which he was now archbishop. Simon the Catholic was put under an interdict, but he forced his priests to say mass, and marched his soldiers into the city with drawn swords, from which the archbishop, who had come out with all his paraphernalia to overawe them, ran away in terror. Despite this irreligion, as great as that for which the Languedocians had been robbed and murdered, Montfort's title to the conquered territory was solemnly confirmed by the pope, two patriarchs, seventy-one primates, four hundred and twelve bishops, eight hundred abbots and priors, the ambassadors of Christian sovereigns, free cities, and universities, and the other members of the great Lateran council of 1215, famous for establishing the doctrine of transubstantiation, and the practice of annual auricular confession, by which girls of twelve and boys of fourteen were made use of as spies against their parents; but most famous, or rather infamous, for giving the solemn sanction of Christendom to wholesale massacre and violation of all law and order for the purpose of punishing toleration and maintaining persecution.

Even Innocent III., however, could not refuse the Languedocian princes permission to reconquer their inheritance. Raymond, son to the count of Toulouse, and then but nineteen, crossed the Rhone early in 1216, and helped the citizens of Beaucaire regain their citadel. Montfort did his utmost to assist the garrison but was compelled to cede the city. He returned to Toulouse in such a rage that he murdered the envoys she sent to pacify him, and his troops joined those of her bishop, and would-be destroyer, Fulk, in slaying and ravishing the people. In September, 1217, Count Raymond appeared before the gates, and all the citizens armed themselves with clubs, sickles, and plowshares, slew the tyrant's mercenaries and welcomed in their rightful lord. Then came ten months of siege which ended soon after Montfort's death, on June 25, 1218, by a stone from a catapult worked by women.

In the fourth act of the drama the stage was filled mainly with sons and successors of the original characters. The young Montfort was aided by the anathemas of the new pope, Honorius III., as well as by the arms of the Dauphin, afterward Louis VIII. Raymond VI. died in 1222, kissing the cross, and giving every sign of orthodoxy, but his body could not be buried, and his skeleton might be seen at Toulouse a century ago. The more warlike count of Foix passed away about this time and was succeeded by his son, Roger Bernard, who had fought gallantly against the crusaders, and who afterward distinguished himself by declaring that religion ought to be free to all, and that no one's liberty of worship should be interfered with, even by the pope. In 1224 the young counts of Foix and Toulouse regained Béziers and Carcassonne for the son of the murdered viscount, and forced Amalric de Montfort to retire from the field.

The last act of the drama opened as the cession of the Montfort claim to the French crown caused the beautiful and energetic Queen Blanche to send down a swarm of crusaders in 1228, to destroy all the houses and vineyards around Toulouse. Bishop Fulk and his clergy sang psalms while the laborers plied spade and ax. Raymond VII.'s dominions were incorporated in 1229 with the Kingdom of France, which was thus extended to the Mediterranean. Toulouse itself he retained during his lifetime, but only by letting himself be publicly scourged in Notre Dame, offering rewards for the arrest of heretics, taking the red cross for Palestine, and making war on the count of Foix. The latter soon submitted, and was stripped of his inheritance, as was the young viscount of Albi and Béziers. Thus closed that twenty years' struggle to establish persecution in Southern France, which destroyed her poetry, liberty, and industry, and changed her from the home of the troubadour to that of the guerrilla and the inquisitor. Myriads of lives were sacrificed in order to put down tolerance, which Christendom was taught to think more sinful than perjury, treachery, robbery, arson, rape, murder, or massacre.

III.

All this time persecution went on steadily, the crusaders being accustomed to order any one they suspected of heresy to kill a chicken, and putting whoever refused it to death at once as a Catharist. More systematic investigations were also carried on, and resulted in the establishment, during 1233, of the terrible Dominicans, the blood-hounds of the Lord, as inquisitors in Southern France. The ancient rule of the Church, to condemn no one as a heretic until he obstinately refused to give up opinions which his judges declared erroneous, had been given up during the Languedocian crusades, and the new tribunal was much more ready to convict than acquit the accused. Thus at Toulouse in the next year, 1234, we find a man sent to the stake while protesting that he had never ceased to be faithful to the Church of Rome. Twenty-two men, eleven women and six children were burned there in one day, and on that of the canonization of Dominic, August 4, 1234, the grand-inquisitor was about to sit down to dinner with the recently-appointed bishop of Toulouse, when they heard that a dying woman near by was about to receive the Catharist consolation. They hastened away from their repast

to her chamber, which they entered without a word. Dimness
of sight made her mistake them for friends, and she proceeded to
recite her creed. They soon interrupted her, and bade her recant her heresies. On her refusal, they had her carried through
the streets in her bed and flung at once into the flames already
lighted for others. This excited an indignation, which grew
still greater when the practice of digging up and burning the
remains of people whose orthodoxy was suspected became
general. In 1235 the inquisitors were expelled from Toulouse
by the magistrates, but they soon returned. Repeated insurrections are recorded at Narbonne, Carcassonne, and Albi, and
many inquisitors were assassinated, but still their work went on.

There were three grades of punishment. The lowest, con-
sisting in compulsory pilgrimages, fines, and wearing of yellow
crosses, was inflicted for listening to heretic preachers, or
neglecting to denounce others for doing so. Thus Alexandris,
aged eleven, was sentenced in 1315 to wear this cross, holier
than the red one of the crusaders, for failing to inform against
her own mother. Similar sentences against young girls who
had not betrayed their parents are frequently recorded, and
among other wearers of the yellow cross was a man who had
taken off his hat to a heretic, and another who had spoken
twice during six years to his heterodox brother. Graver
offenses, such as worshiping with heretics, washing their
clothes, shaving their beards, repaying money borrowed from
them, giving them food, shelter or money, or accepting their
offers of marriage were punished with imprisonment for life ;
and this was so common that the council of Narbonne complained
to the pope in 1243 that there were cities where sufficient
stone and lime could not be found for building prisons enough
for all those who ought to be confined for life. (See Lamoth
Langon, *Histoire de l'Inquisition*, vol. ii., p. 530). The extreme penalty of burning heretics alive, or their bodies taken
from their graves, was usually reserved for preachers or other
noted or obstinate disbelievers, but we find it inflicted in
1249 on a young maiden of Carcassonne, named Madeline,
who was a zealous Romanist, but had given her father, whom
she had not seen since her childhood, food and shelter, suffered

him to hold heretical worship in his own house, been present at it, though without participating, and given no information to the inquisitors. Of the number who perished thus we may judge from the fact that in Moissac, a city of 8,000 inhabitants, 200 people, including one entire family of grandfather, grandmother, father, mother and four children, one in infancy, were burned alive during the year 1234.

The strict Catharists were originally non-resistants, but even the Perfected were gradually forced to take up arms against the Inquisition and join the fugitive cavaliers, who lurked in the caverns and forests at the foot of the Pyrenees, and often succeeded in saving a preacher from the flames, or a maiden of rank from the arms of some soldier of fortune. Monségur still sheltered the fellow-believers of Esclarmonde in its almost unapproachable walls, beneath which flourished Albigensian schools, convents, hermitages and hospitals. From this mountain-fortress came, in 1242, the avenging band who assisted Hugo d'Alfar, bailiff of Avignonet, near Toulouse, to slay eight inquisitors sojourning there with clubs, swords being thought too honorable. This caused the last stronghold of free thought to be besieged by a French army, for whom the bishop of Albi built a movable tower, which gradually rolled nearer and nearer the ramparts, the soldiers interchanging arrows, as the priests and preachers did anathemas. The Perfected gave the Consolation to their defenders as they fell beside them, and did not refuse to aim the cross-bow or catapult. The women, too, among them, some of high rank, kept at work pouring down boiling oil, pitch and Greek fire. Six months of hard fighting and labor brought the bishop's tower close to the ramparts, and gave a part of the wall on the opposite side into the hands of the royalists, whom some shepherds led by night along a secret path up the precipice. Four of the Perfected were then chosen to drop down from the ramparts by a rope, and make their escape through ravines and caverns, carrying with them the treasures and traditions of the sect. The others received the Consolation from their bishops, who led the procession that marched out the next morning to meet their enemies. Two hundred and five men and women were burned at once without trial, though it was Holy Week, March 12, 1244, and many more were sent to prison.

After this we hear of Albigensians only as fugitives into Italy, or as individual victims of the inquisition. The last execution of note in France, that of the preacher, Pierre Autier, who held the heresy that the resurrection-body is merely spiritual, was in 1311; and other Catharists were on trial as late as 1357. Still the sect ceased to be formidable in France soon after the middle of the thirteenth century; and what is most remarkable in the subsequent records of the inquisitors, as we shall see, is the high testimony they bear to the morals of their victims.

In Germany we hear little of Catharism after the terrible persecution carried on by Conrad of Marburg, who had already made himself infamous by checking the charities and encouraging the suicidal self-tortures of the saintly Elizabeth, and who in 1233 sent so many innocent victims to the stake, on no better evidence than that of the ordeal by red-hot iron, that his assasination, like that of a kindred spirit, Droso of Strasburg, whose familiar claimed to be able to tell heretics by their looks, called forth such general approbation as made heresy-hunting rather difficult.

Catharists ruled Brescia in 1225 and Viterbo still later, killed the bishop of Mantua in 1235, drove the inquisitors about this time out of Piacenza, formed one-third of the population of Florence in 1240, and flourished in Lombardy until 1259 under the protection of Eccelin the Cruel. Rome saw a terrible Sermon or *auto-da-fé* in 1231, as Verona did two years later; and an equestrian statue was erected to the governor of Milan, with an inscription, stating that he had done his duty in burning the Catharists.. (Catharas ut debuit, uxit).

The most notorious inquisitor was a Dominican named Peter, who made himself the terror of Lombardy and then of Florence, in which city he organized the Champions of the Virgin, who carried red crosses on their bucklers, and on the front of their white tunics, and who helped him send many of the Perfected, both men and women, to the stake, and drive out their supporters, in 1245, after bloody battles in the streets. Seven years later Peter gained his title of Martyr by being assassinated near Como for his cruelties, as has been pictured by Titian and other painters. Even the vigilance of the inquisition did not prevent Hermann, or Armanno, Pungilovo of Ferrara, from devoting his great wealth, popularity and energy for many years to spreading Catharism, to which he had been won by the heroism with which he had seen one of the Perfect perish in the flames. Pungilovo died in peace, and was laid by crowds of mourners in the Cathedral of Ferrara, 1269; miracles were reported to take place at his tomb; an altar and statues arose in his memory; and the canons begged the pope to make the Catharist preacher a saint. The inquisition, however, now discovered his heresy; but the canons would not admit it. Only after much litigation did the pope finally decide in 1301, that the putative saint was really a heretic. So his bones were dug up and burned, his tomb, altar, and statues broken to pieces, and his memory cursed. The Italian city which most successfully resisted the inquisition at this time was Venice, where it was not introduced until 1289, and then kept under the control of the Doge. Nothing is heard of Catharism in Italy after 1330.

Thus Dualism, which had organized most of the opposition made thus far to Romanism, having successively inspired the Gnostics, Manichæans, Paulicians, and Catharists or Albigenses, ceased to be formidable before the end of the thirteenth century, and has had little subsequent influence on European thought. It was an appeal to reason against the Church, but the persecutions inflicted during the Middle Ages have not been atoned for by any advocacy of much importance in later and more enlightened times. Reason has refused to amend the doom which the Church pronounced on one of her first friends. The suppression of Catharism was largely due to the liability of the Perfected, on account of their dislike of marriage, meat, and slaughter of animals, to detection by the inquisition. But both Waldenses and Pantheists have since won great popularity, while nothing better than neglect has encountered Dualism. The difference is largely owing to the greater harmony of these new sects than the old one with the Bible, but partly also to the failure of Catharism to solve the problem of evil by speculative assumptions. Freedom from biblical or ecclesiastical authority enabled the Albigenses to develop several systems of thought, which existed peaceably within its fellowship, and which all agreed in representing this world as much less favorable to moral growth than is really the fact. Our progress during the last five hundred years has encouraged the hope that evil is only transitory and must ultimately be transformed into good. Faith in the present reign of infinite and eternal goodness has driven out the fancy of an everlasting conflict between two hostile principles. Those who most humbly confess the insoluble difficulty of reconciling the existence of evil with a Divine Providence must pronounce the solution offered by the Dualists peculiarly unsatisfactory, if only on account of the excessive asceticism which was its consistent result; and those who see how sacred is the duty of making themselves and their neighbors happy here on earth can look with little favor on any theory which would hinder this, however serviceable a weapon it may have proved in the earlier battles of the yet unended war against religious tyranny.

IV.

While the Albigenses and their protectors were being robbed and murdered, first by the crusaders and then by the inquisitors, no better fate met the Mystics, who were striving to supplant Dualism by teaching the unity of all creatures and things in God. Amalric of Bena, indeed, saved himself from the stake in 1204 by recanting some propositions thought by the University of Paris and the pope to make salvation depend on the faith of the individual instead of the decrees of the Church, and then died of a broken heart. In 1209, the year of the Béziers massacre, his body was dug up and flung into the Seine at Paris, and ten of his disciples burned alive, for holding that the reign of the Spirit was about to

succeed that of the Son, which is Christianity, even as this
had come in place of Judaism, the reign of the Father; that
as the temple and synagogue had been supplanted by the
church and the Law by the Gospel, so must all visible shrines
and revelations give place to the invisible; that the pope was
Anti-christ and would soon be dethroned by the king of
France; that heaven, purgatory and hell are merely states of
mind; that Jesus was no more divine than any other man may
become, and no more really present in the sacramental wafer
than in other bread; that pagan poets had the same inspiration as the Church Fathers; that salvation comes through the
inner workings of the Spirit, not through outward acts; and
that he who is risen into the newer life can not sin. Some of
these views may have been learned by the leader, William the
Goldsmith, from Joachim. They certainly did not hinder
these martyrs from leading blameless lives, as is acknowledged
by the persecutors. David of Dinanto saved himself by
flight from the penalty of representing God alone as really
existing, but his book of *Quatrains* was now utterly destroyed; while the works of Erigena, Aristotle, and Averroes were also condemned, though with less unfortunate
results.

This was only one wave in a great flood, for but three years
later Ortlieb, of Strasburg, was discovered to have founded a
sect whose reverence for the indwelling spirit led them to
care nothing for church sacraments or gospel history, and to
say, "There is no crucifixion but sin, or resurrection except re-
pentance." "He who converts another reveals the Father, as
the convert does the Son, and the conversion the Holy
Ghost." "Leave behind you all that is outward and follow
the Inner Voice! Trust to that for salvation, and do not
trouble yourselves about good works!" These Ortlibarians
suffered with some friendly Waldenses in the persecution of
1212, when five hundred heretics were arrested in Alsace, and
eighty perished in the flames, including twenty-three women
and thirteen priests. One of the latter, John, was spokes-
man, and when asked if he were willing to abide by the
ordeal of red-hot iron, answered, "Thou shalt not tempt the

Lord thy God." "Are you afraid of burning your finger?" scoffed the heresy-hunters. "Nay, I have the Word of God, and for that I am willing to give not only my finger, but my whole body to be burned." Then he confessed that he and his followers cared nothing for pictures and images, fasts, absolutions, and masses for the dead, for the intercession of the Virgin and the saints, or for the authority of the pope; and held that priests should marry and give the laity the chalice in communion; that sacraments avail only to the penitent; and that salvation is to be sought solely through the merits of Christ. To the customary charge that their meetings ended in debauchery, this Waldensian replied: "How could we die, as we are about to do, if we had done such iniquity?" The threats of their judges and entreaties of their brothers, sisters, wives and children were in vain. All the eighty took their places in a deep pit, still shown in Strasburg as the Heretics' Trench. This was filled up with wood which was set on fire, and then the martyrs sang their last hymn together.

The year of the butcheries of Paris and Béziers was also that of the foundation of the Franciscans, who eagerly welcomed the prophecy of the coming reign of the Holy Ghost, called themselves its destined inaugurators, and spoke of the writings of its chief prophet, Joachim of Floris, as the *Eternal Gospel*. Under this title appeared at Paris in 1254 an edition of his writings, probably much abridged as well as interpolated, with an *Introduction*, supposed to be the work of a friar named Gerard, and announcing that this new Gospel would take the place of those hitherto sacred, and that the kingdom of the Spirit would be established in 1260, when Anti-christ would dethrone the pope, and then be himself overthrown by an inspired emperor. The three successive reigns of Father, Son and Holy Ghost, were said to be those of star-light, moon-beams, and sunshine, of nettles, roses, and lilies, of slavery, family government, and full liberty, of fear, faith, and love. Every body at Paris read these books; but they were soon suppressed, Gerard imprisoned for life, and his friend, John of Parma, forced to resign the generalship of the Order. The

Introduction to the *Eternal Gospel* is no longer to be found, and a consistent mystic would find it hard to believe that an eternal gospel could be written; for books are transitory.

Hitherto the Holy Spirit had been thought to speak mainly through men, but the claim of woman to inspiration was now asserted at Milan by a Bohemian visionary named Wilhelmina, who was supposed to be the Comforter foretold by Jesus, to be appointed to save Jews, Moslems, and unbelievers, even as he did the Christians, and to be a new incarnation, very God and very woman. On her death in 1281, she was believed to have ascended into heaven, mass was said at her altar by the spotless and beautiful English nun, Mayfred, whom she had consecrated as pope, miracles were reported at her tomb, and her biographers hoped to be able to supplant Matthew, Mark, Luke, and John. Not until 1301 did the inquisition succeed in committing Mayfred with Wilhelmina's bones to the flames.

Segarelli, an insane enthusiast who tried to imitate not only the poverty but the garb of the first disciples, and who was burned at Parma in 1300 for asserting an individual inspiration independent of the church, had founded the sect of the Apostolic Brethren, soon to wage open war against authority under the leadership of Dolcino, the John Brown of the Middle Ages.

The most famous Mystics were those Franciscans whom hope of establishing the kingdom of the Spirit encouraged to enforce strict obedience to the rule resting on the vow of poverty, and forbidding any property to be held either by individuals or by communities in the Order. More politic brethren wished the rule relaxed in favor of communities, as was actually done by the popes soon after the death of Francis. Thus his monks sank, like the others, into the hypocrisy of requiring every new brother to swear that he will live in perpetual poverty, though he and they know that he is going to be a member of a wealthy and luxurious community. This pious fraud, of taking a vow of poverty, while firmly intending to break it, has been kept up for many centuries, but it was promptly condemned by many Franciscans, like Peter John Oliva, one of the first to find in the *Apocalypse* a prophecy of papal corruption. The death of their patron, Pope Celestine V., in prison under Boniface, 1296, greatly provoked these Mystics, soon to be cruelly persecuted as Fratricelli.

Thus Mysticism kept showing itself in new but transitory forms, and laying the foundations on which great organizations were ere long to rise.

v.

The persecutions described in this and the previous chapter soon provoked such unbelief as had not been seen in the thousand years since Lucian. Early in the thirteenth century a great satire on religion appeared simultaneously in Flanders, Germany, and France, one of the earliest authors, Pierre de St. Cloud, having been arrested with the Mystics at Paris in 1209 and saved his life by turning monk. No blow so deadly was struck at Christianity during the middle ages, as the portrayal of that arch-robber, murderer, and adulterer, Reynard the Fox, singing a psalm at his creation, baptising his whelps to cure their illness, teaching the creed to the rabbit whom he is thus able to pounce upon, turning hermit in order to kill the chicken, at whose tomb are wrought miracles, saving himself from the gallows by going on a pilgrimage, during which he confesses his sins to the pope and obtains absolution, conquering the wolf in a judicial combat, and tricking his enemies by a mock-funeral, where the ass officiates as bishop. Everything then held sacred : pilgrimages, prayer, miracles, baptism, absolution, funerals, trial by battle, monarchy, prelacy, and papacy itself are laughed to scorn in this unholy bible.

And the name of Bible had already been given to two satires, the most noted being by Guyot of Provence, a monk, who, in 1203, declared that every crime came from Rome, where silver was almighty, and called on all Christians to join in destroying this nest of vermin. A troubadour of Avignon now composed a comedy called the *Heresy of the Fathers*, who were allowed to appear in public to expose the errors of the popes. Pierre Cardinal, who was neither Catharist nor Catholic, but said God ought to kill the devil and not put any one into hell, denounced the Albigensian war, which drove him into Arragon, as the victory of perfidy, cruelty, and iniquity, over honor, love, and truth. "The priests," he says, "call themselves shepherds, but are only butchers, and what they dare to do, I do not dare to speak." Figueira, who fled from Toulouse, and entered the service of Frederic II., exclaims, "I do not wonder that men err, for thou, O Rome, art the guide to all iniquity! Thou forgivest sins for money and feedest on the flesh of the simple. No man may trust thy words; and the devil greets thee as his bosom-friend." One of the crusaders who drove these minstrels into exile, Thibauld, Count of Champagne, complains, "Our pope has made all the Church suffer. The priests have left their sermons to fight and slay; they shall pay for it in hell."

Even German piety did not prevent Walter of the Vogelweide from calling Innocent III. a new Judas, who lays snares for bishops with the help of Satan, and sets up competitors to the crown that he may fill his coffers.

"O Father in heaven how long wilt thou sleep?
The lord of thy treasury is only a thief;
Thy shepherd's a wolf who devoureth thy sheep;
Thy judge is of robbers and murderers chief!"

(*Der Roemische Stuhl* in Pfiffer's, *Walter von der Vogelweide*, p. 216.)

A contemporary with the name, possibly assumed, of Freidank, Free Thought, issued a collection of proverbs, exhorting men of humble birth to make themselves noble by virtue; and declaring that the pope can not forgive sin, and if he could he ought to be stoned for suffering a single mother's son to go to hell; that to say he can not sin himself is a lie; that he cares not who shears the sheep so long as he gets the wool; and that it is fortunate for the peace of the church that Rome is too far away for the Germans to know what is done there. When Frederic II. was excommunicated, Freidank declared that his emperor was doing as well as he could. Then it was that Reinmar of Zwetel, distinguished himself by praising conjugal fidelity and the sanctity of marriage; by declaring that he alone is truly noble whose life is pure, and that thought should be free even from the control of the emperor; and by denouncing the Church in which Christ is sold a second time, the cardinals, who are too wicked to choose a holy pope, and the papal ban which is too much the work of anger to have come from God. One of these loyal poets actually placed in Gregory IX.'s bed-chamber, 1239, the prophecy of what was to come three centuries later.

"Rome staggering long, through various errors led,
Shall cease to be the universal head."
"Roma diu titubans, variis erroribus acta,
Totius mundi desinet esse caput."

Meantime a mightier force than satire or Mysticism had come into the field. Among the victims of 1209 were Aristotle's scientific and metaphysical works, reading which was forbidden until 1237, as was the perusal of Averroes. From these teachings and those of Abelard sprang the materialism which was condemned by the bishops of Paris in 1240, 1269 and 1277. This embraced such doctrines as that what was contrary to the Catholic faith might yet be true in philosophy (the theory of a double truth); that philosophers could not as such believe in the Trinity or the resurrection of the body; that Christianity hinders knowledge, and is founded like other religions on fables; that authority is not a sufficient reason; that man may be saved by mere morality; that the world is eternal and creation impossible; and that human souls are united too closely for individual immortality. The last two propositions soon become famous as the chief errors of the Averroists, among whom was Michael Scott, whose law of study caused him to be charged with sorcery. So bold was the new philosophy that Thomas Aquinas was obliged, soon after the middle of this century to state, and try to refute, the proposition, that miracles could not have happened, because any violation of the order of nature would imply that God acts against himself and that he makes the universal good give way to that of individuals. This controversy mingled at Paris with the endless strife about the reality of abstractions, and the thirty years war of the University against the mendicant friars who finally triumphed in 1259, and had previously suppressed the attack on them by William of St. Amour, a professor who argued in his *Perils of the Last Times*, that beggary should no more be tolerated among the clergy than the laity.

Under such influences Roger Bacon was educated, who also learned much from Bishop Grostête, famous for encouraging the study of Greek in England, and for maintaining his right to reject the pope's commands whenever they did not agree with the teachings of the Apostles. Bacon unfortunately supposed, as some people do still, that monasticism favored study, and became a Franciscan, but his fondness for natural science, and preference for experience rather than metaphysics as a way to truth soon awoke the hostility of Bonaventura, an orthodox mystic and head of the Order; his lectures at Oxford were suspended; and in 1257 he was imprisoned for ten years at Paris, where he was put on bread and water whenever he dared to write. Often has Mysticism shown itself thus blind to all truth not found in its own dizzy path. Bacon was permitted to publish in 1263 a book on the calendar, proposing the reform made three hundred years later, of ceasing to count years divisible by 100 and not by 400 as leap-years; but he had not been able to write any thing he thought important before 1266.

Then a letter from Clement IV. prompted him to compose his greatest work, the *Opus Majus*, where he complains of the general ignorance and the lack of real knowledge, even among famous philosophers like Aquinas, Albertus Magnus, and Alexander Hales, the Franciscan, and points out the two fundatal defects in all medieval and much modern scholarship, namely, blind submission to authority, and reliance on metaphysical reasoning instead of observation and experiment.

No one had yet shown the full value of experience as a guide to knowledge; and Roger Bacon was really the founder of modern science. Again and again he insists on original investigation. " Would you know Aristotle or the Bible? Don't read translations, but study the Greek and Hebrew text. Would you understand the laws of nature? Don't buy books, but get instruments and make your own experiments. Would you be a philosopher? First, master mathematics, for this is the alphabet of philosophy." The Renaissance would have come a hundred years earlier, if the rulers of the Church had been enlightened enough to have Greek, Hebrew, mathematics, and the sciences studied as Roger Bacon recommended. This *Great Work* also contains proposals for reforming the calendar; many discoveries, for instance, of the cause of the rainbow, of the use of the magnifying glass, and of the fact that the motion of light is not instantaneous; daring criticisms on Aristotle and the Ptolemaic system; eloquent though fanciful descriptions of the triumphs to be achieved by using gunpowder, magnetism, and other forces then but imperfectly known; and those passages from Aristotle, Strabo, and Seneca, which were copied by Cardinal d'Ailly, and thus inspired Columbus to cross the ocean. Bacon unfortunately spoke of the Vulgate version of the Bible as inaccurate, and his zeal to bring all phenomena under the reign of law led him to ascribe the rise and fall of religions to planetary influences, as had been done by the Arabs, and to say that Jupiter's conjunction with Mercury gave rise to Christianity, and that with Venus to Islamism, while that with the moon would herald the downfall of all religions. Otherwise the *Great Work* like its supplements and abridgments, the *Opus Minus* and *Opus Tertium* sent soon after to Rome, are fully orthodox, Averroism, especially the doctrine of a double truth, being vigorously combated, and the pope extolled as a human god.

Clement IV. ordered the scholar's release in 1267, and five years later he was able to publish his *Compound of Philosophy*, or *Book of the Six Sciences*, an encyclopedia of philology, mathematics, perspective, alchemy, experimental science, and logic. It was too advanced a work to be suffered to reach us except in fragments. Further publication of his researches was prevented by his imprisonment a second time, in 1278, for no immorality or heresy, but merely because he brought forward suspicious novelties. Only the death, in 1292, of this new persecutor, who had finally become Pope Nicholas IV., permitted Bacon, now nearly 80, to issue from prison, and publish his last plea for science and protest against authority, the *Compend of Theology*. That Bacon's imprisonment for twenty-four years, because he loved science, was really the act of the whole Church, is shown by the unwillingness of contemporary and later authors, for instance Dante, to mention his name, by the mutilated condition of his writings, said to have been nailed down to the shelves by his brother-monks, and by the failure to publish them until after the Reformation. When we further consider that the thirteenth century saw Hebrew manuscripts burned by the cart-load, reading the Bible and discussing theology forbidden to the laity, study of civil law, chemistry, or medicine prohibited to priests, dissection made criminal as soon as it was introduced, tolerant people massacred by the thousand, and the terrible inquisition set up to crush all freedom of thought, we cannot wonder that Christianity has been denounced as an enemy of knowledge.

There are no rationalistic writers in Italian until long after 1300, though many Ghibellines were free-thinkers, for instance the Eccelins of Mantua, Salinguerra Torello of Ferrara, and Farinata of Florence, who won the battle of Monte Aperto in 1260 over his fellow-citizens, who had expelled him, then saved the city from destruction by his own allies, and is placed in hell beside Frederick Second as an Epicurean by Dante. That this emperor would rise from the grave, conquer the Holy Land, convert the Jews, humble the priests, destroy the monasteries, make the nuns marry, and thus bring in the Good Time, was now prophesied by a German poet, named after the rainbow. And it was between 1260 and 1270 that Rutebœuf made an opponent of the crusades urge that God may be served as holily at Paris as at Jerusalem; represented a serf, who was shut out of heaven for poverty, as forcing Peter and Paul to let him in, by reminding them of the denial of Christ and martyrdom of Stephen; and wrote a song against the Franciscans and Dominicans full of lines like these:

> "Who dares the two orders disobey,
> And is not willing to be their prey,
> They laugh his virtues all to scorn,
> And say such a villain never was born.
>
> "Of goodness their sermons make a great show,
> But what they practice, I do not know.
> I only know they are ready to praise
> The virtues of him who freely pays."

Passing on to 1288, we find the *New Reynard*, a satire whose hero makes himself and his whelps masters of the four great orders of Dominicans, Franciscans, Templars, and Hospitallers, so that this incarnation of fraud is enthroned as religious ruler of the world. Somewhat later, but before the end of the century, did that popular love-poem, the *Romance of the Rose*, receive a famous addition from the pen of a priest, named Jean de Meung, from his birth-place, and from his lameness, Jean Clopinel. This satirist speaks only with scorn of women, a mob of whom once attacked him, when he saved himself by shouting, "Let her who is most unchaste strike the first blow!" Equally plain is his hatred of the monks, whom he charges with heaping up wealth in violation of their vows, and eating up men with envy while they keep Lent all the year. His sweeping censures do not spare even the *Eternal Gospel*, and Hypocrisy is made, in one of the passages translated by Chaucer, to boast that he finds no dress so suitable as a cowl and no servants more zealous than bishops, abbots, and abbesses.

Jean de Meung struck against the two main props of monasticism, as he declared marriage holier than celibacy and labor than mendicancy. "The honor we owe to nature we pay when we work." "Pensez de nature bien honorer, servez la par bien laborer." Here he stood above the Church, and so he did when he said that no man is ignoble except through his vices, that nobleness depends on goodness of heart, and that without such virtue high birth avails nothing.

> "Nul n'est vilain fors par ses vices,
> Noblesse vient de bon courage ;

> Car gentilesse de lignage
> N'est pas gentilesse qui vaille,
> Si la bonti de cœur y faille."

"The Golden Age had no kings or princes, rich or poor, but faded away as monarchy and property were introduced; and the first king was merely a peasant whom the rest chose on account of his superior strength, that he might preserve order," says this poem, which deserves its name, by being rosy with the dawn, as is seen in its praising science, placing the sun in the center of the system, and rebuking the fancy that comets, meteors, and eclipses threaten harm. Thus popular literature took up ideas, soon to establish themselves in institutions.

VI.

In this century we find more vigorous resistance than ever before offered to the papal anathemas. The followers of Henry IV. and Arnold of Brescia had quailed before interdicts. Prohibition of public worship in France had forced Philip Augustus, in 1200, to leave the woman he loved for one he hated. But we have seen that the friends of the Albigenses cared little for the ban of the Church, and that their deadliest foe, Simon the Catholic, openly defied it in his greed for their spoils. Still more stubborn opposition was made in England. Richard the Lion-hearted had died under excommunication in 1199. John found little censure at Rome for dismissing his wife or robbing and murdering his nephew, but his refusal to accept the archbishop of Canterbury appointed by Innocent III., caused the latter, in 1208, to lay an interdict upon the kingdom. The English churches were closed for six years, not being opened even for funerals or marriages; church festivals were discontinued, social life was overshadowed to an extent now incomprehensible, the sorrow of the mourner was deepened cruelly, and the bliss of love was disturbed by superstitious fears. But the people suffered in silence, and most of the barons, with three of the bishops, openly supported their godless king, who made the interdict an excuse for plundering the Church, a course which enabled him to hire great bands of mercenaries. Ere long he was excommunicated by name, but without effect. Then his throne was pronounced vacant and offered to Philip Augustus. Even after this, such an army gathered together in England as showed that a popular king might safely have defied France as well as Rome. John's cowardice, tyranny, and licentiousness had alienated his subjects, and it was fear of them rather than of Philip or Innocent that made him, in 1213, own this pope as his liege lord, receive the archbishop, and promise to indemnify the plundered clergy, free the priests from the control of the courts, and let the high places in the Church be filled by orders from Rome.

The triumph of the papacy seemed complete; but the people of England soon proved more formidable than the king. A league against the royal tyranny was made by the new archbishop, Stephen Langton, and other prelates, the leading barons, and the citizens of London, who had now begun to elect their mayors. John was forced to swear at Runnymede, on June 15, 1215, that he would keep the "Great Charter," according to which no taxes were to be levied without the consent of Parliament, no one was to be punished except by due process of law, widows and orphans were protected against spoliation, the tyranny of the barons was as much checked as that of the monarch, and rebellion was made legal in case the king should break his faith. To this perfidy John was openly exhorted by Pope Innocent, who promptly declared Magna Charta null and void, excommunicated its supporters, and laid his interdict on the city of London. The citizens went on holding public worship in defiance of the pope, and Magna Charta has never ceased to be in force. Innocent III.'s dislike of this great charter of liberty soon cursed England with a horrible civil war and a French invasion; but her people would not suffer him to make them slaves.

Italian democracy found the popes more friendly, but only because they were still waging against the emperors the two hundred years war for supremacy begun by Hildebrand. Innocent's wish, that Germany should be ruled in his own interest, had devastated her with ten years of internecine bloodshed before 1212, when he consented, while John was still under excommunication, and Toulouse was resisting Montfort's first attack, to let the empire pass under the sway of Frederic II. This monarch's loyalty to the Church made him take the cross for Palestine at his coronation in Aix la Chapelle, 1215. On receiving at Rome, five years later, the golden diadem which fully confirmed his imperial authority, he promised to put down heresy, to give the clergy full exemption from state taxation and jurisdiction, and speedily to head a crusade. The expedition was delayed with the papal consent for several years, during which Frederic was restoring order to his empire, and discovering who had done most to trouble it. He kept sending men and money to Palestine, and at last set sail thither in August, 1227, but soon returned in consequence of a dangerous illness. The next month he was excommunicated, without being heard, by Gregory IX., who had but just become pope at the age of eighty-five. Then Frederic wrote to all the other sovereigns of Europe, complaining of the injustice, done not only to himself, but to John of England and Raymond of Toulouse, by the popes, whom he calls wolves in sheep's clothing, and leeches ever athirst for gain. This first public rebuke of the Church won general favor; Gregory was driven out of Rome by the citizens; the bishops, princes, and large cities of Germany, Naples, and Sicily, remained loyal almost without exception; and the other Italians continued divided as before into Guelfs and Ghibellines.

The next summer Frederic led an army into Palestine, in spite of papal prohibition, and succeeded by his own diplomacy in making a treaty with the Sultan of Egypt, which gave the Christians Jerusalem and the road thither, as well as Bethlehem and Nazareth, for the next ten years. Thus Christianity gained possession for the last time of her sacred places, and the first use made of them by her religious rulers was to put them under an interdict, in consequence of the presence of the emperor, who had won them without bloodshed, and was on this very account cursed all the more deeply by the ferocious old pope. Prominent among Gregory's supporters were the Templars, whose zeal led them to try to betray the emperor into the hands of the Saracens. Frederic's own behavior was singularly mild and patient, but his tolerance to Moslemism and sarcasms on church sacraments gave great offense in Christendom. After crowning himself as King of Jerusalem, in the Church of the Holy Sepulcher, which no other sovereign of Western Europe has entered during twelve centuries, he returned to find Naples invaded by the papists, armed with a false report of his death. Frederic's subjects were so loyal, that Gregory had to consent to a peace in 1230, when the papal ban was revoked.

Rome's unwillingness to have Germany and Italy under the same power prevented the emperor's doing much for the former country, but the loyalty of her free cities led him to sanction and increase their privileges. His real sentiments toward popular liberty were unfriendly. The democracies of Lombardy and Tuscany were mostly his enemies. Nor did he give any aid to the Stedingers, those gallant peasants, living on the marshes near Oldenburg, who began early in this century to protect their wives and daughters against the robber-knights by destroying the castles. A priest to whom a Stedinger matron had given a groschen, when he expected more, put it into her mouth instead of the communion-wafer, and was slain by her husband, Bohlke. His friends would not give him up; so the whole country was put under an interdict in 1207, at which all the priests were driven out. Army after army of mounted and mail-clad crusaders was now driven back by the light-armed peasants; and it was not until May 27, 1234, that Bohlke and his companions sank under overwhelming numbers.

Meantime Frederic was making Naples and Sicily the most flourishing countries in Europe. In 1231, he published his code, establishing a strict and equable system of jurisprudence and taxation, to which both priests and nobles were made amenable, ecclesiastics not being allowed to become judges, and no special jurisdiction being left to nobility or clergy, except that the latter could still control marriages.

Trial by ordeal was abolished, wages of battle and torture narrowly restricted, private war and wearing weapons in time of peace prohibited, practice of medicine forbidden, except to properly educated physicians, the tools and oxen of peasants guaranteed against seizure, female chastity protected, and women's rights of inheritance secured. Greeks, Jews, and Moslems were tolerated and protected by law, but the Catharists and Waldenses were persecuted cruelly, and nearly all driven out of Southern Italy. The shelter given to these ascetic heretics by the Lombard and Tuscan rebels must have been doubly distasteful to the emperor's lax morals and to his stern despotism. Jews, and only they, were permitted to take interest, but not more than ten per cent., and all taxes on trade were abolished. The cities were freed from the tyranny of bishops and nobles, but kept dependent on the crown. Their representatives were twice summoned to meet those of the clergy and nobility, but only to assist the emperor to levy taxes according to his own sovereign will.

Frederic II. gave special attention to practical improvements, like that of the breed of horses and cattle, and introduced the culture of the sugar-cane, cotton, dates, and indigo, the latter being grown by Jews invited from Africa. The Saracens, who had been rebels in Sicily, were transported to Lucera in Northern Apulia, and made the most loyal of soldiers, especially against the pope, whose mercenaries they opposed, fighting side by side with German crusaders, who had just returned from Palestine and still wore the red cross. The friendship of Moslem sovereigns enabled Frederic to keep a menagerie, containing an enormous elephant, a giraffe, camels, dromedaries, lions, tigers, hyenas, rare owls and falcons, etc. How well he had studied the forms and habits of birds appears in his treatise on falconry, still extant, and containing some corrections of Aristotle. This author, however, he greatly esteemed, and had his works, with those of Averroes and Avicenna, translated by Michael Scott, as well as by Hebrew and Arab scholars. During the crusade Frederic had asked the noted Moslem philosophers to tell him about the eternity of the world, the immortality of the soul, and the foundation of religion. So bold were his questions that a Moorish rationalist said he dared not answer them, except orally, and either to the emperor in person or to some confidential messenger. The earliest Italian poetry was written by Frederic and his courtiers; he spoke seven languages, Latin, Greek, Arabic, French, German, Italian, and Sicilian; he was well versed in diplomacy, as we have seen, and also in mathematics; and to him we owe the foundation of the universities of Naples and Padua, as well as the revival and reorganization of the great Medical School of Salerno. Rightly was he called "The Wonder of the World," *Stupor Mundi*. He was by far the most generous and enlightened patron of knowledge in the Middle Ages. If he had been suffered to go on preparing the way for Roger Bacon, and if the latter had been permitted to labor in peace at Naples, where he and scholars like him would have been glad to gather under such patronage, the Renaissance and the Reformation would have come at least a hundred years earlier. That all this did not take place is mainly due to that great enemy of light which, just before imprisoning Bacon for twenty-four years, kept Frederic under excommunication for fourteen, and met all his plans with a steady opposition which made them fruitless.

Gregory Ninth's rage at seeing the clergy and laity of Southern Italy made equal before the law, at finding Moslems tolerated, and at being hindered from seizing on Sardinia, led him to pronounce a second excommunication on March 20, 1239. Once more did Frederic appeal to all the kings, princes, and prelates, protesting his loyalty to the Church, and the injustice of his sentence by that man of blood and patron of heresy who called himself pope. Gregory retaliated by charging him with preferring Moslemism to Christianity, with calling Jesus, Moses, and Mahomet, the three great impostors, and with asserting that nothing should be believed which is contrary to the laws of reason and nature. These charges were formally denied, but were probably not groundless. Yet Elias, the successor of Francis of Assisi, took the emperor's side, and on being deposed for this from the generalship of the Order, which like the Dominican, was full of papists, excommunicated the pope ; the kings of France and England interceded warmly for their brother monarch ; the bishops of Bavaria trampled on the pope's letters and turned their backs on his legate ; the archbishop of Salzburg anathematized Gregory as the Anti-christ ; other German prelates preached against him ; and the clergy and parliament of England would let no contributions be levied for the war against Frederic. Italy and Germany took sides so generally with the emperor that he was able to lay waste the States of the Church up to the very gates of Rome, and prevent a hostile council from being held there in 1241, by causing nearly a hundred prelates to be captured by his Pisan allies, in a seafight against the fleet of Genoa.

Thus he showed such a determination to resist the highest authority in the Church, which places a general council above even a pope, as gives him the right to a prominent place among the champions of free thought. But thus he exposed himself to the hatred of his pious contemporaries, especially in France, whence had come many of the imprisoned delegates. His true policy would have been to send all the prelates who were his friends to the council with sufficient escort, and then appeal against Gregory, who died soon after, at ninety-nine.

The next pope, Innocent IV., had been the emperor's friend, but was forced by his position to become an enemy. After some delusive negotiations for peace, the pontiff fled to Lyons, and there packed a council, in which, on July 17, 1245, he declared Frederic not only excommunicated but deposed. This assembly was so small, and made up so generally of enemies of the emperor, that he still found much sympathy in Germany, Venice, Switzerland, and Sicily. It is possible that a sovereign of spotless character, known piety, and personal popularity might have been able to resist the authority of both pope and council, and even to organize in these countries a new church of which the emperor should be the head. There is some reason to believe that Frederic and his counselors actually discussed such a plan ;

but it would certainly have been frustrated by the general knowledge of his irreligion, perfidy, cruelty, profligacy, and hostility to political freedom. His contemporary, Saint Louis of France, was able to oppose the pope successfully, as we shall see; but only saints could do so in that superstitious century. The five years of Frederic's life after his deposition were so full of desertions and defeats, that his cause had evidently become hopeless. All his talents and titles did not prevent his vices from making him too weak for reforming, or even for resisting the Church. No one had been so free from superstition for nearly a thousand years; but this independence seems to have co-operated with his exalted position and despotic character in making him insensible to the pressure of public opinion in favor of morality. He was in all probability a free-thinker, despite his constant protestations of orthodoxy, but the historian of free thought must hesitate about including him among her martyrs, though he certainly deserves a place among her champions.

His son Conrad could not maintain himself as emperor; but Manfred, though but eighteen at the death of his father, whom the ban of the Church had prevented from marrying his mother, ruled Southern Italy with great skill, courage and success. Innocent IV. tried to sell Naples and Sicily to the earl of Cornwall, who replied, "The pope might as well ask me to buy the moon of him." This nobleman's brother, King Henry III., was anxious to make the purchase for his son Prince Edward, but Parliament refused the money. Finally, Charles of Anjou was persuaded by Bacon's patron, Clement IV., to seize on a kingdom to which neither of them had the slightest claim. Manfred was defeated and slain at Benevento, February 26, 1266, and denied burial by the pope, who suffered Frederic's grandson, Conradin, to be beheaded as a criminal on October 29, 1268, for trying to recover his inheritance from an usurper in honorable warfare. Thus died the last of the Hohenstaufen, who for more than a century had maintained the authority of the empire against the papacy. The war between pope and emperor seemed ended in the supremacy of the Church. Sicily freed herself from her tyrants, whom the popes permitted to abuse her women without restraint, by that bloody, popular uprising, the Sicilian Vespers, March 31, 1282; and the pope's refusal to let the island become a republic under his protection only resulted in the establishment of the dominion of Arragon. Naples, Tuscany, Lombardy, and Germany remained under the rule of sovereigns friendly to the papal power; and the States of the Church were extended over Ravenna, Ferrara and Bologna by Nicholas III., who taught the Franciscans how to hold vast wealth while professing poverty.

The accession of the docile and bigoted Hapsburgs to the imperial throne was preceded by an interregnum of twenty years, which gave the German cities a grand opportunity to extend their liberties. To do this, Cologne and Aix-la-Chapelle had to conquer their archbishop in pitched battle and keep him for two or three years in an iron cage, despite a papal interdict. Liege, Strasburg, Augsburg, and Würzburg were equally successful in making war against their bishops; and a great league of sixty Rhenish and Swabian towns succeeded in keeping in check, not only the prelates, but the robber knights. There were eighty of the cities of Northern Germany in the Hanseatic League, which was fully organized in 1268, and had previously conquered the king of Denmark, in spite of his support from Innocent III.

Among other popular movements destined henceforth to be often imitated, may be mentioned the great revolt in 1251 of the Shepherds in France. These peasants marched from Flanders to Marseilles, under a leader who called himself the Master of Hungary, and was possibly a Catharist, slaughtering the monks and priests, and administering the sacraments to all who wished them. More permanent opposition to Rome had already been organized by the French barons who, after Frederic's excommunication in the council of Lyons, 1246, formed a league to resist every ecclesiastical anathema pronounced unjust by their own leaders, one of whom, the duke of Brittany, was nicknamed, on account of his hatred of the clergy, Mauclerc. Six years later, Queen Blanche, who had sent out the last crusade against Toulouse, on hearing that the canons of Notre Dame had imprisoned their serfs for not paying taxes, and punished the complaints of the men to the crown by shutting up the women and children also, led her soldiers to the dungeon, smote with her own hand against the gates to encourage her men to break them open, and then declared all the rescued peasants free. Her son, not unjustly called Saint Louis, forbade laymen to use any argument except the sword against unbelievers, and ordered all debtors to the Jews to repudiate their debts for the good of their souls. Yet even he, shortly before departing for the crusade in which he perished, enacted the Pragmatic Sanction of 1268, according to which no prelate could be appointed, or money collected in France by any pope without the consent of her king and bishops. So strong was Louis through his piety and virtue, that neither the pope nor his people showed any displeasure at this great blow to papal tyranny.

Even Denmark felt something of the new spirit, and we find Christopher I. imprisoning the archbishop of Lund for disloyalty in 1257, and successfully resisting an interdict until it was taken off by the pope ; so that the prelate had to resort to poison to overcome his monarch.

In England, Magna Charta was maintained against kings and popes, and the exactions of these potentates sternly resisted. Parliament refused to help conquer Sicily in 1255 ; and the bishop of London, on being threatened with deposition for prohibiting contributions for Rome in his diocese, said to the king, "If your pope takes off my miter, I shall put on my helmet." Robert Grostête, bishop of Lincoln, and an early patron of Roger Bacon, took the lead in resisting the intrusion of unfit foreigners into English benefices, and so far anticipated the Reformation as to declare openly, that only such mandates as were in accordance with the New Testament should be regarded as issued by a successor of the Apostles.

The main war for liberty was waged against Henry III. ; and what was called, from its audacity, the Mad Parliament of 1258, undertook to place the power in the hands of a committee of barons, leaving the king only the name of sovereignty. A wiser step then taken was that confirmation of Magna

Charta called the Provisions of Oxford, the leader in gaining which was Simon de Montfort, earl of Leicester and younger son of the usurper of Béziers and Toulouse. The pope forbade Henry III. to keep his oath to his subjects, and encouraged him, as did Louis of France, to raise a great army, which was totally defeated at Lewes, Sussex, May 14, 1264, by Leicester, whose soldiers wore white crosses on breast and back. Among the prisoners were King Henry, Cornwall, and Prince Edward, who had fought with reckless fury against the Londoners. This victory led to the supremacy of the committee of barons, to uphold whom Leicester arranged for frequent sessions of parliament, and made it, for the first time in English history, contain representatives of the cities as well as of the landed gentry. That famous despoiler of the monks, Robin Hood, is said by Scotch chroniclers to have been among these patriots. They paid no attention to the pope's bull of excommunication, except to have it torn up at Dover, so that it could not be published in England. Prince Edward soon escaped from captivity, gathered an army of royalists, surprised part of the rebel force at Kenilworth, and totally defeated the main body at Evesham, near by, on August 4, 1265, when Leicester fell, fighting so desperately that the minstrels said he would have saved the day, if he had had six men like himself.

Liberty was too strong in England to be suppressed by royal victories or papal anathemas. Scarcely had the prince who won Evesham mounted the throne when the cities sent their representatives to parliament, as they have done ever since, the Statutes of Westminster were enacted in 1275 as safeguards against oppression, and the great Covenant of Freedom was solemnly and finally confirmed in 1297 by this king, who showed himself during his long reign the patron of the liberty against which he had fought as his father's champion.

Despite some slight checks, among which may be mentioned the failure of Boniface VIII. to establish, in 1296, by his bull *de Clericis Laicos* the exemption of the clergy from a taxation on which the kings of France and England insisted, the

papal power was still at its height in 1300, when this pope, who
had won his tiara by frightening the superstitious Celestine
V. into abdication, and had but just suppressed with pitiless
cruelty the opposition of the Colonnas headed by two cardinals, invited all Christians but his own enemies to visit Rome,
and thus gain plenary indulgence. The whole number who
sought remission of their sins is estimated at two millions;
and the contributions were enormous. So extravagant were
the claims to political sovereignty now made by Boniface, that
he is said to have appeared in public, during this first of papal
jubilees, with the imperial sword, orb, scepter, and diadem,
but this is probably a myth. There is good reason to believe
that he did add a second crown to the single one hitherto worn
in the tiara. The next chapter will tell how high his pretensions really were, and how successfully they were resisted in
the first great victory over papal Rome.

VII.

In relating the destruction of Catharism, the crusades
against the Languedocians and Stedingers, the first atrocities
of the inquisition, the persecution of the early Mystics, the
discoveries and imprisonment of Bacon, the appearance of the
Reynard satires and other anti-papal poems, the humiliation of
King John, the establishment of Magna Charta, the fall of the
Hohenstaufen, the uprising of Sicily, and the growth of liberty
in Germany, it has been necessary to pass through the century
four times. So it will be well to look at the chronological relations of these events.

The first great work which was then undertaken by the
church was the destruction of the heresy of the Albigenses or
Catharists. For this end we see the crusaders massacre all
the people of Béziers in 1209, when King John has brought
England under an interdict, when the Stedingers have been
for two years under the ban, when the Parisian Mystics are
being led to the stake, after trial, in company with one of the
authors of *Reynard,* and when Walter von der Vogelweide
is denouncing Innocent III. for plundering Germany, and

keeping her in civil war. The crusaders keep on devastating Languedoc, and the ban darkening all social life in England; the Mystics of Strasburg, among whom are many Waldenses, are burned in 1212, and this year brings Frederic the Second to Germany, where he makes himself emperor with the papal approval. The next year sees the abject submission of King John, and the total rout of the protectors of the Albigenses at Muret. Then, in 1215, Magna Charta is extorted from John, despite papal interference, and the Lateran council, composed of fifteen hundred dignitaries of the church, sanctions the dethronement of the Languedocian princes as a punishment for their tolerance, greatly to the indignation of Pierre Cardinal, Figueira, and other troubadours. Next follow the wars of the disinherited Languedocians to recover their lands from Montfort, and of the English patriots against King John, who is sustained by the pope in the breach of his promise to observe Magna Charta. Frederic is now busy restoring order and encouraging learning, too busy to fulfill his vow of leading a crusade. This delay brings him under the ban, but in 1228, when the king of France subdues Languedoc and so closes the twenty years' war, the excommunicated Emperor goes to Palestine, despite papal prohibition, and throws Jerusalem open to Christendom by treaty, greatly to the anger of Gregory IX., whose violence and injustice are openly blamed, not only by kings and prelates, but by Freidank, Reinmar, and other minnesingers. Frederic is soon freed from the ban but the check given to clerical pretensions by his Sicilian code keeps alive the hatred of the pope. In 1233 the Inquisition opens its career of havoc, in Languedoc, Italy and Germany, and continues to check freedom of thought throughout the century, though somewhat impeded by assassinations and popular insurrections, the slaying of Conrad of Marburg in this year having a peculiarly good effect.

Frederic is excommunicated again in 1239, saves himself from dethronement at a council by the unpopular step of imprisoning its members, falls under this doom six years later, finds his vices make him weak before the pope, and at his death in 1250, leaves his dynasty unable to maintain itself, so that after two hundred years of struggle for supremacy, the papacy gains a temporary victory over the empire. Meantime that daring form of anti-christian skepticism, afterwards known as Averroism, has been discovered in Paris in 1240.

Monségur, the last fortress of the Albigenses, has been destroyed in 1244, and they have suffered terrible persecutions in both France and Italy, in the former of which countries the unsuccessful revolt of the Shepherds may be ascribed to their instigation. The Dualist heresy, which has maintained itself in various shapes ever since the first century, ceases to be formidable about the middle of the thirteenth, and falls into an oblivion, revival from which is prevented by its falsity. This simultaneous triumph over Catharists and Hohenstaufen is the great event of the period.

The latter half of the century shows no such brilliant victories of the papacy, but no serious defeats. Only concealment saves the Waldenses from extermination, and the pantheistic Mystics find themselves unable either to inaugurate the reign of the Holy Ghost now prophesied in the *Eternal Gospel*, or to raise woman to the priesthood instead of man. Vainly do the polemics of William de St. Amour, and the satires of Rutebœuf assail the corruptions of the mendicant friars, whom the popes permit to hold property in violation of their vow of poverty, a pious fraud still kept up. The progress of constitutional liberty in England is temporarily checked by the defeat and death at Evesham in 1265, of the son and namesake of the Languedocian tyrant, Simon de Montfort. The next year, Roger Bacon, who has been nearly ten years in prison because he loves science, writes his great work, and Frederic's gallant son, Manfred, is defeated and slain by the French, whom the pope has tempted into invading Naples. Conradin, last of the Hohenstaufen, mounts the scaffold for trying to recover his inheritance, in 1268, when the exactions of the popes in France are checked by the Pragmatic Sanction, whose author, St. Louis, owes his success in resisting Rome to his character, as Frederic does his defeat; and the same year sees the Hanseatic League fully formed, while the interregnum of twenty years, previous to the accession of the Hapsburgs in 1273, enables the German cities generally to enlarge their liberties, despite the anathemas and bloody attacks of their prelates, one of whom has to be kept in an iron cage, from which the pope's interdict can not set him free. That great popular revolt, the Sicilian Vespers of 1282, takes place during the second imprisonment of Bacon, which was the penalty for eleven years of most fruitful liberty. His death, after passing twenty-four years in all in captivity, may be placed in 1294, the year of the accession of Boniface VIII., and it was about this time that Jean de Meung, author of the latter part of the *Romaunt of the Rose*, gave such praise to marriage and manual labor as had not been heard in Christendom. The final and cordial confirmation of Magna Charta by Edward I. is the great event near the close of the century, though 1300 sees the celebration of the first papal jubilee, and the burning of Segarelli, whose follower, Dolcino, we shall soon find famous.

The great victories of the papacy, not only over monarchs, but over heresies, had given it such a prestige, and the power of superstition over the common people was still so great, that the cause of freedom of thought must have now seemed almost hopeless to its champions. They had measured their strength, and had been defeated. All honor to those who kept on fighting still.

CHAPTER VII.

THE REVOLT OF FRANCE AND GERMANY IN THE FOURTEENTH CENTURY.

I.

The conquest of the Catharists and the Hohenstaufen left no powerful organization among the heretics, and no hostile dynasty on the throne; but bitter memories remained of the massacres at Béziers and Lavaur, the perfidy against the Languedocian princes, the opposition to the peaceful acquisition of Jerusalem, and the execution of Conradin. England had not forgotten the interdict on her innocent people, the deposition of her king, or the anathemas against Magna Charta, while much offense had been but recently given by the pope's supporting Wallace. There was general sympathy, both in Italy and in Spain, with the Sicilians struggling against the French, whom Rome had invited to invade the island more than thirty years before, and still upheld. The cruelty and rapacity of the inquisition called forth ever increasing indignation, and the persecuted Mystics and Waldenses found many friends to pity them. Even the most zealous Catholics blamed Boniface VIII. for causing the abdication and hastening the death of his predecessor, for an unprecedented stretch of authority in deposing cardinals, and for his greedy and unjust exactions. His recent use of the papal title, in pronouncing a judgment which he had promised to render merely in his private capacity between France and England, gave great offense to the king and nobles of the former kingdom. And his attempt to have the clergy exempted from taxation had called forth successful resistance in both these countries, as already mentioned. The irritation thus excited was much increased by the circulation of *Reynard the Fox*, the *Romaunt of the Rose*, the songs of Walter Map, Walter von der Vogelweide,

Pierre Cardinal, Figueira, Freidank, and Ruteboeuf. Education was slowly advancing and the imprisonment of Bacon and burning of Aristotle and the Talmud had shown who was most hostile to knowledge. Thus the fourteenth century found the Romish Church apparently omnipotent but full of secret enemies, a mighty tree bearing all manner of fruit, both useful and poisonous, spreading its dense shadow over all thought, but rotten at the core. Her weakness was soon exposed by one of the royal line which hitherto had been most faithful.

II.

Philip the Fair, who ruled France from 1285 to 1314, made himself an absolute monarch, and this involved a battle with Pope Boniface. Not only did the latter claim authority to judge the actions, blame the faults, and take away the crowns of kings, but he controlled the appointment of bishops, regulated the portion of the state taxes to be paid by the clergy on their enormous estates, and exercised unlimited and immediate authority without check from king or bishop over the monastic orders, one of which, that of the Templars, owned a third part of Paris, and kept up such a standing army as could easily have overturned any throne in Europe; their horsemen alone numbering 15,000. When we further consider that the churches and monasteries were rapidly growing in wealth, that these buildings were open as asylums, not only to criminals but to insolvent debtors, that monks and priests were still exempt from secular jurisdiction in France, that here, as elsewhere in Europe, the inquisition was hunting down and burning up heretics without any control from the bishops or the king's judges, and that excommunication called down legal penalties on those who remained for twelve months under the ban, we see that the pope must be checked before the king could become absolute, or the kingdom made independent of foreign control. Hitherto Europe had been a family of nations under the Holy Father at Rome. The time had come for each country to have her own independent government. The pope who resisted this inevitable progress did so to his own destruction.

Boniface VIII. kept for awhile on good terms with Philip, by permitting him to control the election of bishops and abbots, to restrict the right of asylum, to check the growth of Church property, and to submit it to heavy and steady taxation. Some attempt was made before the end of the thirteenth century to interfere with this last procedure, but ineffectually, as has been mentioned. Only by strong protest was the pope able to keep the king from permanently cutting off all supply of money to Rome from France. No opposition was made to the edict issued by Philip in 1301, censuring the Dominicans for condemning innocent people in order to get possession of their property, and commanding that the bishops and also the royal seneschals should control the management of the local inquisitions. This wise monarch had all the cases of imprisonment on religious charges examined by his own commissioners in 1304. (Lamothe-Langon, vol. iii., p.p. 14-25). To this supervision may be attributed the comparative leniency of the sentences published by Limborch, who, according to Maitland, gives the results of fifteen Sermons, as they were called from the introductory discourse, at Toulouse, Carcassonne and neighboring towns between 1307 and 1323, at only forty executions among over six hundred culprits, of whom five hundred were Albigenses and nearly one hundred Waldenses, and a few Pantheists. About one fourth of the culprits was released, and false accusers received heavy punishment. Scarcely any immorality was brought to light among these heretics except the Albigensian *endura*, or practice of hastening the end of sick people and prisoners who had received the Consolation, and might be tortured into recantation or betrayal of their brethren.

Among these martyrs for an almost obsolete heresy we get a glimpse of one of the dimly enlightened pioneers of the scientific method of thought, Pietro of Abano, a physician who had doubts about the raising of Lazarus, and who was twice brought before the inquisition on the inconsistent charges of not believing in devils, and of keeping them in a bottle. The first time he was freed by Philip, and his death during the second trial saved him from the flames, to which, owing to the shrewdness of his maid-servant, Marietta, the Dominicans were not able to send even his body.

The tolerance of Philip, whose real views about religion remain a mystery, gave less offense at Rome than his plundering the Church. In 1301 the complaints of the archbishops of Narbonne and Rheims against the King's rapacity caused one of his most dissolute and disloyal subjects, the bishop of Pamiers, to be sent to him as legate by Boniface. The envoy was arrested as a traitor, and his seizure justified at Rome by one of the new men destined to dethrone popes, and kings also, a low-born, one-eyed lawyer, Pierre Flotte, who, when Boniface boasted of his supremacy, answered, "Your power is a word; my master's is a reality!" So it turned out to be on the publication of the bull, *Ausculta Fili,* in which the pope claimed authority, like Jeremiah's (Chapter i., verse 10), "over the nations and over the kingdoms, to root out and to pull down, and to destroy, and to throw down, to build and to plant," told the king it would be folly for him to deny his subjection to the Head of the Church, reprimanded him, not only for plundering ecclesiastics, but for debasing the coin and otherwise oppressing his subjects, and summoned him to appear in person or by his ambassadors before a council of prelates at Rome. This bull Philip had publicly burned before a great crowd collected by the blast of trumpets at Paris, on Sunday, February 11, 1302. The nobility, clergy, and representatives of the people of France were called together for the first time in her history, and at this meeting of the States General in Notre Dame, April 10, the king was sustained unanimously. So little respect was then paid to honesty that Philip published a forged bull, wherein the pope was made to claim political supremacy, with a reply, saying, "Let your great foolishness know that we are subject to no one in politics." These two letters were produced before the Assembly, to which the king also pretended that the pope had tried to make him his vassal. These charges were grossly unjust, for Boniface had not claimed that all political sovereignty belonged to him, but only that it ought all to be exercised in conformity with religious principles, of which he was the acknowledged interpreter. Imprudent as even this claim turned out to be, it was not inconsistent. The moral law is no respecter of persons; if the pope is empowered to enforce it, he is solemnly bound to pass judgment on all the actions of kings toward their subjects. Philip's position, that the pope's authority extended only to spiritual but not to temporal matters, really amounted to a denial that this rule had any existence, except over those who submitted voluntarily. Thus the real meaning of the burning of the bull and the approval of the States General was that France, as a nation, was no longer subject to the pope. His control over individuals still continued, but was much restricted by the repeal this year (1302) of the royal ordinance imposing legal penalties on the excommunicated, as well as by the salutary check now given, as described, to the inquisition, and by the command that no French prelate should attend the council at Rome.

Only four of the nine archbishops of France were present at this assembly, with whose approval Boniface sent out, on November 18th, his bull, *Unam Sanctam*, wherein, on the authority of the text of Jeremiah just quoted, as well as of Paul's declaration to the Corinthians (1 *Cor.*, chap. ii., verse 15): "He that is spiritual judgeth all things, yet he himself is judged of no man," it was asserted that "There are two swords, the spiritual and the temporal, and both belong to the Church. The former she holds herself, but the latter she allows to be wielded by kings, though only according to her own order and permission. The political authority is subject to the religious, every human being ought to obey the pope, and belief in this truth is necessary for salvation."

Philip replied by calling his nobility, clergy, and lawyers together on March 12, 1303, and presenting, through William de Nogaret, a jurist of Albigensian descent, formal charges that Boniface was not a legitimate pope, that he had murdered his predecessor, and that he had been guilty of heresy, simony, sorcery, and all kinds of impurity. These charges, whose truth we shall consider later, were also stated to the people of Paris in the pulpit. An assembly, containing five archbishops, twenty-one bishops, several of the principal abbots, and most of the great barons, voted that a general council should meet in France to decide on the guilt of Pope Boniface, and that meantime his bulls and anathemas should be utterly disregarded. Appeal from his wrath was solemnly made to the future council and the new pope there to be chosen. To these proceedings 700 certificates of approval were obtained from absent prelates and religious societies, the refusals being very few. Among the King's champions was William of Ockham, soon to become famous in the revolt of Germany, and Pierre Dubois, who urged Philip to abolish not only the temporal power of the pope, but the celibacy of the clergy, and who is also memorable for advocating the education of women. (*Revue des Deux Mondes*, 1871, March 1, esp. pp. 94, 113.)

Boniface now began to issue anathemas, but his messengers were thrown into prison. At last he prepared to excommunicate King Philip in a bull to be published on Sunday, September 8th, at Anagni, the pope's birth-place and summer residence. William de Nogaret had gone to Italy, with full powers to act for his master, and with him was a brother of one of the deposed Colonna cardinals, who was surnamed Sciarra, or *Quarrel*, from his fierceness, which had led him, when captured by corsairs after the fall of Palestrina, to work for four years as a galley-slave, rather than avow his rank, and so run the risk of being sold to his Holy Father, the pope. These enemies of Boniface found allies even in his birth-place, and gathered mercenaries by offering the plunder of his treasures. Early on September 7th, the day before Philip was to be excommunicated, 300 soldiers headed by Nogaret and Sciarra Colonna rushed into Anagni, shouting, "Long live the king of France! Death to the pope!" Many citizens joined them, the pope found few defenders, and most of his cardinals fled. There was fighting in the streets, an archbishop was slain, and the cathedral was plundered and set on fire. That Saturday evening the pope's palace was broken open, and Boniface, then over eighty, was found, sitting on his throne, wearing his tiara and papal mantle, holding the crucifix and keys of Saint Peter, and with a cardinal standing on either side. Nogaret and Colonna told him he must summon a council at Lyons, but he answered: "Behold my neck! Behold my head! I rejoice at insults from the son of heretics." Nogaret only told him he should soon be deposed, and checked Sciarra who would have smitten the pope's face with his gauntlet. Sunday Boniface spent in captivity, refusing to eat or drink, and protesting that he should never yield. Meantime, the soldiers plundered his treasures, said to have been richer than those of all the kings. Booty enough they found to make them ready to disperse on Monday morning, when the citizens rose to deliver their pope. He returned to Rome, but soon died there, actually a prisoner in the Vatican, where he was confined by his own cardinals, to whom his despotism had become unendurable.

It was fortunate for Philip, as well as for liberty of thought, that the successor of Boniface did not realize how much the authority of the Church was endangered by this virtual dethronement of a pope, and take advantage of the general sympathy, expressed even by personal enemies like Dante, to lay an interdict on France, depose her king, invite England, Flanders and Germany, who had long been at war with him, to invade his realm, and call on the Franciscans and Dominicans to preach, and the Templars to lead the crusade. Public opinion was not yet too enlightened for this, but Benedict XI. was too meek. He had been one of the two cardinals who alone were faithful at Anagni, but he thought only of making peace with as little disgrace to the Church as possible, and waited for seven months before even excommunicating Nogaret and Sciarra Colonna. His death soon after was followed by nearly a year's interregnum, and the next pope, Clement V. hitherto a zealous follower of Boniface, had at last found out that the Church was losing ground. All his actions favor the story, that he bought the tiara by selling himself to France, but the particulars of the bargain are beyond our reach. He showed his subjection by letting his coronation take place at Lyons, November 14, 1305, and thenceforth residing in France, until, after ruining every pre-

late willing to entertain him, he established himself in 1309
at Avignon, which as was charged by Petrarch and is confessed by modern Romanists, soon became one of the most
licentious and irreligious cities in Christendom. For more
than seventy years there was no pope at Rome, except for
one brief visit, and this period is justly called the Babylonish
captivity. The king was at once restored, without even a
show of penitence, to full fellowship in the church; his
accomplices at Anagni obtained pardon on the easiest terms;
the bulls, *Ausculta Fili* and *Unam Sanctam* were declared
inapplicable to France; and Clement had not been a year at
Avignon, when he suffered the worst of charges to be openly
presented there against Pope Boniface. That the latter had
hastened the death of Celestine V., sold the high places in the
church, and indulged in adultery and even grosser licentiousness, was strongly attested, and is not intrinsically incredible;
but his reign was stained by no scandal like the intercourse of
Clement with the Countess of Perigord. That a pope who
cared so much for power as Boniface, should have struck at its
foundations by openly avowing his disbelief in the Trinity,
the Virgin, immortality, the inspiration of Christ, and
transubstantiation is altogether unlikely. The testimony on
these points seems very strong, but it may be attributed either
to mystical zealots who had misunderstood their adversary in
the heat of controversy, or to time-servers who had sold
themselves to Philip. He had been a zealous student of the
Bible and the *Decretals*, before his accession, and his courage
at Anagni shows no lack of faith in the creed on which he
stood. All Christendom shuddered as Philip urged that Pope
Boniface should be condemned as a heretic and a malefactor,
his acts annulled, and his body dug up and burned. The
claim of apostolic succession and papal infallibility was almost given up by Clement V., when he issued his bull, of
April 23, 1311, praising the king's righteous though misguided zeal and referring the great scandal to the decision of
the council of Vienne, which met that October,
and, while formally acquitting Boniface, really condemned
him by forbearing to censure any of his assailants. When we

consider these facts, and also that at this very council, on April 3, 1312, Philip forced his pontifical puppet to disband the most trusty and mighty army in the papal service, and that the despot had already seized on its possessions, tortured many of its members into charging it with heresy, blasphemy, and obscenity, and sent others to the stake for protesting its innocence, we see that we have reached a new period in our history. Free thought has no longer to dread an omnipotent Church, secular interests begin to outweigh religious, and kings are mightier than popes.

III.

But were these martyrs free-thinkers? Was there any heresy in the Temple? These are difficult questions on which the best authorities are at variance. The following facts are the most important:

Up to Friday, October 13, 1307, when all the Templars in France were suddenly arrested at day break, the Order had the best of reputations for orthodoxy. Its knights had fought fiercely against the Moslems, opposed Frederic II. in Palestine, and stood almost alone among Frenchmen in support of Boniface. They had refused to pay taxes to Philip, and tried to recover money he had borrowed. This monarch, who was making himself absolute found an army which paid him no allegiance or tribute, garrisoning his cities. Their claim to be subject only to the pope did not prevent their arrest by the king's officers, and torture by the inquisitors, who soon brought many to confess charges, already made by two criminals, who had once been Templars, to the effect that novices were compelled to deny Christ, spit on the cross, give obscene kisses, worship idols, and promise, if priests, to omit from the mass the proof text for transubstantiation, "This is my body," and were then authorized to commit the sin of Sodom. These avowals were produced by tortures, under which thirty-six prisoners perished in Paris alone. The Grand Master, however, made a confession of his own accord before the clergy of Paris, if we may trust the bull issued on November

22, 1307, by Clement V., who also claimed to have received private information from a Templar of high rank, formerly compelled to deny Christ by the Head of the Order. This bull caused the arrest of the knights in Great Britain, Spain, Italy, Cyprus, and other countries, but few confessions were made, except in France. There the States General declared unanimously on May 1, 1308, the guilt of the Order, as on August 12 did the pope, now actually a prisoner in France.

This bull, called *Faciens Misericordiam*, secured a final hearing in Paris, of which the records have been published by Michelet. Nine judges, mostly prelates, sat from August 1309, to May, 1311, and heard 231 witnesses. Most of the Templars at first wished to defend the Order, and many protested they had been tortured into making false confessions. On May 10, 1310, fifty-four who had thus retracted were burned at Paris as relapsed heretics by the king and archbishop. Similar executions took place all over France, each martyr being offered his life and liberty if he would testify against the Order, and each one preferring to die in its defense. Those who had never confessed any thing were sentenced to imprisonment for life. No wonder that confessions became numerous. More than 150 witnesses now said that immediately, or a few days or months after their reception, they had been driven by threats of death or imprisonment to deny God or Christ. Those who persisted in refusing were not harmed, one being told, " No matter. It is only a joke." They were also, they said, required to spit, or in some cases to tread, on the cross, which is variously described as plain, or bearing the Christ, as a large one from the altar, or a small one carried in the hand, as of wood or metal, as carved on the stone floor, as painted in a book, or on a desk, as that worn on the mantle, as a smaller one in cloth, as made of sticks, or of straws. Most of the witnesses finally spat near the cross; but some would not do even this. About half of them were asked to give obscene kisses, but many refused, and none were compelled. There was the same proportion of testimony to the permission of grosser impurity, but not always from the same people who had been asked for kisses; and all the witnesses declared that very few such sins really took place in the Order. The testimony about the transubstantiation text is very scanty, and it evidently was never omitted during worship. A few witnesses spoke of idols, but contradictorily and otherwise incredibly. Several had been told after these disgusting performances, that it was all a joke, and one was only prevented by this assurance from leaving the Order (*Procès des Templiers*, vol. i., p. 510). Secresy was always enjoined, but most of the witnesses had confessed, usually to Franciscans, and easily got absolution. The general testimony is that the alleged occurrences were not common. Usually only the initiator and neophyte were present at the denial, and in no case was this preceded or followed by any heretical instruction.

It is especially to be noticed that no attempt was made by the prosecutors to show any influence from Mystics, Waldenses, Catharists, or followers of Arnold, Abelard, Berengar, Manes, Pelagius, Sabellius, Arius, or any other heresiarch; and no heretical book by any Templar has ever been brought to light. When a general council met at Vienne, near Lyons, in October, 1311, to determine the fate of the Order, nine of its knights appeared as ambassadors from nearly two thousand others, who were ready to testify in its defense. Most of the three hundred prelates wished to hear these envoys, but the pope threw them into a prison from which they never issued, and adjourned the council for five months, during which the king came with troops to his support. Then, on April 3, 1312, Clement announced to the council that he had concluded to abolish with their approbation the Order, not because it had been fully proved guilty, but because this was most expedient. No further protest was made at Vienne, where the violence of Philip against both the Templars and Boniface, as well as the cowardice of Clement, were fully realized. The local councils of Ravenna, Mainz, Treves, Tarragona, and Salamanca declared the Order innocent, and in Spain and Portugal it was kept up under new names. No Templar was executed out of France. Most of the members joined other fraternities or returned to the world. The Grand Master, de Molay, on being brought before the people of Paris, with three more of the dignitaries to receive sentence of imprisonment for life, protested that there was no vice or heresy in the Temple, and that he deserved to die for having been persuaded by the king and pope into bearing false witness. Guy of Auvergne spoke out also, and both were burned that very evening, March 11, 1313, by Philip's orders, in the island of the Seine, where now stands the statue of Henry IV., the crucifix being held before de Molay at his own request.

This was not the death of a heretic. I see no sign of heresy or free thought in these proceedings, though I believe with Michelet, Martin, Schlosser, Gieseler, Hase, and other historians that the denial, spitting, and kissing really did occasionally take place. The great differences among the witnesses as to the time, order and manner of the abominations, and especially as to the form of cross used, seem to me, as do the ease with which all these commands were evaded and the fact that usually nothing of the sort was required, to show that there was no rule of the Order enjoining any such proceedings, and no symbolic meaning. I venture to suggest that those witnesses were right who said it was only a joke, and that young and timid neophytes were occasionally insulted merely for amusement, as is still done in ships, camps, and colleges. Obscene and blasphemous rites were then publicly practiced with impunity at the Feasts of the Ass, of Fools, and of the Abbot of Unreason. One of the last is described in Scott's *Abbot* (chapters xiv. and xv.). If we suppose that these indecent tricks were known only to a portion of the Templars in France, and not practiced elsewhere, the great variation in the testimony is easily accounted for, as are the condemnation by the States General and all other French judges, the acquittal in Spain and Germany, and the slight penalties inflicted in Great Britain and Italy.

IV.

That the Templars were only imaginary heretics is shown clearly by contrasting them with a real one, sent to the stake a few months before their arrest, for asserting the liberty of the Spirit more bravely than was ever done before. Carcassonne, Toulouse, and Monségur had been defended; Dolcino opened the attack. His master, Segarelli, an insane enthusiast who tried to imitate the first disciples in their poverty, as well as in their garb, had founded the sect of Apostolic Brethren on the basis of an individual inspiration outside of the Church, which therefore had him burned at Parma in 1300. Already had Dolcino begun to travel through Piedmont, where he was born, Lombardy, the possessions of Venice, and the Tyrol, where he won the love of a nun of high rank and wealth, the brave and beautiful Margaret of Trent. Many other earnest men and women listened eagerly to his declaration that the time was come for founding a new and spiritual church, whose members were to be joined together only by pure love, and not be subject to any outward bonds of obedience. "Sine vinculo obedientiæ exterioris sed cum interiori tantum," are his own words, bolder than any that had yet been spoken in Christendom. Early in the year 1305 he called his partisans together on the mountains, near Varallo and Campertogno, in the valley of the Sesia. Thousands of men and women joined him, and an army of crusaders was driven back after a fierce fight, in which Margaret took part. Soon they were assailed by a more deadly foe—hunger. The capture of Varallo and devastation of the surrounding villages yielded but a temporary supply, and the attempt to get provisions as ransom for their captives ended in the fulfillment of the threat that these prisoners would be put to death. The following March the Come-outers made their way over almost impassable rocks to a mountain, standing about ten miles north-east of Biella, and then called Zebello or Rubello, though it was afterward consecrated to St. Bernard, in order to allay the ghosts of the heretics. Near by lies Trivero, which was at once surprised and pillaged. The bishop of Vercelli made repeated attacks, but could do nothing more than keep up a blockade. Dolcino gained victory after victory, captured many villages, burned churches and crosses, and made numbers of prisoners, whom he put to death after vainly trying to exchange them for provisions. The next winter saw him unconquered, but hopelessly imprisoned, much as John Brown was at Harper's Ferry. All the country around was in arms against him, and he and his followers were driven to eat rats, dogs, bark, roots, girdles, shoes, leather coats, etc. It is even said that they practiced cannibalism; but it is not said that any of them turned traitor to their cause. In Holy Week, 1307, the bishop led up all the men he could muster, and on March 23, the day before Good Friday, the mountain-camp was finally stormed, more than a thousand of its defenders slain, and Dolcino and Margaret taken prisoner. Both refused every entreaty to return to the Church; and vainly did men of rank ask the hand of Margaret, who had not lost all her wondrous beauty. On June 1st, she perished in the flames before the eyes of Dolcino, whose calm voice strengthened her to show no fear. Neither did he, though he was led that day through the streets of Vercelli, having one member of his body after another torn off with red-hot pincers, before he was finally flung where his ashes mingled with hers.

V.

Nowhere do Dolcino, the Templars, and Boniface still live as they do in the great poem, whose theological tendency is still a difficult problem. Dante's banishment, in 1302, for political reasons by his fellow citizens from Guelfic Florence, forced him to take shelter with the imperialists; and it was in their interest that, about ten years later, he wrote his *De Monarchia*, a treatise arguing that political sovereignty comes immediately from God to the emperor, that popes are entrusted with merely religious sway, and that even this depends wholly on their not usurping temporal power, selling offices, or otherwise plundering their sheep. This book, worthy of Arnold di Brescia, was burned at Bologna in 1329 by a cardinal who sought to have its author's dead body treated likewise; and Catholics are still forbidden the perusal, an offense which very few are now likely to commit. The archbishop of Milan also charged Dante with heresy ; and he was forced to appear in person before the inquisitors, who found the evidence too weak, or his protectors too mighty.

The principal witness we can examine is the *Divina Commedia*, finished just before Dante's death in 1321. This sublime picture of the doom of the wicked and triumph of the redeemed is now highly prized by all Christians, especially Roman Catholics, but was formerly regarded with much suspicion, a Jesuit, named Arduino, even trying to show that so disgraceful a poem must have been forged by some obscure Wycliffite. Here we find the most heterodox ideas of the *De Monarchia* presented in the assertions of the divine right of Cæsar to sit in the saddle and rule Italy, and of the necessity of two suns, one to show the right path in worldly, and the other in religious matters (*Purgatorio*, vi., 76-93, xvi., 106-8).

The first appearance of the papacy is as the :

" She-wolf that with all hungerings
   Seemed to be laden in her meagerness,
And many folk has caused to live forlorn."

We read further that she

" Suffers not any one to pass her way,
   But so doth harass him that she destroys him.
   And has a nature so malign and ruthless
   That never doth she glut her greedy will,
   And after food is hungrier than before.
   Many the animals with whom she weds,
   And more they shall be still, until the Greyhound
Comes, who shall make her perish in her pain."

Of this Ghibelline chief, whose residence is then described, it is said :

" Through every city shall he hunt her down,
   Until he shall have driven her back to Hell,
   There from whence envy first did let her loose."
(*Inferno*, i., 49-111, Longfellow's Version).

Dante says to the ghost of Pope Boniface:

> "Your avarice afflicts the world,
> Trampling the good and lifting the depraved.
> The Evangelist you Pastors had in mind,
> When she who sitteth upon many waters
> To fornicate with kings by him was seen;
> The same who with the seven heads was born,
> And power and strength from the ten horns received,
> So long as virtue to her spouse was pleasing.
> Ye have made yourselves a god of gold and silver,
> And from the idolater how differ ye,
> Save that he one, and ye a hundred worship?
> Ah, Constantine, of how much ill was mother,
> Not thy conversion, but that marriage-dower
> Which the first wealthy Father took from thee."

(*Inferno* xix., 104–117).

Similar denunciation of that alleged donation which was the foundation of the temporal power of the popes is put into the mouth of the heavenly Eagle, who calls it, "The good intent that bore bad fruit." (*Paradiso*, xx., 56, Longfellow).

A little later we find St. Peter, in a glow of indignation which makes Beatrice and all heaven turn red with sympathy, say of Boniface:

> "He who usurps upon the earth my place,
> My place, my place, which vacant has become
> Before the presence of the Son of God,
> Has of my cemetery made a sewer
> Of blood and stench, whereby the Perverse One
> Who fell from here, below there is appeased."

Then he denounces the popes for using the banner bearing his keys in making war against the baptized, a practice necessarily involved in their temporal sovereignty, which Dante evidently wished to have pass away.

Not one of Peter's successors appears in Dante's heaven, but there are two in purgatory for gluttony and avarice, and three of those under whom he lived are doomed to a peculiarly hot place set apart for the punishment of simony, a sin almost confined to popes and prelates. The last words of Beatrice, as she leaves Dante to take her place in the White Rose of the Saints, are a burst of exultation at the damnation of Boniface and Clement. Another contemporary, Celestine V., is left outside of hell among the wretches, "Hateful to God and to his enemies." Many more popes are in hell for avarice, and an archbishop is sunk in the worst of the nine circles, freezing eternally among other traitors, while his victim is ever gnawing at his brain. Still more remarkable is Dante's saying nothing about the pope in his confession of faith to Peter, omitting the article about the Church still repeated in the Nicene Creed as well as in that ascribed to the Apostles, and inserting such tributes to the Bible as are not found in these much honored formulas. (*Paradiso*, xxiv., 93 and 136, xxv., 88.) The triumph of the Church, at the close of the *Purgatorio*, brings in all the writers of the New Testament, but has no place for the pope, who can not be meant, as some Catholics suppose, by the Griffin, since this monster is said to have never plucked forbidden fruit. (*Purgatorio*, xxxii., 43.)

We also find the pope and cardinals blamed for studying the *Decretals* instead of the Gospel. (*Paradiso* ix., 133-7). Christ is said to be daily bought and sold in their court. (*Paradiso*, xvii., 51). A heathen emperor, who had persecuted Christianity, is placed in heaven, and the poet laureate of pagan imperialism is charged with the duty of guiding Dante through two-thirds of his holy journey; but we do not find any of the professions, then customary, that the poem is written in obedience to Church authority, or in the service of the pope. On the contrary, the *Paradiso* begins and ends with the claim of its author to an independent inspiration, coming directly from the Light Eternal and Glory Infinite.

Considering these facts, and also Dante's epitaph, written by himself and still to be seen on his tomb at Ravenna, "Jura Monarchiæ, Superos Phlegetonta Lacusque Lustrando cecini," etc. "I sang the rights of Imperialism, traversing heaven, purgatory, and hell," I think we must believe he meant to condemn the papal injustice by contrasting it with the divine justice which he thought the emperor ordained to dispense. The grim humor of concealing such an attack on the Head of the Church under the mask of pious zeal for her purity, would be in full harmony with the title of the *Divine Comedy*, which is, I suspect, further justified by many puns like that in the opening line of Canto vii. of the *Inferno*, "Papë Satan, Papë Satan, Aleppe," which would mean if printed as "Pap'é Satan," etc., "The Pope is the Devil!"

That Dante was either an unbeliever or a heretic does not follow necessarily. All his language toward God, Christ, Mary, the Saints, the Fathers, and the angels is thoroughly devout, and I believe sincerely so. The treatment of Boniface by Philip he condemns, (*Purgatorio*, xx., 85-91), and of the general damnation of the heathen he professes to become fully convinced—(*Paradiso*, xx., 70-105)—though he makes exceptions in favor of Trajan, Cato, and Ripheus. The two great rationalists, Bacon and Abelard, he does not mention, though they died at peace with the Church; and their persecutors, Bernard and Bonaventura, are placed by him in heaven. There, indeed, we find Sigier of Paris, who, Dante says, taught invidious truth; but Michael Scott is put in hell as a soothsayer. Two more noted unbelievers, Frederic II. and Farinata, are confined in fiery tombs with other Epicureans, though they had been leaders in his own party. That none of the early heretics are with them, except Pope Anastasius, seems to me of little significance in view of the celestial seat given to their cruel enemy, Justinian. That none of the Catharists, Waldenses, or heretical Mystics, except Dolcino, are condemned to hell is more surprising. That Dante had any sympathy with the Albigensians, as has recently been maintained, is altogether unlikely, since he shows no reverence for Satan, admits one of their worst persecutors, Bishop Fulk, of Toulouse, among the blessed saints, and puts this monster in a Heaven of Lovers, which, according to strict Catharism, could not exist. Fulk had treated the Waldenses also so badly, that Dante can not be ranked among

their champions, especially as there is no proof that he knew
much about this sect. He certainly had much of their reverence for the Bible, but so had the Mystics generally.

That Dante had met with heretical Mystics is almost certain, and some sympathy for them appears, not only in his
placing the Bible above the Church, but in his giving one of
their chief authorities, Joachim of Floris, the alleged author
of the *Eternal Gospel*, a place in the Heaven of the Sun,
among the blessed theologians. Still more important is a fact
I have not seen noticed. Dante agreed with those heterodox
visionaries among the Franciscans, who called themselves
Spirituales and were nicknamed *Fratricelli*, in the principal
controversy they were then holding with Pope John XXII.,
and the Dominicans. The Franciscan Mystics maintained that
their founder, in enjoining absolute poverty, not only on his
disciples as individuals but on his Order as a whole, was merely
trying to have such a life led as that actually lived by Jesus,
and therefore that they themselves alone were faithful imitators of Christ. This latter doctrine was explicitly condemned
in the papal bull of January 13, 1317. In 1321, the year of
Dante's death, one of these Fratricelli confessed, during his
trial by the inquisition at Narbonne, that he believed in the
absolute poverty of Jesus. The Dominicans at once passed a
vote of censure, with only one dissenting voice, that of a
scholar who was punished with imprisonment by the pope at
Avignon. The General Chapter of the Franciscans, on Whitsunday, 1322, held that Jesus had really been as poor as Francis, but the pope formally condemned, in a bull of November
12, 1323, this proposition, from which was easily deduced the
corollary that his own life, like that of his prelates, was
Christless. Among the champions of poverty was Ockham,
who was soon obliged to take refuge, as we shall see, among
the pope's open enemies.

It was in the midst of this controversy about how poor
Jesus really was, that Dante finished his *Divina Commedia*
where he says of the marriage of Francis with Poverty:

"She, reft of her first husband, scorned, obscure,

> One thousand and one hundred years and more,
> Waited without a suitor till he came."

> "Naught it availed being constant and undaunted
> So that, when Mary still remained below,
> She mounted up with Christ upon the cross.
> But that too darkly I may not proceed
> Francis and Poverty for these two lovers
> Take thou henceforward in my speech diffuse."
>
> (*Paradiso* xi., 64-75).

In thus maintaining that Jesus lived a life which Francis was the first to imitate, Dante must have known that he was taking side with the Fratricelli, many of whom were in prison as he finished his poems, and four of whom had been sent three years before to the stake. In the next Canto to that just cited (*Paradiso* xii., 124-5) he speaks of the contest actually going on between the mystical Franciscans who wished strictly to enforce the rule of poverty, and their opponents who sought to relax it, and names the leaders on both sides, Casale and Acquasparto. Here, however, he does not seem to agree fully with either party. This, together with Dante's representing Celestine V., who was in special honor with the Franciscan Mystics and was canonized while the poet wrote, 1313, as eternally lost for resigning the papacy, though the reference is somewhat questionable, leads me to believe that Dante did not fully agree with these heretics, though he had more sympathy with them, apparently, than with any one else.

In fact he was too independent to follow any one's lead, whether heresiarch or pope. He thought for himself, as Erigena, Bacon, and Abelard had done, though more devoutly than the two latter. The whole spirit of his writings is in harmony with his breaking the pavement of the Baptistery to rescue a drowning child, and his refusing when he was more than fifty years old, and had been fourteen years in exile, to return to his native city, on condition of doing public penance as an offender. Whatever may have been his precise creed, his example is one of the noblest in our history. His choice of a modern language and a popular theme assisted him in doing more than any one before him in Christendom to make men think freely and boldly. He has pictured not only the medieval theology but the spirit that swept it away.

VI.

We have seen Mysticism inspire the strife of Dolcino against bishops, and of Dante against popes. Among other defenders of evangelical poverty at the beginning of this century was Jacopone da Todi, author of *Stabat Mater* and of the satire saying, "Oh Father Boniface, how much you have deceived the world. You have cast away all shame and rejoiced in scandals as a salamander does in fire. You have fallen like a new Lucifer." This pope had asked the poet, whom he kept for several years in prison, "When do you expect to get out?" "When you get in," replied Jacopone, who lived long enough to see Boniface a prisoner in the Vatican. Another Franciscan Mystic, Bernard Délicieux, persuaded Philip by personal entreaty to check the cruelty of the inquisition, against which he had preached with great power in one of its chief seats, Carcassonne. There, in 1303, he assisted the king's commissioner, Jean de Picquigny, to break open its dungeons, and take its prisoners under the protection of the laws; and he honored this official the next year with a funeral mass and eulogy, despite his having died under excommunication. Benedict XI. had tried to arrest the friar some months before, but this was not permitted by the people of Carcassonne. The next year it was discovered that some of the opponents of the inquisition had thought Philip lukewarm, and tried to get up a revolution in favor of the king of Majorca. Forty-five of these plotters were hung, and Bernard sent as prisoner by Philip to Clement V., who suffered him in 1308 to return to Carcassonne. Nine years later, the old man was summoned again to Avignon, with sixty-three other defenders of the poverty of Christ, among them Casale, whom we have seen mentioned by Dante. All were put in prison, and Bernard Délicieux was tried for assailing the inquisition, plotting against King Philip, and poisoning Pope Benedict. The first offense he avowed at once, the second he confessed under torture, but no torments could make him say he had any thing to do with the pope's death. On December 6, 1319, he was sentenced to imprisonment for life on bread and water, and died soon after. (*Revue des Deux Mondes*, June 15, 1868.) His four brethren, who were burned by John XXII. at Marseilles meantime, May 7, 1318, and whose bones were preserved as relics, led the way for two thousand such martyrs during that century.

There had been little persecution in Germany since the assassination of Droso and Conrad, whose fury had been mainly directed against Catharists, but insubordinate Mysticism was now found in the lay societies existing for prayer and charity under Franciscan oversight. The Lollards, who took their name from singing at funerals, the Beguines, medieval Sisters of Charity not yet wholly extinct, and the Beghards, or Brothers of Mercy, soon became almost as obnoxious as the Spirituales or Fratricelli. All these names are used of heretics who had nothing to do with the Franciscans, as was that of Brothers and Sisters of the Free Spirit.

One of their early leaders, Margaret Porretta, was burned at Paris in 1310, for teaching that the soul which is one with God is free from laws, and may indulge every inclination innocently. Seven years later, men and women were tried in Strasburg for practicing communism, also charged against Dolcino, and holding that God is every thing ; that man may become God and thus save himself as Jesus did ; that the Church and her sacraments are useless; that prayer and fasting check the progress of the soul ; that the good man needs no priest ; that whatever the inspired do is holy ; that it is better to follow the Inner Voice than the written Gospel, which is full of errors and not so good as books yet to be written; that we must give up even God in order to become God ; that there is no angel but Virtue and no devil but Vice ; and that there is no resurrection of the body, and no hell or purgatory, so that even Jews and Pagans are to be saved. Such teachings brought Walter, the first Lollard martyr, to the stake at

Cologne in 1322, and executions of martyrs took place occasionally thenceforth in Germany, but not so frequently as in France and Italy.

These Brethren and Sisters of the Free Spirit sought not to be less but more religious and moral than their neighbors, and set aside all ecclesiastical restraints, only in order to yield more strict obedience to the Inner Light. Some of them are said to have carried their scorn of conventionalities so far as to worship in utter nudity, and the inquisitors, who testify to this practice, are all the more to be believed because they admit expressly that it did not lead to vice. Nor does there seem to have been any thing criminal in the familiar intercourse of the sexes practiced by Dolcino's followers, and afterward by the heretical Mystics in Germany, where they were called Sisterers, *Schwestriones*. Even the view that whatever God has permitted man to do, however wicked it may be called, is right and not to be regretted, seems to have been held without bad results.

German Mysticism owes much to a Dominican, who was in the Church but not of it. John Eckhart was enabled by his study of Greek philosophy, the Bible, the Fathers, and the scholastics to develop about 1300, in Cologne, a system which he called wholly new, though it was like that of Erigena, whom he had not read, and whom he surpassed in boldness of thought as well as in plainness of speech. So clear and grand a proclamation of the soul's essential goodness and her innate capacity for all truth had never before been heard in Christendom. He had stood too high above Church and Bible to attack them, but he set at naught all their claims, as he showed that salvation could come only through the soul's rising independently into oneness with God, and that this could be done by each soul as soon as she pleased. "Blessed," he said, "are they who live by faith, following the Bible and doing what is commanded by the Church; they are children of God. Far more blessed are the Godlike, who live in Him, enjoying such knowledge as no book can give, and doing His will in such perfect harmony, as to have no need of human ordinances." (Lasson, *Meister Eckhart*, pp. 176–7, 290).

"Fasting and scourging profit nothing; love is the essence of goodness, as selfishness is of sin." "Jesus must have placed Martha, who actually lived the life of love, above Mary, who merely thought about it." "They are most holy who make least effort to be so, the highest goodness being that which is most spontaneous." "God loves every soul and keeps no one from Him: only they who choose it remain in outer darkness." "All that comes to pass is according to His will; nothing that is done should be regretted; but even sin must have been a part of His plan; for if there had been no sin, there could be no salvation." "The visible world is a copy of the invisible and ideal, which we know through powers transcending those of observation or reasoning." "Highest of all truths is that divine oneness in which we call ourselves God." Rightly is this forerunner of Emerson represented by Whittier as hearing the Spirit say:

> "Ye bow to ghastly symbols,
> To cross, and scourge, and thorn,
> Ye seek his Syrian manger
> Who in the heart is born.
>
> For the dead Christ, not the living,
> Ye watch his empty grave
> Whose life alone within you,
> Has power to bless and save.
>
> O blind ones, outward groping
> The idle quest forego;
> Who listens to his inward voice
> Alone of him shall know.
>
> Have ye not still my witness
> Within yourselves alway,
> My hand that on the keys of life
> For bliss or bale I lay?
>
> A light, a guide, a warning,
> A presence ever near,
> Through the deep silence of the flesh
> I reach the inward ear

> The stern behest of duty,
> The doom-book open thrown,
> The heaven ye seek, the hell ye fear,
> Are with yourselves alone."
>
> (*The Vision of Echard.*)

No wonder that Eckhart came under the papal censure in 1327. He professed submission and died soon after; but his works continued to be widely read and his ideas have often reappeared, for instance in the *Theologia Germanica* and the *Nine Rocks*, a description of the stages of ascent into a union with the Deity; which even Jews, Turks, and pagans might attain, according to the author, Rudolph Merswin, also noted for founding, near Strasburg, a monastery, which he empowered the comparatively tolerant Hospitallers, or Knights of the White Cross, to keep open as a refuge for men too liberal to be sheltered elsewhere.

Most prominent among Eckhart's followers is the famous preacher, John Tauler of Strasburg, a Dominican who opposed the Brethren and Sisters of the Free Spirit, and tried to keep in friendly relations with the Church, though he taught that her sacraments changed from helps to hindrances, as men rose in spiritual life. He went on preaching and celebrating the Lord's supper, during the twenty-five years when this was forbidden over a great part of Germany, because the emperor had offended the popes. Even the Black Death, which slew nearly half the people of Germany, France, England, and Italy in 1348 and 9, did not move the wicked shepherd to pity his dying sheep. But Tauler and two of his friends published letters exhorting all monks and priests to pay no attention to the pope's interdict, still in force, but give the sick and dying all the comfort they could. "The pope has no power to shut heaven against poor sinners who have fallen innocently under his ban." "When any one confesses his sins and desires the holy sacrament, we ought to give it to him and comfort him, paying more heed to the words of Christ and the Apostles than to the ban which cometh from envy and lust of worldly power." "It is not proper for a Christian shepherd when one man deserves excommunication, to lay his ban on innocent people who have never seen the sinner, and to condemn whole countries, cities, and villages, for this is not commanded by Christ or by the councils, but is done under an usurped authority." "That all those who will not kiss the pope's foot are heretics, that he who takes the name and fills the office of emperor being duly chosen by the electors is an apostate, or that they who yield him obedience, as to a ruler ordained of God, sin against the Church and become heretical is not to be proved from Holy Scripture. Wherefore those who hold the true Christian faith, and sin only against the pope's person are no heretics; but all who have come innocently under an unjust ban are free before God, their curse will change to a blessing and their excommunication and oppression will God lift off."

This caused Tauler, who stands to Eckhart much as Parker does to Emerson, to be driven out of Strasburg by the pope and his servile emperor in 1350, but he went on preaching at Cologne, where he died in 1361. So noble had been his efforts to give the religious consolation forbidden by the pope, that I am glad to find the best authorities against the story of his suspending them for two years, because a mystical layman told him he was not holy.

One of his contemporaries, but not an acquaintance, made the most famous attempt to set up the reign of the Holy Ghost. Rome had been deserted for forty years by her bishops and fallen into utter anarchy, so that rapes, murders, and robberies were perpetrated with impunity, not only by the nobles but by the banditti whom they sheltered; agriculture was insecure, and few pilgrims dared visit what professed to be a holy city. Vainly had the popes been entreated to leave Avignon, which they had made the most shameless of cities, as is attested by Petrarch, who was not prevented, either by his loyalty to the Church or by his own unchastity, from making such terrible charges of licentiousness and rapacity against Clement VI. and his cardinals as had in some cases to be veiled in allegory, and in others were suppressed. Desire to make the streets and roads safe enough to hold a jubilee with great profit led this pontiff to sanction the schemes of Rienzi, the son of a washerwoman, but a ripe scholar, a powerful orator, and an enthusiast for reviving the ancient glory of the eternal city.

The people had been aroused by his orations and allegorical paintings, many citizens had promised to fight against the nobles, and the most dreaded tyrants were absent from the city, when Rienzi invited all the Romans to meet at the Capitol without arms, early on May 20, 1347, the Pentecostal festival of the descent of the Holy Ghost on the Apostles. At nine that morning the deliverer, who had spent the night in hearing masses to the Spirit, appeared in armor, followed by one hundred confederates and preceded by the banners of justice and peace, and the red flag of liberty. Universal applause welcomed his proposal of putting down robbery and murder by a popular government, supported by a militia which was to assemble at the sound of the great bell. He was made tribune, and the nobles had to swear submission, or leave the city. No armorial bearings were tolerated but those of the pope, nor could any one else be spoken of as Lord. Robbers were punished; peasants and pilgrims were protected; order was established in and around Rome; eighteen hundred of its citizens who had been at deadly enmity were reconciled; and so were many husbands and wives who had left each other. A tyrant who offered resistance at Viterbo was promptly overcome. The messengers of the Republic found themselves every where welcomed, and even worshiped, as they traversed Italy with their silvered wands, issuing invitations to a great parliament to meet at Rome on August 1, and establish the unity of the nation. This idea of a united Italy, which Rienzi was the first to proclaim and which has only recently been realized, gave great offense at Avignon, where it was seen to be incompatible with the temporal power. Florence, too, insisted on her own independence. Rienzi, who was sadly in lack of prudent advisers, and far too fond of theatrical display, turned the meeting in August, when delegates from twenty-five cities were present, into the celebration of his own consecration as knight of the Holy Ghost. He began the solemnities by bathing in the porphyry vase said to have been used by Constantine, and finished by issuing a proclamation still extant, and substantially as follows: "According to the authority given us by the Roman people and the pope, we now declare this city free, as are all the others in Italy, and to these latter we now grant Roman citizenship. By this same authority, and the grace of the Holy Spirit, we claim that the right to elect emperors belongs to the citizens of Rome, and we summon Louis, duke of Bavaria, and Charles, king of Bohemia, who pretend to have been chosen emperors, together with the archbishops and other princes in Germany, who call themselves electors, to appear in person before us and the other representatives of the pope and of the Roman people."

The papal legate here sought to protest, but Rienzi bade the trumpets sound so as to drown his voice. The claim thus made of inspiration independent of the Church, was repeated on the 15th, when the tribune had himself crowned, not only with wreaths of oak leaves, ivy, myrtle, laurel, and olive, but with a silver diadem, typifying the gifts of the Holy Ghost. These heretical pretensions, together with the assertion of the independence of Rome, greatly alarmed Clement, who also objected to the use of the vase and the execution of several monks and nobles for their crimes, and who seems to have been especially offended at Rienzi's refusal to favor Queen Joanna of Naples, who had appealed to him as did her adversary, the king of Hungary, by whom she was charged with adultery, and complicity in the murder of her husband. Of these crimes she has been found guilty by most historians; but she was promptly acquitted by the pope and his cardinals, owing to the fascinations of her youth, grace, and beauty, which led the gallant pontiff to give her not only his constant society, but the Golden Rose, annually presented to monarchs dear to the Church, while the pretty sinner rewarded her lover with the sovereignty of Avignon. That city's magistrates wounded one of the tribune's envoys, broke his wand, and tore up his letters; a new and more vigorous legate was sent to Rome early in October, empowered to depose the liberator as a heretic, and seventy of the robber barons were asked to help overthrow the ruler who had checked their crimes.

Meantime Rienzi greatly offended the leading nobles by arresting them at a banquet in his palace as traitors, keeping them all night under sentence of death, and then making them in the presence of their people renew their oaths of fidelity, which in the state of mind shown at Avignon were worthless, so that their release was almost as great a blunder as their capture. Rienzi failed to subdue their revolt soon afterward, but on November 20, their attack on Rome was repulsed with the loss of eighty of their chiefs. Already had the legate made an unfriendly visit to Rome, and Rienzi's efforts to propitiate him and his master were useless. On December 3, appeared the papal bull, denouncing Rienzi as a criminal and a heretic, and exhorting the Romans to shake off his yoke. Still more alarming was the pope's delay to proclaim the jubilee which would crowd the city with wealthy visitors. Vainly did the great bell ring on the 15th, though only 150 soldiers had revolted. The small force Rienzi was able to send against them was repulsed, and he did not dare attack them himself, but resigned his power, leaving Rome to relapse into anarchy, despite the efforts of other patriots, who had no support from the pope.

Several years were spent by Rienzi in company with other Mystics who lived as hermits on Monte Majella, in the wildest part of the Apennines. At their command he went to Prague in July, 1350, and announced to the emperor Charles, whom three years before he had threatened to depose, that the reign of the Holy Ghost was near at hand. Clement was to be put to death by the people of Avignon, and the new pope would be a holy man who, in company with Charles and Rienzi, would rule over all the earth. The emperor answered the invitation to invade Italy by throwing the prophet into prison at Prague, whence he was sent to Avignon in July, 1352. Clement died while he was on trial, and Innocent VI. had as little scruple about releasing a heretic in order to gain power at Rome, as he had about annulling on his accession the constitution which he had just before sworn to observe, and which would have placed the Church under an aristocracy of cardinals.

On August 1, 1354, Rienzi returned as the pope's servant to the city where, just seven years before, he had sought to become knight of the Holy Ghost. He still did his best to put down the patrons of robbers, but to one of them, a soldier of fortune, the Fra Moreale, he had been so much indebted for aid to return, that his execution looked like ingratitude. Still more offense was given by the death of a highly respected citizen named Pandolfo, as a traitor. Rienzi's fondness for wine increased his unpopularity, and his attempt to augment the taxes on wine and salt led to a general insurrection, in which he was murdered while trying to escape in disguise, on October 8, 1354. His body was hung up for insult during several days, and then burned by some Jews to ashes, which were scattered. So ended the attempt to restore Rome to her ancient liberty and grandeur by making her the capital of the reign of the Holy Ghost.

Rienzi, Tauler, Eckhart, Margaret Porretta, Bernard Délicieux, Jacopone da Todi, Dante, and Dolcino show us the boldness of Mysticism. So indeed does the more orthodox Raymond Lully, who thought his method of teaching, which for a time proved extremely serviceable, had been specially revealed to him by Jesus, and who was stoned to death in 1315 by Moors whom he was trying to convert. Waldensianism had now become thoroughly penetrated by Mysticism, and it is by no means certain which name belongs to the 114 martyrs at Paris in 1304. Nor can we tell which influence preponderated in the Masonic lodges, or Bauhütten, which had formed since the twelfth century a great secret organization of workingmen, with its center at Strasburg, and which came under the papal censure in 1326. Catharism had been so thoroughly suppressed that there were no heretics of any importance, except Mystics, in the fourteenth century, until near its close.

VII.

The opposition, already noticed, of Germany to the pope was largely due to his insisting on being allowed to confirm or annul the election of her emperor. After the death of Clement V. the cardinals had refused for more than two years to fill the vacancy, and it was only under compulsion from the French government that John XXII., the son of a cobbler, and persecutor of the Fratricelli, was chosen on August 7, 1316. Meantime, Louis of Bavaria and Frederic of Austria had been simultaneously chosen King of the Romans, the title held by emperors previous to coronation by the pope. These rivals preferred the arbitration of war to that of the Church, and the battle of Morgarten, where the Swiss asserted an independence which William Tell seems to have done very little to achieve, was incidental to the strife which ended in the complete victory won by Louis at Mühldorf, September 28, 1322. A few days afterward, John XXII., who had from the time of his own election claimed political authority over the empire, on the pretext that there was an interregnum, issued a process, or as Louis called it, an excess, declaring this emperor's election null and void, because not confirmed at Avignon, and bidding him cease to rule, under penalty of excommunication. On January 22, 1324, he made a formal protest at Sachsenhausen, saying that he needed no confirmation from the pope, that the latter had no authority during vacancies, that "John XXII., who calls himself pope," was so great a heretic and enemy of all peace as to have forfeited the tiara, and that a general council must decide between them.

Now appeared the *Defensor Pacis* of Marsilius of Padua, a jurist who maintained that the New Testament is the highest authority; that this forbids the papacy; that all bishops are equal in rank, unless one be temporarily elevated above his brethren by the emperor, the true defender of peace; that the power to give absolution belongs to God alone; that the pope is no successor of Peter, who probably never entered Italy; that only a general council can lay down articles of faith ; that the Church consists of all Christians, not of the clergy only ; and that it is for the state to fill benefices and judge heretics. The daring author was promptly excommunicated, but was made court-physician by Louis, who had himself come under the ban on March 23, 1334, as did his subjects on July 11. Five German bishops still adhered to him, the Franciscans and Knights of the Black Cross were generally on his side, and so were most of the large cities, now rapidly becoming democracies. Strasburg and Augsburg forced the clergy to keep up public worship for twenty-five years in spite of the interdict, as is still commemorated in a song of the period:

> "Do soltent sie ouch furbäs singen
> Oder aber us der Statt springen."

("They shall none the less their masses sing,
Or out of the city we'll make them spring.")

Louis was soon able to gain a recognition of his claims from his rival, who was accordingly set at liberty. This treaty John forbade Frederic to observe, but the German's conscience was holier than his pope, and, finding his brother unwilling to make peace, he returned to captivity. Various compromises were proposed, but were defeated by the pope's dislike of any German emperor. One-half of Christendom was under the ban when Louis was invited by the Italian princes to Milan, where he received the iron crown from three bishops on May 31, 1327. Vainly did the pontiff now try to strip him of every thing but his name. Rome, whose people had recently made Sciarra Colonna, the assailant of Boniface, their captain, gladly opened her gates on January 7, 1328. The coronation was decreed by the citizens assembled in the capitol the next Monday, the 11th, and performed on Sunday, the 17th, by bishops from Venice and Corsica, assisted by Sciarra and Castruccio of Pisa.

Thus did Louis put in practice the theories of Marsilius, who accompanied him to Rome and shared the guilt of burning two of John's partisans alive. On April 14 the emperor announced to the people, in the place before St. Peter's, that John XXII. was the Anti-christ and the apocalyptic Rider on the Red Horse, who takes away peace from the earth, and that he was deposed for heresy and treason. Sciarra's nephew made a public protest, but on May 12 the citizens assembled before St. Peter's once more and accepted a new pope, who called himself Nicholas V. Even the soldiers of Louis now thought he was going too far, and on August 4 he had to leave Rome, while the populace, to whom he had sought to give the spiritual rule of Christendom, flung stones and shouted, " Pereat ! " His marshal actually killed himself in trying to force the citizens of Pisa to see John XXII. excommunicated and burned in effigy, on February 19, 1329, by the rival pope, who was soon sent as a prisoner to Avignon. Louis himself was so frightened at his own acts, that he offered, soon after returning to Germany, to abdicate in favor of his cousin, but the king of Naples prevented the pope from accepting the offer.

John's strength had been largely due to his apparent orthodoxy, which had shown itself in persecuting not only Mysticism, but sorcery, for which he burned a bishop soon after his accession, and to which many enemies of the Church seem actually to have resorted during this century. In 1331 he questioned the ability of the souls in heaven to see God before the resurrection of the body, and found himself generally condemned for heresy. He retracted just before his death, December 4, 1334, but his reputation suffered still more by his being then found to have amassed about $50,000,000 by selling not only places in the Church, but licenses to sin, as may still be seen by his chancery registers, fixing the sums for which absolution could be bought by priests, nuns, or laymen, intending to commit adultery, perjury, murder, etc. His successor, Benedict XII., wished to reform the Church, make peace with Germany, and reside at Rome, but he was so completely in the power of the king of France that he was able to leave behind him only the custom of wearing three crowns in the tiara, and the proverb, " to drink like a pope."

Meantime the electoral princes declared, at Remse, near

Coblentz, on July 16, 1338, that their choice needed no confirmation by the pope, and similar action was taken by the Diet at Frankfort, August 6, and Coblentz, September 12. At the latter session, Edward III. of England, then the emperor's ally, was present. These national assemblies also pronounced the papal interdict null and void, which caused public worship to be resumed in many places where it had been gradually discontinued. Louis might have conquered if he had not taken it on himself to have his son married, on February 10, 1342, to the heiress of Tyrol, Margaret of the Pocket-mouth, who had a husband living, and was too nearly related to the prince. Marsilius and Ockham wrote in favor of this assumption of privileges claimed by the pope ; but the German electors took steps toward choosing another emperor. Their purpose strengthened, as Louis offered to make degrading concessions to the new pope, Clement VI., who preferred to have a candidate of his own elected, as was actually done on June 11, 1346. Many princes and cities still were loyal to Louis, but his death, on October 11, 1347, under a ban which was not removed for two centuries, left the throne to Charles IV., who, however, was soon obliged to yield to the spirit of opposition to the power that had made him emperor, so far as to issue, in 1356, his *Golden Bull*, by which the claim that emperors needed confirmation by popes, was set aside forever. Thus the struggle for supremacy, which had lasted for nearly three hundred years, closed without either party's gaining a decisive victory. The papal prestige suffered much. Germany had found out that popes were neither omnipotent nor infallible, but nearly two centuries more elapsed before she became enlightened enough to have a Church of her own.

VIII.

Among the allies of Louis has been mentioned William of Ockham, an English monk who taught at Oxford and Paris, and who said to the emperor, when he fled to him in 1328 from Avignon, where he had been imprisoned for maintaining the poverty of Jesus, "Defend me with your sword, and I will defend you with my pen." To fulfill this promise he wrote his powerful *Compend of the Error of Pope John XXII.* in ninety days, and kept on arguing for the supremacy of emperors over popes until his death in the same year as his master, 1347. His whole system of thought was antipapal, for he denied the reality of abstractions more boldly than had yet been done, contending that even the existence of God could not be proved by reason, or admitted on any other basis than faith. Whether there is one or three persons in the Godhead, he calls as insoluble a question as whether the number of the stars is even or odd. That there is one First Cause seemed to him no more self-evident than that there is an endless chain of causes. The so-called universals, or general terms, have no reality, he said, either in the mind or out of it; for we know only particulars, and these merely so far as they affect us personally, and thus all inferences, even those leading to belief in God, become too uncertain for philosophy. Church authority forced him to admit that theology has found certainties where philosophy could not, so that there is a double standard of truth. But he speaks not only of the pope, but of that yet higher authority, the general council, with such freedom as had not yet been heard in Christendom; so that it is pleasant to find that no scandal can be produced against his life.

"Christianity," he says, "is a law of liberty, and, therefore, forbids us to recognize the absolute authority of the pope, which would make us slaves." "Innovations must be made when their utility is evident; and nothing great has ever been done by men who were afraid of novelty." "We must adhere to the mind rather than the words of Christ." "The Bible is only a part of the opinion of the Church, and so of less authority than the whole. But even general councils are not infallible. Neither the supreme pontiff nor the whole Church of God can make any thing true which is not true or false which is not false."

Ockham's alliance with the Mystics seems to have been little more than a league for mutual defense, like that afterwards formed with the emperor. Yet plainer opposition of all supernatural authority, whether of Bible, Church, or individual inspiration animated Peter of Abano, who was protected first by his king and then by his maid-servant against the inquisition; Cecco d' Ascoli, who was burned at Florence in 1327, for saying that the birth, life, and death of Jesus took place under the laws written in the stars; and Nicholas of Autricuria, who was condemned at Paris in 1348, for questioning the possibility of knowing God, and asserting that men would learn more if they studied nature instead of Aristotle. The great Peripatetic's authority was, however, claimed by the Averroists, now numerous in Northern Italy, especially Venice, where their unbelief in immortality, as well as in the Bible, greatly offended the pious Petrarch, who was himself unconsciously promoting free thought by assisting in the revival of classic study, a movement of which the chief seat during the fourteenth century was Florence. Among other pioneers in the Renaissance was Boccaccio, best known for exposing the vices of the clergy in his *Decameron*. Much is due to the rationalistic Jews in Southern France; for instance, Vidal of Narbonne, Caspi, who tried to explain the raising of the dead by Elijah and Elisha, and the standing still of the sun at the word of Joshua, as natural phenomena misunderstood, and also Leo, or Levi, Gersonides, who dwelt in Avignon under the protection of Clement VI. and who said: "If my reasonings are correct, the blame men give me is really praise." "We must bring truth to light, even if it contradict our law, for that is given only to lead us to truth."

The most formidable opposition thus far made to the Church did not come from students, but from rulers, who cared little for heresy or any other form of religion. Such were those tyrants of Lombardy, the Visconti, one of whom, John, archbishop of Milan, on being threatened with deposition, held up before the pope's messenger in the cathedral his crosier in one hand and his sword in the other, saying: "Behold the signs of my spiritual power and of my temporal also. With the one I shall defend the other."

Another opponent of papal ambition, who has had little

notice from modern historians, is Marzia, wife of Francisco Ordelaffi, who made himself lord of Forli in 1333, by creeping into the city hidden in a load of hay, and who extended his sway over Cesena, Imola, and other places near Ravenna. His subjects loved him for his liberality, especially to orphans, and enabled him to resist the pope's ban for nearly thirty years. When he heard the bell announce a papal anathema, he ordered all the other bells in Forli rung to tell the people that he had excommunicated the pope and cardinals, whom he forthwith burned in effigy. As he feasted his friends, he used to say: "Have this wine and meat lost their flavor on account of the pope's curse?" He forced the priests to violate the interdict laid on his territory, putting to death those who refused to hold public worship; and those of the crusaders sent against him whom he took prisoners, he branded with the sign of the cross on the soles of their feet, saying, as he applied the hot iron: "You have taken crosses of cloth, which will wear out. I want to have you carry crosses that will last." The accounts of his cruelties, must, however, be received with caution, since the monkish chroniclers were trained to disregard truth in the interest of the Church, and some of the worst accusations against him are disproved by the Annals of Forli and Cesena. (*Vita de Rienzo*, note to Chap. viii.)

When the warlike cardinal, Albornoz, who had recently brought Rienzi back to Italy, led a crusade against Ordelaffi, he wrote to his wife, "Cia, take good care of Cesena," where she was staying with her children and a few hundred mercenaries. "My lord, please to take good care of Forli, as I shall take good care of Cesena," replied Marzia, and she watched the walls in armor during the siege, which began early in April, 1357. Francesco now bade her put to death four citizens most friendly to the pope, but two of her leading adherents persuaded her into a delay, during which this order became known. On Saturday, which old writers call the Sabbath, April 29, the citizens rose with cries of "Church and People!" "Viva il Popolo! Viva la Chiesa!" threw up barricades, and seized a gate where they were soon joined by the cardinal's archers. Marzia attacked the rebels promptly, but was driven back into the upper city, or Murata, where she beheaded the two counselors, much to her husband's displeasure. Now she was alone in command, but Albornoz did not dare attempt to storm, though he had a hundred times her force. Ere long his miners drained her cistern, and threw down her largest tower. She filled the turret next in danger with captured citizens, whose wives and daughters forced the cardinal to wait long enough to make a breach. Then, on May 27, Madam Cia retreated with her children and soldiers into the citadel, whose ruins may still be seen high up on Mount Garampe. Thither came her father to bid her surrender, but she answered: " When you gave me to my lord, you told me to obey him above all. I have done so, and intend to do it until my death. He has given this place into my charge, and told me not to abandon it on any account. I shall not do so until he bids me, either in person or by some secret sign. Little care I for death or any thing else, if I can only obey his commands." Her soldiers were less brave, and on June 21, she had to surrender to the cardinal. She asked no mercy, and was kept more than two years in prison, until her husband was compelled to submit on July 4, 1359. Her heroism is commemorated in a drama, called the *Sack of Cesena*, and supposed to have been written by Petrarch.

During her imprisonment took place that revolt of the Jacquerie or French peasants which was chronicled by Froissart, and which, with those in Rome and Switzerland, shows the people were struggling after political independence, the surest guarantee of liberty of thought.

The same spirit will soon be seen in England, where already was manifest such indignation at the papal exactions, as we shall find in the next chapter produce an opposition never to be suppressed. In 1340, Richard Rolle, the hermit of Hampole, and translator of the Psalms, wrote his *Prick of Conscience*, the first book against Rome in English, now coming into use as a literary language, and in 1356, appeared the *Last Age of the Church*, a mystical prophecy erroneously attributed to Wycliffe, and designed to show that simony had become as dangerous as heresy had been formerly and persecution still earlier, and that no worse enemy could come except Antichrist. In 1343, soon after beginning the hundred years' war with France, Edward III. refused to let the pope act officially in making peace. That same year Parliament passed an ordinance which developed in 1351 into the *Statute against Provisors*, wherein the nomination at Avignon of foreigners to English benefices was checked, all appointments infringing on the rights of the king or other patrons declared null and void, offenders threatened with fine and imprisonment, and no appeal to the pope permitted. Similar penalties, and even outlawry, were denounced in 1353 by the *Statute of Præmunire* against all who should carry into foreign courts suits cognizable by the law of England. Another abuse, the interference of the mendicant friars with the parish clergy, as well as with the Oxford professors, called forth such earnest censure from Fitzralph, archbishop of Armagh, that he was summoned to Avignon, where he plead his cause before the pope and cardinals in 1357, and died under surveillance three years later, when the work was taken up by Wycliffe, as we shall see in the next chapter. So violent had the popular feeling against papacy become before 1350, that Clement VI. had to bid his legates be sure to take a strong enough guard to keep them from being stoned.

IX.

In the two previous chapters, we saw the church conquer all heretics and rebels, even on the imperial throne; but we have now seen her suffer a series of famous defeats, while her few and comparatively unimportant victories were due to the imprudence of such assailants as Dolcino, Louis of Bavaria, and Rienzi. Among the earliest events in the fourteenth century were King Philip's checking the cruelty of the inquisition, protecting Peter of Abano, imprisoning a legate, burning a papal bull in public, and even seizing on the person of Pope Boniface, who escaped only to die in the custody of his own cardinals in the Vatican. Soon after we find these daring deeds pronounced praiseworthy by the Head of the Church, then a French official, as pope after pope continued to be for more than a century. The condemnation of the prisoner in the Vatican as a heretic and malefactor was averted with great difficulty, while the fate of the Templars showed that neither pope nor council was strong enough to protect thousands of the most pious and virtuous members of the Church from open robbery and judicial murder. Nor could the great heresy of this century, Mysticism, be suppressed as Catharism had been; though this was partly owing to the strong likeness of heretical to orthodox Mystics. It is not altogether certain in which class we should place Dante, but there is no doubt of his independence, or of his hostility to the papacy, qualities which would have caused his writings to be suppressed in the previous century. Another mystic, Tauler, owes much of his fame to the revolt of the people of Strasburg against the interdict which he openly violated for twenty-five years and at last publicly and formally denounced.

During the second quarter of this century, the German and Italian cities generally took sides with their excommunicated emperor, crowned him at both Milan and Rome, despite papal prohibitions, and would have given him the final victory if it had not been for his rashness in proclaiming an anti-pope, burning John XXII. in effigy, and violating the time-honored marriage laws of the Church, as well as for the yet greater imprudence of his occasional offers to submit. It cost the popes nearly thirty years of struggle to get an emperor after their own heart, and even he had soon to decide the main point of the controversy against them, and declare in his *Golden Bull* that the choice of the Electors does not need to be confirmed by the Head of the Church. Meantime, Rienzi liberated Rome, temporarily, and might have done so permanently if it had not been for his lack of competent advisers, his proneness to Mysticism and theatrical display, his intoxication at his own sudden success, and the fear of the citizens that they might lose the harvest of the jubilee. Greater prudence and courage enabled the lord of Forli and the heroic lady of Cesena to defy for many years the anathemas, and for some time even the armed mercenaries, of the pope. The warlike deeds of Marzia

and Margaret show how weak was the hold of the Church on
the women of the fourteenth century. Still more influential
on the future were the daring treatises against papal supremacy by Marsilius and Ockham, the latter of whom went further than had been done for more than ten centuries in asserting the rights of reason, and claiming liberty of thought. And
while these books circulated with little opposition, we find the
Parliament of England passing anti-papal statutes, and her
people threatening to stone the pope's embassadors. The
Church was plainly losing ground, and finding it so hard to
defend herself as to be much less dangerous to liberty than
before. Only the fact, that the doctrine of the independent
inspiration of all pious souls is the worst possible basis for organization, prevented Mysticism from successfully asserting
her own claim to be the teacher of the nations.

Most of the events mentioned in this chapter, and also in
the two previous ones, for nearly a thousand years, took place
in a triangle which may be formed by drawing lines from
Rome through Cologne into Friesland, thence through Paris
to Tudela in Spain, and back due east through the center of
Corsica. Central and Southern France, Northern Italy, Switzerland, and Western Germany had formed the cradle of free
thought. Here or in Rome has been the chief scene of our
history since the death of Julian, and one of the most marked
features of our subsequent narrative will be the new promi-
nence of England, Bohemia, and Saxony.

CHAPTER VIII.

OPPOSITION IN NAME OF BIBLE AND COUNCILS.

These ninety years may be rapidly traversed, since they contain no rationalist of importance, and no contest of any magnitude except between the champions of rival authorities. The Church had always looked on the Bible as the highest source of truth, and the Waldensians had been appealing to it for two hundred years in opposition to the papacy. This appeal was now to be renewed in England and Bohemia and much more powerfully than before. Liberty of thought was not so directly aimed at in this movement as in either Catharism or the recent Mysticism, but the former had proved too subject to persecution, while the latter had reached its zenith of splendor, and was showing itself unfit either for popular adoption or for permanent organization. The Bible was now found to furnish a broad and firm platform suited for building up a new and purer church. And it also proved to be much more favorable than was expected by its early champions to liberty of thought. The full adoption of its authority means the dethronement of popes and bishops, the downfall of that household tyrant, the confessional, the abolition of the endowments of the clergy, the liberty of preaching without a license, and the right of the people to read the Scriptures freely in their own tongue. All these five points were insisted on from the first, and greatly in the interest of mental liberty, which thus found her best friends among men who had not the least idea of helping her. Authority still seemed almighty, but she was beginning to strike herself fatal blows.

II.

The Waldenses had had so little success that the title of founder of Protestantism really belongs to Wycliffe, who seems to have learned nothing from these obscure predecessors, and who certainly brought such literary genius and practical skill to the evangelical cause, as made it become for the first time a power in Europe, and one destined to grow for several centuries. He was, of course, much aided by the agitation in England, Germany, and Italy, described in the last chapter, and especially by the writings of his countryman, Ockham. Very helpful, too, was the publication in 1362 or 3 of a popular poem on the corruptions of the Church, *the Vision of Piers the Plowman*, whose author, William Langland, is, as Hallam says, "the first English writer who can be read with approbation." Its hero is an honest and pious farmer, who believes in practical morality and manual labor, and honors the Bible more than any thing except reason and conscience, and denounces the corruption of the Church, without sparing even the pope, whose bulls are said to be sealed by Lady Bribery, and to profit nothing without amendment. A second and more outspoken version, published in 1377, exhorts the Holy Father in the name of reason to have pity on the Church and govern himself before he tries to give grace to others; charges him with robbing the Church, making himself king by force, and spilling Christian blood; brings in an angel who cries aloud, that from the temporal power the Church has drunk poison, and makes the momentous prophecy, one hundred and fifty years before its fulfillment by Henry VIII., "A king shall come, who shall confess you monks and nuns, treat you as the Bible telleth for breaking your rule, and put you to penance." A later version, written in 1393, denounces image worship, and all three editions are remarkable for their reverence for the Scriptures, as well as for showing much more respect for reason than did Wycliffe.

This famous Oxonian, who owes his name to his Yorkshire birth-place, took, in 1360, the great step of publishing as part of his *Commentary on the Gospels*, a full translation, afterward embodied in his Bible. Thus Wycliffe and Langland labored together in showing the English laity an authority above the Church. Six years later Parliament rejected the demand of Urban V. for the arrears during thirty-three years of the tribute of one thousand marks annually from Great Britain and Ireland, originally promised by King John, but seldom paid with regularity; and the reasons for this refusal were publicly set forth by Wycliffe, who seems to have been present, and who tells how various speakers maintained that the tribute should never have been granted without consent of the legislature, that to accept money as a condition of forgiveness was simony, that the pope's temporal power was contrary to the example of Jesus, that he did no good to England, but robbed her grievously, and that he was the vassal rather than the sovereign of her king, who had no superior but Christ. Wycliffe professed to be only a reporter, but the place of warden of Canterbury Hall, Oxford, is said to have been taken from him soon after by his archbishop and the pope. He does not appear to have been in the Parliament of 1371, which voted that the clergy be taxed and the prelates excluded from office, but five years later we find the rector of Lutterworth, as he had in the meantime become, taking part in the Good Parliament, so-called partly because it foiled the scheme of John of Gaunt, duke of Lancaster, to become heir to the crown, partly because it checked official corruption, and partly because it denounced the pope for selling bishoprics, often to several candidates at once, letting vicious and illiterate foreigners, who never came to England, hold high places in the Church, and for taking two hundred thousand pounds a year from the realm, nearly five times as much as the king. To check these abuses the papal collectors were threatened with "pain of life and limb."

This same year, 1376, saw the bishop of London retract by proxy, at St. Paul's Cross, his publication, without leave from Parliament, of a papal bull for a crusade against Florence, who, on being attacked by the pope's troops, while her own were in his service, had declared war against him, sent forth a new army with a red banner, on which was written "Liberty," and called on all his subjects to revolt, as eighty towns and cities had done in eighty days. During this contest, which lasted until 1378, the Florentine ambassador, Barbadori, closed a stormy interview with Gregory XI. by kneel-

ing before a crucifix, and publicly appealing to Jesus Christ
against his vicar's blasphemy.

This pope, further memorable for exhorting Henry, bishop
of Liege, to repent of his sins, which included the mainte-
nance of a Benedictine abbess as a mistress and the paternity
of fourteen children in twenty-two months, and for finally
persuading him to abdicate, as well as for letting his soldiers
sack Faenza and Cesena, in which latter city five thousand
citizens were murdered and many women violated, issued, on
May 22, 1377, five bulls for the trial of Wycliffe, who had
already appeared on a summons from the Convocation of
English clergy before the primate in St. Paul's Cathedral, on
Thursday, February 19, when the demand of his friends, the
duke of Lancaster and the earl marshal, that he should
have a seat, brought on a quarrel which broke up the session
and caused a dangerous riot. The nineteen articles condemned
by Gregory assert, that the State has power to impeach the
pope, and to deprive the Church of her endowments; that the
Gospel is a sufficient guide, and that papal censures are valid
only when they conform to the Bible. These charges could
not at first be pressed, owing to the death of Edward and
then to the hostility of Richard's first Parliament, which asked
Wycliffe if it were not lawful to prohibit sending money to
the pope—a question promptly answered in the affirmative.
Early in 1378 the trial came off in the archbishop's palace,
in Lambeth, where, at the request of the queen-mother,
Wycliffe, whose behavior seems to have been rather too submissive, was simply commanded to keep silence, a result largely
due to the strong sympathy not only of the nobility, but of
the citizens of London.

That April, the people of Rome used such violence in order
to get a pope chosen who should reside at his post, that five
or six months later the cardinals were provoked by the new
pontiff's fury against their luxury, into repudiating the election as compulsory, and giving the tiara to a rival who should
dwell at Avignon, an office which fell to the general who had
just sacked Cesena. The unity of the Church was not fully
restored for more than fifty years, during which time the

rival heads were seen attacking each other with anathemas and armed mercenaries, murdering cardinals, openly breaking their promises to resign, defending themselves, often in vain, against the officers of Christian governments and general councils, and plundering all Christendom in order to keep up their armies and courts.

This was Wycliffe's opportunity. Hitherto he had admitted the utility of the papacy, but now he denied its right to exist, and called it Anti-christ. This was in conformity with his theory of Dominion, according to which all authority depends on obedience to God. Henceforth we find him denouncing, in the name of the Bible, not only the tyranny of the popes, but the wealth of the clergy and their pretended celibacy. He tried to abolish the confessional, because it is contrary to Scripture, and enables a man to buy sin like an ox or a cow, and he would have no such nests of the fiend as the abbeys. The mendicant friars might, he hoped, yet do good service as reformers, and it was after their original pattern that, in 1379 or 80, he began to send out his Poor Priests, itinerants in coarse russet gowns, who lived on charity and preached morality and religion, independently of Church authority. About this time he began the translation of the whole Bible from the Latin *Vulgate* into English, a work whose semi-millenial anniversary was celebrated on December 2, 1880. Single *Epistles* and *Gospels* were put in circulation, with the *Ten Commandments*, etc., in 1381, but Wycliffe's Bible was not much known before 1390, when it had been revised after his death by his friend Purvey. During the one hundred and thirty-five years before the printing of a better version, this manuscript volume had a great circulation, despite its price, which can not be estimated at less than $100 in modern currency, and was much higher for finely written copies.

The first check to Wycliffe's influence came from the violence of professed partisans. The loss of nearly half the population in the Black Death of 1349, had caused a rise of wages which Parliament tried vainly to repress. This, with the continuance of serfdom, caused such a discontent that

John Ball began to travel through the eastern counties before 1366, preaching that things would never go well until the serfs should become equal to the lords and all things be in common. "Are we not all sprung from the same parents?

> When Adam delved and Eve span
> Where then was the gentleman?

Why should lords and ladies wear velvet and ermine and we coarse cloth? Why should they eat fine wheaten bread and drink wine, while we have only rye meal and water? It is by our labor that they live." Ere long he adopted some of Wycliffe's views, so that he was imprisoned as a heretic in 1381. Already the indignation at the poll taxes imposed in 1379 and 1380 had become so great that letters were flying about saying:

> " John Ball greeteth you all,
> And he hath rung your bell.
> Now right and might, will and skill,
> God speed every dele."

> "Jack the miller asketh help to turn his mill aright
> He hath grounden small, small;
> The King's Son in heaven shall pay for all."

In May, 1381, the indecency indulged in by the collectors, under pretext of finding out the girls' ages, made a revolt in Essex, and men from this county and others north of the Thames were soon marching upon London. On June 5, Walter the Tyler, so called from his business of roofing with tiles, killed a collector who was insulting his daughter in Dartford, Kent. His neighbors called on him to lead them to London and get justice from the king. On the two mobs went, gathering strength in every hamlet, breaking open jails, burning records, especially in monasteries, and killing the lawyers. Both armies reached London on June 13; when that from Essex, Suffolk, and Cambridge was persuaded to disperse by the royal promise of redress and amnesty. Wat Tyler and the men of Kent entered at the invitation of the city artisans, set John Ball free, burned Lancaster's palace, flinging a rioter who dared to plunder into the flames, beheaded the archbishop of Canterbury as a criminal, and put to death several high officials with many foreign merchants. On Saturday the 17th, the Lord Mayor assassinated Tyler during a pretended negotiation, in the presence of King Richard, who then persuaded these rebels also to disband, by guaranteeing that all their wrongs should be righted, and no one else put to death. Scarcely had they, too, gone home, when all the royal promises were revoked ; thousands of peasants were hung that summer and autumn, as was John Ball on July 15. John the Dyer, who made noblemen serve him on bended knee, and called himself King of Norwich, was put down by the warlike bishop of that diocese. Serfdom, however, died out rapidly, and no such attempts to collect taxes were ever made again in England.

John Ball confessed before his execution that he had been for two years a follower of Wycliffe, whose attacks on clerical endowments had been much praised by the rioters, and whose institution of unlicensed preachers now seemed dangerous to the public peace. It was on their account that hostility now arose between the reformer and the friars, who were further provoked at his attacking transubstantiation, and asserting that the bread and wine remained really present in the communion elements together with the body and blood of Jesus, a view much like that afterward held by Luther. Even this was going too far for some of Wycliffe's friends, while others regretted his turning aside from more dangerous errors. His twelve theses about the eucharist were condemned by the Oxford theologians in 1381, in which year Parliament ordered that all sheriffs be henceforth sworn to "suppress the errors and heresies commonly called Lolleries," an oath which was exacted as late as 1626, though its observance had then come to mean, for nearly seventy years, the destruction of the Church of England. On May 17, 1382, the Earthquake Council, so called from a shock which occurred that day, met in the Dominican convent, which gave a name to Blackfriars and which stood where the London *Times* now has its office, and condemned twenty-four articles opposed to transubstantiation, to the right of prelates to excommunicate, of clergymen to hold property, and of friars to ask for alms, to the necessity of the papacy or of episcopal ordination, to the sanctity of sacraments performed by vicious priests, and to the institutions of the mass and the confessional. Many Wycliffite preachers were driven to submission and temporary silence that summer, under a pretended Act of Parliament, which was pronounced null and void in October, because the Commons declared they had not sanctioned it. Hereford, who had helped translate the Bible, now appealed to the pope at Rome, where he was imprisoned until released by the populace in 1385. Wycliffe appears to have been summoned thither, but the favor of the king's wife and mother as well as of the men of the eastern counties, who are said to have been one half Lollards, prevented him from having to do more than appear in person at a synod in Oxford in November, 1382. About this time he petitioned Parliament to open a way of escape from monastic vows, tax the clergy, and grant liberty in the pulpit. Soon after he wrote his famous *Trilogus*, a Latin dialogue where Truth and Wisdom declare, in opposition to Falsehood, that the pope is Anti-christ, his infallibility the abomination of desolation, and his indulgencies blasphemies; that transubstantiation is a heresy, the confessional and the mendicant orders evils, and church endowments contrary to the law of Christ ; that there is no mediator or intercessor but Jesus ; that the Bible is above all other authorities, and that there should be no restraint on setting forth its truth. Persecutions in previous centuries Wycliffe nowhere seems to regret, nor does he give reason more than a subordinate place, but distinctly condemns those who claim a special inspiration enabling them to find a new and peculiar meaning in the Bible, as false disciples. He was no Mystic or rationalist, and his views of predestination resembled Luther's and Calvin's, but he did not hold their doctrine of justification by faith. His demand for liberty to read and expound the Bible, as well as his attacks on clerical endowments, the confessional, and the authority of bishops and popes gave powerful, though undesigned, aid to the cause of free thought ; and his own special work for biblical authority was so well organized, as not to be interrupted by his death. This took place the last day of 1384, in consequence of a paralytic stroke suffered while hearing mass.

His cause went on prospering during the rest of the century. Lancaster asserted before Parliament, in 1390, the right of the people to the Bible in their own tongue, the *Statutes against Provisors* and of *Præmunire* were renewed shortly afterward, and the Lollards petitioned in 1395, the time of their greatest strength, against the temporal power, transubstantiation, auricular confession, vows of chastity, prayers for the dead, pilgrimages, exorcism, and other abuses, which they wished to have thoroughly reformed as commanded by the New Testament. Similar aims inspired two anonymous poems written about this time, *Piers Plowman's Crede*, which is marked by its disbelief in the monks, and the *Plowman's Tale*, where the Pelican, who represents the reformed Church, is assisted by the Phœnix to destroy the papacy, which is typified in the Griffin, for whom fight the birds of prey. The author of the work thus imitated, the *Plowman's Vision*, had already given it its final form, though he survived to write about the deposition of Richard II. in 1399, as a punishment for attempting to make himself absolute.

The great name in early English literature of course is Chaucer. The *Canterbury Tales*, which he left unfinished at his death in 1400, have nothing of the moral and religious purpose of the works just mentioned, but seek simply to give interesting pictures of contemporary life. This makes it all the more noteworthy, that his pilgrims, among whom are several monks and nuns, amuse themselves with licentious stories, that rakes and swindlers preponderate among his clergymen, and that the best friend to virtue and piety in the party is a Lollard. This character is indeed represented as preaching in favor of the confessional, but his language is in great part taken from a book written a century before by a French monk ; and the *Parson's Tale* is so much longer than the others, as well as so excessively dull, that there is much in favor of the opinion advanced by Mr. H. Simon in an essay published by the Chaucer Society, that some unscrupulous Romanist has made interpolations in the interest of the Church. It is undoubtedly Chaucer who makes the Wife of Bath rest nobility on character, not birth, so that those who do gentle deeds are gentlemen, and he who acts vilely is a churl, though born a duke, and who speaks strongly for female capacity in his *Legend of Good Women*, as well as in the *Tale of Melibœus*.

During the fourteenth century the Lollards had suffered but little persecution, owing largely to their submissive behavior under arrest. On February 24, 1401, a priest named Sautré, was sent, for revoking his recantation, to the stake at Smithfield, near London, by Henry IV., whose desire to strengthen his weak title by clerical support led him next month to sanction the passage of the *Act for Burning Heretics*. The first victim under this statute, a tailor named John Badby, was burned in a barrel on February 26, 1410. In the previous year the circulation of the Bible in English, of Wycliffe's other works, and of unlicensed publications generally, had been strictly forbidden by the Convocation of Clergy. Disobedience to this edict caused Sir John Oldcastle, Lord Cobham, to be sent to the Tower, in 1413, by Henry V., whose boon-companion he had formerly been, according to a story followed by Shakespeare in his earliest version of the *First Part of Henry IV*. On his trial on September 25, Oldcastle said: "For the sins of my youth I was never blamed by these priests, but see how I am troubled for showing dislike of their traditions." Then he avowed his agreement with Wycliffe, and thanked him for help in becoming virtuous. Citizens of London enabled him to escape to Wales, where he was hidden for three years, though a thousand marks were set upon his head; but December 14, 1417, saw him hanging from a gallows over the flames. A law of 1414 had enabled the secular courts, as well as the episcopal, to condemn heretics, and executions were frequent for more than a hundred years in both England and Scotland, so that Erasmus complained, in 1511, of the incidental rise in the cost of fuel. But Lollardism continued strong enough to do much to cause the insurrections under Jack Sharp in 1431, and Jack Cade in 1450. And we shall find Luther's great protest even more welcome in England than Germany.

III.

Nowhere were the tendencies of the Bible movement more clearly manifested than in Bohemia, which the marriage of a Czech princess to Richard of England brought under the influence of Wycliffe's writings before 1390. Among their open admirers was John Huss, who became a popular preacher in Prague at the beginning of the fifteenth century, and in 1405 exposed the pretended miracles ascribed to some sacramental wafers, covered with red animalcules, but supposed to be stained with the blood of Christ. Four years later he deprived the Germans, who hated Wycliffe, of the control of his University, and they left it to found that of Leipsic. Earnestly did he strive to persuade the pope and prelates to reform the Church, but they excommunicated him in Prague, July 18, 1410, two days after publicly burning Wycliffe's books. These works he at once defended openly, and spoke so vehemently in Bethlehem Chapel against the pope's charges that his hearers shouted, "He lied." He asked if they would stand by him, and they answered, "We will!" The pope put Prague under an interdict, but Huss and most of the other clergymen went on holding public worship. He refused to go to Rome for trial, appealed publicly from the pope to Jesus, and wrote on the walls of his chapel, "No excommunication can harm the innocent."

In May, 1412, came the sellers of indulgencies, promising safety from purgatory to whoever would contribute to a crusade against Naples. Huss announced a public discussion before the University on June 7, when he and his friend Jerome maintained, that it was contrary to the Bible for the Church to levy war, or to sell forgiveness to the impenitent. On the 24th, a procession of armed students marched past the royal and archepiscopal palaces, escorting a comrade, dressed like a harlot and bearing on his bosom the pope's bull of indulgence, which at last was burned publicly. Soon afterward they turned out again for the burial at Bethlehem Chapel of three young mechanics, beheaded on July 11 for interrupting the traffic in pardons on the Sunday previous. Huss was now persuaded by the king to leave Prague for retirement, in which he wrote *De Ecclesia*. Here he says that Jesus is the only Head of the Church, that the papal power comes from the emperor, that an infallible pope would be a fourth person in the Trinity, that only the elect belong to the true Church, and that the clergy must be reformed by the State. He did not oppose the confessional, or clerical endowments, or transubstantiation, and it was largely due to his moderation that he carried nearly all Bohemia with him.

Only zeal for his cause led him to attend the council of Constance, whither he went, asking only for free speech and expecting to be put to death. Neither his safe conduct from the emperor, nor his guard of honor, prevented his treacherous arrest by the pope and cardinals on November 28, 1414, or his confinement for six months without a trial, his first prison being a convent where he nearly lost his life from bad air, and his second a castle in which his feet were fettered, and his arms chained every night to the wall. Plainly did the council declare, as the Church of Rome has always done, that no faith should be kept with heretics. Heresy, it must be remembered, consists not so much in having embraced peculiar views, as in refusing to give them up when commanded. The council, while censuring the disrespect of Huss for the papacy with a violence scarcely to be expected in the dethroners of three popes, and further blaming his censure of persecution and his fondness for Wycliffe, differed from its victim mainly as to its right to compel him to recant. This he refused to do, because some of the propositions complained of seemed to him scriptural, and others were not really his, so that he could not say he renounced them without committing perjury. Here he differed from those Episcopalians who say they renounce the devil, though they do not believe that he exists. Steadily he resisted all threats and entreaties at his trial, June 5, 7 and 8, during the month given him for consideration, at the full session in which he was sentenced, and even at his execution which took place forthwith, on Saturday, July 6, 1415, a day kept sacred in Bohemia. What he taught is of little importance compared with his being the first to defy the highest authority in the Church, and to give his body to the flames rather than say he renounced what he had never believed. He did not call himself a free-thinker, but he stands high among our martyrs, and his paper miter with its painted devils was really the cap of liberty.

In Bohemia there was great indignation, which increased as Jerome of Prague also was burned, May 30, 1416. A convenient emblem had already been furnished by another Bohemian, Jacob or Jacobel of Mies, who discovered before the close of 1414, that the Bible gives all Christians a right to the communion cup. This view was condemned at Constance, but was sanctioned by the University of Prague on March 10, 1417, after which the mode of celebration known as utraquism became general. Insult to a procession of the friends of the cup, on Sunday, July 30, 1419, caused Zizka to lead them to the slaughter of seven of Prague's magistrates. The king's death shortly after was followed by a general plunder of churches and cloisters, so that Bohemia was flooded by coins, made from candlesticks and chalices, and thence called calycles. The next heir, that Sigismund who had betrayed Huss at Constance, refused to grant the demands made by the citizens of Prague, that each communicant should partake of the wine or not as he might choose ; that all observances should be regulated by the opinions of those immediately concerned ; that clergymen should have no office in the State ; and that the word of God should be freely preached. Both parties now prepared for hostilities which began on November 4, by the royal troops dispersing a party of armed pilgrims, close to Prague, where a bloody contest followed, the rebels being again led by Zizka, who gained two victories over vastly superior forces early in 1420, by his invention of a movable fort, made by chaining together wagons fitted with very high sides and filled with musketeers. He was the first general to use gunpowder with effect; his officers ranked according to ability and fidelity without regard to birth; the soldiers were drilled as no others had been for centuries; pillaging, gambling, drunkenness, and outrages on women were suppressed as they never were among the crusaders; and prostitutes were excluded with a strictness unknown at Rome, or Avignon, or even in Constance during the great council. The same purity was enforced in the city of Tabor, which he founded at this time for his adherents, who gave up most of the Romish ceremonies, especially auricular confession, prayers to the saints, and masses for the dead; rejected many doctrines not in the Bible, for instance purgatory; held public worship in the Czech language, without gorgeous vestments and in any place convenient; permitted women to preach and working men to celebrate the Lord's supper, of which even children partook; kept no day but Sunday; called each other brother and sister; had every body taught to read and write, and governed themselves democratically. So indeed, did the more moderate citizens of Prague and other large towns, who are known as Calixtines because they insisted chiefly on the cup. To this latter party belonged most of the nobles. Taborites and Calixtines united to defend Prague in 1420 against Sigismund, who brought nearly a hundred thousand crusaders from every part of Western Europe. His attempt to capture what was thenceforth called Zizka's Mountain, failed through the resistance made by twenty-six men and three women on Sunday, July 14, when the red-cross knights were driven back by the Hussite cannon. The victors now bound themselves to maintain the famous *Four Articles,* namely, the cup for all Christians, liberty of preaching, confiscation of church property, and reformation of all sins and abuses contrary to Scripture. The crusaders soon dispersed, and their friends were conquered by Zizka, so that Sigismund had to retire from Bohemia, early in 1421. That June the diet of Caflau made Zizka regent with another Taborite, five knights, five nobles, and eight representatives of various cities. The archbishop had already joined the Calixtines, who had many friends in Moravia, Silesia, Saxony, and Poland. No opposition was made to transubstantiation before 1421, when a Taborite called Hauska, or Loquis, denied the real presence and was flung into boiling oil by the orders of Zizka, who had already sent two parties of men and women to the flames, which they entered smiling in hope of reigning that day with Him who never stooped from heaven to become a bit of bread. Similar unwillingness to worship the host provoked the Taborites to the destruction with fire and sword, before the end of 1421, of a colony of Mystics who were called Adamites, and charged with worshiping naked and having their women in common, but who apparently did nothing worse than claim to be led by immediate inspiration like Adam. Their island, in the river near Tabor, was only taken after a desperate defense led by a blacksmith named Rohan. Thus the most devoted followers of the Bible thought themselves justified in persecution. Meantime a second host of crusaders, who had committed the worst of outrages on the peasantry, fled at the approach of Zizka, who became totally blind on March 29, 1421, but was able on the sixth of January following to rout Sigismund's great army of Hungarians and Moravians, whom he surprised in winter quarters. Soon after, the Taborites and Calixtines began mutual hostilities, which were interrupted in the summer of 1423 by the appearance of the third horde of crusaders, who scarcely dared to enter Bohemia. The next year is called the bloody one, because Zizka slaughtered the Calixtines cruelly, and was with difficulty persuaded not to sack Prague.

After his death October 11, 1424, his immediate followers called themselves Orphans, and accepted no other permanent leader, though they readily co-operated with the other Taborites, who soon found almost as brilliant a general, and a much more tolerant and far-sighted statesman in Procopius. Early in 1426 we find Taborites, Orphans, Calixtines, and Catholics in council together at Prague, and on February 6, Procopius and his followers declared that they were fighting only to defend their country, and would gladly be at peace with all who would permit the observance of the *Four Articles*. On Sunday, June 16, the city of Aussig was recovered from the Germans, whose chivalry was routed by the peasants' cannonade. Next year another crusade ended a new panic, as did the fifth and last of these ecclesiastical invasions in 1431. Bohemia had now determined to force her neighbors to make peace. Austria and Bavaria were overrun in 1428, Saxony devastated the next year, Nuremberg and Bamberg forced to ransom themselves in 1430, Berlin threatened in 1432, and the Orphans' banner carried to the Baltic in 1433.

The Church now saw for the first time the necessity of tolerating heresy, at least temporarily. In October, 1431, the Hussites were invited by the council of Basel to send ambassadors, who should have every privilege, even that of holding public worship. On Sunday, January 4, 1432, fifteen leading Calixtines, Taborites, and Orphans entered the city, which had been purified for their reception by the suppression of public dancing, gambling, and street-walking. The citizens saw worship held with the utmost simplicity, and heard the new views preached in German. All Christendom knew that cardinals, Dominicans, and doctors of divinity were talking theology, feasting, and even going to church with men who had disowned the pope, abolished almost all the ritual, plundered monasteries, and massacred crusaders. Three months were spent in debates held in the Dominican convent, where Procopius defended the use of the cup, the Taborite bishop denounced the sins of the Church, Peter Payne, an Englishman, attacked the temporal power, and another of the Orphans pleaded for a free pulpit. The Hussites were charged with saying that Satan had founded the monastic orders. "I did tell Cardinal Cesarini so in private," answered Procopius. "But let me ask this. You claim that the bishops represent the Apostles, and the priests the seventy disciples, but there is nothing in the New Testament in favor of those able-bodied monks, who live in idleness rather than work. Whence can they come except from the devil?" Another time the great Taborite on being asked, "Who can interpret the Bible better than a council like this?" answered, "Each man's conscience must be his own interpreter." In

November, 1433, the envoys of the council announced to the Diet of Prague, that the Church would permit all Christians in Bohemia and Moravia to partake of the chalice. Heresy had conquered the Church.

The Bohemian nobles now determined to restore Sigismund, and put down the Taborites and other democrats. Procopius had resigned his command in consequence of being wounded in the face and imprisoned by his own soldiers, among whom success had brought many reckless adventurers, but he returned to his post, and fell with 13,000 warriors in the fratricidal battle of Lipan, August 30, 1434. Tabor held out until 1452, just before which time a future pope describes it as " a place where there are as many heresies as heads, and every man may believe what he likes." The fierce sect was afterward merged in the meek Moravians. Peace was finally established in the Diet of Iglau, on July 5, 1436; and the communion was celebrated in both ways for nearly two centuries, despite the opposition of Pius II., the pontiff just referred to. Thus was Bohemia the first Christian nation to protest against this privilege of the priests, and assert the right of each individual to worship as he pleases. In that blood-stained chalice lay precious seeds.

IV.

While English and Bohemian reformers were being driven out of the Church, pious Frenchmen tried to reform her from within. The University of Paris declared to the king on January 25, 1394, that the rival popes at Rome and Avignon should both resign, or a general council must be called. The French clergy asserted their independence in 1398, and Benedict XIII. was besieged that fall at Avignon. Neither he nor his Italian opponent would resign, and at last the cardinals on both sides united in calling the council of Pisa. This lasted from March 25 to August 7, 1409, and was largely attended by French, English, German, and Italian bishops, abbots, and professors. Its leader, Bishop d'Ailly, the Eagle of France, boldly asserted its supremacy: and so did another prominent Nominalist,

Gerson, chancellor of the University. His tracts in favor of the absolute sovereignty of a general council, and its right to depose popes, had great influence, but his presence at Pisa is almost as doubtful as his authorship of the *Imitation of Christ*. (Schwab, *Johannes Gerson*, pp. 231, 244, 782.)

The council declared its supremacy on May 29, deposed both popes on June 5, and chose a new one on June 26. Its choice was not universally accepted, and thus there were three heads to the Church. To end this schism, and check the rapid growth of heresy and immorality, the emperor persuaded John XXIII., successor of the Pisan pope, to call the council of Constance.

This opened November 5, 1414, and was attended by about fifty cardinals and archbishops, some two hundred bishops, as many abbots, nearly four hundred doctors of divinity, twenty-eight kings and princes, more than six hundred barons, one hundred and sixty ambassadors, mostly from the universities and free cities, and seven hundred and eighteen harlots. About eighteen thousand of the clergy were present, and every Western nation sent delegates. Pope John soon took fright and fled, dressed as a groom. Three days later, March 23, 1415, Gerson preached, at the request of the other Frenchmen and the emperor, a sermon declaring the superiority of a general council to the pope, and its right, not only to meet without his consent, but to depose him in order to end the schism. Similar propositions were passed on March 29, and more deliberately on April 6, by the whole council which now declared its power to reform the Church in both head and members. Pope John was arrested by German soldiers, was found guilty of heresy, simony, fraud on poor students, rape of nuns, adultery, and poisoning his predecessor. He was deposed on May 29; a second pope resigned on July 4; and Benedict found no support, though he was not deposed until two years later.

Thus was the schism ended by this council, which would have made the Church a limited monarchy, if the plan adopted on October 9, 1417, of having such meetings held at regular intervals, even without the papal consent, could have been carried out. Gerson and d'Ailly took the lead in all these proceedings, and also in the condemnation, not only of Wycliffe's books but of his bones, May 4, 1415, and in the burning, two months later, of John Huss. Then this proclamation was posted up: "The Holy Ghost to the Fathers at Constance, Greeting! Do your work as you can. I have business elsewhere." Scarcely had the council finished burning heretics, and deposing pontiffs, when it found itself subject to a pope of its own making, and obliged to close on April 22, 1418, without doing much for reform, except proposing future gatherings.

Accordingly a third great council opened at Basel, on August 27, 1431, and in such a temper that the pope tried to transfer it to Italy. The messenger bearing his bull was imprisoned; the council declared, on April 29, 1432, its indissolubility except by its own consent; and the decrees of Constance, including that providing for decennial gatherings thenceforth, were reaffirmed, provincial synods arranged, and threats of deposition freely uttered. Bohemia had been reconciled by almost unexampled tolerance, before Pope Eugenius sanctioned the sessions. This was early in 1434, when one hundred bishops and abbots had met with eight hundred other clergymen. Attempts to prevent his extorting money, making his nephews cardinals, issuing interdicts, and appointing prelates, soon revived his hostility and divided the council. Many members of high rank withdrew, and with them Nicholas of Cusa, who afterward tried to revive the Pythagorean theory of the motion of both earth and sun round a common center, as well as to establish the system of philosophy which was developed into Pantheism by Giordano Bruno. Eugenius was suspended on January 4, 1438, soon after calling together a rival council, which advised all Christians to plunder merchants carrying goods to Basel, because the *Wisdom of Solomon* says, "Therefore the righteous spoiled the ungodly, and praised thy holy name, O Lord." The bishop of Strasburg persuaded a band of six thousand robbers to march against the council, but they were cut off by his peasants. The Church was once more divided, as were the nations, England holding with the pope, Germany being neutral, and France being with the council, as appeared in the re-enactment of her Pragmatic Sanction, in 1438.

A fatal error was committed on June 25, 1439, when Eugenius was deposed by less than forty bishops and abbots, and three hundred of the lower clergy, the latter now holding the main control. Basel was already smitten by a pestilence, which slew five thousand people there, and is still commemorated in the pictures of the *Dance of Death;* but many of the fathers still held their post. On November 5, the Duke of Savoy was made pope, but Felix refused to pay his own expenses, and the council was obliged to sanction the very extortions they had condemned. Even France refused to plunge into a second schism; and only the heroism of the Swiss prevented her army from capturing Basel in 1444. Two years later Germany was brought to declare against the council by the craft of Æneas Silvius Piccolomini, who had taken part in the deposition and defended it in a *History*, to which he afterward added another, written from the opposite standpoint. The emperor forced Basel to give up sheltering the council, and it emigrated in 1448 to Lausanne, where it dissolved itself on May 7, 1449, after accepting the abdication of Pope Felix the Unlucky, and confirming the recent election of his rival, Nicholas V. This pontiff quietly disregarded all that was done at Basel, and Æneas Silvius, when he became Pope Pius II., openly repudiated, not only his own words in the council, but also its decrees of supremacy, the Pragmatic Sanction, and the grant of the cup to the Hussites, who, however, were protected by their king, George Podiebrad. All the old abuses went on unchecked, and reform from within seemed hopeless. Councils could do much in a schism, but nothing against a regular pope. The papacy was too much revered to be restricted constitutionally. Henceforth the only choice lay between despotism and revolution. Real reform must begin by throwing off the papal yoke.

V.

That form of Mysticism which had freed itself from subjection to the Bible, the Church, or any other authority but that of individual inspiration, was now taught by the virtuous and eloquent Joan of Aubenton, who was burned at Paris in 1373, with others of the Brothers and Sisters of the Free Spirit, who in France were called Turlupins, probably because they had to hide like wolves in the woods. A similar sect, that of the "Men of Understanding," was propagated in Belgium, by an illiterate man, called Giles the Singer, and a scholarly monk, William of Hildesheim, who was charged at his compulsory abjuration, in 1411, with having taught, that there is no resurrection of the body, that all men and angels will be saved, that sin does not stain the soul, and that Christianity was then to be superseded by the reign of the Holy Ghost.

Penitential scourging without permission of the Church had been introduced in 1260, and kept up despite papal prohibition; and in 1414 the Saxon Flagellants were found so confident of their ability to save themselves, and of the worthlessness of ecclesiastical sacraments, that Conrad Schmidt was burned with one hundred and twenty of his followers. Those German Mystics who were affiliated with the Waldenses suffered cruel persecutions at Mainz in 1395, at Strasburg in 1420, and at Worms and Spire soon afterward, in all which cities they were known as Winkelers, or dwellers in corners. Another type of German Mysticism, which was more friendly to the Church, though not dependent on her guidance, is expressed in the *Theologia Germanica*, probably written shortly before 1370, and published with high praise by Martin Luther in 1516. The aim is to show that the highest religious life may be led without depending on priest or sacrament, as well as without opposing them to the extent done by the Brethren and Sisters of the Free Spirit. The same love of conformity without servility characterizes the *Imitation of Christ*, which the best authorities suppose to have been written by the Dutch monk,

Thomas à Kempis, about 1425, and which has been more read by Christians than any other book, except the Bible. The best known Mystic in the latter half of the fourteenth century, with the exception of the docile and philanthropic Catherine of Siena, is Nicholas of Basel, a pious layman who has been supposed to have been Tauler's spiritual guide. He was probably too young for this office, however, and the best authorities do not hold that he ever claimed it. He did found the Friends of God, a secret society of men and women who were willing, like Tauler, to use the church sacraments as help to cultivate an independent but friendly spirituality. Such companies existed in various cities on the Rhine, and the visits and letters of Nicholas were received with the strictest secrecy, his messenger to Strasburg, for instance, being wont to make himself known by a peculiar kind of cough, in the church frequented by the brethren. The most advanced dwelt on a hill between Basel and Constance, under shelter of a papal permission obtained in 1377 by Nicholas in a personal interview with Gregory XI., then much under the influence of the saintly Catherine. These recluses were so excited by the Great Schism as to hear angelic voices and receive other supernatural revelations of the speedy end of the world. This fate Nicholas began to preach openly in 1383, but soon found his own at the stake in Vienne near Lyons. One of his disciples, a priest named Martin, met the same fate at Cologne in 1393, on a charge of placing him above the Apostles or the Ten Commandments.

Shortly afterwards a famous instance was seen at Orleans of martial courage and military genius, developed in an illiterate peasant girl, under the joint stimulus of patriotic fervor and faith in special revelations through angels and saints. Joan of Arc is described as having a large, powerful, and well proportioned body, a round face, large gray or brown eyes, very small mouth and chin, very white complexion, chestnut hair, and a soft voice. (Hirzel, *Jeanne d'Arc*, p. 10, in Virchow und Holtzerdorf's *Vorträge*, vol. x.)

All accounts agree that she had no feminine weakness, except a great readiness to weep. She was only thirteen when she began to have visions of the warrior-angel, Michael, and the virgin-patronesses, Catherine and Margaret. At first they merely bade her be a good girl and go to church, but ere long they told her God would send her to drive the English out of France, then almost wholly in their power. Of these apparitions she said nothing, even to her pastor or her parents, though in other respects she was a docile Catholic to the last. In May, 1428, she spoke for the first time of her mission. This was to a French officer at Vaucouleurs, in Lorraine, where she met several repulses, but was finally given a a horse, male attire, necessary to her safety among soldiers, and an escort to her sovereign. To him she declared, on March 8, 1429, that she was sent to free Orleans, then likely to be captured, see him crowned at Rheims, and drive out the English. Six weeks were spent in deliberations, among whose results was the full sanction of her mission by the archbishop of Rheims and other clergymen. During this time she was probably taught to ride and use weapons. The duke of Alençon afterward testified that he saw her practicing with the lance, and was so much pleased with her dexterity as to give her a horse. (Quicherat, *Procès de Jeanne d'Arc*, volume iii. page 92). This prince also speaks highly of her knowledge of war, especially in the management of artillery. Nothing contributed more to her success than the strict moral and religious discipline under which she kept her troops.

I need not tell how she raised the siege of Orleans, taking herself the lead in storming the English bastions on May 6 and 7, how on June 18, she won a pitched battle against Talbot and Fastolf, or how she brought her rather reluctant monarch to Rheims, where she saw him crowned on Sunday, July 17. Her attempt to take Paris the next September failed, owing partly to the king's retreating after the first repulse. After this she was not entrusted with any large body of troops. On May 24, 1430, she was taken prisoner by the Burgundians, and sold to the English a few months afterwards.

Early in 1431 their tool, Bishop Cauchon, had her tried at Rouen, for sorcery, heresy, and disobedience to both Bible and Church. The king, whom she had saved, made no attempt to rescue her by force, ransom, or appeal to Rome, and did not even send her a lawyer, while the archbishop of Rheims declared, possibly not altogether without truth, that her fate was a judgment on her refusing to take advice. The bishop left her in the hands of soldiers, whose licentiousness strengthened her determination to retain her male dress. He meant to make her out guilty of violating *Deuteronomy*, xxii., 5, "The woman shall not wear that which pertaineth unto a man, *** for all that do so are abomination unto the Lord thy God," and so transgressing canons similar to laws still in force. She was repeatedly asked, during twenty-four hearings, between February 21 and May 24, inclusive, if she would change her dress, but she refused to do so until permitted by God and the saints. She also made a fatal admission that she had given faith to these visions before asking guidance from the Church. Still her conduct in both respects had been formally sanctioned by the archbishop of Rheims, Bishop Cauchon's immediate superior. An eminent jurist, who visited Rouen, declared that for this reason, as well as the neglect to provide the prisoner with counsel, and the evident intimidation of the judges by the English, the whole trial was illegal; on which the bishop threatened to have him murdered. A clergyman who refused to take part in such a mockery of justice was imprisoned, and menaced with death, as was every judge or official who gave Joan any help.

The charge of sorcery could not be sustained, for evil spirits had no power over maidens. That of heresy was pressed with the most unscrupulous craft. The illiterate peasant was subjected to hour after hour of cross-examination, planned so skillfully that trained theologians could scarcely have escaped condemnation. Learned and impartial prelates who studied the records twenty-five years later, declared her orthodoxy blameless. Her devout faith and quick wits often baffled the most captious questioning. She did not at first understand what authority was claimed by the pope, but after she did so she professed such submission to him and desire for his opinion, as ought to have prevented further proceedings without his sanction. Of councils she knew nothing, but when told about that soon to meet at Basel, she asked to be judged by it, a request which the bishop would not suffer to be recorded. The case really turned on the claim made by him, and the conspiring abbots and professors, that Joan should recognize them as representatives of the visible Church, and adopt their opinion of her visions and her dress. Her refusal to do so was not strictly heretical in view of the previous decision of the archbishop of Rheims, and the manifest partiality of the so-called judges, but it showed the noblest of courage in a friendless girl, not yet twenty, loaded with chains, suffering from illness, and in constant danger of death as well as dishonor. Again and again she said :

"Lord Bishop, you say you are my judge ; I do not know if you are ; but take heed not to judge badly ; for you would run in great danger ; and so I warn you that I may have done my duty, if our Lord should punish you." "I am willing to testify about what I have done, but I have had revelations of which I shall not tell you, even if you cut off my head." Here she refers to a secret seriously affecting the title of her king, who had left her to perish. The speedy expulsion of the English from France she predicted so boldly, that Lord Stafford drew his dagger to stab her in open court, but Warwick staid his hand. "I know that my king will conquer all France ; I should die, if it were not for this revelation, which comforts me daily." "I am sent of God ; I have nothing to do here ; let me go to Him." "I have taken no man's advice ; I have not worn this raiment or done aught else, save by command of our Lord and his angels." All the clergy of Rouen and Paris can not condemn me, unless it is just." "If I see the gate open, it will be a dismissal from the Lord." "If you refuse to let me hear mass, our Lord is able to let me hear it without you." "As firmly as I believe that our Lord Jesus Christ has suffered to save me, so firmly do I believe that our Lord has sent his saints, Michael, Gabriel, Catherine, and Margaret to comfort and counsel me." "I honor the Church militant with all my might, but as to what I have done, I refer myself to the Lord, who made me do it." "Nothing in the world could make me say that I did not do those deeds in obedience to God." "What He bids me I will not fail to do, in spite of any man who lives." "If the Church were to wish to make me do aught contrary to the word given me of God, I should not consent, whatever may come to pass." "I think I am obedient to the Church on earth, but God must first be served." "I await my judge, the King of heaven and earth."

She was questioned in full view of the instruments of torture, and said: "If you were to tear off my limbs, I should say nothing but what I have always done: and even if I were to, I should always say afterward, that I was forced to do it." "I have asked my voices, if I ought to submit to the Church, and they have said, 'If you wish to have God help you, look to Him in all things.' I asked my voices if I am to be burned, and they answered, 'Trust in our Lord and He will help you'" So dauntless was her courage, that torture was pronounced useless. As the trial drew near its end, she said: "As I have always spoken, so I wish to speak still; if I saw the fire lighted and were standing in it, I should hold to all I said, until the death."

False friends begged her to submit, and promised that she would then be set at liberty, though otherwise she must be burned. On Thursday, May 24, 1431, she was set on a scaffold, amid a great crowd of soldiers and people; before her were many princes and prelates; and beside her was the executioner ready to carry her to the stake. The customary sermon was preached from, "The branch can not bear fruit of itself except it abide in the vine." She interrupted the preacher, when he blamed the king, who had deserted her. Thrice she was solemnly asked if she would submit to the Church. She only answered: "I have acted in obedience to God. I refer myself to Him and to our Holy Father the pope." Then the bishop began to read her sentence. Midway she broke in with: "I submit to the Church; I will do what you wish, I will give up my visions, and dress as other women do." A statement to this effect, some six or eight lines long, was read aloud, and repeated by her, and it is testified by eye-witnesses, that she was tricked into making her mark, not on this paper, but at the end of the indictment, in twelve long articles, charging her with falsehood, worship of evil spirits, idolatry, blasphemy, heresy, attempt at suicide, etc. She was then told she was to be imprisoned for life on bread and water. She begged she might at least be confined in a convent, where she thought her honor would be safe ; but the bishop had her led back to the ruffianly soldiers, who soon made her dread the worst injuries in her change of dress. Before she rose next Sunday morning, they took away her woman's dress and left only the man's clothes they had kept ready. She lay until noon, asking in vain for other garments. At last she rose, and dressed herself as she could. The next day the judges came to condemn her, as a relapsed heretic. She said, with many tears, "I put on this dress, because you have not kept faith in me. Let me be in a proper prison among women, and I will be good, and do as the Church bids me." They asked what her voices said. "That I have committed treason against God, and damned my soul to save my life. They bade me answer that preacher boldly. The truth is, that God did send me." "Do you believe that your voices are those of Saint Margaret and Saint Catherine ?" "Yes, and I believe that they come from God." "You denied this before the people." "I did not know it. Whatever I said was in fear of the fire. It was contrary to the truth. I had rather do penance, once for all, and die, than stay in prison. I will give up about the dress, but I can do nothing more." To Cauchon she said : "Bishop, I die through you. If you had put me in a church prison, this would not have happened. I appeal from you to God."

On Tuesday, May 30, 1431, she was brought into the public square, still called by her name, and after a second sermon, handed over to the executioner with illegal haste. Many of the by-standers wept with her, as she bade them pray for her, and said she forgave those who put her to death, but that Rouen would suffer judgment. She kept her faith in her voices to the last, as is attested by her confessor, who stood by her on the pyre, until she bade him descend, and hold up the cross before her eyes. Those who see nothing supernatural, either in visions which promised she should take Paris,

drive the English out of France, and escape from prison, or
in victories, plainly due to her dauntless courage and military
genius, as well as to the English superstition, then proverbial,
(O'Reilly, *Les Deux Procès de Jeanne d'Arc*, volume ii., page
406), must give all the more honor to the heroism which made
her victorious over the prejudice against her sex, over conquering armies, and finally over judges who professed to hold
the keys of heaven. No one has done more to emancipate
woman. It is well to mention here that the probable year of
her birth, 1412, was that of the death of the great Queen
Margaret, whose courage, love of justice, and genius for government had enabled her to mold Norway, Denmark, and
Sweden into one united kingdom, which she ruled with singular ability and success. Neither Joan nor Margaret was a free
thinker, but they did much to encourage women to think and
act for themselves.

VI.

The medieval period may be subdivided, in reference to its
enslavement of thought, into five ages. From the destruction
of classic philosophy until 1000 A. D., differences of opinion
are almost unknown in Western Europe, the Paulicians and
Motazalites being too far removed to attract notice, and
Clement, Claudius, and Erigena too far in advance of their
contemporaries. During the eleventh and twelfth centuries,
the common people, especially in France and Italy, are stirred
up against the clergy by an agitation in the name of morality,
which is exerted most powerfully by the stainless Catharists,
who continue to increase, despite frequent executions for
heresy, now for the first time often punished capitally all over
Christendom. Meantime scholars are aroused to unwonted
activity by the attacks on the theory, necessary for the existence of the Church, of the reality of abstractions made by
Roscellin and Abelard, neither of whom speculates more boldly than Heloise. The twelfth century also produces Averroes, Maimonides, and the Waldenses; and Moslem, Jewish,
and Christian visionaries are already in close communication.

The third age is that of the rapid spread, despite cruel persecutions, of the Mysticism which we have just seen develop itself, and which is greatly assisted, not only by that opposition to rationalism shown in the crusades against the tolerant Languedocians, the suppression of Catharism by the inquisition, the imprisonment of Bacon, and the excommunication of Frederic II., but by those satires on the vices of the clergy now frequent. Next comes the successful revolt of France and Germany, in the fourteenth century, against the papacy, which is reduced to captivity at Avignon, and robbed of its most faithful servants, the Templars; while Dante, Eckhart, Tauler, Ockham, and Petrarch are enabled to assail it with a boldness hitherto impossible. Before the close of this century we see the endless conflict transferred to new territory, as Wycliffe is unconsciously serving liberty, in setting up the authority of the Bible against the papacy, already much weakened by the Avignon scandals, to whose damaging effect is now added that of the Great Schism. The founders of English literature, Langland and Chaucer, also do much to help the new movement, which, however, has little success until transplanted to Bohemia, where it gains not only famous martyrs, but victorious warriors. The red-cross knights dare not face the Hussite peasants, and the pope's bulls prove powerless against Zizka's bullets. At last the Church has to make peace with the heretics, and let them worship as they please. This unheard of tolerance is due to the temporary sway of men who wish to reduce the papacy to a limited monarchy, by establishing not only the supreme authority, but the continual activity of universal councils. The two movements against absolutism, in the name of the Bible and of the councils, have come into fatal antagonism, when Huss is burned by the men who have dethroned three popes ; and the treaty at Basel can only check the resulting animosity. Little can be accomplished by any opposition to the pope so long as it is believed that however wicked he may be, he holds the keys of heaven. The last medieval council is dispersed ignominiously, the Lollards are reduced to obscurity, and the Hussites have finally to submit on all points, except the use of the cup.

Mysticism suffers greatly from persecution, and there is but little reliance on special revelations, and visions unsanctioned by the Church, after the martyrdom of Joan of Arc. The year 1450 finds the pope still an absolute monarch, with every known enemy at his feet. We shall see in the next chapter that new and dangerous elements of hostility have already developed undetected.

The Middle Ages are particularly worthy of study, because they form a period when the Church was more powerful and Christianity more universally honored than in any century before or since ; when bishops were princes and popes the masters of kings and emperors ; when there were scarcely any grand buildings but churches, or large armies except for crusades; when there was little writing except about theology, or scholarship outside of monasteries ; when the sick had more trust in monks and priests than in physicians, and the clergy stood above the law ; when the Church owned nearly half the wealth of Europe, knew all the secrets of every family, and was looked up to as the main source of happiness here and hereafter; and when open unbelief was seldom seen and always punished. All this mighty power the Church wielded in the name of the Bible and as the representative of Christ. The ideal of Jesus has never been fully realized, but the Apostles and their successors did their best to embody it as they thought he wished. They saw the need of resisting persecution and conquering the heathenism, first of the Roman emperors and then of the barbarian invaders, and so they built up a strong organization, which ultimately found its needed center in the papacy. They expected to be saved by faith, and so the bishops were authorized to meet in councils and declare the correct belief. The people needed not only instruction but discipline, so power to administer both was given to the priests, and their fidelity was watched over by the bishops and popes. I see nothing unchristian in all this. There was certainly no intention of departing from the teachings of Jesus, but merely of developing them into the institutions most favorable to Christianity. The *Gospels* and *Epistles* represent the Church as made up, not of free-thinkers, each of whom believes only what seems true to him individually, but of teachers and taught, shepherds and sheep, all believing in the words of Jesus and his Apostles, but some authorized to tell others what to believe and do. These ten centuries, from about 450 to 1450, were as truly Christian as any others before or since. Certainly there has never been a time when Christianity was so little interfered with by heathenism, worldliness, or unbelief. The prophecy in the *Apocalypse*, that the saints were to rule the earth for a thousand years was much more truly fulfilled then, than it has been since, or seems likely to be. This was the real millennium. Christianity reigned with such power as she never had afterward. Let us consider what use she made of it.

One great end aimed at by the Church then, and since also, has been keeping the people in subjection to their rulers. The influence of Christianity was certainly directed toward order and obedience during these thousand years, and this was highly beneficial during the first half of the period, when Europe needed nothing so much as the restoration of stable government. Soon afterward came to be felt a further need, namely, that there should be liberty of progress. Now we find the Church taking sides with the rulers, except when it was her interest to promote liberty, as was the case in most parts of Italy. Even there she showed little sympathy with Rienzi, and her own rule was as despotic as possible. Only anathemas fell on the pious Englishmen who won Magna Charta from a godless and vicious tyrant; and the free cities of Germany found their bishops their worst enemies. As liberty advanced, the restraining influence of Christian institutions became more and more unfortunate.

Freedom of thought found her natural enemy in the Church. Before the year 1000, there were few heretics to persecute; but after that we find the executioners, crusaders, and inquisitors kept busy in checking mental progress. Even men who wished to avoid heresy, like Bacon and Abelard, were punished merely for introducing new ideas. Knowledge of the creed, the ritual, and the canon law, the Church had to give her priests, in order to maintain her power; but in promoting all other learning the influence of Judaism and Moslemism was much mightier during the ninth and tenth centuries than that of Christianity. Medical culture is mainly due to the Hebrews. What education there was in Christendom, even in the fourteenth century, was for the priests rather than the people at large. It is not to popes and bishops, but to kings and emperors that we owe the great universities, like Bologna, Padua, Prague, Salamanca, and probably Paris. For popular education, however, we must look to Moslem lands. Christian education was mainly for a privileged few, who were kept within safe limits by savage punishments for originality, and who were prevented from exerting much influence by being shut up in monasteries, and forbidden to have children. The medieval Church treated scholarship just as modern society does crime. It is true that many books were preserved in these monasteries, but I fear that more were wantonly destroyed. We owe it largely to monkish carelessness, that few ancient authors have come down to us entire, and very many survive only in name, while there are sad gaps in some of the most famous and useful books. Medieval Christianity found it for her interest to appear more friendly to knowledge than to liberty, but she did not love it for its own sake ; nor was this required by the New Testament.

What that book most prizes is morality, and for this the ancient Church labored faithfully according to her light. There is little fault to find with her intentions, but some of her methods were sadly unwise. Too much stress was certainly laid on rites and creeds, and far too little room given for free growth. Especially bad was the practice of keeping all peculiarly virtuous men and women unmarried, and shut up where they could have little influence. Sanctity, like scholarship, was hindered from propagating itself through inheritance and family life in the Middle Ages, just as crime is at present. The prohibition of marriage was designed to raise the clergy above worldly relationships and domestic ties into living like Christ and the Apostles, but the result was not only to check the propagation of virtue, but to encourage that of vice. Forbidding innocent relations with women brought about guilty ones. The Eastern Church refused to prohibit the marriage of her priests, and so kept free from scandal. The Western Church deliberately took a different course from her sister's, and persisted in it after its evil results had become manifest; because she cared less for purity than power. She knew that an unmarried clergy was inevitably licentious, but she also knew that no other would serve her interests so faithfully. The same wish to be powerful, rather than pure, caused Becket and other prelates to contend for the immunity of the clergy before the law, the result being that the teachers of the people became not models of virtue but monsters of vice. Another pernicious result of the belief, that morality could be maintained only by keeping up the power of the Church, was the practice of pious fraud, of which we have noticed many instances, perhaps the worst being the systematic acceptance for six hundred years of the *False Decretals* as the basis of temporal power. All the hundred pontiffs who sanctioned this forgery before it was disclosed in the fifteenth century may not have known it to be one, but any of them could have detected it on examination. In other cases of pious fraud, the Church must have known that she was sacrificing morality to power, and wholly without New Testament authority. Still more plainly was this the case with the crusades and other consecrated wars which gave a most unfortunate sanction to some of the worst tendencies of the age. Wars against heathens and unbelievers were, however, so far in accordance with the spirit of the Old Testament and the *Apocalypse* as not to seem unchristian in the Middle Ages, despite the inconsistency with the *Sermon on the Mount*.

But even this loftiest part of the New Testament had nothing to repress another great error of medieval Christianity, the consecration of beggary, and consequent discouragement of the industrial virtues. Whether the evil effects of the mendicant orders, the crusades, the pious frauds, the exemption of the clergy from legal jurisdiction, the check of sanctity from propagation or domestic influence, and the profligacy of the priests fully counterbalanced all the good done by preaching and church discipline, it is hard to say.

At all events the moral condition of Europe at the time of the thousand years' Reign of the Saints was not particularly creditable to medieval Christianity, as must be plain to the readers of this history, of Dante, or of Boccaccio. Knowledge and liberty were advancing, but it was in spite of the Church. The plan of educating the people by keeping them under priests, as sheep following shepherds, had been tried faithfully, and with scarcely any opposition, for ten centuries, and, despite some success at first, had on the whole proved a failure. Europe could not advance either morally, mentally, or politically, until some better system came into use.

CHAPTER IX.

THE REVIVAL OF LEARNING, LITERATURE, AND ART,
1450–1517.

Less than seventy years sufficed to do away with the state of thought and feeling on which the pope's throne had hitherto stood firm, and to establish such mental independence as opened the way for attacking his supremacy with a success never before possible.

I.

This momentous change began with a sudden and great increase of attention to the Latin classics, as well as with a wholly new interest in the Greek language and literature, hitherto almost unknown to Western Europe. The brilliancy of these great authors was extremely valuable in mental discipline; their distance from Christianity made escape from Church authority easy; the protests against tyranny and superstition in Plato, Cicero, Lucretius, Seneca, Plutarch, Lucian, and other ancient philosophers proved singularly well fitted for drawing attention to existing evils; study of the New Testament became possible without resort to commentaries written in the papal interest; and some of the new school of writers struck deeply and skillfully at monks, priests, and popes. Thus Christendom had to look back beyond its origin in order to learn how to take its first great step forward.

Study of the Latin classics had been greatly encouraged during the latter half of the fourteenth century by Petrarch and Boccaccio, and the latter's pupil, John of Ravenna, had traveled through the Italian cities, training scholars, who soon distinguished themselves not only as expounders and translators, but also as discoverers of almost unknown works by Cicero, Quintilian, Tacitus, Plautus, and Lucretius. Among the early patrons in Florence was Coluccio Salutato, who met the monks' attacks on the classic poets by showing that the Bible was at best poetry, and sometimes not the most chaste.

Greek had hitherto been studied only by isolated scholars like Erigena, Heloise, Frederic II., Bacon, Petrarch, and Boccaccio; but in 1396 Emmanuel Chrysolaras began to teach it in Florence, where he found many pupils, as he did afterward in other cities of Italy. About 1405, Guarino of Verona came back to teach what he had learned at Constantinople, as soon after did other Italians, some of whom brought hundreds of manuscripts, including Homer, Plato, Aristotle, Thucydides, Plutarch, Lucian, and the great dramatists. Translations were eagerly made, especially by that denouncer of clerical hypocrisy, Leonardo Bruni. The council held at Ferrara and Florence in 1438, in order to break up that in Basel, though ostensibly to unite the Eastern and Western Churches, brought to Italy not only that future cardinal and powerful champion of Plato, Bessarion, but also that would-be inaugurator of a new religion based on Neo-Platonism, Gemistus Pletho, whose principal book was destroyed by the patriarch of Constantinople about 1455, but whose lectures before Cosimo dei Medici led to the establishment, later in the century, of the Platonic Academy. Many other learned Greeks came over after the capture of Byzantium in 1452, when many thousand manuscripts perished, and visits from western scholars became very difficult. Generous patronage to letters and art was now given, not only by the Medici, but by Pope Nicholas V., who collected the five thousand volumes which were the basis of the Vatican library, and who had translations made from Homer, Plato, Aristotle, Chrysostom, Thucydides, Ptolemy, etc., as well as from the Hebrew and Greek books of the Bible.

Among the scholars thus employed was Lorenzo Valla, who at twenty-five had risked his life by exposing the false pretensions to knowledge of a rival professor at Pavia. Coming thence to Rome about 1443 he published a Dialogue inviting men to live according to reason, rather than authority, by suggesting the identity of the laws of virtue with those of happiness, and brought himself into new danger by his *Declamation on the Donation Falsely and Mendaciously Ascribed to Constantine.* The lies in question had been told, at least implicitly, by all the popes for six hundred years. Not only does Valla refute their claims to temporal sovereignty, but he denounces them as examples of wickedness, most unrighteous Pharisees, who sit in Moses's seat and do the deeds of Dathan and Abiram ; who live like emperors, and make war on their fellow Christians ; and who will suffer speedy vengeance, unless they confess their frauds and cease from usurpation. Only the protection of King Alfonso of Naples saved him from the inquisitors, who actually put him on trial for denying the authenticity, not only of the Creed still alleged to have been written by the Apostles, but of the equally fictitious letters between Jesus and Abgarus, and who had to release their prisoner on his saying, "Mother Church knows nothing about these matters, but I believe as she does." While still at Naples he attacked Augustine, in a treatise on Free-will, which supplied arguments to Leibnitz, and wrote comments on the Greek Testament which were of much use to Erasmus. When Nicholas V. assumed the tiara, in 1447, he summoned Valla to Rome, not to be burned as a heretic, but to be pensioned, authorized to open a school, and employed as a translator, in which work he died.

Poggio, too, who brought to light Quintilian, part of Lucretius, eight orations by Cicero, twelve comedies by Plautus, and several minor authors, qualified himself, by spending fifty years as papal secretary, for severely censuring the monks and priests for avarice and hypocrisy. In his Dialogue on the latter vice the chief speaker is Carlo Marsuppini, known not so much for his Latin verses as for his refusal to accept the sacrament on his death-bed. In another Dialogue, about nobility, he shows that this rests on merit and not birth, with a plainness worthy of a citizen of Florence, where hereditary rank was treated as a political crime. His most famous work is the *Liber Facetiarum*, a collection of ridiculous stories about the clergy, which was published during the Jubilee of 1450, and widely circulated. No persecution touched the author, though soon after attacking clerical avarice, in 1429, he wrote to a cardinal, who censured his loose morals and advised him to reform and enter the priesthood, that nothing worse could be said of him than was openly avowed by abbots, bishops, and higher dignitaries. This letter closes thus :

"As to your advice on my future plans of life, I am determined not to assume the sacerdotal office ; for I have seen many men whom I have regarded as persons of good character and liberal dispositions degenerate into avarice, sloth, and dissipation in the priesthood. Fearing lest this should be the case with myself, I have resolved to spend the remaining term of my pilgrimage as a layman ; for I have too frequently observed that your brethren, at the time of their tonsure, not only part with their hair, but also with their conscience and their virtue" (Shepherd, *Life of Poggio*, p. 200).

Another sign of the times is the rescue in 1452 by an armed band, sent by a Knight of St. John, of Nicholas of Verona, then on his way through the streets of Bologna to be burned for denying that any miracle was wrought by the priests at the communion. About twenty-five years later Pope Sixtus saved Galeottus from the stake to which he had been doomed for saying: "He who lives uprightly and follows the law that is born in him will go to heaven, whatever may be his nation."

Among the Humanists, or Friends of Man, as the scholars of the fifteenth century called themselves, was Stephen Porcaro, a Roman noble, who was banished for opposing the papal yoke, to Bologna. There he prepared, by enlisting three hundred mercenaries and four hundred conspirators of rank in Rome, for setting the papal stables on fire during the celebration of Epiphany, putting Pope Nicholas in golden chains, seizing his treasury, the Castle of St. Angelo, and the Capitol, and proclaiming the Republic. Stephen's premature departure from Bologna awoke suspicion ; soldiers were sent to seek him ; his sister tried vainly to hide him in a chest on whose lid she sat ; and on

January 9, 1453, he went to execution saying, " O my people, this day dies your liberator ! "

On December 26, 1476, the anniversary of an earlier martyr of the same name, and in his church at Milan, Duke Galeazzo Maria Sforza, whose tyranny had become especially galling through his unbridled sensuality, fell under the daggers of three young noblemen who had learned to love liberty by studying Cicero and Plutarch. Two were slain on the spot, and the third, Olgiati, died in tortures, during which he said to a priest who urged him to repent : " I have sinned otherwise, but as to this deed for which I die, it gives my conscience peace ; and I trust that on this account the universal Judge will pardon all my other offenses. No base desire led me, but only the wish to remove a tyrant whom we could bear no longer. Far from repenting, if I had to come to life ten times in order to die ten times by these torments, I would still consecrate all my blood and strength to this noble end."

So revolutionary and rationalistic seemed to be the tendencies of Humanism, that Paul II., the first of five very wicked popes, declared that religion and knowledge are natural enemies, and imprisoned the members of the Roman Academy, in 1468, on a false charge of treason, for which several were tortured to death before his eyes.

More fortunate was the Platonic Academy, which began its meetings at Florence about 1475, and continued them until 1522, when it was thought too incendiary. Its leader, Ficino, had been educated for his post by Cosimo dei Medici, and gave to the press in 1482 one of the best translations of Plato ever executed. Among the members who celebrated the anniversary of the birth and death of the great individualist, on November 7, were the poet Politian, the architect Alberti, Machiavelli, and Michael Angelo. Among the visitors was Count Pico of Mirandola, who in 1486, when but twenty-three, published in Rome nine hundred theses, for which he was at once condemned as a heretic by Innocent VIII., though he was finally absolved by a yet more famous judge of pure religion, Alexander VI., the father of Cæsar and Lucretia Borgia, as well as of the censorship of the press, which he inaugurated in 1501. Pico did much to expose astrology and was busy at the time of his premature death, 1494, trying to reconcile Christianity with Moslemism, and Judaism, which last he had studied in the Hebrew originals. Ficino, meantime, was expounding Plato's doctrine of immortality in opposition to Averroism.

This theory, that all souls are too intimately united in essence for the division into individuals to be more than temporary, had been encountered by Petrarch in the fourteenth century at Venice, one of whose monks asserted it in Bologna, before the general Chapter of Augustinians in 1429. Five years later, the fondness of the Marquis of Villena for Averroes and Lucretius had caused the destruction of his library by Spanish priests. The great strength of Averroism was in Padua where Vernias taught it publicly from 1471 to 1499, when he had to recant; but its character was greatly moderated after its condemnation by the Lateran council, December 19, 1513.

Among the lecturers in support of this scholastic form of heterodoxy appears in 1480, Cassandra Fidele, one of a score of learned ladies mentioned by Tiraboschi, who tells us how famous for their knowledge of Greek were Ippolita Sforza, and Battista da Montefeltro; how the latter conquered other philosophers in discussion, and made orations to the Emperor Sigismund and Pope Martin V.; how Isotta, a poetess of Verona, demonstrated in public discussion, 1451, that Adam was more to blame than Eve; and how Lucretia, the mother of Lorenzo dei Medici, suggested to Pulci his *Morgante Maggiore*, the best known poem of the century.

That a new era was opening for women had already been shown by Joan of Arc and Margaret of Denmark. Let me speak here of Caterina Sforza, who is called "The First Lady of Italy." When she married Jerome Riario, Lord of Forli, in 1477, her hair was brighter than her coronet. His tyranny forced his subjects to murder him and take her prisoner. The citadel still held out, and she offered to go, and have it surrendered, leaving her children as hostages. No sooner was she inside, than she ordered the cannon to be loaded and pointed against the rebels. Her sons were at once threatened with death, but she shouted from the rampart : "I shall have others to avenge them." Her friends soon came to her relief, and she reigned with great ability and energy until 1502, when, after making a desperate defense, she was dethroned and imprisoned by the papal general, Cæsar Borgia.

One of the purest and bravest of women, Isabella of Castile, was queen from 1474 to 1504. It is pleasant to think of her sitting enthroned at Madrid every Friday, to deal justice to all who asked it, offering to pawn her jewels to fit out Columbus, or riding in armor amid her soldiers to conquer Granada. But this noble woman was forced by her dark creed to torture her own daughter for heresy, to let the inquisition enter Spain in 1480 and burn two thousand victims the next year, to drive away her most intelligent and industrious subjects, the Jews, whose number is estimated at least one hundred and sixty thousand, and to banish the unconverted Moslems, contrary to her own plighted faith.

Italy enjoyed from the death of Paul II. in 1471, to the revival of the inquisition by Paul III. in 1542, an unexampled tolerance, except for the wholesale destruction in the valleys of the Alps and Appennines of the witches, whose increase may be attributed to loss of faith in the power of the Church to control evil spirits, and for a few isolated executions like that of Savonarola in 1498, and that of Georgio Novara at Bologna soon after, for denying the divinity of Christ. Doctor da Solo was merely obliged to take back in 1497, his assertions, that Jesus died for crime, that his miracles were wrought by planetary aid, that he is not present in the sacramental bread, and that Christianity is soon to pass away. The posthumous publication, in 1480, of a demonstration of the falsity of the *Decretals* and the *Donation*, by Antony of Florence, did not prevent his canonization in 1523. Boccaccio's brilliant exposure of clerical corruption was printed at Florence about 1470, and passed through a dozen editions during the century, no resistance being made by the Church before 1573, when the pope had the heroes of some of the worst stories changed from monks and priests to laymen. Among the countless authors of equally discreditable tales are Masuccio, who really hated sin, especially when in the Church, and Bandello, who had no moral antipathies, and so was made a bishop, while the early Protestants found plenty of ammunition in his *Novelle*, now best known, like those of his contemporary, Cinthio, for the precious ore they supplied to Shakespeare. Sannazzaro, Mantovano, Pontano, and Michael Angelo were permitted by Alexander VI. and Julius II. to write the bitterest of satires against them. Comedy did full justice to the inferior clergy, who were charged with advising adultery out of mere avarice in the confessional by Machiavelli and other scoffers, whose filthy ribaldry was enacted before the guests of Pope Leo X. and amid his bursts of laughter. Much as the grossness of these dramas and stories must be regretted, it was well that women should be put on their guard against clerical seducers, and that every body should be shown whither priestly guidance led.

Among the best known of the early laborers in a no less popular and fertile field was Pulci, a Florentine who, in 1481, published his *Morgante Maggiore*, a poem giving the legend of Charlemagne and his paladins, the special favorites of the lower ranks of Italian society, with a vivacity which often runs into an irreverence, contrasting strangely with the pious phrases which open and close the cantos. Thus Orlando, as he goes into his last battle against the Moslems at Roncesvalles, says that all things have their limits, as one rises another falls, and this may be the case with Christianity.

The giant Margutte, a caricature of the irreverent and vagrant scholar, replies to the question whether he believes in Christ or in Mahomet: "In neither, but in a chicken, whether roasted or boiled, also in butter, and above all in good old wine. I have faith that whoso trusts therein will be saved." He is ready to rob the saints in heaven, if there are any, and he has, besides all known sins, the theological virtues, namely perjury and forgery.

Then there is a forerunner of Mephistopheles, Astarotte, who says that the earth is round and inhabited on both sides, as well as that it is very inconsistent for the angels to be punished pitilessly for one offense, while men can wash all their sins away with a single tear, and may yet find mercy even in hell. Boiardo's *Orlando Inamorato*, which makes fasts, penances, and sacraments trifles, compared with honor, courage, courtesy, and truthfulness, has been little read, except in the version made by Berni about 1535. The most famous of these epics is Ariosto's *Orlando Furioso*, first published in 1516. Canto xiv. sends the archangel Michael to seek Silence in a monastery; but she has fled, as have Love, Peace, Piety, and Humility. Avarice, Pride, Anger, Gluttony, Envy, Idleness, and Cruelty have chased them away. Fraud, too, is there, and Discord, who later in the poem sets the friars, at the yearly election of officers, to throwing prayer-books at one another's heads. The temporal power of the popes is represented as a heap of flowers, once sweet but now noisome. And these poems, dramas, and tales were most serviceable to mental progress by stimulating the imagination to such activity, especially in regard to man's earthly life, as had been unknown since the fall of Paganism.

II.

The most original thinker of the fifteenth century, and one of the boldest investigators in any age, was Leonardo da Vinci, whose high fame is slight compared with what lay within his reach. The only work of his that has been published, the *Treatise on Painting*, is too technical to interest ordinary readers; his Last Supper and Battle of the Standard were painted in colors which soon faded away; his colossal equestrian statue was never any thing but a model, of which not even a trustworthy drawing has come down to us; his stupendous plans in architecture and engineering found no patron to execute them; few of the machines he designed were ever constructed; none of his scientific discoveries was announced by himself; no full account of them has ever been published or ever will be; and no competent judge ever made a thorough examination of his writings, which, like his drawings, have been but imperfectly preserved. "But serious students assure us that he was one of the very greatest and most clear-sighted, as well as one of the earliest of natural philosophers. They declare him to have been the founder of the study of the anatomy and structural classification of plants; the founder, or at least the chief reviver, of the science of hydraulics; to have anticipated many of the geometrical discoveries of Commandin, Autolycus, and Tartaglia; to have divined, or gone far toward divining, the laws of gravitation, the earth's rotation, and the molecular composition of water, the motion of waves, and even the undulatory theory of light and heat. He discovered the construction of the eye and the optical laws of vision, and invented the camera obscura. Among useful appliances he invented the saw which is still in use in the marble quarries of Carrara, and a rope-making machine, said to be better than any even yet in use. He investigated the composition of explosives and the application of steam power; he perceived that boats could be made to go by steam, and designed both steam-cannon and cannon to be loaded at the breech." (*Encyclopædia Britannica*, Ninth Edition, vol. xiv., pp. 461-2.) Among his other drawings are plans for canals, military bridges, flying machines, clock-work, and the parachute, of which he was undoubtedly the inventor. Probably he did not reach the telescope or the pendulum, but he took important steps toward them. He knew how to make hygrometers, vessels proof against cannon-shot, diving-suits, and machines for wire-drawing, file-cutting, plate-rolling, and silk-weaving. He found out the correspondence of the circles in wood, not only to the age of the trees, but to the relative moisture and dryness of successive years, the law of arrangement of the leaves, and the fact of their respiration. Lyell mentions that he was "one of the first who applied sound reasoning to the question of the origin of fossils," which was not settled before the close of the last century. The great recent discovery, that heat is a mode of motion, he so far anticipated as to speak of "force as a cause of fire." He found out the impossibility of perpetual motion, studied the laws of acoustics, combustion, and friction with great care, and reached not only special results, but general principles of the utmost value. "Force," he says, "is a power, spiritual, incorporeal, and impalpable, which occurs for a short period in bodies which, from accidental violence, are out of their natural repose. I call it spiritual, because there is in it an invisible life, and incorporeal, because the body in which it originates increases neither in form nor in weight." (Mrs. Heaton, *Leonardo da Vinci*, p. 146.) "Mechanics is the paradise of the mathematical sciences, because therein one attains their fruit." "Experience never deceives." "Do not trust authors who wish to interpret between nature and men through their own imaginations, but trust only those who have exercised their understanding upon the results of their own experiments." (Mrs. Heaton, *Leonardo da Vinci*, p. 121.) "Vainly have they labored who have followed any one but Nature, the Mistress of Masters." "Many will think themselves warranted in blaming me, alleging that my proofs are contrary to the authority of certain men whom they hold in high reverence, * * * not considering that my facts are obtained by simple pure experiment, which is our real mistress" (Mrs. Heaton, *Leonardo da Vinci*, p. 126). These were new and needed truths in 1500. No wonder that the priests blamed him, as he tells us, for "working at his art on feast-days, and investigating the works of God." Vasari says he was led by his study of botany and astronomy "to form such heretical ideas, that he did not belong to any religion, and thought it better to be a philosopher than a Christian." His Mss. often speak of "those Pharisees who heap up great riches and pay for them in invisible coin; sell publicly things of value which were never theirs, and without any license from the owner; avoid hard work or poor fare, and live in palaces by exalting the glory of God." A still plainer proof of his freedom from theological prejudice is his spending several years, between 1480 and 1484, as engineer in the service of the Sultan of Egypt. Knowledge of his heterodoxy naturally made him slow to publish. He says himself of some otherwise unknown persecution: "When I made the Lord God an infant, you imprisoned me; now if I make Him grown up, you will treat me worse." One of his Mss. bears the motto, "Fly from Storms;" and he gave the credit of one of his own most original inventions, the steam-cannon, to Archimedes. It is impossible to know how much science lost by that dread of persecution which silenced Leonardo da Vinci, and probably many other investigators whose very names have perished. Much allowance must also be made in his case for incessant occupation and premature old age. This latter, with long illness, led him to submit to the Church, and receive her sacraments nine days before his death, which took place on May 2, 1519. No thinker had freed himself so completely from superstition and deference to authority since the establishment of Christianity, and scarcely any one else advanced so far before the eighteenth century. It is, therefore, pleasant to know that he was a devoted son to his low-born mother, an industrious laborer in his profession, a diligent and generous teacher, a genial and faithful friend.

Science can show no other name so illustrious among the predecessors of Copernicus. That the earth moves in her orbit was actually suggested by the Cardinal de Cusa, also noted for urging the Council of Basel to reform the calendar. In 1494 appeared the first printed book on algebra and geometry, that by Lucas de Burgo, who goes as far as quadratic equations. Ptolemy's geography had been reprinted, with copper-plate maps, sixteen years earlier, and an encyclopædia called the *Margarita Philosophica*, was published in 1486. The description of Asia, written by Pope Pius II., is particularly important for its influence over Columbus, who was also greatly aided by the intelligent sympathy of Toscanelli.

The most famous, or perhaps infamous, book written in prose during the period covered by this chapter is the *Prince*, by Machiavelli. He had served republican Florence with a zeal which caused him to be put on the rack, after Pope Julius II. restored the Medici. Desire to regain office under these despots, as he says himself, led him to present to them in 1516, his manuscript, telling how a city which has once been free may be most easily and securely kept enslaved.

Nothing could have better served the tyrants, especially as the book was left to their private study for sixteen years before its publication. No attention was paid to its only redeeming point, the closing plea for a united Italy, defended by a national militia, ideas so novel and important as to be commemorated in the tablet erected by the author's country on the fourth centenary of his birth, May 3, 1869. It is significant that a treatise written to get office mentions Alexander VI. as a ruler who was always practicing fraud, and warns his Prince not to trust to the alliance with any pope. The *Discourses on the first ten books of Livy*, where Machiavelli ventures to express his real opinion of the infamy of enslaving a free city, plainly declare the convictions of the keenest and shrewdest observer of the age :

"The nearer people are to the Church of Rome, which is the head of our religion, the less religious are they." " The evil example of the Court of Rome has destroyed all piety and religion in Italy." "We Italians then, owe to the Church of Rome, and to her priests, our having become irreligious and bad ; but we owe her a still greater debt, and one that will be the cause of our ruin, namely, that the Church has kept and still keeps our country divided " (*Discourses*, Book i., chapter xii., Detmold, *Writings of Machiavelli*, vol. ii., p. 130).

The year of the presentation of the Mss. of the *Prince* by Machiavelli to the Medici, and of the first publication of Ariosto's *Orlando Furioso*, 1516, was also that of the printing of one of the boldest books thus far written in Christendom, the *De Immortalitate Animæ*, by Pomponatius. This physician and professor of philosophy at Bologna and Padua was born September 16, 1462, and died May 18, 1525, with "an unsullied reputation for virtuous conduct and sweetness of temper" (Symonds, *Renaissance*, vol. v., p. 461, Am. Ed.). He was thrice married, but not even on these occasions did he discontinue for more than a few hours the study of Aristotle, concerning which he says: "This drives me and straightens me : this makes me sleepless and insane." His diminutive size caused him to be nicknamed Peretto, and called a pigmy warring against heaven, by bigoted monks against whom he was protected by friendly cardinals. One of these latter gave him an honorable burial in Mantua, where his tomb may still be visited.

His little treatise on *Immortality*, after attacking the Averroist view, that the only part of us which survives death has no individuality, makes a thorough examination of the belief then and now orthodox, namely, that each soul is one indissoluble and immortal personality. Pomponatius protests that he has no doubt of this, since it is plainly taught, not only by the Bible, which is above all human reason, but by the incontrovertible Thomas Aquinas, and that he is only acting as a questioner, seeking to bring truth into full light, when he states such objections as the following: "If the soul's independence of the senses in some respects proves her immortality, so does her dependence in others disprove it. And there are more of her faculties which imply mortality than immortality, as may be seen in the low mental condition of savages, as well as of women generally. Nor can we prove that the soul is able to think without the body, a capacity expressly denied by Aristotle, or understand her connection with the body except by assuming her materiality. Finally, since each soul is admitted to have a beginning, she can not be a partaker of eternity, wherein is neither beginning nor end, but must be finite in her end as well as in her beginning." After giving these and similar objections at some length, in chapter viii., Pomponatius sets forth his own view, that "the soul may be called immortal in so far as she is a form of pure thought, which latter is independent of sensation, and therefore both immaterial and eternal, but that she is mortal in reality, since she is affected by the mortality of the body, which is necessarily with her, not as the subject, but yet as the object, of her acts." A series of objections to this view are proposed in chapter xiii., and answered in chapter xiv., as follows:

"1. If man is mortal, he has no adequate object for exertion and no superiority over the lower animals.

"2. If this earthly life were thought our only one, we should not be willing to sacrifice it for any duty.

"3. If there is no reward for goodness or punishment for sin but what is seen here on earth, then there is no government, or at least no just one, by God.

"4. All religions have taught immortality.

"5. There are many accounts of apparitions, as well as of visions, like that at the close of Plato's *Republic*, and of heavenly dreams, some of which latter had happened to Pomponatius himself.

"6. There is also testimony in favor of demoniacal possession.

"7. Some passages of Aristotle imply belief in immortality.

"8. All who denied it have been wicked and godless men; for instance, Aristippus and Sardanapalus."

But—

"I. As all the members of the body are necessary for its life, so are all those of the human race, living for which is the individual's destined end and aim; and as for superiority over the brutes, that is secured by our intelligence, one spark of which is worth more than all bodily pleasures.

"II. Nothing is more precious and advantageous in itself than virtue, and nothing more ruinous than vice; so that goodness is always to be chosen for its own sake, and wickedness to be shunned.

"III. Virtue is its own true reward, and does more than all things else to make us happy, while vice is its own worst punishment.

"IV. Of the three religions founded by Jesus, Moses, and Mahomet, two at least are false, and perhaps all of them, while the wisest legislators, as is shown by Plato and Aristotle, have not cared for truth, but only for virtue, in teaching future rewards and punishments, and have acted like physicians who deceive the patient for his good.

"V. Some of the stories of ghosts are mere fables, others illusions, and others fabrications by priests, many of whom turn the four cardinal virtues into ambition, avarice, gluttony, and lust. Apparitions, not to be accounted for thus, may be those of angels or demons who never were human. Visions and dreams prove only that God is watching over us.

"VI. What is called demoniacal possession may be only disease.

"VII. Aristotle may be explained otherwise.

"VIII. Many great sinners are known to have believed in immortality, and among those who rejected it have been many good and wise men, like Homer, Simonides, Hippocrates, Galen, Alexander of Aphrodisias, Pliny, and Seneca."

"It is commonly said," adds Pomponatius, "that if the soul is mortal, a man ought to give himself up to bodily pleasure, and do any wickedness he may think expedient, while worship of God would be wholly useless; but it is enough to answer that, since it is our nature to seek happiness and shun misery, and since happiness consists in virtue and misery in vice, it follows not only that we should worship God, which is virtuous, but that we ought to abstain from murder, robbery, theft, and other vices which turn men to beasts. Remember that he who works earnestly, and seeks no reward but virtue herself is much more virtuous and noble than he who looks for some reward besides; and so he who flees from vice on account of its baseness only is much more worthy of praise than he who avoids it merely through fear of punishment. Thus those who make the soul mortal are seen to preserve the honor of virtue better than do they who call themselves immortal, for hope of reward and fear of punishment bring in something selfish."

In the concluding chapter, Pomponatius says, that though these arguments from reason do not decisively establish either the mortality of the soul or her immortality, yet he himself believes in the latter as taught in the Bible, the creeds, the Fathers, and the Doctors, especially Thomas Aquinas, and submits himself completely to papal authority. Thus he closes: "On September 24, 1516, the fourth year of the pontificate of Leo X. to the praise of the Holy Trinity."

This pious conclusion did not save the book from being publicly burned at Venice, but the favor of Cardinal Bembo prevented the persecution of the author, who was obliged to publish, two years later, an *Apology*, in which he says that Christianity is the only religion which can consistently teach immortality, because this creed alone asserts the resurrection of the body.

Much of the power of the *De Immortalitate* lies in the suggestion that Aristotle, who was considered almost as infallible as the Church herself, really differed from her so much, that one or the other must be given up. That this dilemma also exists about the miracles is shown in his *De Naturalium Effectuum Causis or De Incantationibus*, first published in 1556. Here he is not so argumentative or metaphysical as in the work just described, but gives much space to stories of biblical, classical, and medieval prodigies, especially those said to be wrought by evil spirits. Pomponatius speaks with great respect of the order of nature, and plainly declares that many alleged violations of it are really due to the power of the imagination and other natural causes. Such explanations can not, he thinks, be given of the multiplication of the loaves, the raising of Lazarus, the darkening of the sun at the crucifixion, etc. Here he comes to the dilemma, one side of which he states thus: "The principle laid down by Aristotle is false, that God can not act except according to the universal order of nature. We know that Aristotle and Plato were ignorant and sinful mortals ; wherefore it is foolish to put faith in all they say, especially in what they say contrary to Christianity." (Chapter xiii., p. 320 and 321, Ed. of 1567). He has to leave it to the reader to see the other alternative, which Pomponatius evidently thinks peculiarly probable in regard to demoniacal agency. Perhaps the boldest passages are these: "Every thing is now growing cold in our faith, and miracles cease, except fictitious ones, for the end is near." (Chapter xii., p. 286, Ed. of 1567). "All knowledge is the perfection of the intellect, and good in itself, useful, and honorable." (Chapter iv., p. 64, Ed. of 1567).

These last words show what there was in Pomponatius, as well as da Vinci, Bacon, and Abelard, which was most dangerous to the Church. She held knowledge good or bad, according as it helped or hindered her work. This had been her view from the beginning, and there is not a word, even in the New Testament, to show that intellectual culture is a duty, or that knowledge is valuable for its own sake, or that truth is to be reached by any natural process of thought. These ideas had not yet been recognized by Christianity, but they were common-places in classic literature. Hence the revival of letters necessarily and immediately brought about habits of thought incompatible with the authority of the Church, and indeed of Christianity itself, as then understood. The earlier manifestations of this spirit had been repressed by persecution, but love of truth had now become irrepressible.

Especially favorable to the power of literature was the invention of printing, whose origin was north of the Alps, but whose first early success was in Italy, two thousand eight hundred and thirty-five books having been published at Venice between 1470 and 1500, nine hundred and twenty-five at Rome, and six hundred and twenty-nine at Milan; while Paris had seven hundred and fifty-one, Cologne five hundred and thirty, Strasburg five hundred and twenty-six, no other place more than four hundred, and London had only one hundred and thirty. Printing-presses had been set up in seventy cities of Italy before the end of the century, and had published five thousand works, among which were two editions of Lucretius, the first being placed about 1473. Lucian appeared at Florence in 1496, and in 1503 at Venice, where the Aldine press had now become famous. Wood-cuts, which are believed to have been made in 1406, and copper-plate engraving, which seems to have been in use as early as 1440, assisted in preserving and diffusing every result of thought, though their chief value was as servants of beauty, rather than of truth.

III.

Strongly helpful to liberal views was the artistic culture, which developed rapidly in Italy during the fourteenth and fifteenth centuries, and culminated early in the sixteenth, when Raphael, Michael Angelo, Leonardo da Vinci, Correggio, Titian, Andrea del Sarto, Benvenuto Cellini, Bramante, and many other painters, sculptors, and architects, produced works which I can not criticise. I venture only to suggest how they favored mental progress.

In the first place, great attention was early paid to pagan subjects. Raphael's School of Athens, Galatea, and Psyche, Michael Angelo's Bacchus, Cupid, and Brutus, Leonardo da Vinci's Leda and Medusa, Correggio's Io, Danaë, and Diana, Titian's Bacchus and Ariadne, Perugino's Leonidas and Cato, Signorelli's Pan, Mantegna's Triumph of Cæsar, and many similar but less famous works, were admirably adapted to show how much pleasure, beauty, and truth there is outside of Christianity. So were the newly discovered ancient masterpieces, like the Laocoön, the Belvidere Apollo, and the Vatican Venus.

"Art proved itself a powerful coagent in the emancipation of the intellect; the impartiality wherewith its methods were applied to subjects sacred and profane, the emphasis laid upon physical strength and beauty, as good things and desirable, the subordination of classical and medieval myths to one æsthetic law of loveliness, all tended to withdraw attention from the differences between paganism and Christianity, and to fix it on the "goodliness of that humanity wherein both find their harmony." (Symonds, *Renaissance in Italy*, volume iii. *The Fine Arts*, p. 8, Am. Ed.).

Moreover, these ancient statues were none the less honored because they were nude, as for instance were the Graces which a cardinal set up in his family chapel, and the Venuses which popes valued more than any crucifix. Naked figures were introduced by Signorelli before the end of the fifteenth century, into a painting of the Madonna, as they were later by Michael Angelo, into his Last Judgment, while the houses of wealthy Florentines were profusely ornamented with nudities destitute of religious meaning. Here was a wide departure, not only from ecclesiastical ideas of purity, but from that disparagement of the body hitherto characteristic of Christianity. Paul was then thought the author of "Bodily exercise profiteth little," as well as of "In my flesh dwelleth no good thing," "Our vile body," etc. The dislike of gymnastics, expressed in *Maccabees*, i., 14 and 15, had never been recalled canonically. Bathing, much insisted on by ancient Jews, Greeks, and Romans, almost went out of use until after the crusades. Monks, nuns, and hermits who never washed, or even looked at their bodies, were thought peculiarly holy. Thus the Church was committed to views of the body which Art showed to be puerile.

Then again even the professedly religious pictures often were only portraits of voluptuously beautiful women, notorious for profligacy. Raphael is not the only artist whose mistresses became Madonnas, and Leonardo da Vinci painted a Virgin from one of the Grand Duke's favorites, whose name was appended to the masterpiece. Such pictures did much to make intelligent church-goers irreligious.

No one understood the spiritual condition of the fifteenth century better than Savonarola, and he had many of its artistic productions burned publicly. A century later we find deep conviction of the irreligious tendency of Italian pictures expressed by Michael Angelo and Vittoria Colonna. (Clement, *Michael Angelo, Leonardo da Vinci, and Raphael*, p. 135.) The Puritans felt in the same way; and these people certainly knew more than any one can at present about the effect on themselves and their associates of the paintings and statues around them.

And, finally, that Art, while professing to serve the Church, should only make use of her to her ruin, was inevitable from the fact that their aims are irreconcilable. Art delights to honor physical beauty, and glorify this earthly life. The Church seeks to raise thought and feeling above worldly objects. She has said from the beginning, "Turn away mine eyes from beholding vanity." "Love not the world, neither the things that are in the world. If any man love the world, the love of the Father is not in him. For all that is in the world, the lust of the flesh, and the lust of the eyes, and the pride of life, is not of the Father, but is of the world." "Set your affection on things above, not on things which are on the earth." "Look not at the things which are seen, but at the things which are not seen." Art, on the other hand, speaks directly to the lust of the eyes, and says,

"Rejoice in the beauty you see around you. Be satisfied with what I show you here on earth." There is nothing in the New Testament to favor artistic culture, or love of natural beauty. Jesus speaks of the lilies of the field, but only to blame thought about attire. Paul would have us think of "Whatsoever things are lovely," but both context and classic usage show that he really refers to what is amiable. Biblical and medieval Christianity thought nothing lovely but piety and morality, looked at earth only as a step in the way to heaven, and scorned the body in order to save the soul. Thus the progress of art implied the decline of Christianity, as then understood. The change was for the moment unfavorable to purity, which, however, had not been very successfully cultivated by the Church. Morality could not thrive until the laws of Self-culture were brought into harmony with those of Purity, Justice, and Love.

And not only the artistic and literary, but the commercial activity of the fifteenth century involved disbelief in Christianity. "Blessed be ye poor, for yours is the kingdom of God." "But woe unto you that are rich, for ye have received your consolation." "Take therefore no thought for the morrow." "If thou wilt be perfect, go and sell that thou hast, and give to the poor." "Lay not up for yourselves treasures upon earth." "It is easier for a camel to go through the eye of a needle, than for a rich man to enter into the kingdom of God." Thus spake Jesus, and his words had been taken literally by ancient and medieval Christianity. The whole monastic system, and especially the great Franciscan order, was simply an attempt to follow the Gospel teaching of the superior holiness of poverty, and the peculiarly dangerous temptations involved in the possession of wealth. The early satirists had seldom done more than ridicule the monks and priests for striving to make money, blaming every one who did so. *Piers Plowman's Vision* is one of the first declarations of the intrinsic holiness of honest industry. It was long before the rights of merchants, bankers, and manufacturers were fully recognized by either literature, theology, or legislation. Usury, which then meant merely lending on interest, was considered sinful and criminal for centuries after the first advocate of its innocence was burned as a heretic in 1388. This necessary branch of business was quietly carried on, however, by the bank of Venice, established in 1171; by those of Barcelona and Genoa, whose dates are 1401 and 1407, and also by many individual Lombards and Florentines. The most powerful men of Florence, as well as of other cities in upper Italy, France, Germany, Flanders, and England, were bankers, merchants, and manufacturers, who treated the Church with sincere respect, as well as lavish generosity, but yet gave unconsciously an irresistible demonstration of the extravagance of some of her plainest precepts.

Commerce, art, and literature helped make the spirit of the age secular, and so did oceanic discovery. Nothing did more to show how worthy of study this earth is, and how little was known of it by the saints and sages of the past, than the discovery of America by Columbus, Friday, October 12, 1492. Diaz had reached the Cape of Good Hope in 1486; Vasco di Gama went on as far as India in 1498; the Cabots discovered North America in 1497; Balboa saw the Pacific in 1510; Cortez conquered Mexico in 1519, and Magellan set sail that very year to circumnavigate the globe. Spain and Portugal, which fitted out most of these expeditions, made larger gains commercially than intellectually, but the quickening influence was felt all over Europe.

Scholars, authors, printers, painters, sculptors, merchants, bankers, and navigators, all did something to make the ruling spirit at the beginning of the sixteenth century secular, but no one did so much as the popes. Papal history for more than two hundred years had been an almost unbroken series of scandals. The trials of Boniface and the Templars, the debaucheries at Avignon, the contests of the perjured usurpers who reigned there and at Rome in a rivalry not to be ended except by that great council which exposed the iniquity of John XXIII., and the steady resistance of his successors during the next fifty years to even moderate reform, had been followed by the reign, between 1464 and 1513, of five notoriously licentious, bloodthirsty, and perfidious tyrants. The first of them, Paul II., the persecutor of the philosophers, had openly violated the pledges with which he mounted the throne, and made no secret of his sensuality. Nor did Sixtus IV., who sold his offices openly, starved his subjects by a monopoly of wheat, had murder committed during public worship in Florence, sanctioned the entrance of the inquisition into Spain, as well as the expulsion of the Jews, put the archbishop of Carniola into the prison where he perished, for trying to call a second council of Basel, and died himself of rage at seeing peace return to Italy. Then came Innocent VIII., who openly violated his oath to rule constitutionally, publicly acknowledged his bastards, and loaded them with the wealth he gained by selling pardons for every sin. All previous scandals were surpassed when Alexander VI. turned the Vatican into a harem, looked with delight at gladiatorial combats among his own guards, stirred up unjust wars to aggrandize his atrocious son, betrayed his allies with an effrontery hitherto unknown, sold cardinals' hats openly, and poisoned brother clergymen for their wealth, until, as there is good reason to believe, he drank by mistake his own venom. Then, passing over the few days of Pius III., we have that drunken, sensual, and ambitious lover of war, Julius II., who would not have a book placed in the hand of his statue, but a sword, and who led in armor his soldiers to the sack of Mirandola. It was a great relief when these monsters were succeeded, in 1513, by Leo X.; but he really finished their work, by an utter indifference to religion, which made him sanction the publication of the books of Pomponatius and Erasmus, delight in licentious comedies which brought the worst of charges against the Church, give his main attention to theatricals, feasts, hunting, fishing, and the purchase of naked statues and pagan manuscripts (objects for which he freely spent the profits of the sale of indulgences,) favor a cardinal who advised a bishop not to read Paul's epistles lest their barbarisms should hurt his style, permit preachers to speak of God as Jupiter Optimus Maximus, of the Virgin as a Goddess, as well as of the popes and saints as Gods, and finally suffer himself by mere negligence to die without the sacraments. No one was thought a man of culture who did not scoff at the doctrines of the Church. Priests at the altar delighted in burlesquing the formula of consecration at the communion, and saying, "Bread thou art; bread thou shalt remain!" Even the names of the people were becoming pagan, as is shown by the frequent occurrence of Cæsar, Hector, Achilles, Lucretia, Portia, and Hippolyta. We have seen that Machiavelli believed Catholicism to have been destroyed in Italy. Thus the sixteenth century opened more propitiously for the growth of free thought than any of its predecessors for more than twelve hundred years. No wonder that Leo and his successors were unable to suppress the Reformation. But why did Germany, and not Italy, take the lead in this movement, and why was it most active in countries north of the Alps? This is the question to be answered in the remainder of the chapter.

IV.

The problem, at first, seems all the darker because medieval habits of thought lingered nearly a century longer in Germany, France, England, and the Netherlands, than in Italy, whither northern scholars came to study Greek and Latin at the beginning of the sixteenth century.

Poggio could find no good books in England in 1420, not even in the monasteries, where there were many men given to sensuality, but very few lovers of learning, and those caring for little but quibbles and sophisms. Chaucer found no worthy successor, and all culture languished during the Wars of the Roses, which lasted until 1485. The first English book, the *Game of Chess*, was printed by Caxton, in 1474, and this century reared Eton, King's, Queen's, and St. John's Colleges at Cambridge, and Lincoln, All Souls', and Magdalen at Oxford. The Cabots had begun their discoveries before 1500. Not until late in the sixteenth century did the English renaissance reach its height. Among its best friends in the fifteenth were the merchants who had commercial treaties made with Spain, Flanders, the Hanse towns, Brittany, Florence, and other cities of Italy, with all which places, as well as with Scotland and Ireland, trade was brisk.

Rather before 1450, Bishop Pecock, whose name accords well with his vanity, fell unawares into heresy in his attempt to take more reasonable ground than the Lollards. Their objections to all ceremonies not commanded by the Bible, he met substantially as follows: "It does not belong to Holy Scripture to be the foundation for any practice or belief which the reason of man is able to find out naturally." (*Repressor of overmuch blaming the Clergy, page* 10). "All knowledge of God's moral law may be had from reason; and all the virtues may thus be known sufficiently." (*Repressor*, pp. 12 and 13). "Where doth Holy Scripture give a hundredth part as much about matrimony as my book, all whose teaching is little enough?" (*Repressor*, p. 15.) "Before any positive law was given by Abraham or Moses, people were bound to all the moral truths which had been learned from natural reason." (*Repressor*, p. 18). "The moral law still abiding among Christians is not founded in Holy Scripture, but in that book which was written in men's souls by the finger of God, before the days of Moses and Jesus." (*Repressor*, p. 20).

"And if there be any seeming discord between the words written in the outward book of Holy Scripture and the judgment of reason, written in man's soul and heart, the word so written outwardly ought to be expounded and interpreted and made to accord with the judgment of reason in the matter, and this judgment should not be made to agree with the outward writing in the Bible or any where else." (*Repressor*, p. 25–6).

"If any man be afeard, lest he trespass against God, if he think over little of the outward authority of the Old Testament and of the New, I ask why he is not afeard, lest he make over little of the inward scripture of the law of nature, written by God himself in man's soul, when he made it in his own image." (*Repressor*, p. 51–2). "Let Holy Scripture abide within its own limits, and not enter the rights of the law of nature, or usurp that fundamental authority which belongs to moral philosophy." (*Repressor*, p. 70). "Holy Scripture, as the law of faith, is not so worthy in itself, nor so necessary and profitable unto man, as is the moral law decreed by reason." (*Repressor*, p. 84).

Such advanced ground had not yet been taken by any Christian teacher, except Raymond of Sabunde, or Sabieude, a medical professor at Toulouse, who said, about 1435, of the Book of Nature, "This is the source and fountain of all truth, so that he who has it needs no other." "It does not rest on the authority of the Scriptures, but confirms them." "It cannot be falsified or wrongly interpreted, neither can it make any one heretical, but the second book, namely, the Bible, may be falsified and misunderstood. Yet they both have the same author and agree among themselves." (Owen, *Evenings with the Skeptics*, vol. ii).

Raymond's *Liber Creaturarum* attracted little notice before the middle of the next century, and does not seem to have been known to Pecock, who soared higher than any one else had done for twelve hundred years, when he said, in answer to the Lollard doctrine, that whatever is clearly taught in the Bible should be admitted without discussion :

"This is like the law of Mohammed, where it is most unreasonable." (*Repressor*, p. 99). "No truth can be known without argument." (*Repressor*, p. 97). "A conclusion of belief is not worthy of being held true, if it can not be sustained by proper evidence, and if sufficient answer can not be given to all objections which may be made against it. God forbid that any man should think any doctrine ought to be held true, when it could be proved false by any argument." (*Repressor*, p. 98.) "The more any truth, whether of faith or not, be brought under examination by discussion, the more true and the more clearly true it shall be seen to be." (*Repressor*, p. 99.)

Pecock makes an exception of doctrines plainly revealed, for instance, the incarnation, but there is no other reservation in favor of church authority, which in fact had never yet been set aside so boldly in the name of free discussion. And the book we are considering actually dares to present, as ground for rejecting the legend, quoted by Langland, and very dear to the Lollards, that when Constantine gave political power to the pope, an angel was heard crying aloud, " This day is poison poured into the Church," an elaborate series of arguments proving that this emperor made no such gift. (*Repressor*, pp. 350–66.) This was directly against all ecclesiastical authority, especially that of the *False Decretals*, exposure of which but a few years before had nearly sent Laurentius Valla to the stake. The bishop's wish to argue only from sound premises also led him to admit, as this Italian scholar had done, that the Apostles did not write the Creed which still bears their name. This view is set forth in the *Book of Faith*, which was published like the *Repressor*, about 1456, and which denied the infallibility of councils. For these and other heresies the aged bishop was expelled from the House of Lords shortly before November 11, 1457, when he recanted, because the archbishop of Canterbury threatened him with the stake. On Sunday, December 4, he appeared in full pontificals at Paul's Cross, and read his abjuration, while his books were burned. The rest of his life he spent in a convent-dungeon, where he could see no visitors or have pen, ink, or paper. Nearly three centuries elapsed before any pains were taken to show how far he had advanced, the *Repressor* was not printed before 1860, and the greater part of the *Book of Faith* is still like his other works extant only in manuscript. Few men have been so plainly in advance of their age, and seldom has the Church shown herself so decidedly hostile to liberty of thought. We may regret his cowardice, but we must thank England for being the first, not only to establish biblical authority, but to show how it could be struck down when it had served its end.

France suffered greatly during the fourteenth and fifteenth centuries from civil and foreign wars, amid which we find the earliest of professional authoresses, Christine de Pisan, pleading for peace with an earnestness which does not hinder her delight in the achievements of Joan of Arc. Early in this century we hear Baunet lamenting the slaughter of brother by brother on account of differences of faith, blaming the pride, lust and avarice of Rome for all the strife, and prophesying that the nations who see her sins will soon break her yoke. Strong opposition to the temporal power of the pope is expressed by the authors of the *Good Shepherd* and the *Orchard Vision*, the former of which poems insists that kings ought to live for their people, while the latter says : " No unbeliever should be forced by war or in any other way to come to the Catholic faith; and we ought not to fight against those infidels who wish to be at peace with us, but only against those who attack us." A little later, about 1450, that peculiarly powerful propagandist, the theater, complained, in the pastoral comedy, *Better than Before, Mieulx que Devant*, of the weight of the taxes, as well as the outrages committed by the recently disbanded soldiers, against whom the people are exhorted to take up arms. In 1496, the farce of the *Miller, Le Munyer*, brought before French audiences that character familiar to the readers of Boccaccio, the adulterous parish-priest. These two dramas are still extant ; but no one knows how many similar ones of this period have passed away after doing their part in emancipating France. In the same cause labored many of the popular preachers, for instance Maillard, who when that gloomy tyrant, Louis XI., threatened to throw him into the Seine, answered : " Tell his Majesty that I can go to Heaven more rapidly by water than he can with his post-horses."

Neither of these two countries produced any artists of importance during the period covered by this chapter; and only at its close can Germany show Albert Durer and Peter Vischer, while the invention of oil-painting by the Van Eycks, 1410–20, proved rather unproductive in Flanders ; though this country was then advancing toward the height of prosperity, which she reached before 1470.

Printing with movable types is said to have been invented by Koster at Haarlem before 1430, but this whole story is very improbable, and it is certain that not a single book of importance was published there before 1483. The credit of setting this great servant of thought successfully to work belongs to Gutenberg, who, in all probability, discovered it independently. The only doubt is whether the presses he had set up in Strasburg as early as 1436 were used in printing or only in his ostensible business of making looking-glasses, that is whether the first use of movable metal types was not at Mainz, where he and Faust issued in 1454 the earliest printed work extant, which bears a date, a sheet of papal *Letters of Indulgence,* and where they were then working on a large and superbly executed Bible, which appeared about 1455, and was certainly the first printed book of any size. The stories of persecution of these early printers by the monks do not appear to be founded on fact. Before the end of the century presses had been set up without any opposition of importance in Strasburg, Mainz, Cologne, Munich, Bamberg, Vienna, Basel, Lubeck, Ghent, Brussels, Bruges, Haarlem, Cracow, Stockholm, Copenhagen, Paris, Lyons, Troyes, Rouen, Oxford, London, seventy cities of Italy, and many other places. A dozen editions of the Bible in German appeared before 1500, with other versions in modern languages.

No original book seems to have appeared in Germany before Sebastian Brandt's *Narrenschiff*, or *Ship of Fools,* printed in Basel in 1494, and mainly important for the boldness with which it was used by Geiler of Kaiserberg, a popular preacher who said : "I shall be dead when the reformers come ; but many of you will live to see the building crumble." An extremely anti-clerical *Reynard the Fox*, in Low German, appeared in 1498. I know of nothing by Felix Hemmerlein, a classical scholar, who died about 1464, in prison for censuring the clergy. And the writings of the learned Gregory Heimburg, who was excommunicated and exiled in 1461 for maintaining that it was heresy in the pope to place himself above a general council, and that Jesus had given only spiritual, but not temporal, power to the Apostles and their successors, were not printed before 1595. The opening of the university of Heidelberg, in 1386, was followed during the next hundred years by those of Cologne, Erfurt, Würzburg, Leipsic, Rostock, Greifswald, Freiburg, Treves, Tübingen and Mainz, besides Louvain and Upsala, all at first claimed by scholasticism, but destined ere long to be focuses of the new culture, in whose interest better schools than had been hitherto in use, especially for girls, were now opened in many cities.

Nothing north of the Alps did more to break up medieval habits of thought than the terrible defeats which Germany and French chivalry suffered during the fourteenth and fifteenth centuries from Flemish artisans and Swiss, English, Bohemian, and Saxon peasants. The defeats of King Philip the Fair at Courtrai, 1302; of the dukes of Austria at Morgarten and Sempach, 1315 and 1396; of the nobility of France at Crecy and Agincourt, 1346 and 1415; of five hosts of German crusaders in Bohemia, between 1420 and 1426, and of Charles the Bold, duke of Burgundy, at Granson, Morat, and Nancy, 1476 and '77; were followed by that of King John of Denmark, on February 17, 1500, in the Pass of Hemmingstadt. Here the Ditmarsh peasants, who have had too little notice from historians, gained such a signal victory over an army twice their numbers, and composed mainly of German knights, that they were left to live free under magistrates of their own choice until 1559, as they had done from time immemorial. Less fortunate was Hans Boheim, a young peasant prophet, under Hussite or Mystic teachers, who collected 20,000 armed followers near Würzburg, in 1476, in order to put down popes and emperors, taxes and inequalities of property, so that all men might live like brothers, but who was promptly burned alive by the bishop. Perhaps his plans have been as much misrepresented as are Jack Cade's in *Henry VI*. The English rebel, who was really a physician named John Aylmer, tried in 1450 to reform fifteen grievances, as follows: Kent was to be turned into a forest. The king lived on the commons. Provisions taken for the royal household were not paid for. Justice was denied the poor. Prisoners were confined without trial. Poor men's lands were taken illegally. Traitors of high rank went unpunished. Taxes were collected in ways needlessly burdensome. Sheriffs and bailiffs extorted fees unsanctioned by law, a charge made three times in various forms. Arrests were made without legal warrant. Elections for Parliament were interfered with by men of rank. Members of Parliament took bribes. The courts of justice were held in places difficult of access. These were Cade's demands, according to Holinshed, who says that the citizens of London took his side until they found that his men would not obey his command to abstain from pillage. The closer we look at the popular insurrections in England, France, and Germany, the more reason we shall find to regret that they did not succeed like those in Switzerland. But all these movements did something to make bishops, nobles, kings, and popes see that they could not hope to hold their power much longer without the popular consent.

v.

With the sixteenth century began an unprecedented literary activity in France, Germany, Switzerland, England, and the Netherlands. The reign of Louis XII. from 1498 to 1515, was singularly favorable to authorship, on account not only of his personal tolerance, which permitted the actor of the monologue, still known as the *Passing Pilgrim, Le Pélerin Passant*, to ridicule the royal avarice and other faults in high places, but also of his political hostility to Pope Julius II. whom he tried to depose at the council of Pisa in 1511, when he struck medals saying, "I will destroy the very name of Rome," "Perdam Babylonis nomen." To this period belongs the farce in which Poverty complains that Nobility and Clergy make her wash their dirty linen, stained with all the vices, but will pay her nothing, as well as that in which when the Old World goes to sleep, and a party of fools, led by the Church, try to build a new one, Chivalry proposes that it be founded on Chastity, but his fellow jesters exclaim, "Chastity and the Church are not acquainted." The most original and fertile of early French satirists, Gringoire, wrote in 1510 that censure of the papal fondness for war, called the *Hope of Peace from the Arts of certain Popes*, and also that attack on the pontiff who called himself "Servus Servorum," *la Chasse der Cerf des Cerfs*. During the carnival of 1511 was acted his *Jest of the Prince of Fools, Jeu du Prince des Sotz*. This personage, then well known on the stage, and here typifying the king of France, calls together his nobles, prelates, and burghers to help him resist the Church, whose temporal power is declared incompatible with peace. The bishops acquiesce, especially as they are reminded how many of them keep mistresses behind their curtains, instead of prayer books. The commons object to levying war against St. Peter's throne. A woman who calls herself "Holy Church," enters and confesses that she has lost her most useful fool, Faith. The bishops join her, and fight with her against the nobles, who say, "Our Mother has turned soldier!" The prince bids his servants find out who this sanctified enemy really is, and she is seen to be "Mother Folly" in disguise, "*La Mère Sotte.*" The commons exclaim with delight, "It is not Mother Church who makes war upon us, but only Mother Folly!"

On the death of the bloody Julius, 1513, appeared a satire which was probably written by Faustus Andrelini of Forli, whose title of poet laureate had been gained by a long residence in France, and whose initials, F. A. F., are on the title-page. Some critics have ascribed it to Erasmus and Hutten, both of whom disclaimed it, and neither of whom took its strong position in favor of councils. At all events, an abridged version may here be given with propriety, especially as it has never been translated into English, though it was published in German as early as 1520, and occasionally reprinted afterwards.

Pope Julius II. (Before the gate of Heaven.)—What is the trouble? Don't the gate open? I think the lock has been changed, or is out of order.

Attendant Genius.—See if you have the right key? Why did you bring only that of your money chest?

Julius.—I never had any other, and don't see the need of any.

Genius.—Neither do I, but meantime we are shut out.

Julius.—My blood boils. (*Beats the gate*). Halloo! Halloo! Open the door!

Peter. (*within.*)—It is well the gate is of adamant, or it would be broken down. There must be some giant here.

What a stench! (*Looks out at a window*). Who are you? What do you want?

Julius.—Open the gate! If you did your duty, you would come out to meet me with all the heavenly glory.

Peter.—You are domineering enough. Tell me who you are.

Julius.—As if you could not see for yourself.

Peter.—I see such a sight as was never seen here before.

Julius.—You are blind, or you would know this key, and the triple crown, and the jeweled robe.

Peter.—I see a silver key, very unlike those given me by the true Shepherd, Christ. But what a crown! No one ever tried to enter here with it. And your cloak is nothing to me, who trampled on gems and gold. I see the marks of my namesake, Simon the Sorcerer.

Julius.—You had better stop jesting, I am Julius. You know what P. M. means?

Peter.—Pestis Magnus, I suppose.

Genius.—Ha! ha! He's hit it.

Julius.—Pontifex Maximus.

Peter.—You may be thrice mightiest, but you can not come in, unless you are saintly.

Julius.—Then open the door, impudence! You are only a saint, but I am most saintly in all my bulls—six thousand of them.

Peter.—Do you think it makes no difference whether you are called saintly, or whether you are so? But who are your companions? There are about 20,000, and not one looks like a Christian. How they smell of gunpowder! What a band of robbers! How fierce you look, yourself, and how plain it is that you have lived in lust! I suspect you are that most noxious heathen, Julius Cæsar, returning from hell.

Julius.—Ma—— desi——.

Peter.—What does he say?

Genius.—He is angry. When he makes such a noise, all the cardinals run. They have felt his cudgel, especially when he was drinking.

Julius.—Will you open the gate, or do you want it broken down? I will hurl a thunder-bolt of excommunication at you. I have a bull ready.

Peter.—Bull? Excommunication? Never did I hear such words from Christ!

Julius.—I am still pope, for the cardinals are quarreling over my successor. Open the door!

Peter.—Not until you tell your merits. Have you excelled in teaching?

Julius.—No, I was too busy with war.

Peter.—Has your example led many to Christ?

Genius.—Very many to hell.

Peter.—Have you distinguished yourself by miracles?

Julius.—You speak of what is obsolete.

Peter.—Have you prayed without ceasing?

Julius.—Nonsense!

Peter.—Have you grown lean in fasting and watching?

Genius.—You are wasting your time.

Julius.—I made myself cardinal by my courage, but you were frightened at the voice of a girl. I never gave up hope of the papacy, and at last I gained it by the favor of France, and the power of money. Then I made myself richer than Crassus by selling benefices and other offices. I conquered Bologna, Venice, and Ferrara. Finally I drove the French out of Italy. There is not a king in Christendom whom I have not stirred up to war, and all the treaties which kept them in peace I have broken. My triumphs have been most applauded, and my buildings most magnificent. All this is not owing to my birth, for I don't know who my father was, nor to my education, for I never had any, nor to my popularity, for every body hates me.

Peter.—To what then?

Julius.—To my courage and my money.

Peter.—I never heard any thing like it.—But who are those companions, so covered with scars?

Julius.—My soldiers. I promised them in my bulls that they would fly straight into heaven.

Peter.—Some of them came before with those bulls.

Julius.—And did not you let them in?

Peter.—I? Not one of them! Christ has told me not to open these doors to those who bring bulls heavy with lead, but to those who have fed the hungry, clothed the naked, and sheltered the stranger. Many who have prophesied in his name, and cast out devils, and done many wonderful works, will be shut out; and do you think those are to be let in who only bring a bull in the name of Julius?—But why do you wear a sword?

Julius.—That belongs to a pope. Would you have me go to war without one?

Peter.—I had only the sword of the Spirit, which is the word of God.

Julius.—Malchus does not say so, whose ear you cut of.

Peter.—To defend my master. He bade me sheathe the sword, because war is not proper for Christians. But do men make themselves popes as you did?

Julius.—Seldom otherwise.

Peter.—I should not have let any one become a deacon thus. But what had those Venetians done whom you fought against?

Julius.—They had invaded your patrimony.

Peter.—My patrimony? I left all and followed Christ. And who was your enemy at Ferrara?

Julius.—The son-in-law of that vicar of Christ, Alexander.

Peter.—What! do popes have wives and children?

Julius.—No wives, but children certainly.

Peter.—Have not such things made a council necessary?

Julius.—When I became a pope I had to swear that I would call one, but I absolved myself from my oath. My enemies tried to assemble one and depose me, but popes can never be dethroned.

Peter.—Not for murder?

Julius.—Not for parricide.

Peter.—Nor for lewdness? Nor for blasphemy?

Julius.—No, indeed. Add six hundred other sins. A pope is not to be dethroned for them.

Peter.—A new honor, if he alone may sin and not be punished. Is there nothing for which he can be deposed?

Julius.—Yes. For heresy; but he alone can say what this is.

Peter.—Why do popes fear councils so much?

Julius.—You might as well ask why kings fear parliaments. But their council came to naught. Times have changed since your day. How I wish you could have seen me carried in my golden chair by my soldiers, and heard the cannons! What should you have thought then?

Peter.—That I saw the curse of the Church and the enemy of Christ. He came down from heaven, not to teach philosophy, but to make men scorn pleasure and trample on wealth. You have said a blessing over others, and are yourself accursed. You would open heaven for other men, and are yourself shut out.

Julius.—Then you won't open the gate?

Peter.—To any one else rather than to such a pest. Would you have my advice? Take your men and money, and build yourself a paradise, but take care the devils don't storm it.

Julius.—I have some months more of authority, and that will be enough to conquer you. The sixty thousand souls that died in my wars will follow me.

Peter.—O miserable Church! Are the other bishops like him?

Genius.—Most of them.

Peter.—Then no wonder that so few souls enter here.

That this powerful satire was written in Germany is particularly unlikely, because the emperor had finally become the ally of Julius against the French, and only in manuscript could Hutten circulate his Latin epigrams deriding this pope for his offers to sell a heaven which he had no right to enter, advising men to rob, murder, and ravish, because any one can make himself righteous cheaply at Rome, where God himself is sold, and wondering what will become of the guilty city when Germany opens her eyes. This knightly author did succeed in publishing, in 1517, his *Phalarismus*, a comparison of the duke of Würtemburg with the classic tyrants, and probably took part about this time in the famous *Letters of Obscure Men* (*Epistulæ Obscurorum Virorum*). In 1509, a converted Jew, named Pfefferkorn, had attempted, in concert with the Cologne Dominicans, to destroy Hebrew literature, especially the Talmud. Reuchlin, the founder of Christian study of the Old Testament, published a protest, which was publicly burned at Cologne and Mainz, and which nearly caused his condemnation as a heretic. Learned men in German, French, Italian, and English cities generally took his side, and welcomed the *Letters* published in 1516, and purporting to be written by his opponents, who were made to confess their ignorance, stupidity, and sensuality in the worst possible Latin. One of them has taken off his hat to Jews whom he supposed to be masters of arts, and asks if he must go to the pope to get absolved. Another confesses that there is no justice to be had at Rome without money, and quotes a saying of Wympheling (possibly the author of a *Defense of the Council of Basel*, written by the emperor's order, and published in 1515), to the effect that there are three kinds of monks—first, the holy and useful, who are all in heaven; second, the harmless, who are in pictures; and third, the living ones who do much mischief through their pride as well as their fondness for women. The popularity of this work was, I suspect, largely due to the circumstances which called it forth.

Hutten is supposed to have taken some share, especially in the second part, published in 1517; but the originator appears to have been Jäger, or Crotus Rubianus, as he is usually called, according to the custom then prevalent of translating German names into Latin and Greek ones of similar meaning. Thus Reuchlin was known as Capnio, and it is only as Celtes that we hear of Pickel, or Meissel, who did good service near the close of the fifteenth century in starting literary societies, and who in his Odes, published 1513, says: "You wonder why I do not move my lips in church. There is a Divinity in my heart. You wonder why I go so seldom. God is within us. No need for me to gaze upon His painted image in the temple. You ask why I love the free fields, and the warm sun. Here in Nature shines the glorious image of the Almighty. Here I see His worthiest temple."

Only in letters, which could not be published before the

seventeenth century, did Muth, or Mudt, a canon at Gotha, who called himself, partially in reference to his red hair, Mutianus Rufus, venture to say: "What did men do in the many centuries before the birth of Christ? Did they wander about, wrapped in thick darkness of ignorance, or did they enjoy bliss and truth? I will tell thee my opinion. The religion of Christ did not begin with his becoming man, but was before all the centuries. For what is the true Christ but that divine wisdom which was not given to the Jews alone in the narrow land of Syria, but also to the Greeks, and Romans, and Germans, though they had different religions? Who is our Saviour? Justice, peace, and joy. That is the Christ which has come down from Heaven." "The law of God, which enlightens the soul, has two chapters, love God, and love all men as thyself. This is the law of God, not written on stone or parchment, but poured by the highest teacher into our hearts." "The true body of Christ is peace, nor is there a holier sacrament than that of mutual love." "Not wrong are those Moslems who say that Jesus was never crucified. The real Christ is a spirit not to be seen or touched." "In the Koran we read, 'He who worships the Eternal God, and lives virtuously, wins Paradise, be he Jew, Christian, or Moslem.'" "It is by an upright life that God is honored, and not by change of raiment; for the only true worship of God consists in abstaining from vice. He is religious who has a pure heart; all the rest is smoke." "Only fools seek salvation in fasting." "Jonah's whale was only a bath-house with this sign; and his gourd was a bathing hat. Yet more curious things occur to me, but I can not tell them." "We must never tell our secrets, or shake the people's faith, without which the emperor could not maintain the State, or the pope the Church, or we ourselves our property, but every thing would go back to chaos." "There is one God and one Goddess, but many shapes and names, Jupiter, the Sun, Apollo, Moses, or Christ; Diana, Mother Earth, or Mary. But do not reveal this. Keep it secret, like the mysteries of Eleusis."

Among Germans who kept their original names, one of the most interesting, besides Hutten, is Bebel, who, in 1505, published his *Triumph of Venus*, among whose votaries the first place is given to the begging friars, and the second to the popes, who have wrecked Peter's ship. Next year appeared his *Facetiæ*, a collection of stories making fun of the Church. Thus a student finds his doubts of the Trinity so ill-received by a priest that he says: "Oh, well, I don't insist on my opinion. Rather than make acquaintance with the fire, I am willing to believe in a Quaternity." Two lansquenets on being refused admission by Peter, say: "Why should the wolf blame the fox? You denied your Lord three times. None of us ever did that." Then Peter is so ashamed that he lets them in. A monk stays alone with a dying man, until he is so far gone as to assent to every word. Then he calls in the son, and asks, "Have you bequeathed this to our Order?" "And this?" "And this?" The dying man nods at every question. At last his son says, "Father, shall I kick the brother down stairs?" The usual nod is given, and out he goes. Another monk says he has vowed, "Poverty when I bathe, obedience when I eat, chastity when I am in church."

Among the most original and daring thinkers of the century, was Cornelius Agrippa. He was but twenty-three when, in 1509, he became professor at Dôle, near Dijon and Besançon, and began at once to give public lectures in favor of the Cabalistic philosophy, which had already been espoused by Reuchlin. This system, mainly inportant as setting up an authority independent of Bible or Church, is fully expounded in Agrippa's *De Occulta Philosophia*. The three books composing this work give, first, the Neo-Platonic fancies about planetary influences, magic virtues of plants and jewels, etc., then the Pythagorean superstitions about sacred numbers, and finally the rabbinical dreams about the power of holy names to rule angels and demons. That the bigotry of the monks prevented him from publishing this work before 1531, or continuing his lectures, need not surprise, or greatly distress us.

It was certainly unfortunate that persecution and poverty forced Agrippa to wait twenty years before printing an essay which even when it did appear, 1529, seems to have been by far the earliest plea in favor of the emancipation of women, unless this title be given to Plato's *Republic.* The little treatise, *De Nobilitate et Præcellentia Fœminei Sexus,* still extant in fourteen pages of closely printed Latin, begins by distinctly asserting that there is no sex in souls. " Eandem ipsa mulier sortita est mentem." Woman, rather than man, is then declared to be the latest and noblest work of God. "Mulier autem fuit postremum Dei opus introducta a Deo in hunc mundum, velut ejus regina." Female superiority is further supported by many scriptural, historical, mythological and quasi-scientific arguments, a good summary of which may be found in Morley's *Life of Cornelius Agrippa* (volume 1, pp. 98–110.) Paul's command that "women keep silence in the churches," is set aside as merely temporary. Of Joan of Arc, Agrippa says, "Who is able to praise sufficiently that most noble, though low-born, girl, who, when the English occupied France, took up arms like an Amazon, and, leading the van herself, fought so vigorously and successfully as to conquer the invaders in many battles, and restore the kingdom to the French?" Much indignation is expressed against the injustice by which "Women are forbidden to be literary." Other fine passages, showing how much needed still to be done before one-half of the world could begin to share what little liberty had been already gained for the other half, are translated by Morley as follows : " The tyranny of men, prevailing over divine rights and the laws of nature, slays by law the liberty of women, abolishes it by use and custom, extinguishes it by education. For the woman as soon as she is born, is, from her earliest years, detained at home in idleness, and, as if destitute of capacity for higher occupations, is permitted to conceive of nothing beyond needle and thread. Then, when she has attained years of puberty, she is delivered over to the jealous empire of a man, or shut up forever in a shop of vestals. The law also forbids her to fill public offices ; no prudence entitles her to plead in open court," etc. Women are also said to be treated by the men as conquered by the conquerors, not by any divine necessity, or for any reason, but according to custom, education, fortune, and the tyrant's opportunity.

The man who had the intelligence and gallantry to write thus against that subjection of women, which is still the main foundation of ecclesiastical oppression, was soon to be seen serving in arms against Julius II., and sitting, in 1511, among the fathers of the anti-papal council at Pisa, where the populace mobbed the reformers. He made peace with Leo X., but new storms were soon to gather around his path.

England, too, had her heroes. When the Convocation of the clergy met to punish heresy, Colet, dean of St. Paul's and founder of its school, preached in the cathedral, on February 6, 1512, a sermon which was at once published in both Latin and English, and which ascribed all the trouble to such plain facts as that the priests cared more for sensual pleasure than any thing else, and were blinded by covetousness. Thus was opened the session in which the bishop of London, on being asked for texts commanding that heretics be put to death, quoted, "Thou shalt not suffer a witch to live" (*Exodus*, xxii., 18); and also, "A man that is an heretic after the first and second admonition, reject," (*Titus* III., 10). The last word of the latter verse in the Latin version, *Devita*, he supposed to mean "deprive of life." A year later, on Good Friday, Colet preached in favor of peace, to Henry VIII., who was then making war with the pope against France. The dean used often to say, "Keep to the Bible and the Apostles' Creed, and let doctors, if they like, dispute about the rest." Moses had, he thought, accommodated what he said of the creation to the prejudices of the Hebrews. And even the *Epistles* of Paul seemed to him to grow mean as he admired the majesty of Christ.

His friend, Thomas More, was but twenty-four, when he persuaded Parliament to reject an exorbitant demand of Henry VII., who had his father fined and imprisoned in consequence. Six years later, in 1510, he spoke of Savonarola as a man of God, in his translation of Pico's Life and Works into English. In that peculiarly productive year, 1516, appeared his *Utopia*, which was translated within thirty-five years into German,

Italian, French, and English. In this ideal island, whose name means *Nowhere*, there are no lawyers or monks, property is held in common, nobody works more than six hours, but nobody is idle, every child is educated, the priests are few in number, and either married men or widower; the king is chosen by the subjects, and deposed, if he tries to be a tyrant; other magistrates are elected annually; every one is allowed, not only to hold what religion he pleases without fear of punishment, but to urge others to join it, provided that he use no reproaches or violence, for which offenses he would be liable to banishment or penal servitude. Unbelievers in God and immortality are excluded from office, and forbidden to argue, except with priests, but are not molested otherwise. The true object of life is declared to be earthly happiness, and the Christian monks and priests are repeatedly condemned as useless idlers.

The leader of the Northern Renaissance, Erasmus of Rotterdam, would still be the most readable author of his age, if he had not written exclusively in Latin. His *Praise of Folly*, and his *Colloquies*, lose but little by translation, however, and would justify Charles Reade's calling him "the heaven-born dramatist of his century," if this period be understood as beginning with his birth in 1466 or 7. He was a skeptic but not an unbeliever, and the latter fact gives much weight to his censures of the Church. His *De Contemptu Mundi*, written before 1490, calls the monasteries schools of vice, where no one can keep pure. His own experience also led him to see that they were bad places for study, as he often says in his letters, where he also recommends that parish priests should be permitted to marry, and monks and nuns to recall their vows. His *Adages*, or *Proverbs*, which first appeared in 1500, and grew to great bulk in successive editions, say: "Many of the monks remind you of Paul, with their long beards, pale faces, dark robes, and austere looks. Look within and you will find only a glutton, a vagabond, a rake, or a robber." "The bishops who hold the first rank are often the least worthy of the name. Many a prelate is only a soldier, a merchant, or a despotic prince." "The Vicar of Christ should not be like Cæsar or Alexander, Crassus or Xerxes, those crowned brigands." "What is there in common between Christ and Belial, the miter and the helmet?" "How can he who makes money the basis of his power preach scorn of riches?" "A heavenly-minded man should not burden himself with earthly rule." "Christian princes are more tyrannical than any pagans were, but even this is not so damnable as it is for the priests, who ought to despise money and give freely what they have freely received, to do nothing without pay. You can not become a Christian by baptism, unless you pay for it. Neither can you be married. Confessions are heard only in hope of reward, and the mass is celebrated for hire. The priests will not sing or pray gratis. Scarcely will they pronounce a benediction, unless something is given them. Even their preaching is stained by greed. Nor, finally, will the body of Christ be offered you without a fee. I need not speak of what great harvests come from dispensations, indulgences, etc. Heathens could be buried gratis. Among Christians the dead can not be covered with earth, until a bargain has been made with the priest, and the higher the price the more honorable is the place of burial." Another striking passage is to the effect that kings are justly compared to the eagle, which is not only the most cruel but the most useless and hateful of birds.

The same free spirit marks that protest in favor of the superior sanctity of morality over ceremonies, the *Handbook of a Christian Soldier*, which was further hostile to the power of the priesthood in its denial of the materiality of hell. This book appeared in 1502, and was followed ten years later by the *Praise of Folly*, which passed through twenty-seven editions during the life of Erasmus, and was speedily translated out of the original Latin into the principal modern languages. Its goddess boasts of her sway, over the theologians who think the Church will fall unless propped up with syllogisms, over confessors who say that every sin can be paid for in money, over monks who deem it the height of piety to be unable to read and the worst of sins to break their own rules, while they fail to fulfill Christ's chief command, to love one another; and over godless popes, who destroy souls by their pestilential example and think of nothing but war, which is most unchristian. This censure on the reigning pontiff, Julius II., was repeated five years later in the *Complaint of Peace*. No wonder that the *Praise of Folly* soon came under papal censure, especially as its heroine, after quoting such texts as, "We are fools for Christ's sake," "The foolishness of God is wiser than men," "God hath chosen the foolish things of the world to confound the wise, "Thou hast hid these things from the wise and prudent," etc., says : "Christianity seems to have some likeness to folly, but none at all to wisdom. This is seen in the pleasure children, old people, women, and fools take therein. Moreover the founders of religions have always been men of great simplicity and strong hostility to knowledge. And what can be more silly than to give up one's property, take no notice of insults, make no difference between friend and foe, despise pleasure, and live on fasting, watching, tears, and labor, so as to wish for death?"

That Erasmus did not undervalue the New Testament is plain, not only from the desire he often expresses to have it read by all men in their own tongue, but from the pains he took to make the original text for the first time accessible to readers generally in 1516. He ventured, however, to omit the famous text about the three heavenly witnesses, which was not in his manuscripts, but which he unwillingly inserted afterward, as well as to mention that the Apostles and Evangelists wrote a barbarous Greek, quoted the Old Testament inaccurately, attributed to Abraham (in *Acts* VII., 16) what was really done by Jacob, spoke of a passage in *Zechariah* as if it were in *Jeremiah* (*Matthew* XXVII., 9) and made Jesus mistake the name of a high priest. (Compare *Mark* II., 26 with I. *Samuel* XXII., 1). Even then Erasmus expressed doubts of the authenticity of *Revelation*, as he did later of other parts of the New Testament, every manuscript of which he knew contained some errors. His treatment of texts appealed to for trinitarianism was so impartial, that he was nicknamed Ariasmus and Errasmus. The latter appellation was also due to some hasty work in editing the Fathers, with whom he began by publishing Jerome in 1516. This year, which was that of Machiavelli's Prince, also saw the appearance of his own book with a similar title, but with the aim to teaching kings to govern for their people's good. The exact position of Erasmus will be described when he can be contrasted with Luther. Suffice it for the present to call him an Abelard without any Heloise, and with a fondness for practical morality instead of metaphysics.

Holland had already produced a far bolder thinker, Herman Rysswick, who in 1502 was sentenced to imprisonment for life for firmly maintaining that the world has existed from all eternity, and never been created, what Moses says to that effect being merely a dream; that there is no hell and no other life than this; that Aristotle and Averroes have come nearer than any one else to the truth; that Jesus Christ was a visionary who has deluded the simple and brought the whole world into misery; that all he taught is contrary to reason; that he is not the Son of God; that his coming was not needed for our salvation; and that the Bible is fiction. In 1512 he escaped from prison and wrote several books, but was burned to death with them, steadfast to the end.

The Northern Renaissance, while as hostile to Rome as the Southern, was generally more favorable to the independent growth of religion and morality. Germany in particular showed a remarkably strong faith in a Christianity outside of the Church, as will be more fully seen when we come to speak of her Mystics.

VI.

The most famous martyr of this period for free speech, though no free-thinker, was Savonarola, who risked assassination at Bologna for publicly calling its princess a devil, and told the Florentine magistrates, when they advised moderation, "I see you are sent by Lorenzo dei Medici. Tell him to come and do penance for his sins, for the Lord spares no one. I do not fear banishment, for your city is like a grain of lentil upon the earth. I am a stranger, and he is first among the citizens, but I shall abide and he must pass away," a speech in harmony with the well-attested story, that he refused to give the dying prince absolution, because he would not restore liberty to Florence. There is also reason to believe that his fearless reproof kept the French king from sacking the city. His heroism in opposing Alexander VI., is all the more laudable, because he was a devout Catholic, protesting to the last that no one could be saved outside of the Church, and that the pope was its supreme head. Of justification by faith he knew nothing, but taught that salvation depended mainly on morality, though he was so far from undervaluing monkish observances, that he forbade his monks to have comfortable beds or handsome books, made them often exchange breviaries, clothes, and cells, so as to have nothing on earth they could think their own, and tried to make them desert the stately convent in Florence, decorated by Fra Angelico, for a rude retreat in the wilderness. His novices were encouraged to amuse themselves by questioning him about hell; and his sermons, during the eight years in which they swayed Florence, 1489 to 1497, were directed, not only against the immorality and unbelief then very prevalent, but also against dancing, cards, perfumery, false hair, secular music, classic poetry, ancient philosophy, drawings from the nude, and portraits of living women in sacred pictures. Two immense bonfires of anathematized articles, collected by boys of ten to twenty whom he sent to search shops and houses, blazed in the carnivals of 1497 and 1498, when many valuable manuscripts and works of ancient and modern art were destroyed.

He claimed to be guided, partly by the Bible, which he allegorized in the delusive fashion then almost universal, so as to say that forbidding Jacob to marry a Canaanite meant that Christians should not study Plato and Aristotle, and partly by his own prophetic visions. About the time that Columbus first saw the New World, Savonarola saw an air-drawn falchion, with the inscription, "The sword of the Lord cometh swiftly upon the land," as he thought it did two years later in the French invasion. The black cross of the wrath of God, planted in Rome and reaching to the zenith, was soon shrouded in a thunder-storm, after which the golden cross of the divine compassion was seen rising out of Jerusalem and illuminating all the earth. Thus it was shown, as Savonarola preached constantly, that the Church was to be chastened, and then glorified, and that this was to be done quickly, so that all the earth would be converted in ten years. Very bold was his testimony against the vices of the priests, whom he warned his hearers not to trust with women or children.

The prophet did not spare Alexander VI., who tried vainly to tempt him to Rome, in 1495, by a request to be taught the will of God ; or to bribe him with a cardinal's hat ; whereupon Savonarola told his people, " All I hope for is that bloody hat which Christ has given to his saints." That fall his preaching was prohibited, but soon permitted again at the request of the magistrates of Florence, now a republic under the direction of Savonarola, who recommended this as practically the the best form of government for the city, and denounced all who opposed it as enemies of Christ. A second prohibition, a year later, he set aside at the entreaty of the magistrates, pleading that he obeyed the intentions, though not the words, of the pope, but saying that it might yet be necessary to imitate Paul, who withstood Peter to his face. On May 12, 1497, shortly after the first holocaust of worldly vanities, its author was excommunicated, on which he stopped preaching and wrote his *Triumph of the Cross*. There he asserts the superiority of inward to outward religion, but admits all the established Catholic doctrines, even saying, "He who separates from the Church of Rome, separates from Christ." His popularity was now diminished by his suffering five political adversaries to be executed in violation of a law he had proposed himself. In February, 1498, he reappeared in the pulpit and declared that popes had erred, even officially, and that " He who rejects what I preach combats the gospel law of love and is a heretic."

On the 27th, took place a second bon-fire, in which many ancient busts of Cleopatra and Lucretia perished with portraits of the reigning beauties, an illuminated manuscript of Petrarch, etc. That morning Savonarola appeared in public, with the consecrated wafer in his hand, and called on God to strike him dead if he were not really a prophet. The Franciscans had already proposed that he should submit himself to the ordeal of fire, in company with one of their champions. Savonarola refused, unless the ambassadors of the pope and Christian kings would promise to attend, and, if he should triumph, help him call a council to depose Alexander VI. and reform the Church. Such a council he recommended, on March 14, in letters to the monarchs of Germany, France, England, Spain, and Hungary. Meantime his staunchest adherent, Fra Domenico, volunteered to pass through the fire with a Franciscan; and April 7 was appointed for the ordeal by the magistrates, one of whom, however, proposed taking a tub of water, and seeing if either champion did not get wet. How the trial failed to take place in consequence of the reluctance, first of the Franciscans and finally of Savonarola himself, who insisted that his friend should carry the communion bread into the flames, is powerfully told in *Romola*. That a professed prophet, who had often declared himself ready for martyrdom, should first expose his friend to it instead of himself, and then refuse even this risk, naturally made the disappointed spectators indignant. Only military protection brought Savonarola back to St. Mark's. The signory had already forbidden him to preach, and now they banished him. The next day, Palm-Sunday, he broke both commands; and that night the convent was the scene of a bloody conflict, which ended in his arrest. During the trial which followed, he is said, perhaps falsely, to have been tortured into denying his own inspiration, but no word of doubt in him could be extorted from his faithful Fra Domenico. Both were hung on May 23, when Savonarola told the bishop, who declared him separate from the Church in heaven as well as that on earth : " From the Church on earth ; but from that in heaven ? No; you have no power for that." So died the principal representatives at this time of that vision-led Mysticism which had already been glorified by Joan of Arc.

The freest form of Mysticism, which followed individual intuition in conscious independence of angels, Bible and

Church, had been temporarily suppressed by persecution. The visionary form, which, while professing obedience to the Church, was constantly seeking guidance from angelic voices and supernatural signs, is represented during this period only by Hans Boheim and Savonarola. That docile type, most in favor with the hierarchy, had now no advocate of importance, except Thomas à Kempis, who died at the age of ninety, in 1471. By far the most important form of Mysticism was that which prevailed in Germany and the Netherlands during the latter half of the fifteenth century and beginning of the sixteenth, and which, while making no very dangerous claims of independence, and insisting too firmly on biblical authority to give any injurious license to individual phantasy and vain credulity, taught the superior holiness of a spiritual to a ceremonial religion, the necessity of complete dependence on God for guidance, and the duty of purifying the Church. All attempts at reform had failed, because most Christians thought they could not be saved without the help of the priesthood, and so were as patient as possible with its iniquities. Vainly had the Church been implored to reform herself voluntarily. She had to be forced to do so by popular pressure, and this could not be exerted except by men who knew that she did not hold the only key to heaven. Hence the foundation of the Reformation was the doctrine that salvation was to be sought from Christ alone, and not from the priests; in other words, justification by faith.

This momentous dogma was dimly taught by John Goch, who died in 1475, at Mecheln, where he had long been abbot. More clear and full teaching was given by John of Wesel, so-called from his birth-place, near Mainz. When the pope held that great sale of indulgences, the Jubilee of 1450, Wesel wrote a book to prove, that God alone could remit the real penalties for sin, those he had himself imposed, that popes and priests could only remove such punishments as they had introduced, and that the traffic had no sanction either from the Bible or the Fathers. To the objection, the Church can not err, he answered, the whole Church can not, but part of her may, and that part which sells indulgences does.

In 1460 Wesel began to preach at Mainz and Worms, and openly taught that the Bible was the only safe guide, and that men must look to Christ himself for salvation, which would be given according to their inward faith, not their outward observances. Among his sayings were these : "I despise the pope, the Church, and the councils, and praise Christ." "I hold nothing sinful which is not condemned in Scripture." "Eat when you are hungry, even roast chicken on Good Friday." "If Peter ordained fasting, it was probably to sell his fish." On Monday, February 11, 1479, Wesel, then very old and infirm, was arraigned in Mainz as a heretic, and urged to recant. This he would not do, until the judges agreed to take the guilt upon themselves. At last he yielded, and was sentenced to life-long imprisonment, under which he died in 1481.

Eight years later died John Wessel, who was not persecuted, except in the destruction after his death of most of his writings. He had taught philosophy at Cologne, Louvain, Heidelberg, and Paris, and won the title of Lux Mundi, "The Light of the World." Luther said: "If I had read Wessel earlier, my enemies would insist that I got all my views from him." Both published Theses against indulgences, and in very similar language. Wessel said, "Purity of heart is the only acceptable penance." The fire of purgatory seemed to him purely spiritual, and the presence of Christ in the eucharist merely symbolic. Justification by faith he taught with the utmost plainness, saying, "He who thinks he is justified by works does not know what justification means."

The same momentous doctrine was taught early in the sixteenth century by Staupitz, vicar-general of the German Augustinians, at whose meals he commanded that the Bible be read aloud, instead of the writings of their patron-saint and reputed founder. Among his monks was Martin Luther, who renounced his brilliant prospects as a jurist and joined the Order in 1505. He was killing himself by trying to carry out rules for self-torture, which had grown more and more cruel because so generally evaded, when Staupitz, whom he henceforth called Father, saved his life and revealed his great mission, by teaching him that salvation could not come through forms and ceremonies but only through faith in Christ. This same lesson Luther also learned from the study of the Bible, which was enjoined on him and his brethren. What did most to emancipate him from ceremonialism was his journey in 1511 to Rome, where he found the clergy openly irreverent and scandalously profligate. The greatest formalism he saw produce the least morality and religion. Salvation by faith alone was the main theme of Luther's preaching, which began in 1515 at Wittenberg, where he had become professor. The next year he published the *Theologia Germanica*, a mystical treatise written about a hundred and fifty years before. "Here," he said, "I have found God as I have not found Him in Latin, Hebrew, or Greek." Still a year later, and his Theses against the indulgences brought on that great contest between formalism and justification by faith, which resulted in crippling the worst enemy of liberty of thought.

VII.

The revival of ancient learning, the invention of printing, the oceanic discoveries, and the new activity in literature, art, and commerce, co-operated with the notorious wickedness and worldliness of the popes in temporarily subverting their authority in Italy, where their cause was so closely united with that of religion, that both seemed hopelessly lost at the beginning of the sixteenth century. The Renaissance of secular art could make no Protestants. Her best service to them was in making the papacy too weak to put them down. Italy's culture was too irreligious for her to be the cradle of Protestantism. Germany was taught by her Mystics, somewhat aided by the Hussites, that religion could live independent of Rome, and German culture had only developed so far as to furnish the reformers with weapons. In England, also, there was too little unbelief to hinder revival of religion, which Lollardism was able to assist powerfully, and which the political liberty, then unequaled except in Switzerland, greatly facilitated. France stood, intellectually as well as geographically, midway between Italy on one side, and Germany and England on the other. The medieval loyalty was preserved only by Spain, now infuriated by recent triumphs over the Moors, and enriched by her plunder in the New World for yet bloodier contests.

Two distinct forms of literary activity now meet us. Valla, Poggio, Pecock, Leonardo da Vinci, Machiavelli, Pomponotius, More, Muth, Celtes, Hutten, and Erasmus labored for the advancement of learning and the diffusion of knowledge, prompted by love of mental culture for its own sake, keeping on good terms with the Church, but freeing themselves as far as possible from the trammels of her authority. Colet, Savonarola, Wesel, Wessel, Staupitz, and Luther sought to make her not only more pure but more powerful, strove to raise her members to the highest spiritual life, and valued intellectual culture only as an aid in preaching spirituality. It was the latter class that was destined to produce the Reformation. The two schools of thought were still friendly, but a time of violent hostility was drawing near.

CHAPTER X.

THE REFORMATION.

I.

The sixteenth century found the Church of Rome ruling a larger part of Europe than ever before or since. Her sway extended over the Spanish and Scandinavian peninsulas, Great Britain, Ireland, Denmark, the Netherlands, France, Switzerland, Germany, Poland, Hungary, and Italy, in which last country the pope was a political sovereign. Elsewhere his power was partly due to the monks and nuns, who held vast tracts of real estate, controlled most of the universities, and were directly under his own government, and partly to that great hierarchy in which the parish priests were marshaled under princely prelates. The latter organization was not so fully subject to the pope as the former, but the members of both were at work, controlling domestic life through the confessional, checking all free expression of thought, defending his authority in the pulpit as well as through the press, and collecting vast sums of money for his treasury. His power was now without canonical limits, councils being wholly out of favor. The laity were merely servants of the Church, which practically meant the pope and his subordinate monks and priests. Out of this Church there was generally supposed to be no salvation, but the German Mystics were already teaching the sufficiency of faith in Christ to save the soul, without the help of priest or rite. Vainly did the Italian free-thinkers try to cut the Gordian knot by showing the ability of man to take care of himself without any help from religion. The popular heart was set on getting salvation, and propitiating the divine wrath. The great question of the century was whether this could be done without leave of the popes. That the pontiffs failed to maintain their religious supremacy was largely due to their neglect to reform abuses, and largely also to their political quarrels with the sovereigns of France, Germany, and England, as well as the incessant wars which these three powers were waging against each other. Germany was peculiarly ready for a schism, on account of the anarchy arising from the efforts of the princes and free cities to establish their independence, of the knights to reatin their perishing privileges, of the peasants and artisans to free themselves from oppression, and of the emperor to maintain his tottering authority. Too many hostile interests were dividing and agitating Europe in the sixteenth century to allow any efficient co-operation in maintaining religious unity against mental independence, recently awakened by the revival of classic learning, and by the unprecedented activity in art, literature, discovery, and commerce, described in the last chapter. And now the printing-press began to show itself mightier than the pope.

II.

It is needless to say who took the lead in setting up not only the authority but the saving efficiency of the Bible, against the Church. Every one has heard of the publication of the Theses against indulgences in 1517, the burning of the pope's bull in 1520, and the heroic refusal to recant at the Diet of Worms in 1521. Especially important is it to remember, that popular feeling in Germany was on Luther's side from the beginning, especially in his native Saxony, in Hesse, and in the free cities. In his early pamphlets, 133 of which were printed in the year 1520 alone and widely circulated, he denounced every form of ecclesiastical despotism, and spoke with great power and plainness for the equality of the clergy and laity, the right of each congregation to choose its own pastor, independent of bishop, presbytery, prince, or patron, and the liberty of each individual to follow the Bible as he might understand it, without danger of punishment. This last view is especially prominent in his *Appeal to the German*

Nobility, published in August 1520, as a reply to the bull in which his condemnation was partly based on his objecting to the burning of heretics.

Luther's main purpose, however, was not to serve reason but faith. From the beginning to the end of his career as a preacher and author, he insisted on the dogma of salvation by faith alone, with a zeal which led inevitably, not only to the disparagement of practical morality, but to the requisition of doctrinal uniformity. That Protestants were unable to remain long at peace among themselves was largely due, as we shall see, to the bigotry with which he treated all who differed from him about baptism or the communion. While he was at the Wartburg, where his prince concealed him after he had been put under the ban at Worms, and where he did his greatest work, the translation of the New Testament, he found that Wittenberg had been invaded by daring Mystics, who pushed the doctrine of salvation by faith alone so far as to abolish the established ceremonies, oppose all institutions of learning, and deny the authority of government. Never did he act more bravely than when he renounced the protection of Frederic the Wise, and showed himself openly at Wittenberg, but in order to re-establish order he had to insist on the submission to rulers enjoined by Jesus, Paul, and Peter, as well as to deny the propriety of abolishing any existing custom or institution not expressly forbidden in the Bible.

As early as 1522 he found himself thus forced by the excesses of his followers into reactionary conservatism, and this position he maintained during his remaining twenty-four years, which are comparatively unimportant, being occupied partly in organizing the Lutheran Church in such subjection to political rulers as has greatly hampered its independence, and partly in carrying on bitter controversies with more liberal thinkers, prominent among whom we shall find Erasmus. The latter had said, "I dislike dogmatism so much that I gladly rank myself among skeptics, wherever this is permitted by the inviolable authority of the Bible, and the decrees of the Church, to which I submit in all things." Luther replied indignantly: "It is characteristic of the Christian mind to delight in assertions." "The Christian wishes to be as certain as possible, even in things which are unnecessary and outside of scripture." "Take away assertions and you have taken away Christianity." Never did Luther speak more plainly from his inmost heart. The dispute in question was brought on by his following Paul so literally as to assert the doctrine now called Calvinism, but hitherto almost unknown to the Church, that sin and damnation arise out of the arbitrary predestination of God. Thus we find him maintain in reply to Erasmus : "The immutable and eternal love and hatred of God toward men existed before the world was made, and before there was any merit or work of free-will." " He crowns a wicked man without any merit, and damns another man perhaps not more wicked." "Our salvation depends entirely on the will of God, in the absence of which all that we do is evil, and we do this necessarily." Even those who believe most firmly in necessarianism, as expounded by Bain and Mill, must consider the theory of Luther and Calvin singularly likely to hinder independence of action and thought. I do not find my own liberty to believe what seems true and do what seems right checked by my belief, that all my present thoughts and actions are the inevitable results, partly of my past life and partly of my immediate surroundings ; but I should be crushed to dust by the fancy, that I am only a tool in the hands of an angry God, who will certainly make me serve His arbitrary will and may possibly fling me into hell fire.

Luther's subjection to the letter of Scripture was made complete by his rejecting the allegorical method, which enables every expositor to justify his own opinions by calling them the mysterious and hidden meanings of the book he pretends to interpret. The servant of literalism was forced to excommunicate merchants who took interest as usurers ; to live in constant fear of the devil ; to sanction, though with great reluctance, the Landgrave of Hesse's bigamy, because it could not be proved unscriptural, to uphold the doctrine of the trinity, despite his own doubts on the subject ; to reject the Copernican theory, on the ground that it was the sun which Joshua bade stand still, not the earth ; and to oppose forming such a league against the emperor as was necessary to prevent the extinction of Protestantism. Luther objected to this alliance, not merely because the New Testament commanded obedience to monarchs, but because such texts as, "This is my body" and "Except ye eat my flesh and drink my blood ye have no life in you," seemed contrary to the views of men whom it was proposed to accept as allies. They agreed with him on other points, and pleaded that here they were only giving the Bible such an interpretation as it required by reason, but Luther answered : " Reason is the devil's harlot, and can do nothing but blaspheme." He refused the hand of friendship which Zwingli offered him with tears in his eyes. Perhaps the speedy defeat and death of the Zurich reformer in the battle of Cappel, October 11, 1532, was due to his being left to stand thus alone against the Roman Catholics. Luther now grew more and more intolerant. In 1538 he advised the banishment of heretics, and he seems to have even consented to their execution. One of his last books urges that the synagogues of the Jews be burned down, their books taken away, their worship suppressed, and their men and women enslaved without pity. We must certainly thank him for doing more than any one else to check the tyranny of Rome ; but to him are also in great measure due that servitude to the letter of the Bible, that hostility to free thought, and that exaltation of theology above morality which have always characterized Protestantism. That this system has not also been marked by the prevalence of predestinarianism and passive obedience is no fault of his. He did greatly help free thought by dividing her enemies into two hostile camps, but this aid was unintentional and they remained her enemies still.

That the Lutherans succeeded in establishing their independence against both emperor and pope, is partly due to the dissension between these two potentates, but partly also to the courage of a leader who would not let himself be fettered by texts. It was the Landgrave of Hesse, Philip the Magnanimous, who in 1529 brought about that declaration of religious independence from which comes the name of Protestant, and who soon after opened the way for this new faith into Wür-

temburg with the sword. He was able, despite the opposition
of Luther, to keep up union enough among the German
Protestants to prevent the emperor from attacking them
before 1546. For the defeat that year at Mülberg, he was
not responsible; the captivity that followed did not crush
him; and at length he was able to crown his labors, in 1555,
by the treaty of Augsburg, which permitted each state and
free city in Germany to maintain its own faith and worship,
without interference from its neighbors or the emperor. This
of course did not hinder any petty prince from persecuting his own subjects, a practice from which Philip himself kept
unusually free. It must further be mentioned to his credit,
that his personal preference was for a congregational system
of church government, which, however, the theologians
around him considered impracticable.

It was fortunate for the German Protestants that Henry
VIII., who had formerly been a stanch ally of the emperor
and a zealous writer for the papacy against Luther, was driven,
by his desire to get divorced from Catharine of Arragon and
married to Anne Boleyn, into a rupture with the pope, which
became final in 1534, when the Parliament declared the king
the only supreme head on earth of the English church. The
clergy had already been forced to acquiesce by threats of prosecution, for violating the statute of 1353 against appeals to
Rome, and their submission was insured by the suppression
of the monasteries, whose gross licentiousness was fully proved
in parliament, and whose vast wealth was so freely distributed
among the nobility and gentry, that they were firmly bound
to the new policy. Great was the desire, especially among
the Lollards, to have the Reformation made as complete in
England as in Germany and Switzerland; and that such a
change was not carried out before the death of Henry VIII.,
was due mainly to the vigor with which, at the same time he
beheaded Sir Thomas More and other Roman Catholics as
traitors for refusing to acknowledge his supremacy over the
Church, he burned Protestants as heretics for disbelieving in
transubstantiation. Among the victims sent to the stake in
1546 for denying that a priest could change bread and wine by

miracle into the body and blood of Christ, was a saintly woman only twenty-six years old, whose constancy on the rack saved the lives of many noble sympathizers, among whom was probably the queen herself, and whose only offense was stated thus by herself in Newgate. "The bread is but a remembrance of his death, or a sacrament of thanksgiving for it." "Written by me, Anne Ascue, that neither wish death nor yet fear his might, and as merry as one that is bound toward heaven." A creed as Protestant as Luther's, or even Zwingli's, was enacted during the reign of Edward VI., and too firmly established to be rooted out by Bloody Mary, though she retaliated for the oppression which she had suffered from her father as well as from her brother's ministers, by burning more than three times as many heretics as had previously been put to death in England. This persecution was made peculiarly cruel by the refusal, almost for the first time among Catholics, to spare the life of those who should recant, as for instance did Archbishop Cranmer, who, however, regained his courage at the last. Sympathy with him and many braver victims, like Rogers, Hooper, Taylor, Ridley, and Latimer, did much to make Romanism so hated that Elizabeth found no difficulty on her accession, November 17, 1558, in making England permanently Protestant. The great body of the clergy not only submitted to these four great changes in creed and ritual, made by as many successive sovereigns within thirty years, but preached as their rulers bade them. And the result was the establishment of the present system by which pastorates, when not actually sold in open market, have been filled by official or aristocratic patronage, exerted with very little regard to the wishes of the parishioners, and by which the bishops have been so entirely the creatures of sovereigns and prime ministers as to have no right to call themselves successors of the Apostles, who filled the first vacancy in their own body by a popular vote, instead of accepting a nomination from Tiberius or Pontius Pilate.

Neither in England nor in Germany were the rights of the church-members recognized so fully as at Geneva. This city had cast off the yoke of her bishop in 1535, after a struggle whose hero, Bonivard, had suffered for six years, at Chillon, in a prison from which he issued just in time to oppose the compulsory imposition of Protestantism upon the peasants. The ruling spirit, however, was that of John Calvin, who came to Geneva in August, 1536, shortly after publishing that wonderfully able work for a man of twenty-six, his *Institutes*, which are equally remarkable for uncompromising independence of Romanism, for unreserved submission to the authority of Scripture, and for pitiless plainness in teaching total depravity, arbitrary election, and irresistible predestination, not only of God's favorites to be saved, but of all others to be damned. That in which Calvin differed most widely from other reformers was his hatred of dancing, novel-reading, games of chance, drinking, theatricals and gay attire. All these had been made criminal; and a bride had been put in prison for going to church with her hair hanging down too far, before Calvin's exclusion of the entire population from the Lord's Supper caused his banishment early in 1538. His aid in keeping down Romanism and immorality could not be long spared, and in 1541 he was suffered finally to establish such a proscription, not only of free thought but of amusements, as had never before been seen in Christendom. Staying away from church was now, for the first time, made criminal. In the years 1558 and 1559, four hundred people were punished for dancing, laughing in church, dressing too gayly, and similar offenses. Blasphemy was treated as a capital crime, and far worse than theft, in conformity with the biblical legislation, which was enforced with peculiar severity against witches, of whom one hundred and fifty were burned within sixty years. Calvin had opposed persecution, while in danger of suffering it himself, but how far he followed the Old Testament rule, as soon as he had the power to do so, will be seen on subsequent pages. It must here be noticed that peculiar advantages for detecting heresy were secured by the ministers visiting every house in Geneva once a year to question the inmates about their faith, a custom still surviving in a comparatively harmless form. Books were suppressed so rigidly that Bonivard was unable to publish a history which displeased Calvin, and the latter's own literary utterances were occasionally checked when opponents happened to be in office. A woman was whipped for singing ordinary words to a psalm-tune, a child beheaded for striking his parents, a man imprisoned for reading Poggio, another for calling his little son Claude, when the minister preferred Abraham, and a whole family, including a magistrate, for dancing at a wedding. This opposition to public amusements made the churches the only legitimate places for meeting socially, and so greatly increased the power of the clergy. The same result was promoted by making the Calvinistic ministers much less dependent on the State than were the Lutherans or Anglicans. The single congregations regained much of the liberty they had enjoyed in apostolic times, though they did not go so far beyond this pattern as to encourage individual independence, but on the contrary permitted great despotism to be exerted by the consistory of ministers and pious laymen. Calvin's legitimate successors are the Presbyterians, rather than the Congregationalists, and his immediate followers were so firmly organized as to be able to resist persecution with unusual success, especially in France, Scotland, and Holland.

In these three countries there were still to be bloody conflicts about religion; but Protestantism had reached substantially its present limits in Europe at the time of its establishment by the Scottish Parliament in 1560. It was also supreme in England, Denmark, Norway, Sweden, Prussia, Hesse, Saxony, Würtemberg, and other German states, besides several of the Swiss cantons, especially Geneva, Berne, Zurich, and Basel. In France it was increasing so rapidly that the king had made peace in 1559, with England and Spain, in order to have the latter power co-operate in a general suppression of heresy. Of this attack Holland was already prepared to stand the brunt successfully, and Belgium contained decidedly more Protestants than at present. So did Bavaria and Austria, where there was great tolerance, as was also the case in Bohemia, Poland, and Venice. Rome was now in such danger that she had to reform herself, and give up, finally, the manners of the Borgias for those of the Borromeos. She was also obliged to close that long warfare for larger territory against Catholic sovereigns which had been the safety of Protestantism, to abandon all attempts at domineering over kings and emperors, and to become the accomplice of Philip II. and Catherine de' Medicis. The inquisition had been revived in 1542 by Paul III., under whose sanction the first *Index of Prohibited Books* was compiled five years later by the University of Louvain. The foremost adviser of these measures assumed the tiara, as Paul IV., in 1555, and ruled so intolerantly, that his death in 1559 was welcomed by the burning of the palace of the inquisition by a Roman mob. His policy survived him, however, and mental liberty remained much more restricted, throughout Italy, than during the seventy years after the death of Paul II. in 1471. Prominent among the champions of reaction was the Society of Jesus, which had been authorized by the pope in 1540, despite the belief of the cardinals that monastic orders were too liable to corruption, had made the breach with Protestantism irreparable at the Council of Trent, and had shown singular capacity for destroying freedom of thought, especially among its own members. Alarm at the progress of the Reformation assisted the triumph of the spirit of Loyola and Philip II. over that of Erasmus.

III.

We have seen how much the *Praise of Folly*, the *Christian Soldier*, and the *Adages* did early in the century to expose the sins of monks, priests, bishops and popes, and increase the authority of moral laws. The *Colloquies*, which appeared in a piratical edition, 1521, and in an authorized one three years afterward, are still well worth reading on account of the life they give to such characters as the dissolute soldier with a conscience in perfect peace, because the Dominicans would sell him pardon for any sin, even robbing and murdering Jesus ; the pious girl, driven from the convent by dangers of which she cannot speak ; the pilgrims who have found the rags with which Becket wiped his nose treasured as holy relics ; the prior who goes regularly to brothels but had rather die than eat meat; the dying swindler sent to heaven by monks who fight over his bounty at his funeral; the tavern-keeper whose pastor is his best customer; the learned woman obliged to defend her tastes against an abbot who boasts that there are no books in his room; and the Virgin Mary complaining that her worshipers make prayers too indecent for her to hear. No wonder that this book soon passed under the papal ban, or that in 1527 it had a sale of twenty-four thousand copies. Luther's cause had already been greatly helped by the censures which Erasmus passed on the monks in his second edition of the New Testament, 1518, and a year later, in his *Paraphrase of Corinthians*, on fasting, excommunications, and indulgences. In 1525 he pointed out the lack of biblical authority for confession to priests, as well as the dangers to chastity. Luther had only been married about a year, when Erasmus printed his declaration that matrimony is holier than celibacy, and ought to be permitted to priests. Shortly before his death, which took place in 1536, appeared his *Art of Preaching*, complaining bitterly of the so-called pastors who spent the day in taverns and were ruled by mistresses. In his private letters he never spoke but with indignation of the condemnation of Luther, and the burning of heretics, or neglected to urge the necessity of a reformation. His own plans for this were adopted by the Duke of Juliers with great success.

That Erasmus never became a Lutheran was largely due to his loyalty to principles, some of which are also ours. He believed that progress could best be promoted by popular education, and that the circulation of the Bible and the Fathers of the Church would make all Christians willing to give up indulgences, the inquisition, and other abuses, which would soon be seen to be innovations. It was not only devotion to this plan of peaceable reform, but hatred of the persecutions which he saw Luther and his followers call down upon themselves, that made him blame their violence. Still more fatal to any harmony between Erasmus and Luther was the fact, already noticed, that the former was naturally skeptical and made as much use as possible of what little liberty he

found in the Church, while the latter quitted her communion
because his fondness for dogmatism made him ready for any
sacrifice in order to propagate a new and narrow creed of his
own. Protestantism was too far committed to the literal infallibility of the Bible to have any claim on the impartial and
enlightened critic who kept pointing out the fatal discrep-
ancies, not only between the Old and New Testaments, but
between the various manuscripts of the original Greek, and
who did much to shake belief in the authenticity of *Hebrews,
James*, II. *Peter*, III. *John*, *Jude* and *Revelations*. The *Epistle to the Romans*, which was the most precious part of the
Bible to Luther and Calvin, and was constantly appealed to by
them in support of their darkest doctrines, seemed to Erasmus
too obscure to have much value. The doctrine of the trinity
for which one at least of these fathers of Protestantism was
ready to persecute to the death, was not recognized as scriptural by Erasmus, who even ventured to leave out the only
text strongly in its favor, the spurious passage about the three
heavenly witnesses, until compelled to insert it by the Church.
Of the Old Testament he said frankly that most of it should not
be read by uneducated people, because the history is so obscure
as well as immoral, and many of the riddles are inextricable.

The most powerful advocate of the sanctity of morality in
all that century was never more consistent than in attacking
the doctrine of justification by faith, which has caused belief
to be valued as a substitute for virtue, and creeds to be swal-
lowed as panaceas warranted to heal all diseases of the soul.
But it was only after repeated requests of both pope and emperor, that Erasmus undertook to point out the most dangerous error into which Luther, like Calvin, was led by refusing to consider faith as the reward of virtue, and protested
against ascribing man's spiritual condition and destiny wholly
to the arbitrary choice and resistless will of God. Thus
opened a controversy in which neither side was able to reach
ground which could now be held by mental science, but in
which Erasmus was much more favorable than his adversary
to the process by which a scientific view could be developed.
Justly does Hallam call him "the first conspicuous enemy of

ignorance and superstition," and he may also be placed among the most efficient opponents of persecution, as well as most widely read of liberal writers before Voltaire. Others have spoken more boldly, but no one ever led a larger number of his contemporaries on into more advanced ideas than they could have reached without his help.

Many other Roman Catholics were able to remain within the communion and yet do good work for tolerance, as well as for the kindred doctrine that morality is holier than forms and creeds. Of the author of *Utopia*, which, during this period was often reprinted and translated into modern languages, I need only say that the loyalty to truth with which he mounted the scaffold, rather than take an oath recognizing the king as Head of the Church, and as lawfully divorced, forces me to put full faith in his own declaration that he was not himself guilty of persecution, as has been alleged.

That daring defender of the truth of Neo-Platonism and the capacity of woman, Cornelius Agrippa, was expelled in 1520 from Metz, where he had been laboring usefully as a physician, because he saved a poor woman from condemnation for witchcraft by the inquisition. Ten years later, he called down on himself the poverty and exile in which he died in 1535, by publishing an elaborate exhibition of the vices and errors of monks, lawyers, doctors, professors, nobles, and kings. Morality he declares more conducive than learning to happiness. Religion seems to him essential for public welfare and to consist in faith rather than ceremony, yet not in faith alone, as taught by the Protestants, but in faith combined with brotherly love. His censures fall not only on the monks, who ought to have ropes around their necks instead of their waists, and the popes, who have turned the house of prayer into a den of thieves, by waging war and selling impunity for sin, but on the heretics, who would divide the Church. Among the most original and useful passages are those showing that nobility was originally a reward for serving the anger or lust of monarchs, that the noblest of animals, trees and metals, like lions, tigers, eagles, dragons, laurels, and gold, are always the most useless, and pernicious ; that heraldry is

right in giving noblemen the figures of cruel monsters and
birds of prey, and that the royal court is a hot-bed of licentiousness.

The tolerance advocated by Agrippa, More, Erasmus, and
other writers under the reign of bigotry, was not put into
legislation until 1561, when the French chancellor L'Hôpital,
secured the enaction of laws permitting the Huguenots to
hold public worship, and making such provisions against their
suffering or offering sectarian violence, as might have averted
the civil wars which began soon afterward. France had few
men wise enough to agree with him when he said, in the
king's name, on December 13, 1560: "God does not wish to
have his cause defended by weapons." "Not by their help did
our religion begin, nor is it to be preserved." "The dagger
has no power over the soul." "Let us do away with those
diabolical names, words of faction and sedition, Lutheran,
Huguenot, and Papist. Let us keep the name of Christian."

With these great men should be mentioned Dumoulin, whose
exposure of the abuses in papal appointments to office
caused his house to be mobbed at Paris, and whose lectures
on theology proved so unwelcome in Protestant Germany that
he had to return to France; Cardinal Contarini, who died of
grief at his failure to reconcile Lutherans and Catholics by
mutual concessions in 1542; and that bishop of Macon, who,
when asked by a French cardinal, if he thought he behaved
episcopally in interceding for heretics, answered, "I speak
like a bishop, but you act like an executioner."

And high among the Roman Catholics who labored in vain
to make their Church pure and tolerant stands the Queen of
Navarre and sister of Francis I., Marguerite d'Angoulême,
who protected Marot, Dolet, Desperriers, Rabelais, and other
liberal authors, against persecution, and who probably received help from them in composing her sprightly comedies,
as well as a collection of stories somewhat resembling the
Decameron, but written with much more regard for morality.
Her liberality in relieving the sufferings of the refugees at
Geneva and Strasburg was all the nobler because it was not
the act of a Protestant but of a tolerant Romanist.

There is strong reason to believe that it was mainly the unwillingness of Queen Juana, daughter of Ferdinand and Isabella, and mother of Charles V., to hear mass or see heretics burnt alive, which caused her to be put to the torture even in her girlhood, and to be kept for nearly fifty years in a prison where she never saw the light of day, nor received a single visitor. That her alleged insanity was merely a pretext for her exclusion from the throne of Castile, is shown by the letters of her jailer to Charles V., by the offer of marriage made by that shrewdest of monarchs, Henry VII., shortly after her incarceration, and also by her demeanor during the three months for which she was set at liberty by the patriot-chief, Padilla, who might possibly have established her permanently on the throne, if she had consented to sanction his opposition to her undutiful son. The cardinal, who afterward became Pope Adrian VI., saw her at this time, after she had been fourteen years in prison, and wrote to his sovereign that all her attendants were confident that she was then as capable of reigning as her mother, Isabella, and had always been so. It may have been desire to please Charles V., which led him to express some doubts about her complete sanity, which had, perhaps, by this time been impaired by long seclusion from fresh air and daylight. Only the wish to prevent another sedition seems to have led the nobles, who put down the rebellion, to break their promise to her, and send her back to prison, where she remained until her death. (See *Revue des Deux Mondes*, June 1, 1869.)

Her persecution, like that of Savonarola and the German Mystics, and like the failure of Erasmus to reach lucrative preferment, shows that the best element in the Church was too weak to take the lead, or even to protect itself against most atrocious cruelty. Love of power forced the Church to reserve her high places for men of unscrupulous and pitiless craft. Sanctity was a secondary consideration, as is manifest from the fact that scarcely any of the medieval or modern popes were pronounced fit for canonization, even by the most partial judges. Men and women who would not serve the inquisition, were fortunate if they escaped its fangs.

IV.

Meantime the innovators whom Luther drove out of Wittenberg, in 1522, had discovered that infant baptism is not sanctioned, either by the Bible or by the principle that nothing is a sacrament to any one who does not believe in it. Accordingly they had insisted that all Christians should receive the rite on reaching mature years and without regard to any previous celebration. This doctrine soon gained thousands of followers who were called Anabaptists, and underwent terrible persecutions, especially in Bavaria, Austria, and Holland. Many fugitives from this last country were burned alive in 1535 and afterward in England, where Joan of Kent was among their disciples. Their general disbelief in the Trinity and endless misery, and their faith in morality as necessary for salvation did much to make them hated; as also did the disregard for marriage and other social institutions, and readiness to encourage insurrection, which characterized many of the early leaders. Prominent among these was Melchior Hoffmann, whose disciples, the Melchiorists, became infamous at Münster, but whose own imprisonment, which proved fatal at Strasburg in 1540, was largely due to his teaching that Jesus is not God but only His prophet, and that the atonement still leaves much for men to do in order to be saved. Among his sayings are these: "It would be a mischievous God who should call all men to His supper, and yet will that some should not come." "It would be a lying God who should openly give a man grace, but yet secretly prepare hell for him." The first result of importance from Anabaptism, however, was the Peasants' War.

The preachers of liberty were nowhere more welcome than among the German peasants, of whom some were still serfs and the rest merely tenants, plundered almost to the point of starvation by heavy rents and arbitrary exactions, denied instruction, punished with lawless cruelty, forbidden to defend their crops against wild beasts, or their families against highborn ravishers, harassed by constant warfare, and deprived of all means of redress except insurrection. Again and again had the *Bundschuh,* or laced shoe-worn only by peasants, been set up as a standard ; and these revolts had been suppressed so cruelly that a fierce thirst for vengeance was added to the hunger for liberty. Luther's New Testament showed the primitive equality of all Christians, and this fact was urgently insisted on by the Anabaptists and other religious innovators, who saw that their only chance of success or even tolerance, was in a democratic revolution. Lay preachers and exiled priests, prominent in which latter class was Münzer formerly of Zwickau, traveled to and fro, showing the peasants that Christianity knew nothing of nobles and landlords, and that all men were equal by the law of God, and should be so by that of man. The age of the Spirit and kingdom of heaven upon earth were declared to be near at hand. Saxony, Alsace, Lorraine, Baden, Würtemberg, Bavaria, Austria, and the Tyrol heard the new gospel of revolution ; and some of its preachers were sent to the stake early in 1524 by the Roman Catholics. The friends of freedom were now binding themselves together from village to village, gaining partisans in many cities, and preparing for a general rising.

The revolt was precipitated by a certain countess Helena, in Southern Baden, who used to call on her peasants to cease harvesting, or resting on feast-days, and pick strawberries and snail-shells. On St. Bartholemew's day, August 24, 1524, twelve hundred rebels took the field at Waldshut, near Basel, under the black, red, and yellow flag, often to wave in Germany thenceforth. The number of this Evangelical Brotherhood, as it was called, rose to six thousand men before the end of the year, and no one dared attack it, especially as no violence was committed, and nothing asked for except the redress of manifest grievances. The peasants of Baden, Würtemberg, and Bavaria, had risen generally on Sunday, April 2, 1525, and presented twelve articles which would have given parishioners power to choose and dismiss their pastors, reduced tithes and rents, abolished serfdom, illegal punishments, and arbitrary exactions, and permitted hunting, fishing, and cutting of timber. Luther at first approved of these demands, most of which have since been granted. The first blood shed was in routing a band of Würtembergers who bore a black and red banner with a white cross. The red flag was also flying in this state, where there were many defeats and executions, but no redress. It was in retaliation for these cruelties, that castles and convents began to be plundered and burned, and images of saints and crucifixes to be broken up ; for the Church was known to be on the side of the oppressors.

A great army gathered in the Neckar valley, where the Counts of Hohenlohe had to grant the Twelve Articles, and shake hands with the peasants, who called them "Brother Albert and Brother George." Two knights, who loved liberty and hated priests, Götz von Berlichingen, who has been immortalized by Göethe, and Florian Geyer, joined the rebels, and took the lead on Easter Sunday, April 16, in storming Weinsberg. The commander, a Count of Helfenstein and son-in-law of the Emperor Maximilian, had murdered straggling peasants, and tried to burn villages, while he professed to carry on negotiations, and had finally fired on the ambassadors of the rebels. He and most of his knights and soldiers were, however, permitted to surrender to the peasants, who abstained from plundering, and shouted as they entered the city, "All the burghers will be safe in their houses." Most of the leaders wished to keep on good terms with the nobles, that they might help each other curb the tyranny of the princes, and seize on the wealth of the clergy. Only speedy vengeance was thought of by the band which had the charge of the prisoners, all of whom were slaughtered before sunrise, without the knowledge of most of the host, and greatly to the indignation of Florian, who at once departed with his own followers. This bloodshed called out general indignation, and even Luther was provoked into calling on the princes to slaughter the rebels without pity, like mad dogs. Never again was he as popular as before, and long afterward he found it unsafe to visit his dying father, lest this sanction of slavery and massacre should be remembered against him. The princes, however, thought their best policy was to promise redress, and secretly gather mercenaries. The revolution had now spread from Salzburg to Lorraine, whose duke is especially infamous for making a treaty, and then commanding a massacre. The central body, which had many women in its ranks, was under the nominal command of Götz von Berlichingen, who was either unable or unwilling to organize his forces sufficiently to avoid a ruinous repulse at Würzberg, on May 15. The most northerly focus of revolution was Mühlhausen, in Saxony, where Münzer declared that the reign of the Holy Ghost was to be inaugurated, reason to be placed above the Bible, all men to be recognized as capable of inspiration, Jesus to be considered only a great prophet, heaven and hell to be no longer looked for except on earth, and all opponents to be slaughtered, as had been the enemies of Israel. A too eager associate hurried him into action, before he had time to drill his men or buy weapons, especially powder, for which he had sent in vain to Nuremberg. His fortress of chained wagons was stormed on May 15, by the Landgrave of Hesse, his rainbow banners taken, and five thousand peasants slaughtered in the massacre, after which came merciless executions. Münzer seems to have maintained the justice of his cause, even on the rack. As he mounted the scaffold he told the princes before him that they must set their people free, or perish like Saul and Ahab. Other disasters followed rapidly. Florian died fighting to the last. The Weinsberg murderers were burned alive, as were many of the captured preachers. Götz von Berlichingen saved himself by betraying and deserting his comrades. Wendel Hippler, the most far-sighted and moderate of the leaders, perished in a dungeon. A hundred thousand peasants were put to death that summer, besides the women and children who died of hunger. The survivors were heavily fined, and the old abuses kept up except in Baden. But few of the thousand castles and monasteries which had been burned were ever rebuilt, however, and it must have been due in part to the peasants being treated better than before, when the first storm of fury had spent itself, that they never afterward made such an insurrection.

The revolt of the populace of Münster, under Anabaptist leaders, who had been ordained for very different work

by Hoffman, did not extend beyond that city, where,
after horrible excesses of tyranny and licentiousness, it
was cruelly suppressed in June, 1535. The immediate
result of this insurrection was that Bucer, the Protestant
pastor of Strasburg, published a book that very year, urging
that heretics ought to be put to death with their wives
and children, like the Canaanites. Similar ground was taken
in 1536 by Melanchthon, with whose decided approbation
three communistic Anabaptists, one of them a tailor, named
Kraut, had been beheaded in Jena on January 27. The Hessian synod of Homburg recommended on August 7 that all
preachers against infant baptism, marriage, private property,
or magistrates be banished, and if they returned, put to
death ; but the Landgrave never went beyond the milder
sentence. Other princes were less tolerant, especially in
Roman Catholic Germany and in Holland, where even the
peaceably inclined Anabaptists, whose leader was Simon
Menno, suffered horribly.

Nothing shows better the degradation of the German peasantry than the fact that they found no champion in literature
until long afterward. Lyndsay did something to emancipate
his own countrymen ; but not before the eighteenth century
did the downtrodden European gain an advocate as eloquent
and zealous as was secured early in the sixteenth by the enslaved American. Las Casas had become aware as early as
1514 of the cruelty and injustice under which the natives of
the West Indies were being exterminated, had set free his
own slaves, and had devoted himself to agitating for the
emancipation and protection of the race. For this purpose
he brought over in 1521 a philanthropic association of colonists, but the plan was frustrated by the general opposition
of the Spaniards, from whom his life was often in danger.
In 1537 he was able to Christianize a large district of Central
America, according to his theory of peaceable conversion, advocated in a treatise which was widely circulated, but never
published. He maintained not only that persuasion is the only
way to make converts, but that it is wrong to wage war
against unbelievers without special provocation. The latter

proposition he afterward defended against Sepulveda, who, in 1550, had upheld the right of conquering the heathen with an extravagance which caused his book to be excluded from Spain by the sagacious Charles V. A similar censure is said to have prevented the publication before 1554 of that indignant rebuke of Spanish cruelty, the *Destruction of the Indies*, which had been written by Las Casas a dozen years earlier. His most elaborate work, the *History of the Indies*, which is still unpublished, contains a frank confession of regret that his sympathy with the horribly oppressed Indians had led him to approve of the request, already urged by other Spaniards, that slaves might be brought from Africa.

So unwilling was this century to listen to new views, even of practical matters of the utmost importance, that a Parisian lawyer, named Spifame, was prohibited from practicing his profession because in 1551 he published his *Royal Decisions*, wherein he recommends beginning the year with January instead of Easter, turning most of the church-bells into coin or cannon, forcing bishops to reside among their flocks, putting copies of every new publication in the royal library, passing sanitary laws, establishing soldiers' homes, free concerts, and respectable pawnbroker's shops, and taxing the nobility and clergy as well as the common people. Adoption of this last suggestion might have averted the French Revolution.

One great obstacle to progress in the sixteenth century was the failure of either the Renaissance or the Reformation to do more than substitute the authority of ancient for medieval literature. The Bible was thought infallible in religion, Aristotle in philosophy, Galen in medicine, Ptolemy in astronomy, and Justinian in legislation. Every path to greater knowledge was blocked up by some old book. Mysticism was trying to pull down some of these idols, though only to set up others. What the age most needed was to see that facts are more instructive than books.

First to show the advantage of direct observation over mere reading were the physicians. Among the most famous innovators of the century is Paracelsus, the Luther of medicine. In ascribing all diseases to natural causes instead of supernatural, he was probably a follower of Hippocrates, on whom he wrote a commentary. His own habits of thought were so independent, however, that in the latter part of his life he read no books, and never entered a church. He used to say, "He who will explore Nature must trample on books." "She must be studied by traveling from land to land." "Where we find a country, there we find a leaf." "Who shall teach us the power of natural things, they who write of it but have not proved it, or they who have proved it but written nothing?" Year after year he traveled over Europe, even as far as Moscow and Constantinople, gathering all he could from hunters, fishermen and miners. At thirty-two he returned to Germany, and opened his lectures as professor at Basel, in 1525, by publicly burning the books of Galen, Avicenna, and other Greek and Arab physicians, all of whom, he declared, knew less than his shoe-buckles. This love of independence is powerfully shown in Robert Browning's tragedy, which probably ascribes to Paracelsus rather too high aims, and much too deep regrets at his own short-comings.

It is not unlikely that he really held that:

"Truth is within ourselves; it takes no rise
From outward things, whate'er you may believe:
There is an inmost center in us all,
Where truth abides in fullness."

In his struggles to keep free from all established systems, he fell, perhaps unconsciously, into Neo-Platonism. And thus he was led to disregard anatomy, as well as what had already been ascertained concerning the properties of drugs, and to rely mainly on new remedies which he thought corresponded mysteriously to the essence of the disease, or the relations of various parts of the body to the sun, moon, and planets. This theory led him to pay much attention to chemistry, by whose aid he discovered some specifics of great value, for instance, antimony and laudanum. With these he performed some marvelous cures, for one of which he asked so high a fee as led to his dismissal; though this, as well as the poverty in which he died, were in great measure due to his habitual drunkenness. Greater regard for the experience of his predecessors might have made him more virtuous and successful, but it was difficult to rebel against the tyranny of tradition without going to the opposite extreme. There could be no progress in medicine or any other field of thought, until the infallibility of all books had been denied boldly and plainly. Rightly, is he portrayed by Browning, as seeing the shades of the ancient physicians gather to mock him around the bed where he dies in shame and misery, and as exclaiming :

> "That yellow blear-eyed wretch-in-chief,
> To whom the rest cringe low with feigned respect—
> Galen, of Pergamos and Hell ; nay speak
> The tale, old man ! We met there face to face :
> I said the crown should fall from thee : once more
> We meet as in that ghastly vestibule :
> Look to my brow ! Have I redeemed my pledge ?"

More weighty opposition to Galen was made by Vesalius, who began to study anatomy when he could get no subjects, except by fighting for them against savage dogs or stealing them from grave-yards and gibbets, whereupon he had to hide them in his own bed. One of these thefts drove him forth as an exile from his birth-place, Louvain ; but at twenty-two a professorship was founded for him at Padua, and others at Bologna and Pisa. He had also a lucrative practice in Venice where the worst criminals were placed by the state at his disposal. Thus he gathered materials for a book on the *Fabric of the Human Body,* remarkable for costly illustrations, copious and novel information, and vigorous attacks on Galen, who was charged with giving as descriptions of the structure of men and women, what are merely inferences from what he knew of that of monkeys and quadrupeds. This daring book appeared in 1543, and brought down upon Vesalius, then but twenty-eight, the wrath of all the old doctors. He held public dissections to prove that he was right and Galen wrong, but the prejudice against him was so blind and fierce, that at last he burned his unpublished writings, including many original notes on the effects of drugs, and confined himself for the last ten years of his life to practicing at Madrid. There, he fell into the clutches of the inquisition, apparently because the heart of a patient, on whom he was making a *post-mortem* examination, seemed to beat, and was sentenced to a pilgrimage, during which he died from ship-wreck, at the age of fifty.

With the publication of this work, in 1543, may be said to have begun the great conflict between fact and tradition, for this is also the year in which appeared the *De Revolutionibus Orbium Cœlestium*, written a dozen years before, by Copernicus, who prudently waited until his last days before announcing the motion of the earth around the sun, and thus striking a deadly though probably unintentional blow, at all theories of a local heaven above our heads, or of the ascent of Jesus thither, or of his incarnation for the exclusive benefit of the inhabitants of this single planet. Showing the earth's dependence on the sun was to lead eventually to establishing her independence of heaven. The first result was proving Ptolemy, the Bible, and ancient literature generally, to be so much in error as to have no just claim to infallibility.

This memorable year was also that in which Ramus published his *Censures on Aristotle*, as well as his own *Method of Logic*, which eventually took the place of that by the most idolized of all philosophers. He had attacked this mighty authority in a public discussion at Paris as early as 1536 ; but his books subjected him to a trial there, which ended in their suppression and his condemnation to silence, on March 1, 1544, when he narrowly escaped the galleys. His books were burned, but often reprinted, and his lectures at Paris, where he became professor in 1551, were attended by two thousand hearers. His position was made insecure by his embracing Protestantism, in 1561, and his attempts to establish himself in Germany were frustrated by the devotion of the Lutherans to Aristotle, shortly after which failure he fell a victim in the massacre of St. Bartholomew.

Vives, a friend of Erasmus, had published a book in 1531, showing that the true disciples of Aristotle must investigate facts afresh, as he had done. Similar ground was taken by Cardan, an Italian physician, who, five years later, exposed the malpractice then inveterate among his brethren; and, who, after much petty persecution, succeeded in becoming the founder of algebra in 1545, as well as in doing much to inaugurate scientific methods of thought by his *De Subtilitate Rerum* and *De Varietate Rerum*, which appeared respectively in 1551 and 1552, and represent the world as the result of natural forces, acting according to fixed laws. Some dim ideas of spontaneous variation and natural selection have been found in these books, whose author said: "He who insists that every thing comes into existence merely because such is God's pleasure, dishonors Him, by making Him act unreasonably."

Popular rights found their earliest modern advocate in La Boëtie who, at the age of eighteen, was provoked by the massacre in Bordeaux by command of her king, 1548, to expose the danger of "subjection to a master of whose goodness we can never be sure, because it is always in his power to act wickedly." The power of tyrants is shown to rest on the apathy of the people. "Resolve to serve no more and you are free," exclaims the *Involuntary Servitude*, which was promptly circulated in MS., though not printed before 1576. Knox, when he published his *First Blast of the Trumpet* against the Bloody Mary, in 1558, promised to let his second blast—unfortunately never blown—show that kings can have no right to reign, except from the choice of the people, who may "most justly depose and punish him that unadvisedly they did elect." Another fugitive from Britain, Bishop Poynet, printed that same year a book in favor of regicide, said to have been burned at Geneva. A year later Aylmer, then a refugee, but afterward a bishop, admitted in his answer to Knox, that English monarchs have not the right to make laws. Alciati, who had previously fled from Italy to England, began an important innovation by showing the worthlessness of the confessions drawn by torture from alleged witches. He also went so far beyond his age as to recommend that astrologers should be punished as cheats. Bolder reforms in law were soon to be inaugurated; and the opposition to tradition was already beginning to spread into every field.

V.

Another band of servants of mental progress held little more than a nominal allegiance toward the Church of Rome, but offered their real homage to the Muses. Their hostility to religion seems to have been much overrated, as especially was that of their leader, Rabelais. So skillful, eager, and successful had the hunters after heresy and unbelief become before the middle of the sixteenth century, that no one whose writings and conversation were so grossly irreverent, as are often said to have been those of the author of *Gargantua and Pantagruel*, would have been suffered to die in peace, or even to rest in his grave. That he was imprisoned in 1523 by the Franciscans, whom he had joined, is ascribed by his learned contemporary, Budæus, to his having secretly studied Greek, then called the language of heresy. Bacon had been kept in confinement for twenty-four years on no worse charge by these haters of knowledge. So innocent in reality was Rabelais, that neither he nor the friendly magistrate who broke open his cell, underwent any censure from the pope, who first transferred the young student to the erudite Benedictines, and finally suffered him to cease entirely to be a monk, and become not only a parish priest but a physician. Such a powerful preacher and faithful pastor, as he was at Meudon near Paris until he resigned his charge, when nearly seventy, is scarcely to be reckoned among the enemies of religion and morality. Nor should we give implicit faith to such stories as that, after receiving extreme unction, he said: "I have greased my boots for a long journey," or that he told a visitor who asked how he was, "I am going to seek the Great Perhaps."

There can be no question of his right to a place beside Aristophanes, Lucian, Shakespeare, Swift, and Voltaire. His genius, like theirs, has been much obscured by his filth, but he has the excuse that it was needed to make his work palatable to his sovereigns. The first and second books appeared in 1535 and 1533, their order having been soon reversed, and are a strange mixture of fanciful tales, borrowed from old romances, with daring protests against servility, intolerance, and superstition. High above the smoke of burning heretics and embattled bigots rises the prayer of Pantagruel, "Thou art Almighty, and thou hast no need of us to defend thy cause."

Especially remarkable is the presentation of a far better system of education than had yet been known, or is even now in general use. The old philosophers had relied too exclusively on practice in logic, which had been supplemented in the medieval schools, by such restriction of knowledge to what could be learned from books, and such compulsion to perform irrational ceremonies, as seriously checked the development of originality. Rabelais's young prince goes through year after year of this routine without gaining any real knowledge or ability ; but he makes rapid progress under a system which is briefly this. He rises very early, hears the Bible read aloud ; talks with his tutor, while going through the elaborate toilet then customary, over what they have done the day before ; follows up three hours of study with as many of athletic exercise ; converses during dinner about the origin and properties of various kinds of food, and the opinions on this subject of classic authors ; then plays at arithmetical games, or on musical instruments ; spends three hours more with books and as many in the saddle, or else in bathing, or botanizing ; amuses himself after supper in the same way as after dinner, or in visits to travelers ; and gives his last thoughts to meditating on the revelations of God's glory in his works. In stormy weather the hours of recreation are spent in learning to use tools, and visiting all sorts of workshops and places of business. The king bids his son study, not only Latin, Greek, Hebrew, and Arabic, but also astronomy, though not astrology, and says : "To knowing the facts of nature I would have you devote yourself diligently, so that there shall be no sea, river, or spring of which you can not tell the fish ; as for the birds of the air, the trees and bushes in the woods, all the plants on earth, all the metals under it, the gems of the east and south, let nothing of this kind be unknown to thee; read and re-read the Greek, Arab, Hebrew, and Latin physicians, and dissect frequently, so as to have perfect knowledge of that other world, man." That mind and body should be developed together had already been urged by the Greek philosophers, but Rabelais was the first writer except Roger Bacon to show the advantage of studying things directly, and not merely reading about them in books.

Still more original and anti-ecclesiastical is the description of the Abbey of Will or *Thelema*. This richly endowed institution has no walls, bells, or statutes, the only rule being, "do what you please." "Fais ce que vouldras." Boys of good station and character enter at twelve, as girls do at ten, and stay as long as they please, subject to no restraint in their intercourse except their own honor, on which Rabelais is so much wiser than his age as to rely confidently There is no public worship, and no interference with private devotion. Social amusements and solitary studies are encouraged, as is early marriage.

The third book, which came out in 1545, would have been suppressed by the monks, if it had not been for the favor shown by Francis I. to the author, who left the kingdom two years later in alarm at the surreptitious publication of book fourth. Here Rabelais sends his prince traveling past various islands, on one of which the keepers of Lent appear as ferocious monsters, waging perpetual war with their Protestant neighbors who have the shape of sausages; another is consecrated to Hypocrisy, and peopled by male and female sayers of pater-nosters with their children; and a third is that of the Papomaniacs who ask the travelers, "have you seen him?" "The only one?" "The God on earth?" At last they realize that the pope is meant, and Panurge, the jester of the party, says, "Oh yes, I have seen three, and no good did it do me." He has to explain that he means three successively, and then they are treated with almost divine honors, and sumptuously feasted by the bishop, who has a house full of pretty girls, and who keeps drinking in honor of the seraphic and angelic decretals, boasting that there are no books which bring in so much money to the owner, denouncing fire and sword against the enemies of the pope, whom he calls our decretal God, and exclaiming, "Oh, how will reading but a single passage in the canons and decretals inflame your hearts with love to God, and your neighbor, provided he is not a heretic!" The Protestants are made as ridiculous as the Papists, which must have been one reason that this book was finally published with the royal permission in 1551, two years before the author's death.

Not before 1562, did any one dare to print the fifth and boldest book. This opens at the "Ringing Island," full of birds who look like men and women, but are kept in cages where they do nothing but eat, except that they sing whenever the bells ring that hang above their heads. Their names are derived from those of pope, cardinal, bishop, and abbot, and there are both males and females of each variety. Of course there is but one male among the "Pope birds," but he has several females. Many of these birds come from the countries of "No Bread" and "Too Many of that Sort," and some have flown away from places where they would have been punished for crime. The most greedy and impure are marked with the white cross of the Knights of St. John, or the red, green, or blue ones of other orders. All would be perfectly happy if they were not pestered by fish-eating harpies, whose color is that of the mendicant friars. Near this gay island is the gloomy one of the "Furred Cats of the Law," whose paws are always bloody, whose deathly work is blamed by no one but heretics, and whose tutelar deity carries the sickle of injustice, and a balance with purses instead of scales. Brighter again is the kingdom of Queen Quintessence, who feeds on abstractions, categories, and antitheses, and who professes to heal all diseases with her songs, while her officials keep at work washing blackamoors white, plowing with foxes, shearing asses, gathering figs from thistles, milking he-goats into sieves, and cutting fire with knives. Another island, that of the Sandals, is peopled by monks whose fondness for women is as excessive as their hatred of heretics. One of the visitors speaks of the harm done both to health and to morals by keeping Lent, and Panurge asks: "Is this speaker heretical?" "Very." "Would he be burned

justly?" "Justly." "And in what way?" "Alive."
Close by is an island full of hydras, unicorns, centaurs and
phœnixes, near whom dwells a little old man named Hearsay,
who has seven tongues, each in seven parts, and all chatter-
ing constantly, and as many ears as Argus had eyes, but is as
blind as a mole. At last they come to the "Island of Lan-
terns," or reign of light and truth, and the work closes with
an exhortation to drink freely of the new wine, and seek
boldly underground for treasures of wisdom.

This advice refers less to the study of classic philosophy,
in my opinion, than to that of natural science, but the point
can not be determined with certainty, and it is not unlikely
that both are recommended here, as in the letter already
quoted. It is a great pity that Rabelais did not find it safe
to state what he really believed in, as plainly as he shows his
independence of traditions and formalities, and his hatred of
all tyranny, bigotry, and superstition. Perhaps his disgust
at the hypocrisy of the Church in forbidding her servants to
marry, while she knew that she was thus driving them by the
thousand into concubinage, may have done much to provoke
a coarseness of language, to which he was also driven by the
necessity of pleasing the kings and bishops whose permission
was necessary for the circulation of his book. Whenever he
ventures to speak seriously, it is in favor of pure religion,
sound knowledge, and high morality; and if he had tried to
say more in this strain, his words might not have been suffered to come down to us.

No one else whose methods were so purely literary did
such good service at this time to the cause of liberty. Ariosto
and Machiavelli belong to an earlier period. The former's
satires and comedies, exposing clerical corruption, did not increase the fame already won by that masterpiece in which
the amorous and martial spirit of medieval chivalry still lives,
with nothing of its superstition; but the *History of Florence*,
on which Machiavelli was laboring at his death in 1527, did
much to expose the falsity of the alleged "Donation of Constantine," on which the popes rested their claims to temporal
power, as well as to show their guilt in calling foreigners into

Italy and keeping her disunited, while acting so treacherously that no prince could afford to trust them. Another great historian, Guicciardini, was more fully contemporary with Rabelais, and like him so far emancipated from what was then called Christianity as to declare human nature fundamentally virtuous, from which position he deduced the still more daring one, that it depended on a man's natural disposition whether his faith made him better or worse.

With these famous names might have ranked that of Berni, if all the boldest passages of his *Orlando* had not been surreptitiously destroyed after his death by two personal enemies, one of whom, Aretino, cared nothing for either religion or morality, and took the side of the Church only to gratify his malice. Some of the omitted stanzas are still preserved; and among them is one, saying that it is as likely that the pope and prelates will reform the Church, as that blood should come from a turnip, or that vinegar should become sweet. Similar ground was openly taken by many Italians of less note, for instance, Folengo, whose heroine, Berta, says she will not pray to the saints, nor confess to friars who are thinking only of how to seduce her; Manzolli, or Palingenius, author of the *Zodiac of Life*, Frezzi, Alamanni, Negri, Trissino, who was obliged to suppress promptly whatever was anti-clerical in his *Italia Liberata*, and Gryphius, who went to the scaffold about 1552, for calling the inquisition a dagger drawn against all authors.

Among French authors less brilliant than Rabelais, and perhaps, on this account, more severely persecuted, should here be mentioned Desperriers, Dolet, and Marot. It is hard to see why the first-named should have had his *Cymbal of the World* suppressed with a severity which caused it to be wholly unknown until a solitary copy was found in the last century, and which drove the author to kill himself, in 1544, rather than be forced by the rack to betray his friends, among whom was Queen Margaret of Navarre. Possibly the pope is meant by Mercury in the dialogue telling how he was robbed of the *Holy Book* which the gods wished to keep to themselves. Anagrams of the names of Luther, Bucer, and

Erasmus, also called Girard, may be detected in the scene
where Rhetulus, Cubercus, and Trarig quarrel about the value
of the little fragments into which the philosopher's stone has
been broken, in order to keep man in ignorance. The dialogue, which concludes the little book, brings in the dogs of
Actæon, who have become able to talk by eating the tongue
of their master, a capacity which one advises the other to
conceal, lest they should be whipped and not fed. Little is
known of his real views, or of those of Dolet, who was burned
after having been strangled, on his thirty-eighth birthday,
August 3, 1546, only his reluctantly invoking the Virgin and
his namesake, Stephen the first martyr, having saved him from
being burned alive. This execution, as well as the suicide
just mentioned, were among the results of a system which
on January 13, 1535, actually made it a capital crime to print
or sell any book in France. This prohibition was soon relaxed,
but not so far as to prevent the publication without license of
translations of the Scriptures and the attempt to sell
Calvin's *Institutes* and the *Commonplaces* of Melanchthon from
being among the offenses urged against Dolet, who was also
charged with eating meat in Lent, staying away from church,
and altering a passage in the *Axiochus*, then attributed to
Plato, so that a statement of cessation of earthly life in these
words, "Thou shalt be no more," was made to read, "Thou
shalt be nothing at all." His having studied at Padua may
have increased the suspicion that he rejected immortality, but
his writings show some faith therein, as well as in the existence of God. His boldest words are those which caused his
brief imprisonment at Toulouse in 1534, and which not only
charged this city with not having acquired even the rudiments
of Christianity and being given over to superstitions worthy
only of the Turks, but plainly say that the persecution of heretics is opposed to all semblance of humanity and utterly contrary to justice. The charge of atheism made by Calvin, Castalio, and many others of Dolet's contemporaries is scarcely
to be reconciled with the risk he took in order to circulate
religious books; but it is difficult to determine whether he
really had much respect for Christianity.

Among the friends of Dolet, Desperriers, and Rabelais was Clement Marot, page to Queen Margaret, who took him more than once out of the confinement in which he was put for eating meat in Lent and writing satires against the persecutors, especially that pillar of the Church, Diana of Poitiers, mistress of two royal devotees. The freedom of Marot's pen obliged him to put himself under the protection, first, of the duchess of Ferrara, and then of the republic of Venice. On returning to France in 1536, he wrote his *Balladin*, telling how Christine, the good shepherdess, ever kind, pure and young, and the best of singers and dancers, because she puts her heart in all she does, was driven away by the painted and wrinkled Simone, who dances falsely and cares nothing for the songs she chants, and how, after a thousand years of persecution and exile, light from heaven pierced the darkness, and Christine has left her retreat in Saxony and come back to France. It was not so much this comparison of true and false Christianity as a translation of the *Psalms*, musical enough to please King Francis and accurate enough to satisfy John Calvin, that called forth a storm before which Marot fled to Geneva. There, however, he found such different views from his own that he went to Turin, where he died the next year, 1544.

Gringoire wrote much after 1522 in behalf of the Church he had formerly derided on the stage, but other authors still found there a freedom of speech which could be enjoyed nowhere else in France. It was in the midst of *auto da fés* and on the brink of a religious war, that Jodelle, creator of the French comedy, exposed clerical corruption before the king and court in his *Eugène*, first acted in 1552. Of much earlier date and style is the farce of the *Theologaster*, a personification of the Sorbonne, who pours his lament—that men study Greek, the language of heresy, instead of scholasticism—into the ear of Monasticism, who answers by complaining that his table is no longer supplied sumptuously. Both try in vain to cure Faith of a Sorbonical colic, but she refuses their sermons and decretals and keeps calling for Holy Writ, who at last enters as a decrepit old man, his face so bloody that he is not recognized until cleansed and invigorated by his daughter Reason.

After denouncing the intolerance with which Erasmus and
Melanchthon are treated, Holy Writ heals Faith with a kiss,
and she in return salutes Reason as her sister, a dénouement
evidently belonging only to the beginning of the Reformation,
whose later spirit would have been better shown by making
Holy Writ lay the stick on which he has been leaning across
Reason's shoulders, and adopt Faith as his daughter in her
place.

But the dramatist most worthy of mention here is Sir David
Lyndsay, justly celebrated in *Marmion* for—

> "The flash of that satiric rage
> Which, bursting on the early stage,
> Branded the vices of the age,
> And broke the keys of Rome."

His most artistic poem, the *Dreme*, shows popes and
bishops lamenting in hell that they had been given temporal
power by Constantine, who, according to the *Complaynt of
the Papingo*, or Parrot, had divorced Prelacy from Poverty,
the mother of Chastity and Devotion, and married him to
Lady Property, whose daughter is Sensuality. The last-
named is prominent in the Lion King's great drama of the
Three Estates, which was acted in the vernacular before the
king, clergy, nobles and citizens of Linlithgow in 1540, and
often afterward, all day being occupied in the performance,
and which may still be read with interest, despite its coarseness. The first event is the conquest by Sensuality of the
young King, who is told that he is only following the example
of all the bishops. Popes, too, are said by the lady to be
among her subjects. Vainly does Chastity complain that she
has had no home since the pope became king, and ask hospitality of Bishop, Abbot and Prioress. They put her in the
stocks in company with Dame Verity, whom they call a
Lutheran, and whom Flattery, in the frock of a friar, addresses
thus:

> "What book is that, thou harlot, in thy hand?
> Out, walloway, this is the New Testament,
> In English tongue and printed in England.
> Heresy! Heresy! Fire! Fire incontinent!"

The sisters are soon rescued by Correction, or Reformation, who tells the King, he will lose his crown if he does not send away Sensuality; so that she has to put herself under the protection of the Clergy. Then Poor Man complains of his pastor's extortions and gets into a fight with Indulgence-peddler, who swears at the New Testament for teaching laymen so much truth that there is no more money to be made out of them. At last the three estates of the realm, Clergy, Nobility, and Bourgeoisie, meet in Parliament around the King. John the Commonweal, complains that the Church is governed by Avarice and Sensuality, and both are put in the stocks by Correction. The popular voice also secures the banishment of the great fat friars, who do no work, either religious or manual, but yet live like well-fed hogs. Prioress is discovered to be a harlot in disguise. Bishop and Parson are accused of keeping mistresses and neglecting to preach. They confess their guilt and lose their land. John the Commonweal takes the place of Clergy in Parliament as one of the three estates. Laws are then passed enabling tenants to become freeholders, confiscating the property of the wanton nuns in order to establish new courts of justice, permitting all clergymen to marry, and providing that no benefices be held by men who can not preach, and that no more money be sent to Rome.

That Lyndsay did not embrace Protestantism may be due only to its slight hold on Scotland at the time of his death, 1555. And not until six or seven years later was this step taken by George Buchanan, who had been imprisoned in 1539, on account of a satire against the Franciscans, written at the request of James V. He soon escaped to France, where he wrote several dramas, one of which, the *Baptistes*, shows that Savonarola and Luther were the true successors of John the Baptist, and makes Gamaliel say, "In our order cruelty is unbecoming," and "It is tyranny to oppress a holy man whom you can not convince by reason." Herod, too, tells the Daughter of Herodias that "The law puts a limit to the commands of kings." Among the youths who acted in those dramas was Montaigne. In 1547 Buchanan became Professor of Latin in Portugal, where he was imprisoned for nearly two years in a monastery on account of the *Franciscan*, which, however, was not published until 1564.

VI.

Still another list may be made of men and women who called themselves Protestants, but did not let themselves be bound in Lutheran, Calvinistic, or Anglican fetters. If Hutten had not died at the age of thirty-five, in 1523, it would soon have become plain that he cared little for the Bible or justification by faith, and hated the papacy mainly because it was the worst enemy of free thought. Scarcely had the great Theses appeared when he re-published Valla's attack on the legitimacy of the temporal power, and dedicated the book to Leo X. His fortune depended on the favor of the archbishop of Mainz, but he made up his mind to sacrifice every thing to the cause of liberty, and he took for his motto, "The die is cast." To the pope's bull against Luther, in 1520, he replied by a number of poems and dialogues in both German and Latin, showing the injustice of this sentence, as well as the profligacy, rapacity and tyranny of the Roman clergy, and calling on Germany to break the papal yoke. One of the earliest of these pieces is the *Roman Triads*, where he says: "Of three things Rome has plenty, priests, scribes and harlots." "Three things every Roman loves, short masses, old gold, and sensuality." "Three things are for sale in Rome, Christ, benefices and women." His poem on the burning of Luther's books runs somewhat thus:

> "Here is indulgence given to any
> Sinner who has the needed penny;
> Here are falsehoods freely told;
> Pardon for sin in advance is sold;
> Here the friends of truth are sent to hell;
> And God himself they try to sell."

A dialogue of great vigor brings forward Hutten as the slayer of the Bull which is attacking German Liberty.

He had been excommunicated, and obliged to take refuge with Sickingen, whose castles were open to all the persecuted, before the Diet of Worms, where the two knights are said to have been the authors of a placard, posted up in the streets, and warning Luther's enemies not to touch a hair of his head, for an army was ready to take the field in his defense.

At the same time Hutten tried to set the emperor against the pope. Failing in this, he and Sickingen did their utmost to bring about an anti-Romish league of all the German knights, burghers, and peasants, the co-operation of the last being solicited in a dialogue called *Neu Karsthans*. The first step in carrying out this plan was Sickingen's expedition in the name of gospel liberty, against the archbishop of Treves, in September, 1522. The attack was repulsed, many of the confederates stood aloof, and the most warlike of the Protestants, Philip of Hesse, helped conquer Sickingen, who died in the ruin which cannon had made of his castle, May 7, 1523. Hutten had taken refuge at Basel, but Erasmus would not see him, and the magistrates forced him to depart. Only Zwingli was willing to lighten the load of poverty, sickness, and mortification under which he sank on August 29, writing satire to the last. Thus ended the hope in which he had said, "The minds awake, the sciences bloom, it is a pleasure to live."

In sheltering Hutten, the Zurich reformer showed a liberality which was also apparent in his rationalistic view of the sacramental presence of Jesus, and which was largely due to his education having been received from Erasmus and the old philosophers, and not like Luther's, from the Mystics. Dean Stanley liked to quote Zwingli's prophecy of "the meeting in the presence of God of every blessed spirit, every holy character, every faithful soul that has existed from the beginning of the world even to its consummation." He was not without guilt in the murder by drowning of Felix Mantz, January 5, 1527, for looking at baptism as freely as he did himself at the communion; but his death in battle against the papists, October 11, 1531, prevented him from taking a decided position among the foes or friends of tolerance.

It was in the previous year that Campanus, for denying the personality of the Holy Ghost, the equality of the Son to

the Father, and the inability of the truly converted to commit
sin, was imprisoned by the elector of Saxony, whom Melanchthon
advised to hang him. Luther was more merciful,
and the Unitarian was suffered to return to Zurich where he
was again imprisoned by the Catholics. Others who attempted
to point out the unreasonableness of this dogma
were even more unfortunate. It may have been partly for
licentiousness, that Hetzer was beheaded at Constance in 1529,
but his worst offense was the view he expresses thus:

> "Why ask how many are in me?
> I made the world, and I alone;
> I am but one, I am not three;
> Of persons nothing have I known."

There is no such stain on the name of James Bainham, who
was racked in 1531, and burned early in 1532 at London, for
objecting to transubstantiation and the confessional, and asserting
that "If a Turk, a Jew, or a Saracen, do trust in God,
and keep his law, he is a good Christian man." And it was
merely disbelief in the incarnation that provoked Protestants
to light the fire on May 2, 1550, for Joan Bocher, who had
said to her judges: "It is a good matter to consider your ignorance.
It was not long since you burned Anne Ascue for a
piece of bread, and yet came yourselves soon after to believe
and profess the same doctrine for which you burned her. And
now, forsooth, you will needs burn me for a piece of flesh, and
in the end you will come to believe in this also, when you
have read the Scriptures, and understand them." Another
disciple of the Baptists, George van Paris, who came from
Holland to England, was burned for yet plainer opposition
to trinitarianism in 1531. Arians and Anabaptists were so
numerous in England that a commission was appointed the
year previous, in order to search for them, and many were
forced to recant during this reign and the next. One of the
culprits in 1556, Robert King, was also charged with saying
"That it is not lawful to put a man to death for conscience'
sake." Free-willers, or opponents of predestination, were also
put in prison by the Bloody Mary, who does not, however,

seem to have sent any of them, or of the Arians or Anabaptists, to the stake. Among the documents preserved by Strype, is that in which Archdeacon Philpot, who was burned as a Protestant, 1555, justifies himself for spitting on one of those "rank Anti-christs," "members of the devil," and "enemies of God," who deny that "Jesus is the eternal Son of God."

This last was also a prominent charge against Servetus, whose unrivaled originality made him persecuted by both Catholics and Protestants. He claimed to be self-taught, but he was greatly under the influence of Erasmus, as well as of the early Fathers, when, at the age of twenty-two, he sent out his *Errors About the Trinity*, a book denying that the three persons are more than three dispositions, a view condemned in the third century as Sabellianism, asserting that the real existence of the Son of God began at the birth of Jesus, and warning all Christians, that morality does not follow necessarily and spontaneously from faith, but needs special effort. This book was published near Strasburg in 1531, and read by Luther and other leading Protestants, but it found few adherents except at Vicenza and Venice, which latter city was noted for its tolerance. In Switzerland, where Servetus then resided, his views were so much hated that he had to depart, after publishing a second work, which closes thus: "It would be easy to separate truth from error, if all were allowed to speak in peace. May the Lord destroy all the tyrants of the Church. Amen."

From 1532 to 1553, he lived in various parts of France, under the assumed name of Villeneuve, studying and practicing medicine with such ability that he discovered the circulation of the blood through the lungs, and won the favor of the archbishop of Vienne, where he resided after 1540. In 1542 he published a Latin Bible, with notes written on the new theory, not yet fully adopted, that each passage must be interpreted as what the author designed mainly for the benefit of his own contemporaries, and that readers in later ages have no right to take any text as addressed directly and exclusively to themselves. It was a great step toward real knowledge of the Bible, when Servetus showed that it was David whose star was to come out of Jacob, and whose hands and feet were said by the Psalmist to have been pierced with wounds; that it was Hezekiah who was born of a young woman, as our critic correctly rendered it, and was named Immanuel; and that it was some one who was trying to bring back the Jews from Babylon, who was "despised and hated of men." Only a secondary reference to Jesus was admitted by Servetus, who may contest with Erasmus the title of founder of biblical criticism. It was not in these notes, but in those to an edition of Ptolemy, published in 1535, that the young student had dared to say that Palestine is not fertile, as is asserted in *Deuteronomy* and *Joshua*, but is inhospitable and barren.

He grew more and more independent, as he met with those revolutionary Mystics, the Anabaptists, and as he studied the Neo-Platonists, who made him a Pantheist. So bold were the letters which he sent to Calvin, that the latter wrote, on February 7, 1546, to his friend Farel, that Servetus was thinking of visiting Geneva, but that, "If he does come, and I have any influence, I will never suffer him to depart alive." He who wrote thus became so angry two years later, when Servetus sent him a manuscript copy of his best known, least read, and worst treated book, the *Restoration of Christianity*, that he would never send it back, despite the entreaties of the author.

The work, as printed in 1553, is a pantheistic commentary on the opening verses of the *Gospel of John*, written in a spirit of hostility to the principal rites and dogmas of both the Protestants and the Catholics. It opens with a prayer, that Christ would guide his servant's mind and pen to declare worthily the glory of his divinity. Only as God contains all things in himself is there a union between Him and Christ, who is intermediate between God and man, but did not exist personally before he was born of Mary. God, who was originally the Father only, has finally manifested himself as Son and Holy Ghost, but most of the Trinitarians make three Gods and worship a three-headed Cerberus. Faith in Christ saves us by reconciling us to God, but there is no need of reconciling Him to us. That we are justified, does not depend on His grace and election, but also on the merits of our own deeds and lives. Jews and Pagans are able to practice such virtue as will bring them to heaven. Good works are proper and natural to man, who did not incur the fall of Adam. Unbaptized infants are not lost. It is foolish to say that the salvation of a baby depends on a man's choosing to have it baptized. Infant baptism is an invention of the devil to prevent the true baptism, that of adults. Predestination, Servetus rejects utterly. A clear statement of that new truth, the pulmonary circulation of the blood, is also continued in this work, to which are appended some letters to Calvin and Melanchthon, and an indignant denunciation of all the Romish doctrines, especially trinitarianism and transubstantiation.

While preparing this book, Servetus had written to one of Calvin's brother-ministers, "I am sure I shall die for this; but I do not falter in soul, for I would be a disciple like the Master." Immediate danger he thought he had avoided by sending out the book anonymously, and not giving the printer's name or residence. Before any copies could be sold, a letter came to Lyons, near Vienne, from Geneva, inclosing the opening pages, and telling the real as well as assumed name of the author, who it was said ought to be burned alive. It is probable that Calvin had some share in giving this information, and it is certain that it was he who, when Servetus had been arrested, in consequence of the first communications and discharged for lack of evidence, sent to the Romish inquisitor the private letters written him in confidence by the Unitarian. This at once brought Servetus into prison, and would have sent him speedily to the stake, if he had not escaped, owing, it is said, to the gratitude of the Vibailly for the recovery of his little daughter from a dangerous illness. Soon after this escape, which was on April 7, he was burned in effigy, as were his books. He had reached Geneva, on his way to Italy, and was about to leave the city, when he was arrested, on Sunday, August 13, at the request of Calvin, who always gloried in it. This was his first visit to the city, and there is no evidence that he had been there more than a few days, had then made any attempt to spread his views, or had ever done any thing which could give any one there a legal or moral right to put him on trial.

Calvin took the lead in the prosecution, and drew up the thirty-eight articles on which Servetus was examined August 14, 15, 16 and 17. The chief charges were Sabellianism, Pantheism, the reference to Cerberus, disparagement of Calvin and Melanchthon, denial of the pre-existence of Jesus, of the efficacy of infant baptism, of the doom of unbaptized babies, and of the liability of children under twenty to commit deadly sin, irreverent treatment of *Deuteronomy, Judges,* and the Messianic prophecies, sedition in escaping from prison, and disbelief in immortality. The last accusation was utterly false. Servetus tried to make light of the differences between himself and Calvin, but the latter worked as hard as he could to magnify them, and wrote to Farel, that he hoped the sentence would be capital, though burning alive seemed too cruel. Such was the law, as he knew, when he prosecuted Servetus and preached against him, which he did the Sunday after the arrest. He also tried to argue away the fact, stated by Servetus, that Justin Martyr and other very early Fathers were not Trinitarians. Then the city attorney brought forward a new series of articles, charging the prisoner with immoral life, seditious designs, and sympathy with Jews and Moslems ; but these accusations had to be withdrawn. On the 22d Servetus pleaded that heretics were never put to death until the Church became corrupt, and that he had done nothing worse than present abstruse problems to the consideration of scholars ; but these pleas were treated as insults to all Christians, and his request, that he should either be set at liberty or else be furnished with a legal adviser, was promptly rejected. A heated discussion of the right of governments to put heretics to death took place on September 1, between Calvin and Servetus, who that day refused the request of the Genevese judges that he should give the inquisition at Vienne such information as would enable it to confiscate all sums still due him from his patients. A third set of articles, much resembling the first and written by Calvin's secretary, had already been brought into court. The resolution to ask the opinion of the magistrates and ministers of Bern, Basel, Zurich, and Schaffhausen, caused Calvin to prepare a fourth list of articles, thirty-eight in number and all dealing with the pre-existence of Jesus, except five, one of which repeated the false charge of disbelief in immortality. Servetus was allowed to reply, but did so very hastily, quoting no texts, often speaking obscurely, and frequently calling Calvin liar and ignoramus. The fourteen ministers of Geneva signed a refutation equally abusive, but much abler; and this Servetus answered only by scribbling such epithets, as persecutor, liar, and murderer, on the margin and between the lines. He sent no letters to the ministers in the four cities, but Calvin wrote to them individually. Before the answers arrived, Servetus complained to the judges of the hardships of his confinement, urged that heretics could not be justly put to death, and demanded to have Calvin banished for betraying him to the inquisition and afterward bearing false witness against him. No attention was paid to this petition, nor to the protests against sentencing him to death which were made by Zebedee, pastor at Noyon, as well as by Gribaldi, an Italian lawyer then visiting Geneva. The magistrates and ministers of Basel, Bern, Schaffhausen, and Zurich were found to favor capital punishment, and a majority of the court of twenty-five magistrates voted, in spite of the opposition of Perrin, the president, and a few others, that Servetus be burned alive. At noon the next day, Friday, October 27, 1553, he was tortured to death accordingly, wearing a crown of straw and leaves covered with sulphur, and having the manuscript he had loaned to Calvin, as well as a printed copy of his great book, hanging at his waist. Green wood was used, and his sufferings lasted half an hour. To the last he protested that Jesus was not the Eternal Son of the Father. Much less effort was made to have him recant than would have been made by Roman Catholics; but he had recently been visited by both Farel and Calvin, and the latter had answered his request for forgiveness only by fiercely denouncing his errors. The attempt of the famous persecutor to have his victim beheaded was useless, and he undoubtedly knew from the beginning that conviction meant death at the stake, as was required by the ancient law, then often enforced against witches.

It is to be noticed that the plea of Servetus, that heretics should not be put to death, was treated only as an aggravation of his guilt. His execution was so generally approved of in Switzerland, Germany, and England, that Protestantism was now fully committed to intolerance. However the Church might be divided otherwise, it was still firmly united in hostility to freedom of thought.

Vainly had the guilt of persecution been brought to light by More, Erasmus, Rabelais, Dolet, and Agrippa. What Luther and Calvin had said in their early writings in favor of tolerance was soon lost sight of even by themselves. But the cruel murder of Servetus caused his protest against such atrocities to win unexpected favor. His execution was promptly and openly censured at Basel by people who detested his theology. The Secretary of State at Bern, Zurkinden, wrote, in 1554, to Calvin, advising that the sword should not be used often against enemies of the faith, "because this has always been found to make their partisans more extravagant," and also that he should not defend his treatment of Servetus, for "you would have to support a proposition hateful to every one who thinks." Calvin's disregard of this advice called out the publication that year of a work showing, in both French and Latin, what he himself in earlier years, as well as other Reformers and many of the Fathers, had said against persecution. "Who would be a Christian, when he sees that those who confess Christ are murdered by other Christians with fire and sword, and treated worse than by robbers and murderers?" says this book, which made a great sensation. It bore the name of Martin Bellius, but is ascribed to Sebastian Castalio, formerly a school-teacher at Geneva, where he had showed rare ability, as well as a courage which made him visit the sick during a pestilence which frightened away the ministers. His opinion, that the *Song of Solomon* is immoral, brought on a controversy with Calvin, and some charges which he made publicly against the Genevese clergy, and which were fully justified five years later, when Freron was deposed for adultery, were received so angrily that he had to leave Geneva in 1544. During the rest of his life he suffered much from poverty, but in 1552 he became professor of Greek at Basel, where he published a Latin version of the Bible, showing great originality. His powerful attack on predestination appeared a few years later than the period covered by this volume.

In 1554 was also published a dialogue, in which Vaticanus asserts that if Christ were to come to Geneva, he would be crucified afresh, or else burned alive by the new pope who reigned there. This piece also had to appear without the real name of the author, who is supposed to have been Bolsec, formerly a French monk, but more recently a physician in Geneva, whence he had been banished, on December 22, 1551, for maintaining at a Friday conference, that Calvin's doctrine of predestination made God a tyrant, and lessened the difference between virtue and vice, as well as for admitting during his trial his belief, that faith does not depend on election, that free-will was not lost in Adam's fall, that God calls all men to salvation, and that He has not ordained that some rather than others should be lost. No attention was paid to a petition for his release by Jacques de Bourgogne, Lord of Falais, who on November 9 pleaded, what had never before been heard in Christendom, namely, that "Free speech ought to be permitted to all Christians." It seems to have been the intercession of Bern and Zurich which saved the life of Bolsec, who wrote a poem during his imprisonment, charging Calvin with seeking his death, and who afterward revenged himself by writing the *Life* of his persecutor, with that of a minor bigot, Beza.

Among the publications of 1554 were two other censures of the murder of Servetus, one by Occhino, formerly a popular preacher at Naples, but then a refugee for Protestantism, and soon to be banished from Zurich for Unitarianism at the age of 76, and the other a Latin poem by a fugitive from Sicily, named Camillo Renato, who had been on trial in the Grisons for Sabellianism and denial of the resurrection of the body. He now charged Calvin with an inexpiable crime, warned him that though the man had perished, the opinion remained, and advised him to spare men and destroy only error. Minos Celso of Siena also wrote at that time with singular force as well as moderation against capital punishment for heresy, but his work was not printed until thirty years later. Similar opinions were expressed by Lælius Socinus, uncle of the founder of the Socinians, on his arrival at Geneva, as a fugitive from Bologna in 1554. Strong ground in favor of tolerance was also taken by Vergerio, formerly a bishop, and by Cellarius, professor of theology at Basel, where the proposition was under discussion by the clergy in 1555. That same year Foncelet was banished from Bern, for a French poem making out Calvin worse than Caiaphas. Then, or even earlier, Lyncurt of Spain wrote an apology for his compatriot. A dozen protests had now been made against persecution, which was thenceforth indulged in more sparingly among Protestants. Gribaldi was punished for his Unitarianism only by banishment from Geneva in 1555, as he was two years later from Bern, to which city he finally returned to die in prison. Blandrata and Gentilis were exiled for the same offense in 1558 from Geneva, where Gentilis might have mounted the scaffold if he had not recanted, bare-headed and bare-footed, clad only in his shirt, and holding a lighted torch. Blandrata soon made his way to Poland, where Unitarianism had been taught before the accession, in 1548, of the tolerant King Sigismund, under whom, eight years later, every nobleman who admitted the authority of the Bible was granted the privilege of worshiping as he pleased in his own house. The *first* persecution was in 1564, when Occhino and Gentilis, who had recently arrived, were driven forth, the former soon to die in prison, and the latter to be beheaded two years later at Bern, where he suffered with great courage. Such were the French, Spanish, and Italian refugees who tried to liberalize Calvinism.

The liberal Protestants in Germany were mostly Mystics, the only exception of importance being Thamer, pupil of Luther, and chaplain in the Schmalkald war. There the soldiers answered to his reproofs of their lewdness and drunkenness: "You tell us yourself that we must be justified through the merits of Christ alone, that none of our acts can possibly please God, and that good works avail nothing toward salvation. Why then trouble us about morality?" This opened Thamer's eyes, and in 1547 he offered to maintain the saving efficacy of morality in a public discussion at Marburg, where he was pastor and professor. The discussion was prohibited, and his sermons to prove virtue indispensable caused his banishment on August 15, 1549. The archbishop of Mainz gave him a pulpit, which he soon lost by placing conscience above the Bible. After many wanderings he was driven into the Roman Catholic Church about 1557, and died professor of theology at Freiburg.

Of the steadfast followers of the Inner Light the most famous is Sebastian Franck, whose popularity as an author did not prevent his passing the latter part of his life in poverty and exile. He had to leave Nuremberg in 1531, on account of his incorporating in his *Universal History* a laudatory *Chronicle of Heretics*, which name he says has always been given to those who have taught true wisdom. In the preface to the whole work he exclaims: "God be thanked, I can read every author without prejudice and am not so far gone in any sect, that all pious men do not please me heartily, though they err in unessentials." "Neither have I sworn by any man's words, for I hold only to God, and under Him to my own reason." "I reject no heretic, but separate the gold from the dross." "There is scarcely a heathen or a heretic who has not some good thoughts, wherein I find my God, who lets his sun shine on the evil and the good, and pours out his blessing on them all."

No wonder that Luther called Franck the "Devil's Mouth," especially as he also said: "In each man a love of liberty is implanted by the free God." "There can be no sin against Him, for we can injure only our fellow men." "We were more at liberty to blame the vices of princes under the papacy than we are at present." "Each sect treats all others as heretics, but God is no respecter of sects, and whoever does

His will is acceptable in His sight." "The heathen were originally more tolerant to Christians than Christians are to Christians at present." "Reason is the fountain of all the rights of man." "God has no anger, but we, each of us, find Him angry or friendly, according to what we think of Him, just as for the blind the sunshine is darkness." "There is no need to reconcile God to men, for He is all love." "Surely, Jesus would not have had to come to us, if we had known how free God is from wrath." "He has implanted His light in every human soul, so that each man is able to know the truth and judge between evil and good." "By this aid wrote Job, Plato, Seneca, and Plotinus." "God is nature, and all nature is in itself divine. He can do nothing contrary to nature, for that would be to deny Himself." "There is no definition of God." "We are not fallen so far as not to be still divine. Each of us has good and evil principles in him, and can choose which to follow." "We need love as well as faith in order to be saved." "He who thinks ceremonies still necessary for the people is no Christian, but only a Jew." "Without the Inner Word the outer one is dead and barren, and only a source of error." "We can not trust to any book, not even Holy Writ, unless we have learned judgment from God." "It is wrong to say, Israel carried on war and therefore it is right for us. On the contrary, we should say, Israel waged war according to the old covenant, and therefore we, who are in the new, should not." "We need something higher than a Bible to reach to heaven." "God's Word is eternal, but many books of Scripture have been lost." "Surely they have not the Word and Wisdom who appeal to the Bible for themselves, as a thousand sects do among Christians, and as the Turk does to the Koran, the Jew to the Talmud, and the Papist to the Decretals, while each man calls the others heathens and heretics." "Let each one think that others also can quote Scripture, and take no rest until he has been taught of God." "If the Bible were necessary to salvation, then would those children have been lost whom Jesus blessed." "With the letter of Scripture have scribes and Pharisees slain the prophets and apostles." "The letter is the sword of Anti-christ, wherewith he fights against the saints."

We might say that we have not yet advanced much further than this, but it must be remembered that such opinions now make preachers popular in many sects, whereas Sebastian Franck was driven from city to city, under a hatred greatly increased by his declaring that he could not sign any creed, even one written by himself, or take any name but that of Christian. No serious attempt was made to suppress his books, among which were a *History of Germany*, tracts against war and drunkenness, collections of proverbs and paradoxes, two mystical treatises entitled the *Golden Ark* and the *Book with Seven Seals*, and translations of the *Praise of Folly*, by Erasmus, as well as of the *Vanity of Arts and Sciences*, by Cornelius Agrippa. All these works were printed before 1540 and most of them passed through several editions. No one has done more to purify religion and morality in Germany.

Many other Germans were also freed by faith in the Inner Light from bondage to ceremony and dogma. The simplicity of Protestant worship is largely owing to Carlstadt, who was one of the first reformers to marry, and who lived in great poverty after his banishment from his parish of Orlamünde, in 1524, at the instigation of Luther, on account of his disbelief in the sacramental presence of Jesus. Special stress was laid as early as 1524 on the immoral tendencies of the doctrine of justification by faith alone, as well as on the duty of taking brotherly love, rather than baptism by water, as the true sign of Christianity, by Schwenckfeld, who was called Stenckfeld by Luther, but who won many followers, owing largely to a holiness of life, which even a Catholic cardinal acknowledged. Bünderlin tried to reconcile the differences among the followers of the Bible, by publishing in 1529 at Strasburg a plea for the authority of the Inner Word. "This it is that saves us, and the Bible can be only a guide to it." "No one can tell whether his neighbor has this Inner Word, and therefore no one should blame another for lack of faith." "Our only duty toward those who differ with us is to teach

them gently." " He errs who says it is only by his own faith
that men may be saved." " Wholly contrary to Christ is it
for Protestants who pleaded for freedom of conscience when
they were contending against Rome, to use the sword against
those who differ with them." "Even the heathen are God's
children, and what the Bible says of His wrath against them is
merely figurative." "Jesus is our Saviour in so far as he helps
us to love God." In 1530 this Mystic ventured to assert that
baptism and all other outward rites are unnecessary and about
to pass away. John Denck, who died of the plague at Basel
in 1528, had already made hundreds of converts there as well
as in Augsburg, Strasburg, and Worms, to his view, that all
methods of baptism and theories about the Lord's supper are
unimportant, and that neither trinitarianism nor endless misery
is true, according to that highest of authorities, the Inner
Word. Apparently he was the first Universalist in modern
times, and he certainly had great learning and integrity, as
well as the grace, rare among religionists in that dogmatic century,
of admitting his own liability to error.

VII.

None of the people already mentioned in this chapter can
be positively asserted to have renounced Christianity, though
this religion had little hold either on the French or Italian
rationalists, especially Desperriers, Machiavelli and Guicciardini,
or on the Munster fanatics. Among the Anabaptist extremists
was David Joris, who disowned the authority of
Jesus, and claimed to have succeeded him as Christ David,
author of revelations which took the place of all that had been
known before, and set believers free from all outward laws and
institutions, particularly marriage. His tongue was bored by
the Dutch in 1528, and soon after publishing his *Wonderbook*,
in 1542, he took refuge under an assumed name in Basel,
where he propagated his views by correspondence, and died
in peace in 1556. No sooner was his record known than his
books and bones were burned together by the city executioner,
May 13, 1559.

Similar views are ascribed to the Libertines, who, perhaps, were successors of the Brethren and Sisters of the Free Spirit, and who are said to have appeared at Antwerp in 1525, to have made four thousand converts in France, where they were protected by Queen Margaret, and to have spread to Geneva, where, however, it is probable that this name was applied by Calvin to more rationalistic opponents.

One of these, Jacques Gruet, who had made himself obnoxious by wearing the same style of breeches that was in favor in the tolerant city of Bern, was arrested on Monday, June 28, 1547, for putting into one of the principal pulpits at Geneva an anonymous letter, threatening that the clergy would be assassinated, and declaring that, " We will no longer endure so many masters," an offense which he did not confess until he had been put on the rack, with Calvin's full approval. Gruet's books and private papers were examined, and he was found to have written in the margin of a chapter on immortality in Calvin's works, " All nonsense." Among his notes were these : " Moses says much and proves nothing," and " All laws, whether divine or human, were made by man's caprice." A letter, which had not been sent, urged a friend to complain to the king of France against Calvin, who was spoken of as a great hypocrite that wished to be worshiped like a pope. A draft of a petition to the Great Council contained this novel proposition : " If a man chooses to spend his property freely, other people ought not to interfere. If I wish to dance and enjoy myself, what has justice to do with that? Nothing ! Too severe laws will only make trouble." Never before had the punishment of conduct injuring only the agent been denounced as wrong in principle. Among the questions at the trial, and his answers, were these : " Does not he who says that we ought not to watch over the honor of God, but only to chastise such evil as is committed against men, show that he despises God and has no religion?" " He who says this may possibly have religion and a conscience, and agree with Scripture." "Are not the commandments of God more credible than those of man, and do not all who break them deserve punishment ?" " I know nothing about that."

Gruet protested that he did not really believe what he had written about Moses and the origin of morality, that he did not object to Calvin's doctrine of immortality, but only to his reasoning, and that he recognized him as a preacher of truth, though he thought ministers should confine themselves to expounding the Gospel, and not meddle with worldly affairs. The only witness was a clergyman who had held a private discussion with Gruet, commenced by the latter and running thus: "Where is the prohibition of fornication?" "It was given to Moses." "How do you know that?" "By Holy Scripture." "Was Moses present at the creation of the world?" "No." "Then, who said it to Moses?"

This is all that was brought up against Gruet, and no blame was ever cast upon his moral character. The indictment charges him with blasphemy against God and Moses, in saying that the latter proves nothing; in making all laws spring from human caprice; and in maintaining that only offenses against men ought to be punished, but not the violations of the divine commandments. "Thus he evidently seeks to annul all divinity; such a crime is more execrable than any heresy that has ever appeared; and only a monster in human shape could speak thus," urged the prosecutor who begged that Gruet might be punished according to *Deuteronomy*, xviii., 20, which directs that the false prophet shall die. The relatives of the prisoner now presented a petition in which he confessed his faults, implored mercy, and promised reformation. This would probably have saved his life, if he had been in the hands of the inquisition. Roman Catholic tribunals did not put to death heretics who could be persuaded to recant, and much pains was often taken, for instance with Huss and Bruno. Calvin had shown not the slightest desire to have Gruet turn from his ways and live. He had petitioned the court, immediately after the arrest, to strike at all slanderers of the ministers or magistrates, for the honor of God; and now we find him expressing regrets, in a private letter, that the trial lasts so long, and the judges are so timid. On Sunday, July 25, 1547, however, they voted that Gruet had blasphemed against God, insulted His servants, and committed treason against the state. "Wherefore, having God and the Holy Bible before our eyes, we, in the name of the Father, the Son, and the Holy Ghost, sentence you, Jacques Gruet, to be carried to the place of execution, and there to have your head cut from your shoulders, your body fastened to the gallows, and your head nailed up in this place." And thus, on the next day, perished as a criminal the first man who denied the right of the state to punish conduct which injured nobody, and was merely contrary to Scripture.

More than two years after Gruet's execution, some repairs on his house brought to light a treatise in his hand-writing, alleging that both Moses and Jesus were criminals, that the latter was not born of a virgin, that his miracles were delusions or deceptions, that he deserved to be put to death, and that the Bible has no more truth in it than Æsop's Fables. Such at least is the account given of this book by John Calvin, who falsely charged Servetus with disbelief in immortality. He had this manuscript publicly burned before the former home of its author on Friday, May 23, 1550. This book is often referred to as a mitigation of the guilt of shedding Gruet's blood, but no such sentiments were ascribed to him on his trial. The real offense for which he was murdered was disbelief in persecution.

That same year Bishop Hooper says, "England is afflicted by heresies. There are some who say that the soul of a man is no better than the soul of a beast, and is mortal and perishable. There are some who dare in their conventicles not only to deny that Christ is our Saviour, but to call that blessed child a mischief-maker and a deceiver." These unbelievers were possibly Baptists, for this sect is known to have had great influence over Servetus, Denck, Hetzer, Joan of Kent, and George van Paris. Two Anabaptists were banished from Geneva in 1537 for denying immortality. The same doom fell July 27, 1553, on a Frenchman who had said "There is no devil or hell but ourselves," and "The Holy Scripture is not paper and ink, but the human heart." Another was expelled in 1557, with his children, because he thought nothing of the Gospel, and both men were to be scourged if they returned.

Conradin Bassen was beheaded at Basel in 1529 for denying the divinity of Jesus, his miraculous birth, and the efficacy of prayer. The same fate would have been suffered at Chur in 1540 by Tiziano, if he had not recanted his assertion that Jesus is simply human and the Bible without authority. No persecution seems to have fallen on Postel, a Parisian professor, who maintained the superiority of natural to supernatural religion, and the need of a female Messiah, nor on Ludovici, a Venetian poet, who in his *Triumph of Charlemagne*, published 1535, makes Nature say : "As for that part of you which is called immortal, I do not make it ; nor do I know if God makes it, or what it may be. This may be some good gift which it did not please Him, when I made the body, to give to that part of you which, after your death, is resolved into Him."

These scattered instances, from Italy, Switzerland, England, Holland, and France, show that there was more opposition to Christianity in these countries than ever before, though not so much as if the bigotry of the Protestant and Catholic clergy had not kept on the alert.

VIII.

In this account of the forty-three years between Luther's theses and the general triumph of the Evangelical reformers, less attention has been given to those great though narrow men than to their more enlightened contemporaries. Of these really liberal men and women we may make five classes. Section III. was devoted to Erasmus, More, Agrippa, L'Hôpital, Queen Margaret, Queen Juana, and other sincere but tolerant Roman Catholics, whose failure to reform the Church from within goes far to prove all such attempts impossibilities. The second group is much more heterogeneous, for it includes a great variety of practical reformers, of whom some, like Münzer, Florian Geyer, and Wendel Hippler, joined in a concerted but fruitless effort to emancipate the German peasantry ; while others, like Las Casas, Spifame, La Boëtie, and Poynet, made more peaceable opposition to political abuses, and still others labored single-handed and with great success against different mental despots, Paracelsus and Vesalius attacking Galen, Ramus assailing Aristotle, and Copernicus showing the falsity of the Ptolemaic theory, whose fall shook all the systems of theology and philosophy hitherto revered. Next come the rationalists whose Romanism was only nominal, and whose tendencies to Protestantism or unbelief caused most of them to be persecuted. Here the great name is that of Rabelais, who was unusually fond of science. It was the influence of ancient philosophy apparently which ruled Pomponatius, Machiavelli, Guicciardini, Berni, Folengo, Manzolli, Gryphius, Desperriers, Dolet, Marot, and Lyndsay. The same tendency may be detected in many Protestants, like Hutten, Zwingli, Buchanan, Castalio, and Servetus, as well as assumed in Gribaldi, Bolsec, Occhino, Renato, Vergerio, Socinus, Celso, Cellarius, Lyncurt, Blandrata, and Gentilis; but Mysticism preponderated with Franck, Carlstadt, Schwenckfeld, Denck, Hetzer, Bünderlin, Hoffmann, Mantz, and Menno, as well as, in all probability, Joan Bocher and George van Paris. These two sets of liberal Protestants could not easily be distinguished apart so clearly as to form two classes; and no such division is necessary, for they all agreed closely enough, in stopping short of utter unbelief, for us to study them together. None of them can be called rationalists as correctly as could be most of the members of the previous class. And far beyond all these groups is that in which stand Joris, Postel, Ludovici, Gruet, and Tiziano who were led by either Mysticism or rationalism to give up the authority of Christianity more completely than had ever been done before. Gruet is our first martyr for the truth, that no one should be punished criminally, except for injury to his fellow men.

Having thus studied each group of thinkers by itself, we must next consider the chronological relationship of their leading members, and look at the Reformation as a drama in five acts, as follows :

First comes that great deliverance from papal tyranny, which gives a name and character to the whole period, but which is substantially achieved between 1517 and 1522, when

Luther, Erasmus, Hutten, Zwingli, Carlstadt, and the other liberals are working together in perfect harmony against their common enemy.

Early in 1522, Luther comes into conflict with other Mystics who are destroying old institutions too rapidly, and thus begins the second act of the drama, the strife of Lutherans against revolutionists. Soon we see the most martial of the Protestant princes, Philip of Hesse, in deadly warfare with the knights-errant of the Reformation, Hutten and Sickengen. Still more bloody are the battles of Lutheran despots against Baptist rebels in 1525, a supplementary scene of the same character being enacted ten years later in the horrors of Münster. These thirteen years are also marked by bitter controversies among the reformers. Erasmus keeps active to the end in assailing the bigotry, superstition and immorality of the Romanists, but does not neglect to censure the same faults, as he sees them among Protestants. Thus he comes into angry disputes with Hutten and Luther. The latter is now destroying the unity and imperiling the very existence of Protestantism by his intolerance against Carlstadt, Zwingli, and every one else who thinks rationally about the sacraments. Banishment from Protestant cities is incurred, not only by Carlstadt for this liberality, but by Schwenckfeld for showing the immoral tendencies of trusting to justification by faith alone, by Servetus for criticising trinitarianism, by Franck for asserting the right of heretics to tolerance, and by Paracelsus for publicly burning the books of Galen, Avicenna, and other medical authorities, which deed made him the first to show that facts outrank traditions. The transitoriness of all religious institutions is declared by Bunderlin, while Protestantism is gaining its name at Spire and its creed at Augsburg. The first murders caused by its bigotry are those of Bassen at Basel, and Mantz at Zurich. The Reformation has now securely established itself in Germany, Switzerland, and the Scandinavian peninsulas, while its advocates are becoming numerous in Holland, Belgium, France, Italy, and England. Henry VIII. becomes head of the Church and carries on a double persecution of both Catholics and Protestants, those liberal men on each side, More and Bainham, being among his earliest victims. At this time takes place the first martial victory of Protestantism over Romanism, the conquest of Würtemburg by the Landgrave of Hesse.

The third act is a comparatively peaceful one, except for the persecutions which continue in all Catholic lands, as well as in England, but are as yet rare and slight among Protestants. It extends from 1536 to 1546, over the last ten years of the life of Luther, who is now almost inactive, the leading theologian of Protestantism being Calvin, while the politics of the Reformation are controlled by the mighty Landgrave. Now it is that Desperriers publishes his *Cymbalum Mundi*, the opposition to which drives him to suicide, and Servetus lays the foundation of rational criticism in those notes on the Bible, soon to be numbered among capital offenses. Nothing worse is yet done in Geneva, however, than to inflict fines, exile, and imprisonment for unbelief, irreverent behavior, dancing, and staying away from church, the two last offenses being now made penal for the first time in Christian history. Especially important are the simultaneous, but wholly independent, attacks of Copernicus, Vesalius, and Ramus on Ptolemy, Galen, and Aristotle. Hitherto the battle against tradition has been mainly carried on by rationalistic philosophers and Mystics. Thenceforth, they have the mighty aid of science.

From the burning of Anne Ascue in July, 1546, to that of Servetus in 1553, is a reign of terror. Among the murdered are also Dolet, Gruet, Joan Bocher, George van Paris, and Gryphius, while Bolsec and Thamer are among the banished. Most of these victims are treated all the worse, because they and their friends plead the right of heretics to tolerance. La Boëtie protests vainly against the cruelty of despotism. The half-way policy of Henry VIII. is superseded by a more Protestant but not more tolerant administration. Rabelais and Servetus finish their great works, one to be universally read, even by the tyrants it ridicules, and the other to be suppressed almost entirely.

The last seven years covered by this chapter form a fifth

act, less tragic than the fourth, except for the reign of the Bloody Mary, after whose death, in 1558, England has a few years of unusual tolerance. What is most characteristic of these seven years is the series of protests called out by the murder of Servetus. Among the speakers and writers against persecution are Zebedee, Gribaldi, Zurkinden, Castalio, Bolsec, Occhino, Renato, Celso, Lælius Socinus, Cellarius, Vergerio, Lyncurt, and Foncelet. Calvin and Beza write fiercely on the other side, but Protestantism now does nothing worse than burn the books and bones of that most daring of Mystics who has called himself Christ David. To make up a list of twelve apostles of tolerance, may be added to the names just given that of L'Hôpital, author of the first edicts designed to make Catholics and Protestants live together peaceably.

The boldest writers during all this period, Copernicus, Agrippa, Bünderlin, Servetus, Franck, Ludovici, Desperriers, Berni, La Boëtie, Joris, Gruet, Dolet, Marot, and Rabelais, did their best work between 1530 and 1550. Before the latter date thinking independently had become too dangerous in Protestant as well as Catholic lands to be carried on openly, but there is every reason to believe that it went on actively in secret. It is hard to say whether intellectual liberty up to the middle of the sixteenth century, was more indebted to the Mysticism which arose in Germany and Holland out of the Bible and Tauler, or to that French and Italian rationalism which sprang from the revival of the classic philosophy. At all events, mental progress was now more rapid than ever before since the age of Cicero and Lucretius. It is needless to say how rich and bright, especially in England, was the new literature to which all this conflict of opinions soon led.

CHAPTER XI.

CONCLUSION.

We have seen how easily liberty of thought conquered classic polytheism, how completely it was crushed by the emperors and the Church, how cruelly it was persecuted as it slowly revived during the latter part of the Middle Ages, and how rapidly it grew during the Renaissance and Reformation, though not to its former stature.

In this narrative, I have sought simply to state the important facts accurately and clearly, and have left it for each reader to draw his own conclusions. Though fully confident of the incomparable advantages of greater liberty and activity of thought, than have ever yet been reached, I have not had a single specific proposition before me, as desirable or possible to be proved. It was not until I had finished the previous chapters, that I inquired what I had found out. In the final revision, I saw that some general principles had been well enough established to be worth mentioning, if only in order to show how the facts should be interpreted.

The independent thinkers I have mentioned may properly be divided into two schools. The first exercise of mental liberty was in the search after scientific knowledge of natural phenomena. This pursuit was carried on by those earliest of Greek philosophers, the Ionians; and their results, with some attained by more idealistic speculators, enabled the Epicureans to free themselves from supernaturalistic fetters, by asserting that all phenomena take place according to laws necessarily involved in the properties of matter, and that all the distinction between right and wrong arises out of intrinsic differences in human actions. This position was strengthened by the labors of Peripatetics, Stoics, astronomers, and physicians, and one of these last, Galen, who lived to 200 A.D., was able to develop scientific positivism into agnosticism. Thought was already becoming less free than before. More than a thousand years elapsed before fondness for science reappeared, and then only to call down twenty-four years of imprisonment on Roger Bacon. Positivist principles were soon after taught more obscurely and safely in the latter part of the *Romance of the Rose;* but they did not become much known until the publication of the great works of Copernicus, Vesalius, Rabelais, and Cardan, in the middle of the sixteenth century, taught people to study facts instead of books.

Nearly as early in origin, and much more prominent in classic literature, was that form of philosophy which recognizes no higher authority than the deductions of the individual reason, unverified by scientific investigation, and has thus been led to insist with peculiar earnestness, on the greatest possible liberty and activity of thought, as a necessity for both mental and moral growth. The most famous champion of this view, though not the earliest, is its great martyr, Socrates. His views have come down to us mingled with theories peculiar to his brilliant biographer; but the liberatory tendency remained predominant in ancient philosophy. Pyrrho showed the bliss of keeping independent of all authorities, whether theological or metaphysical, and thus founded a school of skepticism, which soon conquered the Platonists, whose reliance on intuition instead of experience was found to result in utter uncertainty of opinion. Cicero gave this view a permanent place in literature, and it was rapidly supplanting the more scientific one, when both sank beneath the pressure of imperialism, Neo-Platonism, and Christianity. It was at the close of the eleventh century that this metaphysical skepticism first reappeared, as Nominalism began to demonstrate the unreality of abstractions, a truth which Ockham was ere long enabled by imperial protection to maintain against the pope. The same tendency showed itself in the emperor Frederic II., and also among the bold expositors of Averroism at Paris. Its spirit may also be detected in *Reynard the Fox*, and other medieval satires. The sixteenth century gave it a powerful champion in Pomponatius, and placed

Rysswick and Gruet among its martyrs. Neither philosophic nor scientific thought had done so much up to that time to liberalize Christianity, as had been accomplished by less irreligious heresies.

Faith in the soul's capacity for receiving direct light from God, and coming into union with Him, led during the thirteenth, fourteenth, fifteenth, and sixteenth centuries to such disbelief in the need of salvation by the help of the Church, that Dolcino levied open war against her, Rienzi tried to establish at Rome the reign of the Holy Ghost, predicted in the *Eternal Gospel*, and the revolutionary agitation, carried on, first by the Brethren and Sisters of the Free Spirit, and then by the Anabaptists, showed itself in the Peasants' war, as well as in the excesses at Münster. Meantime a more peaceful but not less independent type of Mysticism had been developed by Eckhart, Tauler, and other Germans, whose influence may be seen in Luther, but much more strongly in Paracelsus, Schwenckfeld, and Sebastian Franck.

Before the appearance of heretical Mysticism, a more rationalistic form of piety had shown itself in the Gnostics, Manichæans, Paulicians, and Catharists, the last of whom were suppressed with peculiar cruelty. The same position was taken by many individual scholars, some of whom, like Origen, Abelard, Heloise, Erasmus, and Servetus, did good service as biblical critics.

These four movements of scientific positivism, philosophic skepticism, heretical Mysticism, and pious rationalism, all received great though unmeant help from the Wycliffites, Hussites, and Protestants, for the Roman Catholic Church had trained herself so skillfully and armed herself so powerfully for the destruction of intellectual liberty, that even Calvinism has proved much less pernicious. The natural hostility between Protestantism and rationalism had, however, become unmistakable before the establishment of the Reformation.

It is hard to say whether it is to the Christian rationalists, the Mystics, or the classic philosophers that we are most indebted for teaching the duty of tolerance. This principle is necessarily involved in the teachings of Socrates and Seneca; but it was not stated by either of them formally. Its first exercise was by the Buddhists; and its earliest expression west of India seems to have been in A.D. 25, when Cremutius Cordus told the senate, who sentenced him to death for freedom of speech, that "Errors in words should be punished by words only." Hadrian and Antoninus Pius were taught by philosophy to practice it, as was Zenobia. She and Galen are among the few Pagans who are known to have judged fairly and intelligently of Christianity. The first Christian rulers who tolerated differences in opinion were those Languedocian princes who were dethroned and murdered on this account. Roger Bernard, Count of Foix, went so far as to declare that religion ought to be free to all, and that no one's liberty of worship should be interfered with, even by the pope. His instructors were the Catharists, a sect whose persecution was severely censured by Hildegard, the prophetess. She also spoke, as did Abelard, in behalf of the Jews, who were not hunted down systematically like the heretics, but yet were much worse treated in Christian than in Moslem lands. They suffered greatly from German and English mobs at the departure of the crusades; and such stories of the murder of Christian children in the synagogues as stain the pages of Chaucer, and have been ineffectually revived in our own day, often exposed them to massacre. They were expelled successively from England, France, and Spain, and where they were permitted to remain, it was only to be insulted and plundered without redress. Still, the worst of their sufferings are of rather early date, and their condition in those parts of Western Europe which they were allowed to inhabit in the sixteenth century, was so much better than before, as to call out savage denunciations from Martin Luther when most reactionary. Previously he had made strong protests against this and all other persecution. So for a while had Calvin, whose share in the murder of Gruet for denial of the right of the state to punish conduct not injurious to any one, as well as in that of Servetus for innovations in theology, is peculiarly culpable, because the Church of Rome had made peace with the Hussites more than a century before, and had perpetrated but little persecution for seventy years, while More, Erasmus, Dolet, Rabelais, and Cornelius Agrippa had made the guilt of intolerance manifest. When a blameless scholar was burned to death for his opinions by his fellow-Protestants, there was such loud remonstrance as had never been heard before. Thenceforth differences in opinion were punished less severely, especially by Protestants. Spain was incorrigible, and Rome took a great step backward as late as 1555, the year when Mary of England incurred her epithet of infamy. This persecution, however, ceased three years later, when that in Southern Germany was discontinued, as was also that in France in 1560. Venice had always quietly permitted her subjects to worship as they chose. Tolerance had also been practiced by Sigismund of Poland and Margaret of Navarre, as it probably would have been by Juana of Castile, if her disposition that way had not caused her to be deprived of her throne, and kept by her own father and son in prison for nearly fifty years. No scholar who encouraged persecution after 1555, can have been ignorant that good and wise Christians had pronounced it wicked. The correspondence between the growth of tolerance and that of unbelief is so close as to show that religious faith is largely due to compulsion, exercised by people who have been educated into loyalty to the Church. It is also true that scarcely any nation has ever given up persecution until it has begun to grow irreligious.

The increase and diminution of intellectual liberty, in its various forms, has also been accompanied by corresponding changes in the condition of women. Theano, Aspasia, Arete, and Hipparchia, stand almost alone as female students of philosophy during the period when it was still liable to persecution at Athens. Plato's proposition, that women should be educated, like men, for a share in the government, was as far in advance of the age as was that confidence in intellectual activity which he had learned from Socrates. The increase of enlightenment, which permitted Epicurus to teach openly, brought Leontium and many other women into the Garden. The decay of ancient institutions gave the Roman ladies a liberty which would have been complete if they had been less superstitious. Early Christianity was equally successful in restoring marital supremacy and unreasoning faith. Those heretics, the Gnostics and Montanists, permitted women to preach ; but no ancient Christian of unblemished orthodoxy showed himself so friendly to female independence as the skeptical Seneca, Plutarch, Pliny, Hadrian, and Antoninus Pius. Clement of Alexandria, who lost his place in the list of saints more than a century ago on account of his liberality, urged that women have as much right as men to study philosophy, and gave high praise to Miriam, Sappho, Theano, Aspasia, and Leontium. These names, with those of Portia, Livia, Agrippina, the Arrias, Fannia, Sulpicia, Zenobia, and Hypatia, show that more female ability had been developed before the establishment of Christianity than can be found afterward for centuries. Women had almost ceased to figure in history, except as devotees, when they appear among the most zealous propagandists of Catharism, whose sacraments they administered to the dying, and whose deadliest enemy fell before a stone from their catapult. This is the time when Heloise and Hildegard wrote, when Averroes declared the frailty of women due to their habit of depending on men, and when Waldensianism went so much beyond Moslemism, Catholicism, or even Catharism, as to permit female preaching, which afterward became customary among the Taborites. The ardent Mysticism of the thirteenth century found a new Messiah in Wilhelmina, and a similar fancy appeared in the sixteenth. Pierre Dubois advocated female education, as well as marriage of priests, and suppression of the papal sovereignty. His contemporary, Dolcino, found Margaret as eager as himself to abolish all bonds of outward obedience, and as steadfast in the fierce battle, the long struggle with famine, and the final tortures. The fourteenth century, which suffered not only her but Marzia Ordelaffi to wage war against the pope, produced also that philanthropic author, Christine de 'Pisan, that eloquent and virtuous heresiarch, Joan of Aubenton, and that great Queen Margaret, who brought Norway, Sweden and Denmark together beneath her sway. Well might Chaucer celebrate female capacity, which was soon to receive a new illustration in Joan of Arc. Among the glories of the Renaissance are the gifted women of Italy, like Cassandra Fidele, the Averroist lecturer, and Caterina Sforza, the defender of Forli against the Borgias. Cornelius Agrippa showed his rare originality and independence in asserting the natural nobility of the female sex, and its right to disregard Paul's command of silence in the churches, to write books, to hold offices, and to plead in the courts. I should perhaps have mentioned in the previous chapter that the sixteenth century was as favorable to female scholarship in England as the fifteenth had been in Italy. Thus female activity and other forms of independence increased together, and on account of the growing weakness of the Church.

Equally close is the connection between political and religious liberty. Both flourished together in Athens, and then in Rome, where imperialism showed itself to be their common enemy. Both revived in the second century, but they vanished together after the establishment of Christianity. As they slowly re-appeared during the Middle Ages, they found their best friends in the same cities in Southern France, Central and Northern Italy, and Western Germany. This volume has mentioned many patriotic rationalists and heretics like Empedocles, Zeno the Skeptic, Cicero, Brutus, Seneca, Arnold of Brescia, Jean de Meung, Dolcino, Rienzi, Erasmus, Hutten, Cornelius Agrippa, Carlstadt, Münzer, and Sebastian Franck. That William Rufus, John, Frederic II., Philip the Fair, and other despots became unbelievers, is largely due to the fact that the Church stood in the way of their ambition. England was able to attain political freedom earlier than intellectual, but she has since been pre-eminent in both kinds of liberty.

The question is somewhat complicated by the fact that a man seldom becomes a rationalist, without such culture as has been confined, until very recently, to the upper and privileged classes, whose interests are aristocratic. Socrates, indeed, was of humble origin; but his patrons and friends were, for the most part, wealthy men of high rank, and his death was due to a sudden revolution in favor of the democracy, in whose previous ascendency had occurred the persecution of Anaxagoras and Alcibiades. Not only Socrates, but Plato and Aristotle found nobles and monarchs so much more friendly than the common people, as fully accounts for their disapproval of democracy. At Athens, and all over the Roman empire, philosophy soon gained such ascendency among people of rank and wealth, that Christianity had to begin by converting the lower classes, for whose benefit it taught the unimportance of social distinctions, except that between subject and emperor, said to be ordained by God. The humble rank of Jesus and his Apostles also did much to give early Christianity leveling tendencies, which gradually disappeared as it gained dominion over the upper as well as the lower classes.

How completely the common people in Western Europe had come under the power of the medieval Church is shown by the failure, first of Catharism and then of Mysticism, to establish itself, except for brief periods and in regions of limited extent. Vainly did Dolcino call upon the Lombard peasants to break every yoke, or Arnold of Brescia and Rienzi exhort the Romans to restore the republic. Even less popularity was won by those scholars who labored wholly for intellectual liberty, like Erigena, Berengar, Roscellin, Abelard, Peter of Bruis, Henry of Cluny, Averroes, Maimonides, Joachim of Floris, Amalric of Bena, Bacon, Ockham, Marsilius, and Gerson. Peter of Bruis was actually murdered by a mob, as Hypatia had been. Berengar, Roscellin, and Abelard ran great risk of perishing likewise. Peasant revolts began to be formidable as early as the thirteenth century, but were generally provoked by the pressure of material grievances, though knowledge of the leveling doctrines of the New Testament proved dangerously incendiary in England, Bohemia, and Germany. This influence did much to give Wycliffe, Huss, Luther, and Zwingli a popularity which is also due to their not attempting to diminish the national faith, but merely to direct it to worthier objects. Even that could not be done before the closing years of the fourteenth century.

And in the sixteenth the dogmatism of Luther and Calvin was much more acceptable to the common people than was the rationalism of Pomponatius, Cornelius Agrippa, Gruet, and Servetus; while the popularity of Erasmus and Rabelais was greatest in the upper classes, who were the most severely lashed by these satirists.

Among the rationalists and reformers mentioned in this volume, are the physicians, Empedocles, Democritus, Hippocrates, Galen, Maimonides, Cade, Pietro of Abano, Cornelius Agrippa, da Solo, Manzolli, Paracelsus, Rabelais, Servetus, Bolsec, Vesalius, Cardan, and Copernicus. More than fifty clergymen, friendly to religious and political liberty, have also been commemorated in these pages, but I need here only name Arnold of Brescia, John Ball, and Münzer. Almost all the other champions of progress, especially in the fifteenth and sixteenth centuries, are remarkable for love of books. Some of the early philosophers, like Diogenes, and possibly Socrates, educated themselves mainly by conversation; but Xenophanes seems to have been the only classic thinker of importance who could be called self-taught. Thales had studied in Egypt. The Buddha had received some instruction, and so had most of the Hebrew prophets. Amos seems to be the only one whose mission found him utterly unprepared. Jesus is said to have sought instruction of the learned men in the Temple when he was only twelve; and there is no reason to suppose that he did not often do so afterward. We also read that he was in the habit of expounding the Old Testament in the synagogue at Nazareth; and his sayings show great familiarity with that work, as well as with Hebrew literature generally. There is also some reason, as we have seen, for supposing that he was under Buddhist influence, as well as that he did not rise so far above Judaism as is represented in the Gospels. (See pp. 2 and 67). Still he can not be called a scholar, nor can his Apostles, with the exception of Paul, whose learning made him by far the most original, energetic, and liberal.

The only medieval heresiarchs who worked independently of books seem to be Tanchelm and Segarelli. Eon could quote the Bible, though not very rationally; and Waldo had the help of scholars. It is not unlikely that Dolcino had some instruction from his priestly father. Leutard and Hans Boheim seem to have acted under instruction; Wat Tyler had been preceded by John Ball; and the other peasant revolts were largely due to Catharist, Mystic, Lollard, or Anabaptist instigators. Paracelsus had learned much from his father, who was a physician, and from other teachers, had studied Hippocrates and the Neo-Platonists zealously, and finally gave up reading books to his own destruction.

In short, the work of discovering truth, exposing error, and attacking oppression during the twenty centuries covered by this history has been almost entirely performed by scholars, or under their direction. Wendell Phillips was sadly mistaken when he said in his recent Phi Beta Kappa address: "I do not think the greatest things have been done for the world by its book-men." This volume has been mainly occupied with what book-men have achieved, despite continual persecution, which uneducated people seldom tried to mitigate, and generally approved heartily. Another statement of the brilliant orator who has done so much to make New Englanders think for themselves, is that, "Almost all the great truths relating to society were not the result of scholarly meditation." He forgot the services of Plato, Aristotle, Tacitus, Averroes, Rienzi, Jean de Meung, More, Erasmus, Cornelius Agrippa, Hutten, Carlstadt, Münzer, Lyndsay, Las Casas, Rabelais, Franck, Spifame, La Boëtie, Knox, and Bishop Poynet. All that was known about social rights in the sixteenth century was due to these and other scholars. Still, Mr. Phillips was more than half right, for most of the members of his own class have always been conservative. So-called education has commonly been perverted into teaching pupils to take for granted the authority of teachers and text-books. Schools and colleges are still busy making people think, as they did in the Dark Ages, that knowledge must be got by studying books. The really liberal education, of looking at facts directly and independently, has scarcely been inaugurated. The scholar's livelihood has usually been gained in the service of obstructive institutions; he has seldom succeeded in rising above the need of guidance, a feat never accomplished by the illiterate; and he has often been provoked, by the indifference of the masses to new truth, into doubting their capacity for self-government. During the period covered by this volume, however, the scholarly class contained nearly all the friends of progress; and their number has increased rapidly with the rise of the standard of scholarship, while the illiterate class has proved conservative throughout, except when material grievances have made it revolutionary.

The general connection of the progress of culture with that of political and religious liberty, is undeniable. All three flourished together at Athens, were suppressed together at Rome, struggled together to emancipate themselves from medieval bondage, and made their inspiration felt in the literature of the sixteenth century, as had not been done for ages previously. And to show how much all three gained from the decline of ecclesiastical tyranny, I must here refer to some facts opposed to the common fancy that monastic life has favored scholarship. The Church did her best to check study outside of the cloister, but inside it was constantly interfered with by fasts, vigils, scourgings, lengthy devotions, for which sleep was interrupted incessantly, prohibition to travel in search of books, objects of study, or learned society, and punishment for reaching unfamiliar results. Gottschalk was imprisoned for conversing more logically than his brother monks; Abelard was scourged for finding out new facts in history and was compelled to turn hermit in order to study safely; Bacon's fondess for scientific methods of thought kept him idle for twenty-four years in convent dungeons; Poggio could find few scholars in the English monasteries; Erasmus had to get papal permission to quit the cloister before he could study properly; and Rabelais' literary activity is due to a similar favor accorded to him after he had been sentenced to life-long confinement for trying to learn Greek.

The whole effect of such a system must have been to make

scholars conservative, and their seclusion from the world outside was particularly well adapted to prevent sympathy with the people's wrongs. Thus the Renaissance, in making it possible to get books and teachers outside of the monasteries, at once increased, not only the amount of culture, but the interest in political and religious freedom among scholars.

No form of scholarship gained more by this emancipation than biblical criticism. The earliest work had been done by heterodox or else pagan critics. Thus the incredibility of Moses' account of the creation, and the immorality of mobbing tradesmen busy in the service of the worshipers in the Temple were pointed out by Origen in the third century. So was the real origin of the *Book of Daniel* by the kingly Porphyry; but his work was promptly destroyed, with that in which Julian brought to light the discrepancy in the Gospel genealogies. Then biblical criticism slumbered, except among Jews like Chivi of Baikh, for eight hundred years, until Abelard and Heloise began to write what could not be published, about the doubtful genuineness of *James*, the misquotation of the prophets by Matthew, the uncertainty of the original text of the New Testament, and the improbability that Jesus cursed the fig-tree, or that Moses related his own death and burial. No such speculations could be safely circulated before the fifteenth century, and Valla said much less then than other critics did soon afterward. It is a significant fact that Erasmus was in high favor among Roman Catholics, despite his striking out as spurious the text about the. "three that bear witness in heaven," attacking the authenticity of *Hebrews* and other *Epistles*, and exposing the barbarous character of the apostolic Greek; while the attempt of Servetus to make rational criticism of the Bible possible, by taking each passage as addressed by its author directly to his own contemporaries, rather than to readers in later ages, and the application of this principle by its discoverer to the so-called Messianic prophecies, were among the charges on which he was burned alive by the Genevese Protestants. Idolatry of the Bible rendered them even more unwilling than the Papists to have it made intelligible. Merely translating it literally was but half of the work. The other half, that of interpreting it rationally, has been slowly accomplished during the last three centuries, on the principle discovered by Servetus, and amid the constant opposition of the legitimate successors of his murderers.

This inveterate, though diminishing dislike of the majority throughout Christendom to have the truth told about the Bible, together with the repeated decision of many countries in Europe for papistry rather than heresy, shows such a strong inclination toward theological conservatism, as results, I think, from the joint action of several causes. Total and sudden change of deep-rooted opinion is a painful process, especially for those who have not been trained to reason logically. We all need to be taught by our fellow-men, and he who never learns any thing from others is an ignoramus. The advantage of getting what information we can, and holding fast to all we get, is so great, that people are apt to forget that, in order to know the truth, it is also necessary to compare carefully all the knowledge we can get from any quarter, and discard whatever is shown to be untrue by the light of reason and experience. Then again, clear and positive statements are so much more valuable, when justified by fact, than vague ones, that dogmatic assertions are apt to be received with a favor beyond their due. The attempt to take away definite opinions without putting others equally definite in their places, is usually treated as mischievous. People do not consider that the more firmly settled and clearly defined any error has become, the worse is its influence, and the greater is the benefit of getting rid of it. The advantage of having settled opinions which are true, over remaining unsettled, is so great as to make people forget that even this last is better and safer than settling down on what is false. Error must be unsettled, before truth can become fixed. And it is not always possible to introduce well-grounded certainty as fast as the ill-grounded is taken away. The settled theory, popular as late as the sixteenth century, that diseases are due to evil spirits and other supernatural agents, was given up long ago; but we have not yet got any other theory as definite on the subject, and perhaps shall never have any. Dante and other Roman Catholics have given minute descriptions of hell, which have gradually come to be regarded as incredible, not because more probable narrations have been generally adopted instead, but because believers in future torments are now inclined to consider their nature as indescribable. Very many Christians have ceased to hold the *Athanasian Creed*, but have not attempted to put any such precise statement in its place. This creed is upheld, however, by people who can not believe it fully and literally, but who had rather have even this definite statement, though incorrect, than none at all. Luther showed this spirit when he rebuked Erasmus for confessing an inclination to be as skeptical as the Church permitted, and declared that for his own part he wished to be as certain as possible, even about trifles. "The Christian naturally delights in assertions," he added. "Take away assertions, and you have taken away Christianity." There is a great deal of this feeling still, and it is the basis of the success, not only of the dogmatic theologian, but of the demagogue and the maker of almanacs. It is this love of precise and minute statements which causes the agnostic, who can not make them about theology, to be falsely charged with inability to be sure of any thing.

Another reason why liberty of thought has been disliked, is that it has been associated by Christian teachers with moral guilt, ever since Paul put heresy into the same black list with murder, adultery, and other "works of the flesh." Such charges are still so common, that it is pleasant to find that most of the early rationalists had an extremely good reputation. Empedocles, Parmenides, Protagoras, Gorgias, Pericles, Socrates, Euripides, Plato, Antisthenes, Crates, Aristotle, Pyrrho, Epicurus, Lucretius, Brutus, Virgil, Messala, and Cicero were among the best men of the age, as were the Epicureans generally, according to the not altogether friendly testimony of the author last mentioned. There is not much to be said for Aspasia or Leontium, however, and the depravity of Alcibiades, Critias, Aristippus, Horace, Catullus, and Julius Cæsar must be admitted. Still there was a gratifying preponderance of virtue among the unbelievers, wnen they had flourished long enough and had attained sufficient freedom, for the tendency of their views to become fully manifest. History had thus far justified the opinion of Socrates, that nothing is so favorable to morality as intense mental activity and perfect liberty of thought. Imperialism, by lavishing wealth and honor on its unscrupulous tools, permitting the foulest tyrants to indulge their passions almost with impunity, treating strength of character as criminal, checking literary activity, and encouraging demoralizing amusements, brought about a general decline of morality from which rationalists were not exempt, though Epictetus, the Plinies, Antoninus Pius, and Galen were exceptionally virtuous. The general character of the Paulicians, Catharists, Waldenses, Mystics, Lollards, and Hussites was much better than that of the church people. Simeon, Bernard of Clairvaux, Hildebrand, and Innocent III. had to admit the purity of their victims. The inquisition was unable to ferret out much vice, even among such enthusiastic scorners of conventional restraints as the Brethren of the Free Spirit. Pungilovo, the Catharist, was so virtuous as almost to gain canonization, an honor which had been already given to the Buddha. The most hostile scrutiny of Erigena, Roscellin, Farinata, Bacon, Dolcino, Dante, Eckhart, Ockham, Joan of Aubenton, and Joan of Arc could bring nothing discreditable to light. Abelard and Rienzi were most virtuous when least orthodox. The only vicious unbelievers I know of during the middle ages were tyrants, who hated the Church because she interfered with their ambition, avarice, and sensuality, and who despised the populace all the more on account of its superstition. Irresponsible power has seldom been found compatible with virtue, as is proved by the history of the orthodox emperors of Byzantium, of the pious Louis XI., and of the popes. Liberal thinkers in general were liable to unusually severe punishment for irregularity of conduct, so that they were as strongly restrained from vice as any one could be by the Church.

Papal iniquity was the main cause, according to Machiavelli, of the immorality which sullied the brightness of the Renaissance, and which is sufficiently accounted for by further considering how profligate and unscrupulous were the invaders whom the popes had summoned into Italy, how strong was the taste of the leading ecclesiastics for obscene literature, and how cruelly the Church had checked the spread of better teaching than her own. Poggio thought his morals would be injured by taking orders; Hutten and Aretino were no worse than most of the contemporary priests and bishops; and among the best men of the age were the heretic, Savonarola, and the skeptics Leonardo da Vinci and Pomponatius. The latter pronounces disbelief in immortality highly favorable to morality. The reformers were saintly men, despite their general bigotry, the treachery and falsehood of Calvin toward Servetus, and Cranmer's cowardice. The Münster depravity was exceptional, even among visionary fanatics. Hetzer was the only rationalistic martyr whose character could not stand the efforts made by both Protestant and Catholic persecutors to justify themselves by showing the immorality of their victims, the rest of whom like Münzer, Bainham, Anne Ascue, Dolet, Gruet, Servetus, Gribaldi and Gentilis, are stainless. Joan Bocher should probably be placed in the same category, though she did not escape calumny. Paracelsus was guilty of nothing worse than intemperance. The most unfriendly criticism could detect no serious fault in Erasmus, Bünderlin, Carlstadt, Rabelais, Franck and Bolsec; while Denck and Castalio attained rare excellence, as did Schwenckfeld, whose holiness of life was acknowledged by a cardinal. The general character of the rationalists and come-outers recorded in history is good enough to show that Socrates, Lucretius, and Pomponatius were right in teaching that skepticism is peculiarly favorable to morality.

Such facts as that Pyrrho and his followers during several centuries found the greatest possible mental peace in keeping free from belief in any theological or metaphysical views; that unusual happiness was enjoyed by Epicurus, Lucretius, and their friends, and that extreme old age was reached by

Thales, Xenophanes, Protagoras, Democritus, Diogenes, Pyrrho, and Timon, together with all accessible knowledge about other independent thinkers up to the present time, force me to believe that Mallock is altogether wrong in asserting, as he does in *Is Life Worth Living?* chapter IX., that there are any "high-minded unbelievers" who say not only that religious belief is false, but that unbelief is miserable. Change of views in any direction usually causes some pain at first, especially when accompanied by loss in family harmony, social standing, or professional prospects; but it often happens that the pleasure of mental activity and victory preponderates from first to last; and the cessation of inner conflict in the establishment of any form of belief or disbelief, always brings joy and peace. The only distress of importance caused by unbelief is to believers. Rationalists and come-outers find their views singularly conducive to happiness.

Groundless as are these prejudices, they have united with the limitations which still restrict scholars, with popular fondness for definite creeds, with trust in the sufficiency of learning from others without criticising, and with aversion to changing views already fixed, to form that strong tendency toward conservatism, which has resisted every attempt to liberalize thought, and is likely to continue to do so, though with increasing feebleness. The apprehensions expressed in Count Goblet d'Alviella's richly-stored history of Free Religion, *L'Evolution Religieuse Contemporaine*, and in other liberal publications, that liberty of thought is likely to be eclipsed again, as in ancient times, by the rise of some new religion, will not be felt by those who remember that classic unbelief was confined to the upper classes; that the Roman emperors sought to suppress mental independence; that science was then in its infancy; and that culture had not become so general as at present. This phase of history will never be repeated. A century hence thought will be much more free than at present, but it will still be far from having reached the full liberty which is its ultimate destiny. Ability to think for one's self has been made more common than in the Dark Ages by that long struggle, a part of which is recorded in this volume. Who can say how many more centuries of effort will be needed to make the capacity universal? Our path will never again be lighted by blazing faggots; but it can be carried forward only by such courage, patience, and wisdom as have done the work that lies behind us. No longer do our champions have to put forth all their strength to defend themselves from destruction; but there is still enough for us all to do in liberating the enslaved around us.

That every yoke will yet be broken, and the doors of all prisons be unbarred, cannot be doubted by those who see how many movements are working together for emancipation. There are the various schools of thought which I have described as scientific positivism, philosophic skepticism, independent Mysticism, and pious rationalism, which last might be called liberal Christianity, if it did not include such other movements as independent theism, and progressive Judaism. Then, besides the efforts to establish these ways of thinking, there is the labor now going on for the growth of biblical criticism, the destruction of intolerance, the emancipation of women, the increase of political and social liberty, and the improvement of general culture. Here are nine distinct movements, all working for universal liberty of thought. When any of these culminates, its force will be incorporated in the rest. That all the progressive movements should fail together is no longer a possibility. No one of these movements has ever before reached its present perfection, or it could not have been swept away. There is no more danger of the return of the Dark Ages than of the relapse of New England into Indian hunting-grounds, or of the revival of the mastodon and icthyosaurus. Complete emancipation of thought may still be distant, but it must surely come.

AUTHORITIES.

Important authors have been studied in their own writings; the standard Encyclopædias, Biographical Dictionaries, and Histories of Philosophy, Literature and the Church constantly consulted; and the following books on special subjects found to possess peculiar value.

Chapter I.

Edwin Arnold.—The Light of Asia.
St. Hilaire.—Le Bouddha et sa Religion.
Köppen.—Die Religion des Buddha.
Wassiljew.—Der Buddhismus.
Stäudlin.— Geschichte des Skepticismus.
Lange.—History of Materialism.
Lewis. — Astronomy of the Ancients.
Lassalle. — Philosophie des Herakleitos.
Zeller. — Presocratic Philosophy.
Littré.—Œuvres d' Hippocrate.
Funck-Brentano. — Sophistes Grecs.

Wecklein.—Die Sophisten.
Grote.—Plato and the other Companions of Socrates.
Zeller.—Socrates and the Socratic Schools.
Krohn.—Socrates und Xenophon.
Alberti.—Sokrates, ein Versuch nach den Quellen.
Zeller.—Plato and the Older Academy.
Simon.—Theodicée de Platon et d' Aristote.
Grote. — Aristotle. Fragments on Ethical Subjects.
Lewes.—Aristotle.
Stahr.—Aristotelia.
Geier.—Alexander und Aristoteles.

Chapter II.

Zeller.—Stoics, Epicureans, and Skeptics.
Cicero.—Philosophical Treatises.
Gassendi.—De Vita et Moribus Epicuri.
Guyau.—Morale d'Épicure.
Diogenes Laertius.—Lives of the Philosophers.

Sellar.—Roman Poets of the Republic.
Veitch. — Lucretius and the Atomic Theory.
Mallock.—Lucretius.
Delambre.—Historie de l' Astronomie.

Chapter III.

Schmidt. — Geschichte der Denk- und Glaubensfreiheit im ersten Jahrhundert.
Boissier. — L'Opposition sous les Césars.
Merrivale. — History of the Romans.
Beulé. — Tibere et L'Heritage d' Auguste. Le Sang de Germanicus.
Lecky. — History of European Morals.
Friedländer. — Sittengeschichte Roms.
Renan. — The Apostles. St. Paul. L'Antichriste. Marc-Aurèle.
Matter. — Histoire Critique du Gnosticisme.
Baur. — Die Christliche Gnosis. Drei Ersten Jahrhunderte.

Chapter IV.

Hoyns. — Geschichte der Dreissig Tyrannen.
Barbeyrac. — Morale des Peres de l' Eglise.
Mücke. — Flavius Claudius Julianus.
Ammianus. — Roman History.
Laurent. — Histoire de l' Humanité.
Redepenning. — Origenes.
Lea. — History of Sacerdotal Celibacy.
Milman. — History of Latin Christianity.

Chapter V.

Sprengel. — Geschichte der Arzneikunde.
Baur. — Kirche des Mittelalters.
Taillandier. — Scot Erigène.
Kremer. — Culturgeschichte des Orients.
Hammer-Purgstall. — Literatur-Geschichte der Araber. Histoire de l'Ordre des Assassins.
Schmidt. — Histoire des Cathares ou Albigeois.
Lea. — Superstition and Force.
Grätz. — Geschichte der Juden.
John Owen. — Evenings with the Skeptics.
Cousin. — Philosophie Scholastique. Ouvrages Inédits de Abélard.
Rémusat. — Abélard, sa Vie, sa Philosophie, etc.
Hauréau. — Philosophie Scholastique.
M. et Mme. Guizot. — Abailard et Héloise.
Berington. — Literary History of the Middle Ages.
Wright. — Latin Poems, commonly attributed to Walter Mapes.
Reumont. — Geschichte der Stadt Rom.
Francke. — Arnold von Brescia.
Herzog. — Romanischen Waldenser.
Maitland. — Facts and Documents, Illustrative of the History etc., of the Albigenses and Waldenses.
Melie. — Origin, etc., of the Waldenses.
Renan. — Averroes.
Schmölders. — Documenta Philosophiæ Arabum.
Müller. — Geschichte der schweizerischen Eidgenossenschaft.
Reuter. — Geschichte der religiösen Aufklärung im Mittelalter.

AUTHORITIES. 405

Chapter VI.

Sismondi.—The Crusade against the Albigenses.
Guizot.—Memoirs Relatives a l'Histoire du France, Trois Chroniques.
Peyrat. — Histoire des Albigeoises.
Lamothe-Langon.—L' Inquisition en France.
Molinier.—L'Inquisition dans le Midi de la France.
Preger.—Die deutsche Mystik.
Rousselot. — L'Evangile Eternel.
Potvin.—Le Roman du Renart.
Diez.—Die Troubadours.
Pfeiffer.—Walther von der Vogelweide.
Kurz.—Handbuch der poetischen Nationalliteratur.
Charles.—Roger Bacon.
Jubinal.—Rutebœuf.

Besant.—French Humorists.
Lenient.—Satire en France au Moyen Age.
Barbazan.—Tableaux et Contes Françaises.
Chaucer. — Romaunt of the Rose.
Hurter.—Innocent VIII.
Huillard-Bréholles.— Historia Diplomatica Frederici Secundi.
Kington.—History of Frederick the Second.
Schirrmacher.—Kaiser Fredrick II.
Cherrier. — Lutte des Popes et des Empereurs.
Stubbs.—Constitutional History of England.
Pauli.—Simon de Montford.
Prothero.—Simon de Montford.

Chapter VII.

Boutaric. — La France sans Philippe le Bel.
Drumann.—Geschichte Bonifacius des Achten.
Tosti.—Vita di Bonifazio VIII.
Christophe.—La Papauté pendrant le XIVe. Siècle.
Wilcke.—Geschichte des Ordens der Tempelherren.
Raynouard.—Monumens Historiques Relatifs a la Condemnation des Chevaliers du Temple.
Michelet.—Procès des Templiers.
Addison.—The Knights Templars.
Mariotti.—Fra Dolcino.
Longfellow.—Dante's Divine Comedy.
Foscolo.—Discorso sul Testo di Dante.
Witte.—Dante Forschungen.
Aroux.—Dante Hérétique.

J. Rossetti.—Spirito Antipapale.
Lasson.—Meister Eckhart.
Susanna Winkworth.—History and Life of Tauler.
C. Schmidt.—Gottesfreunde im 14. Jahrhundert. Johannes Tauler von Strassburg.
Pappencordt.—Rom im Mittelalter.
Gregorovius.—Rom im Mittelalter.
Zefirino Re.—Vita di Rienzo.
Du Cerceau.—Conjuration di Gabrino.
Müller.—Ludwig der Baier.
Häusser.—Die Sage von Tell.
Hissly.—Recherches Critiques sur Tell.
Reilliet.—Origines de la Confederation Suisse.
Muratori.—Annales Cæsenates.

Chapter VIII.

Skeat.—Longland's Vision of Piers' Plowman.
Lechler.—Johann von Wiclif.
Vaughan.—Life of Wycliffe. Tracts and Treatises of Wycliffe.
Eadie.—History of the English Bible.
Simon.—Chaucer a Wickliffite?
Morley.—English Writers.
Sinding.—History of Scandinavia.
Otté.—History of Scandinavia.
Dahlmann. — Geschichte von Dänemark.
Creighton.—Papacy during the Reformation.
Denis.—Huss et la Guerre des Hussites.
Gillett.—Life and Times of John Huss.
Palacky. — Geschichte von Böhmen.
L'Enfant.—Histoire du Concile de Constance. Histoire du Concile de Basle.
Lukavecz et Pelhzinow. — Chronicum Taboritarum.
Bonnechose. — Reformers before the Reformation.
Schwab.—Johannes Gerson.
C. Schmidt.—Essai sur Jean Gerson.
Wessenberg.—Kirchenversammlungen.
Voigt.—Enea Silvio.
Clemens. — Giordano Bruno und Nicolaus von Cusa.
Hirzel.—Jean d'Arc (Virchow und Holtzendorf's Vorträge Bd. X.)
Quicherat.—Procès de Jeanne d'Arc.
O'Reilly.—Les Deux Procès de Jeanne d'Arc.
Janet Tuckey.—Joan of Arc.
Wallon.—Jeanne d'Arc.

Chapter IX.

Hallam.—Introduction to the Literature of Europe.
Voigt. — Wiederbelebung des Alterthums.
Symonds. — Renaissance in Italy.
Burckhardt.—Renaissance in Italien.
Schultze.—Georgios Gemistos Plethon.
Nisard.—Gladiateurs de la Republique des Lettres.
Shepherd.—Life of Poggio.
Prescott.—Ferdinand and Isabella.
Mrs. Heaton.—Leonardo da Vinci.
Detmold.—Writings of Machiavelli.
Francke.—Moralistes et Philosophes.
Niceron.—Memoirs des Hommes Illustres.
Buhle.—Geschichte der neuern Philosophie.
Rio.—Poetry of Christian Art.
Hoffmann. — Geschichte des Handels.
Anderson. — Origin of Commerce.
Lewis.—Life of Pecock.
Fournier.—Theatre Française avant le Renaissance.
Humphreys.—History of the Art of Printing.
Schmidt.—Geschichte der Pädagogik.
Münsch.—Epistolæ Obscurorum Virorum, with which is printed the Julius Exclusus.
Hagen.—Deutschland's literarische und religiöse Verhältnisse im Reformationszeitalter.
Geiger.—Johann Reuchlin.
Mayerhoff.—Reuchlin und seine Zeit.

Strauss.—Ulrich von Hutten.
Morley.—Cornelius Agrippa.
Seebohm.—Oxford Reformers.
Durand de Laur.—Erasmus.
Stichart.—Erasmus von Rotterdam.
Jortin.—Life of Erasmus.
Milman.—Savonarola, Erasmus, and other Essays.

Villari.—La Storia di Girolamo Savonarola.
Perrens.—Jerôme Savonarola.
Elizabeth Warren. — Savonarola, the Florentine Martyr.
Oliphant.—Makers of Florence.
Ulman.—Reformatoren bevor der Reformation.

Chapter X.

Ranke.—Geschichte der Reformation.
Häusser.—Zeitalter der Reformation.
Baur.—Kirchengeschichte der neueren Zeit.
Lindsay.—The Reformation.
Seebohm.—Era of the Protestant Revolution.
Lecky.—Rationalism in Europe.
D'Aubigné.—History of the Reformation.
Hallam.—Introduction to Literature of Europe.
Bunsen.—Life of Luther.
Köstlin.—Martin Luther.
Hare.—Vindication of Luther.
Henry.—Leben Johann Calvins.
Wessenburg.—Kirchenversammlungen.
Cayley.—Memoir of Sir Thomas More.
Morley.—Cornelius Agrippa.
Taillandier.—Recherches sur L'Hôpital.
Lenient.—Satire en France au XVIc. Siecle.
Gebhart.—Rabelais, La Renaissance et La Reforme.

Fleury.—Rabelais et Ses Œuvres.
Noel.—Rabelais et son Œuvre.
Arnstadt.—Français Rabelais und sein Traité d'Éducation.
Christie.—Etienne Dolet.
Douen.—Etienne Dolet.
Morley.—Clement Marot.
Irving.—Memoirs of George Buchanan.
Hess.—Vie de Zuingle.
Trechsel.—Antitrinitarier vor F. Socin.
Strype.—Memorials.
Willis.—Servetus and Calvin.
Roget.—Histoire du Peuple de Genève.
Hase.—Sebastian Franck.
Hagen.—Deutschland's lit. und rel. Verhälttnisse.
Van Braght.—Martyrology.
Zimmermann.—Geschichte des grossen Bauernkrieges.
Bebel.—Der Deutsche Bauernkrieg.
Morley.—Jerome Cardan.
Morley.—Vesalius.
Waddington.—Vie de Ramus.
Daru.—Histoire de Venise, vol. XV. (on Ludovici).

CHRONOLOGY, B. C.

(Earliest Dates Doubtful.)

640. Birth of Thales.
610. Birth of Anaximander.
585. Eclipse said to have been foretold by Thales.
562. Death of Thales.
547. Death of Anaximander.
544. Ionia conquered by the Persians.
540. Xenophanes begins to teach.
535. Birth of Heraclitus.
509. Pythagorean Order suppressed.
502. Death of Anaximenes.
500. Birth of Anaxagoras.
483. Birth of Gorgias.
480. Greece invaded by Xerxes. Birth of Euripides and Protagoras, also, according to some, of the Buddha, whose death is placed here by others. Coming of Anaxagoras to Athens.
475. Death of Heraclitus.
469. Pericles begins to rule at Athens.
468. Birth of Socrates.
460. Birth of Democritus and Hippocrates. Arrival of Zeno and Parmenides at Athens.
450. Death of Epicharmus.
448. Birth of Aristophanes.
444. Birth of Xenophon and Antisthenes.
435. Birth of Aristippus.
432. Meton proposes his calendar; Anaxagoras and Damon have to leave Athens; Aspasia and Phidias tried for impiety; The latter dies in prison.
431. Outbreak of the Peloponnesian war.
430. Death of Empedocles.

429. Death of Pericles; Battle of Potidæa; Socrates begins to teach about this time.
428. Death of Anaxagoras in exile.
427. Birth of Plato; Coming of Gorgias to Athens.
423. Aristophanes attacks Socrates in the *Clouds;* Thucydides is banished.
420. Democritus writes his *Microcosmos*.
415. The Mercuries mutilated, and Alcibiades sentenced to death.
413. Defeat at Syracuse; The Eclipse, Aug. 27.
411. Protagoras is banished and Diagoras flees from Athens, where a price is set on his head.
409. Euripides driven from Athens.
407. Alcibiades condemned the second time; Plato becomes a pupil of Socrates.
406. Death of Euripides; Birth of Eudoxus.
405. Athens taken by Lysander; The Thirty Tyrants; Death of Alcibiades.
403. Thrasybulus liberates Athens.
399. Socrates put to death.
388. Plato in Sicily.
386. The Academy founded; *Banquet* written.
384. Birth of Aristotle.
376. Birth of Pyrrho.
372. Birth of Theophrast.
370. Death of Antisthenes.

367. Plato in Sicily a second time.
364. Defeat and death of Pelopidas.
361. Plato's third visit to Sicily.
360. Plato sold as a slave.
359. Dion dethrones Dionysius.
356. Death of Aristippus; Birth of Alexander.
353. Death of Dion and Eudoxus.
347. Plato dies; Speusippus head of the Academy.
342. Aristotle teacher of Alexander.
341. Birth of Epicurus.
339. Speusippus succeeded by Xenocrates.
337. Statues erected to Æschylus, Sophocles, and Euripides at Athens, and their works preserved at the public expense.
335. Aristotle founds the Lyceum.
334. Alexander invades Asia.
332. Alexandria founded.
323. Death of Alexander and Diogenes; Aristotle has to leave Athens; Ptolemy Soter becomes ruler of Egypt.
322. Death of Aristotle.
320. Stilpo teaches at Athens.
316. Birth of Arcesilaus; Zeno in Athens.
307. Censorship over the philosophers attempted at Athens.
306. Epicurus begins to teach at Athens; Ptolemy Soter, founder of the Alexandrian library and museum, assumes the crown of Egypt.
304. Eristratus discovers the valves of the heart.
300. Megasthenes visits India.
288. Death of Pyrrho.
287. Birth of Archimedes; Death of Theophrast; Strato head of the Lyceum; Its library is buried.
283. Death of Euclid.
280. Chrysippus born; Aristarchus observes the summer solstice.
276. Birth of Eratosthenes.

271. Death of Epicurus.
263. Zeno dies, and Cleanthes becomes head of his school.
260. Callimachus chief librarian at Alexandria.
250. Birth of Apollonius of Perga; Death of Eristratus; Invention of Greek accents and punctuation marks by Aristophanes of Byzantium; Hymn of Cleanthes written; Buddhism made a state religion by King Asoka, about this time.
241. Death of Arcesilaus.
240. Death of Callimachus.
239. Birth of Ennius.
219. Birth of Pacuvius.
212. Death of Archimedes.
207. Death of Chrysippus.
203. Birth of Polybius.
195. Death of Eratosthenes.
190. Birth of Hipparchus.
186. Bacchanalia suppressed at Rome.
173. Alcæus and Philiscus banished from Rome as Epicureans.
170. Birth of Attius.
169. Death of Ennius.
168. Victory at Pydna in consequence of prediction of eclipse, June 21, by Gallus.
161. Rationalistic philosophers and rhetoricians banished by the Roman senate.
156. Carneades in Rome.
150. Panætius teaching at Athens.
148. Birth of C. Ennius Lucilius.
146. Hipparchus observes the vernal equinox.
139. Chaldæan astrologers driven out of Italy.
133. Tiberius Gracchus murdered; Lyceum library brought to light.
129. Death of Pacuvius.
121. Death of Polybius.
120. Death of Hipparchus.
106. Birth of Cicero.
102. Lutatius consul.
100. Birth of Julius Cæsar.

99. Birth of Lucretius.
97. Human sacrifices prohibited by the senate.
82. Death of Scævola.
74. Julius Cæsar becomes Pontifex Maximus.
70. Birth of Virgil.
65. Birth of Horace.
63. Birth of Octavius, afterward Augustus; Julius Cæsar declares before the senate that death is an eternal sleep.
55. Accession to power of First Triumvirate; Death of Lucretius, and publication of his poem.
48. Pharsalia.
47. Varro's book on religion.
46. Cæsar reforms the calendar.
45. Cicero writes his philosophical treatises.
44. Cæsar assassinated.
43. Cicero murdered; birth of Ovid.
42. Philippi; Birth of Tiberius.
38. Horace gains the friendship of Mæcenas.
31. Actium.
30. Death of Antony and Cleopatra; publication of the *Georgics;* Opening of the first public library at Rome in the Temple of Liberty.
29. Octavius returns to Rome and begins the Restoration of Polytheism.
28. He builds or restores ninety-two temples; Death of Varro.
24. Virgil is working on the *Æneid.*
23. Horace publishes three books of Odes.
22. Number of gladiators restricted legally.
21. Worship of Isis forbidden at Rome.
19. Death of Virgil, Sept. 22.
17. The Secular Games celebrated, and the *Æneid* published.
12. Octavius, now Augustus, becomes Pontifex Maximus, and destroys 2,000 Sibylline Books.
8. Death of Mæcenas and Horace.
7. Birth of Seneca.
4. Birth, about this time, of Jesus.
2. Ovid's *Art of Love* published.

CHRONOLOGY, A. D.

4. Death of Pollio; Augustus banishes slanderers and burns their books.
8. Banishment of Ovid and Cassius Severus, and burning of the latter's history.
11. Death of Messala.
12. Labienus starves himself to death, because his history is publicly burned, as are other independent books.
14. Death of Augustus, Aug. 9; Accession of Tiberius.
16. Magicians expelled from Italy.
18. Death of Ovid and Livy.
19. Temple of Isis at Rome destroyed, her image thrown into the Tiber, and her worshipers banished, as are the Jews.
20. Manilius completes his poem.
21. Lutorius Priscus murdered in prison for his elegy on a prince who did not die; Unsuccessful attempts to prevent wives of governors and generals from taking part in politics.
22. Ælius Saturninus thrown from Tarpeian Rock for poems disliked by Tiberius; Birth of Pliny the Elder.
25. Cremutius Cordus condemned to death for freedom of

speech, by the Senate, who orders his *History of the Civil Wars* to be burned by the Ædiles.

26. Tiberius leaves Rome, where Sejanus carries on a reign of terror.

28. Jesus begins to preach, according to Luke.

29. Crucifixion of Jesus, March 25; Death of Livia.

30. Asinius Gallus imprisoned for rivalry in both love and politics to Tiberius.

31. Fall and execution of Sejanus.

33. Cassius Severus starved to death in exile and Asinius Gallus in prison.

34. Mamercus Æmilius Scaurus has to kill himself for verses in ridicule of Agamemnon.

35. Conversion of Paul.

37. Tiberius dies March 16, and is succeeded by Caligula; Birth of Nero; Name of Christian first used at Antioch.

39. Carrinas Secundus and Thrasymachus banished for orations in praise of tyrannicide.

41. Assassination of Caligula, Jan. 24, and accession of Claudius, who banishes Seneca to Corsica.

42. Death of Pœtus and Arria.

43. Laws against Druidism.

45. Apollonius of Tyana visits India.

49. Seneca recalled from exile and made tutor of Nero.

50. Birth of Plutarch about this time.

51. Birth of Domitian.

52. Paul preaches at Athens, and writes the *Epistles to the Thessalonians*, the oldest books in the New Testament.

54. Claudius poisoned, Oct. 13, by Agrippina, who makes Nero emperor; Birth of Tacitus; Banishment under Claudius of the Jews from Italy.

55. Murder of Britannicus by his brother, Nero.

57. Pomponia Græcina accused of practicing a foreign superstition, possibly Christianity; Paul's *First Epistle to the Corinthians* written.

59. Nero murders his mother; Paul writes the *Epistle to the Romans*, and is soon after imprisoned at Jerusalem; Death of Domitius Afer.

60. Demetrius teaches in Corinth; the *First Epistle of Peter* is written about this time.

61. Paul enters Rome; Birth of Pliny the Younger.

62. Antistius tried for satire on Nero by the senate, who are persuaded by Thrasea to spare his life, against the emperor's wish; Veiento banished for writing against the priesthood, and his books burned; Death of Persius and Burrhus; Murder of Octavia and of Plautus, the Stoic, by Nero.

63. Seneca writes his *Questions about Natural History*.

64. Burning of two-thirds of Rome, July 19-25; Cruel persecution of the Christians afterward.

65. Failure of Piso's conspiracy; Among Nero's victims are his wife Poppæa, Lucan, Seneca, Gallio, and probably Paul and Peter.

66. Petronius Arbiter forced by Nero to kill himself; Thrasea, Soranus, and Servilia condemned to death by the senate; Helvidius banished, as are Rufus, Cornutus, Apollonius, and all the other philosophers; the Romans are driven out of Jerusalem.

68. Rebellion of the armies in Spain, Gaul, Germany, Palestine and Africa; Nero is condemned by the senate to be

scourged to death, and kills himself, June 10; Galba becomes emperor, and the *Revelation of John* is written during his reign.

69. Galba murdered, Jan. 15; Wars of Otho with Vitellius, and of the latter with Vespasian, who is acknowledged emperor after Dec. 22; Helvidius tries during this year and the next to assert the privileges of the senate against both Vitellius and Vespasian.

70. Jerusalem taken by Titus.
71. Helvidius put to death.
74. Philosophers banished.
79. Pliny the Elder dies.
81. Domitian becomes emperor.
90. Philosophers driven from Rome, on which Sulpicia is supposed to have written her satire.
94. Reign of terror; Juvenal's second satire written.
95. Persecution of Christians.
96. Assassination of Domitian, Sept. 18, and accession of Nerva; Clemens Romanus writes about this time.
98. Accession of Trajan.
104. Pliny the Younger writes about persecuting the Christians, (some say 112.)
115. Martyrdom of Ignatius.
117. Accession of Hadrian.
118. Death of Tacitus.
120. Death of Plutarch.
125. Birth of Lucian; Teaching of Basilides in Alexandria.
130. Birth of Galen.
138. Antoninus Pius becomes emperor.
140. Valentinus teaching at Rome.
144. Marcion comes to Rome.
150. Lucian comes to Rome; Death of Demonax; Justin Martyr's *First Apology* and Polycarp's *Epistle to the Philippians* written; Rise of Montanism; Ptolemy and Numenius flourish about this time.

161. Marcus Aurelius begins to reign, and the empire to suffer a series of calamities.
164. Death of Justin Martyr.
165. Lucian begins to write.
166 or 169. Martyrdom of Polycarp.
168. Marcellina comes to Rome; Suicide of Peregrinus Proteus.
170. Montanists declared heretics.
177. Persecution at Lyons.
180. Death of Marcus Aurelius; Pantænus begins to teach in Alexandria; Celsus writes against Christianity.
182. Lucian writes about Alexander the False Prophet.
185. Birth of Origen.
192. Dec. 31, Commodus assassinated.
200. Galen and Lucian die; Tertullian and Clement of Alexandria are now teaching and writing.
201. Ammonius Saccas teaches at Alexandria; Diogenes Laertius writes his history during the first quarter of this century.
212. Persecution of the Peripatetics commanded by Caracalla, who now has 2,000 of his subjects massacred.
217. April 8, Caracalla assassinated.
220. Death of Tertullian and Clement of Alexandria.
222. Accession of Alexander Severus, who permits much liberty in teaching and worship.
250. Persecution of Christians recommenced.
251. The Emperor Decius defeated and slain by the Goths.
254. Death of Origen.
258. Martyrdom of Cyprian.
259. Christianity tolerated in the West.
261. Toleration all over the empire.
263. Odenathus acknowledged as associate emperor.

267. Athens plundered by the Goths; Porphyry comes to Rome; Zenobia begins to reign; Perfect toleration at Palmyra.
270. Porphyry writes against Christianity; Death of Plotinus.
273. Capture of Palmyra; Death of Longinus.
274. Birth of Constantine.
275. Tacitus elected emperor by the senate.
276. Tacitus succeeded by Probus.
277. Death of Manes.
282. Murder of Probus, last emperor who is controlled by the senate.
284. Accession of Diocletian.
303. Persecution of Christians.
305. Death of Porphyry; Origin of Monasticism by Antony.
306. Constantine proclaimed emperor.
308. Five emperors actually ruling, and a sixth nominally in power.
312. Constantine master of the West.
313. Edict of Milan, by Constantine and Licinius, establishing toleration throughout the empire; Death of Diocletian; Rise of the Donatists.
315. Churches exempted from taxation by Constantine.
318. Property of the Donatists confiscated; Arius begins to preach.
319. Pagan rites still permitted by the edict of Constantine.
321. Observance of Sunday prescribed.
323. Constantine sole emperor.
324. Constantinople founded.
325. Council of Nicæa; Arius condemned, and possession of his writings made a capital crime; Nicene creed imposed; Marriage of priests permitted.
326. Constantine murders his son and wife, and confiscates several temples; Athanasius becomes bishop.
331. Birth of Julian.
336. Banishment of Athanasius; Death of Arius; The *Apostles Creed* drawn up about this time in Jerusalem.
337. Baptism and death of Constantine.
338. Constantine's sons murder their relatives.
340. Constantine II. murdered by the soldiers of his brother, Constans.
341. Constantius forbids sacrifices; Athanasius banished again.
346. Sacrifice made a capital crime; Temples closed, but not permitted to be destroyed.
349. Bishop Gregory murdered at Alexandria in a sectarian tumult.
351. Julian becomes a pagan at Athens.
352. Paul, bishop of Constantinople, murdered by the Arians; Great loss of life in this contest.
354. More bloodshed at Constantinople, and also in Paphlagonia, arising from favor given by the emperor to Arianism.
355. Julian sent into Gaul; Pope Liberius and other partisans of Athanasius banished, and compelled to recant.
356. Sacrifice made a capital crime, by an edict to which Julian's name is appended by the emperor.
357. Great victory of Julian over the Germans at Strasburg.
360. Julian proclaimed emperor by his victorious army.
361. Death of Constantius leaves Julian supreme.
362. Julian proclaims toleration, but makes paganism the state-religion in place of Christianity, annuls the laws against sacrifice and in favor of observ-

ing Sunday, recalls the bishops, restores all the places of worship taken from pagans, Jews, or Athanasians, restricts liberty of teaching, and connives at the murder of George, bishop of Alexandria, and other Christians.

363. Death of Julian in battle against Persia, June 26; Jovian restores Christianity to supremacy, but tolerates paganism.
364. Empire divided between Valens and Valentinian.
365. Valens, the emperor of the East, issues an edict against the monks.
366. Damasus elected pope after a bloody strife with the other candidate.
367. Valens persecutes the Athanasians.
372. Many philosophers murdered by Valens on the charge of sorcery.
373. Death of Athanasius.
376. Valens attempts to force the Egyptian monks into his army.
378. Valens slain by the Goths.
379. Theodosius emperor of the East.
380. Feb. 23, Theodosius, Gratian, and Valentinian II. command all their subjects to hold the faith taught by the Apostle Peter and Pope Damasus; A series of edicts in this and subsequent years prohibits heretic and pagan worship, makes the sacrifice of animals a capital crime, orders temples to be closed and books destroyed, threatens death against Manichæans, Arians, etc.; Many temples destroyed.
385. Bishop Priscillian executed at Treves, then under the rule of Maximus, for heresy, with six followers, one of whom is a woman; This judicial murder is blamed by Ambrose and Martin of Tours.
386. Siricius becomes pope, and does much for the celibacy of the Latin clergy during his pontificate.
389. Alexandrian library destroyed, with Temple of Serapis, by Theophilus the patriarch.
390. Jovinian excommunicated by Ambrose.
395. Death of Theodosius, who has suppressed paganism.
396. Alaric invades Greece.
397. Death of Siricius, Ambrose, and Martin.
400. Alaric invades Italy.
402. Innocent I. becomes pope.
404. Gladiatorial games end at Rome; Chrysostom goes into exile.
405. Pelagius begins to teach; Vigilantius opposes celibacy and worship of relics.
406. Jerome declares that Vigilantius ought to be put to death; Gaul is overrun by Goths and Vandals.
407. Death of Chrysostom.
408. Siege of Rome by Alaric; All pagan ceremonies prohibited by its emperor, Honorius.
409. Spain invaded by Goths and Vandals.
410. Rome sacked by Attila.
411. Augustine begins to write his *City of God;* Public worship of heretics made a capital crime in the Western Empire.
412. Birth of Proclus.
415. Hypatia murdered with the connivance of Cyril, patriarch of Alexandria.
416. Pagans excluded from office in the Western Empire.
417. Persecution of the Donatists defended by Augustine; Pelagius condemned by Pope Innocent I.
418. Honorius banishes the Pelagians from Rome and other cities, at the request of Augustine; thus it is made a crime

to say that men are naturally capable of virtue.
420. Death of Jerome.
422. Simeon Stylites mounts his pillar.
423. Doubt expressed in an imperial edict if there are any pagans left.
428. Augustine's *City of God* finished.
429. The Vandals invade Africa, and are joined by the Donatists.
430. Death of Augustine; Nestorius and Cyril ask Pope Celestine to decide between them.
433. Patrick preaches in Ireland.
435. Nestorius is banished with his followers, by Theodosius II., who has the works of Julian and Porphyry destroyed.
440. Nestorius dies in exile; Vandals invade Sicily; Leo I. becomes pope.
441. Attila invades the Eastern Empire.
442. Africa ceded to the Vandals.
444. Manichæans outlawed by Leo and their books burned.
445. Semi-Pelagianism introduced by Bishop Faustus.
449. Robber-council of Ephesus, when the patriarch of Constantinople is murdered by the patriarch of Alexandria in presence of three hundred bishops, and the oneness of Christ's nature asserted; Saxons enter England.
451. Council of Chalcedon makes the doctrine that Jesus has two natures united in one person orthodox; Attila defeated at Chalons.
452. Attila invades Italy; Rome saved by Leo.
453. Death of Attila.
455 Rome sacked by the Vandals.
476. End of the Western Empire.
483. Death of Patrick of Ireland.
484. The pope of Rome and patriarch of Constantinople excommunicate each other in a quarrel brought on by the latter's tolerance; Death of Proclus.
486. Clovis invades Gaul with his Franks.
489. Nestorian school at Edessa broken up by the Emperor Zeno.
492. Accession of Gelasius, who strongly asserts papal supremacy.
493. Theodoric the Ostrogoth becomes king of Italy, and shows great tolerance.
494. Benedict becomes a monk.
496. Baptism of Clovis in consequence of his victory at Tolbiac.
500. Persecution of the Jews prevented by Theodoric.
506. Alaric II., the Visigoth, publishes the *Breviary of Roman Law*.
507. Alaric defeated and slain by Clovis.
510. Paris seat of monarchy of Clovis.
511. Death of Clovis.
512. Religious riots in Constantinople against the Emperor Anastasius, accused of heresy and persecution on account of his tolerance.
514. Civil war waged by Vitalianus against Anastasius with the approval of the pope.
515. Sigismund, king of the Burgundians, becomes orthodox.
525. Boethius and Symmachus put to death by Theodoric.
527. Justinian becomes emperor.
528. Benedictine Order founded.
529. Justinian suppresses the schools of philosophy, issues edicts against pagans and heretics, and publishes his *Codex* of imperial edicts.
533. The *Pandects* or digest of early law, published.
534. Africa conquered and *Nicene Creed* imposed by Belisarius.

540. Italy temporarily subdued by Belisarius.
554. Italy becomes a province of the Eastern Empire.
565. Deaths of Justinian and Belisarius; Monastery of Iona founded.
568. Lombard kingdom established in Upper Italy.
570. Birth of Mahomet.
589. King Richard of Spain adopts *Nicene Creed*.
594. Death of Gregory of Tours.
597. Austin arrives in England.
607. Death of Austin.
610. Mahomet begins to preach.
612. Sisebert begins to reign in Spain, and forces the Hebrews to receive baptism or emigrate.
622. July 16, The Hegira, or flight of Mahomet from Mecca.
632. Death of Mahomet.
634. Capture of Damascus by the Moslems.
637. Jerusalem captured.
638. Antioch captured; Council of Toledo expels Jews from Spain.
639. Egypt invaded by the Saracens.
640. Alexandria captured.
651. Pope Martin dies in exile; Origin of Paulicianism.
658. Beginning of the Gaonic Period among the Hebrews.
662. A monk named Maximus murdered as a heretic by the Monothelite emperor Constans.
675. Council of Braga forbids bishops to strike priests, except for deadly sins.
680. Death of Cædmon, first British poet.
684. Constantine, the founder of Paulicianism, stoned to death.
690. Simeon, who directed this execution, is burned to death with other Paulicians among whom he has lately become chief prophet.
693. Council of Toledo decrees divine right of kings and forbids the Jews to hold real estate.
694. All the Jews in Spain enslaved.
697. First doge elected at Venice.
711. Spain conquered by the Saracens.
723. Jews and Montanists persecuted by Leo the Isaurian.
726. Leo issues an edict against image-worship.
727. Leo resisted by the pope.
732. Saracens driven back by Charles Martel at Tours.
750. Abasside caliphs begin to rule over Persia, Syria, Arabia, and Egypt.
751. The Lombards take Ravenna and end the rule of Byzantium over Italy.
752. Merovingian kings overthrown by Pepin, son of Charles Martel. with the approval of the pope.
755. King Pepin makes the pope a temporal prince.
756. Cordova becomes the capital of the Western caliphs.
758. Baghdad founded by Almansor.
768. Charlemagne becomes king.
774. The Lombards conquered by Charlemagne.
778. Charlemagne's rear-guard defeated at Roncesvalles.
779. Birth of Agobard.
787. Image-worship re-established by the Empress Irene.
792. Felix of Urgel condemned by Charlemagne and the Council at Ratisbon.
794. Felix condemned again at Frankfort, and imprisoned for life, because he will not recant Adoptianism.
800. Charlemagne crowned by Pope Leo III., on Christmas morning in St. Peter's.
814. Charlemagne dies.
818. Death of Felix, bishop of Urgel, in prison for heresy.
820. Fabrication of the so-called *Athanasian Creed*.

839. Death of Claudius, bishop of Turin.
840. Death of Agobard, bishop of Lyons; Accession of Charles the Bald in France.
842. Final restoration of image-worship.
843. Erigena invited to Paris.
845. Revolt of Carbeas the Paulician; First quotation of the *False Decretals;* Synod of Meaux attacks the Jews.
848. Gottschalk condemned at Metz for ultra predestinarianism.
849. Synod of Rheims has Gottschalk scourged and imprisoned for life.
850. Persecution of the Motazalites about this time.
855. Council of Valence condemns Erigena.
868. Gottschalk dies in heresy.
871. Tephrica, the Paulician strong-hold, captured by the Emperor Basil; King Alfred wins the battle of Ashdown against the Danes.
877. Death of Charles the Bald, who has recently become emperor of Germany.
909. A great hospital built in Baghdad, with Rhazes, discoverer of alcohol, as chief physician and examiner of would-be practitioners.
959. Dunstan becomes archbishop of Canterbury.
961. Al-Hakim II. begins to reign in Andalusia, and to patronize literature and science.
963 Deposition of Pope John XII. for his iniquities by Otho the Great.
965. Aaron the Jew, professor of medicine at Cordova, now the seat of a great university.
970. Paulicians transported to the Danube.
976. Death of Al-Hakim, who has established eighty public schools in Cordova, and an immense public library.
978. Birth of Avicenna in Bokhara.
987. Accession of Hugh Capet.
990. A public library in Baghdad.
993. Opening of the University of Baghdad.
998. Birth of Berengar and Peter Damiani.
999. Sylvester II. becomes pope after studying at Cordova.
1000. Persecution of Leutard and Bilgard.
1004. Foundation of University of Cairo, still extant.
1010. Jews driven out of Limoges.
1012. Jews expelled from Mainz.
1020. Murder of Caliph Al-Hakim of Egypt, founder of the Druses; Birth of Avicebron.
1022. Stephen and twelve other Catharists burned to death in France.
1030. Gerard and other Catharists burned at Milan.
1037. Death of Avicenna.
1039. German emperor at his height of power.
1049. Hildebrand's influence supreme at Rome.
1050. Berengar condemned, and his book burned; Avicebron writes his *Fountain of Life.*
1052. Catharists hung at Goslar, Hanover.
1056. Henry IV. becomes emperor.
1058 Birth of Al-Gazali; Peter Damiani becomes cardinal.
1059. Berengar recants at Rome.
1066. Norman conquest of England.
1072. Death of Peter Damiani.
1073. Hildebrand becomes Gregory VII.
1075. Berengar nearly murdered by a mob at Poitiers.
1076. Jerusalem taken by the Turks.

1077. Humiliation of Henry IV. before Gregory VII., at Canossa, Jan. 25-27.
1078. Berengar's second recantation at Rome.
1079. Birth of Abelard.
1084. Rome taken by Henry IV.
1085. Death of Gregory VII. in exile.
1088. Death of Berengar.
1090. The Assassins establish themselves at Alamut.
1091. Birth of Bernard of Clairvaux.
1092. Roscellin recants at Soissons.
1093. Anselm archbishop of Canterbury.
1094. The first Crusade preached by Peter the Hermit.
1095. Al-Gazali retires from the world.
1096. Hebrews of Worms, Mainz, Spire, and Treves persecuted by the departing crusaders.
1096. Meeting of Roscellin and Abelard in Loches, Touraine.
1098. Birth of Hildegard.
1099. Jerusalem taken by crusaders, July 15.
1101. Birth of Heloise.
1102. Abelard begins to teach.
1104. Revolt of Henry IV.'s son with the sanction of Pope Paschal II.
1106. Al-Gazali's books burned in the mosques in Spain and Morocco.
1109. Death of Anselm.
1111. Death of Al-Gazali.
1113. Emperor's vicar defeated and slain by Florentines.
1114. Abelard master at Paris.
1115. Irnerius teaching Roman law at Bologna; Tanchelm and Henry of Cluny begin to preach.
1118. Abelard meets Heloise; Orders of Templars and Hospitallers founded.
1119. Basil, the Bogomilian Catharist, entrapped and burned by Alexius Comnenus.
1120. Death of Roscellin.
1121. Abelard condemned at Soissons.
1122. Concordat of Worms between emperor and pope.
1125. Tanchelm murdered by a priest; Peter of Bruis burned by a mob; Death of the Old Man of the Mountain or founder of the Assassins.
1126. Birth of Averroes; Abelard becomes abbot of St. Gildas de Rhuys.
1130. Avicenna, Avicebron, Avempace, and Al-Gazali, translated into Latin between 1130 and 1150.
1134. Arnold preaches at Brescia against the avarice of the Church.
1135. Birth of Maimonides; *Song of Roland* written about this time.
1136. Abelard teaches on Mount St. Geneviève.
1138. Death of Avempace (Ibn Badja) and Irnerius.
1139. Arnold driven from Italy.
1140. Abelard and Arnold condemned by Council of Sens and Pope Innocent II.; Bogomile books burned at Constantinople.
1141. Hildegard begins to publish her Revelations.
1142. Death of Abelard, April 21.
1144. Pope deposed by the Roman Republic.
1145. Pope Lucius killed while attacking the Capitol; Abolition of imperial prefecture in Rome; Arnold comes there; Senate of 56 appointed with Pierleone as patrician.
1146. Persecution of Jews by Moors and Germans; Minna of Spire tortured to death.
1147. The Second Crusade; Gilbert, bishop of Poitiers, accused of heresy; Henricians suppressed in Languedoc.
1148. Henry of Cluny and Eon,

the Star, imprisoned for life; Eon soon dies in prison.
1149. Vacarius lectures on law at Oxford.
1150. Apostolic Brethren burned in Cologne; Peter Lombard's *Sentences* published.
1152. Frederic I. becomes emperor.
1154. Nicholas Breakspear becomes Adrian IV., and puts Rome under an interdict, which causes Arnold to be banished; accession of Henry II. in England.
1155. Martyrdom of Arnold di Brescia at Rome.
1158. Frederic Barbarossa charters University of Bologna.
1159. Gerard and thirty other Catharists branded and outlawed at Oxford, after which they starve to death.
1162. Milan destroyed by Frederic Barbarossa.
1163. Arnold and other Catharists burned at Cologne.
1164. The Constitutions of Clarendon.
1165. Catharists burned at Vezelay.
1166. Persecution of Catharists in England.
1167. Catharist Council at St. Felix de Caraman, near Toulouse; Lombard League formed, and Milan rebuilt.
1170. Becket murdered, Dec. 29; Peter Waldo begins to preach; Birth of Dominic.
1171. Bank opened at Venice.
1176. Frederic Barbarossa defeated at Legnano.
1179. Waldenses condemned by Lateran Council and pope.
1181. Crusade against Viscount of Béziers.
1182. Birth of Francis of Assisi.
1183. Treaty of Florence assures the independence of Lombardy; Waldenses expelled from Lyons.
1185. Death of Ibn Tophail.

1187. Saladin takes Jerusalem.
1190. Frederic Barbarossa and Richard of England embark for Palestine; Persecution of the Jews on the Rhine, and also in England; The Teutonic Order founded.
1194. Dec. 26, birth of Frederic II.; Pierre Vidal is now writing against the Church.
1197. Death of Hildegard.
1198. Death of Averroes; Accession of Innocent III.; First steps toward the inquisition.
1199. John becomes king of England.
1200. Amalric teaches Pantheism in University of Paris, which, like that of Bologna, has been recently founded.
1202. Death of Joachim of Floris.
1203. Constantinople taken by crusaders.
1204. Death of Maimonides; Amalric expelled from his professorship.
1207. Stedingers put under interdict.
1208. Papal interdict on people of England; Peter the Legate murdered.
1209. First crusade in Languedoc; Massacre of Béziers, July 22; Body and followers of Amalric burned at Paris; with them is arrested Pierre of St. Cloud, an author of *Reynard the Fox;* Franciscan Order founded.
1211. Massacre of Lavaur.
1212. Montfort attacks Toulouse; Eighty Mystics and Waldenses burned in the Heretics' Trench at Strasburg; Frederic II. makes himself emperor; Pierre Cardinal, Figueira and Walter von der Vogelweide are writing against the pope.
1213. King John submits to the pope, May 15; King of Arragon and other friends of tolerance routed at Muret, Sept. 12.

1214. Roger Bacon born about this time.
1215. Lateral Council deposes the Languedocian princes for their tolerance, and establishes auricular confession; Frederic crowned at Aix-la-Chapelle; Magna Charta granted by John, Friday, June 15.
1216. Dominican Order founded by new pope, Honorius III.
1218. June 25, Montfort slain.
1221. Death of Dominic.
1222. University of Padua founded by Frederic.
1224. University of Naples also founded; Main action of Browning's *Sordello;* Dethroned Languedocians restored.
1226. Louis IX. becomes king of France.
1227. Accession of Gregory IX., and excommunication of Frederic.
1228. Death of Walter; Departure of Frederic for Palestine.
1229. Frederic gains Jerusalem and Nazareth for Christendom by negotiations; Treaty of Paris gives Languedoc to the crown of France.
1230. Birth of Rutebœuf; Frederic freed from the ban.
1231. Pope forbids laymen to dispute about theology; Frederic's Sicilian Code.
1233. Dominicans made inquisitors; Conrad of Marburg murdered.
1234. Defeat of the Stedingers, May 27.
1239. Frederic again excommunicated.
1240. Many Catharists burned at Milan.
1241. French prelates, on their way to a council, captured by Pisan fleet at Frederic's request; Zurich forbids observance of an interdict.
1242. Inquisitors mobbed in Milan, and massacred in Avignonet.
1244. Fall of Monségur, a Catharist castle in the Pyrenees.
1245. Frederic deposed by Innocent IV. in the Council of Lyons.
1246. Anti-clerical league of French barons.
1247. Alleged death of Robin Hood.
1249. Michael Scott translates Aristotle.
1250. Pietro of Abano born; Death of Frederic, Dec. 13.
1254. Interregnum in Germany begins, and freedom advances in the cities; *Eternal Gospel* and *Introduction* thereto published.
1255. *Eternal Gospel* suppressed.
1256. William of St. Amour's *Perils of the Last Times* published and burned.
1257. Bacon imprisoned by Bonaventura.
1258. Provisions of Oxford; Ghibellines expelled from Florence.
1259. Death of Eccelin the Cruel, and of King Christopher I. of Denmark; The mendicant Orders triumph over the University of Paris.
1260. Florence defeated, and spared by Farinata; Rutebœuf begins to write, and Segarelli to preach.
1264. Death of Farinata; Battle of Lewes won by Leicester over King Henry III. and Prince Edward; Cities and landed gentry represented in Parliament.
1265. Leicester defeated and slain at Evesham; Birth of Dante.
1266. Manfred defeated and slain by French invaders of Naples; Bacon writes his *Great Work.*
1267. Bacon released from prison.
1268. Execution of Conradin, October 29; Pragmatic Sanc-

CHRONOLOGY. 421

tion enacted by St. Louis; Hanseatic League fully formed.
1269. Death of Pungilovo.
1270. Death of Louis IX. in the last Crusade.
1272. Bacon writes his *Compend of Philosophy*.
1273. Rudolph of Hapsburg becomes emperor.
1274. Death of Bonaventura and Thomas Aquinas.
1275. Statutes of Westminster.
1278. Bacon again imprisoned; Jacopone da Todi renounces the world, and afterwards writes *Stabat Mater*.
1279. Nicholas III. orders vow of poverty to be taken, but not kept.
1280. Death of Albertus Magnus.
1282. Sicilian Vespers, March 31.
1283. Peter John Oliva begins to oppose the papacy.
1285. Accession of Philip the Fair.
1288. Giélée's *Renard Renewed* written.
1290. Jews expelled from England; Jean de Meung writes second part of the *Romance of the Rose* about this time.
1294. Segarelli imprisoned; death of Bacon; accession of Boniface VIII.
1295. Marco Polo returns to Venice.
1297. Death of Peter John Oliva; Great Charter confirmed by Edward I.
1299. Destruction of the Colonnas by Boniface VIII.
1300. Segarelli burned; Jubilee at Rome; The name Lollard, first used at Antwerp; Furious party strife at Florence.
1301. Pungilovo's body burned at Ferrara, and Wilhelmina's at Milan; Eckhart begins to write about this time; Quarrel between Philip and Boniface; Pope's bull against the king issued, Dec. 5.
1302. Bull publicly burned at Paris, Sunday, Feb. 11; April 10, Philip sustained in first meeting ever held of States General; Dante banished.
1303. Boniface is arrested, Saturday, Sept. 7; Dies a prisoner in the Vatican, Oct. 11; Bernard Délicieux has the dungeon of the inquisition at Carcassonne broken open by the royal commissioner.
1304. Burning of one hundred and fourteen Waldenses at Paris; Execution of Wallace, Aug. 23; Benedict XI. leaves Rome; Birth of Petrarch.
1305. Dolcino levies open war against the Church; Clement V. crowned at Lyons, Nov. 14.
1306. Death of Jacopone da Todi.
1307. March 23, day before Good Friday, Dolcino conquered; He and Margaret executed soon after; All the Templars in France arrested, Friday, Oct. 11; Supposed conspiracy on the Rütli, Nov. 7, and assassination of Gessler, Nov. 19 or 20.
1308. Jan. 8, English Templars arrested; States General condemns the Templars, May 1, as does the pope in his bull entitled *Faciens Misericordiam*, Aug. 12.
1309. Pope begins to dwell at Avignon; Trial of the Templars by his commissioners at Paris begins Aug. 7.
1310. Margaret Porretta burned at Paris, as also are fifty-four Templars, for retracting their previous confessions made under torture on May 10; Dante's *De Monarchia* written this year or soon after; Trial of Boniface for heresy and gross vice at Avignon; Councils of Mainz and Treves acquit the Templars.
1311. Bull freeing Philip and other enemies of Boniface

from censure, April 23 ; Trial of Templars ends at Paris, May 26, and a few weeks later in England, where no one is executed ; Council of Vienne opens, Oct. 16.

1312. Local councils at Tarragona and Salamanca acquit the Templars ; Clement V. announces the suppression of the Order with consent of the Council of Vienne, April 3 ; Boniface is acquitted.

1313. Birth of Boccaccio; March 11, De Molay, Grand Master of the Temple, and Guy of Auvergne, burned at Paris for retracting confessions.

1314. April 20, Death of Clement V. and June 25, of Philip; Bannockburn, June 24 ; Frederic of Austria chosen emperor, or rather king of the Romans, Oct. 19, and Louis of Bavaria, Oct. 20.

1315. Battle of Morgarten, Nov. 16.

1316. Pietro of Abano dies during trial ; John XXII. chosen pope after an interregnum, Aug. 7.

1317. Jan 23, doctrine of utter poverty of Jesus condemned by the pope ; Bishop of Cahors burned, as a sorcerer, by the pope, May 7.

1318. Four Franciscan Mystics burned at Marseilles, May 7.

1319. Robert Bruce excommunicated ; Bernard Délicieux sentenced to imprisonment for life, Dec. 6.

1320. Death of Jean de Meung, who finished the *Romance of the Rose*.

1321. Sept. 14, death of Dante soon after completing the *Divina Commedia*.

1322. Chapter of Franciscans at Perugia sanctions mystical doctrines, among others that of Christ's utter poverty, on Whitsunday ; Victory of Louis of Bavaria at Mühldorf, Sept.

28 ; Mandeville begins his travels ; Walter, the first Lollard martyr, burned at Cologne.

1323. Nov. 12, Perugia proceedings condemned by pope.

1324. Jan. 22, protest of Louis at Sachsenhausen ; he is excommunicated, March 23, and all places adhering to him are put, July 11, under an interdict, which is generally disregarded in the German cities ; Marsilius writes his *Defender of Peace ;* Wycliffe born about this time.

1326. Gunpowder used by the Florentines.

1327. Edward II. deposed by Parliament.

1328. Flight of Ockham, from Avignon ; Louis crowned at Rome, against the orders of the pope, Sunday, Jan. 17 ; May 12, Louis has an anti-pope chosen by the Roman people, as Nicholas V.

1329. Feb. 19, Louis and Nicholas burn Pope John XXII. in effigy at Pisa.

1331. Pope John XXII. falls into heresy.

1333. Ordelaffi becomes lord of Forli.

1334. Dec. 4, death of John XXII.

1338. Declarations that Germany is independent of the pope made on July 16, at Rense, by the Electors, and on Aug. 6 and Sept. 12, by the Diets of Frankfort and Coblentz ; At the latter is present Edward III., now the ally of Louis.

1340. Rolle's *Prick of Conscience* written ; Death of the learned Hebrew, Caspi ; Birth of Chaucer about this time ; Truce of Tournay mediated by Countess of Hainault, Jeanne de Valois.

1341. April 8, Petrarch crowned at Rome.

1342. Louis gives a dispensation for the marriage of his son on Feb. 10; May 7, Clement VI. chosen pope.
1345. Death of Levi, or Leo, Gersonides and of Jacob van Artevelde of Ghent.
1346. Charles IV. set up as rival of Louis; Aug. 25, battle of Cressy, where cannon are said to have been used.
1347. Death of Louis of Bavaria and Ockham; On May 20, Pentecost, Rienzi liberates Rome; Aug. 1, his consecration as knight of the Holy Ghost; Sept. 14, arrest of the nobles; Nov. 20, their attack on Rome repulsed; Dec. 15, Rienzi resigns under the ban.
1348. University of Prague founded; Nicholas of Autricuria condemned at Paris; Avignon obtained by Pope Clement from Joanna of Naples; The Black Death carries off nearly half the population of Italy and France.
1349. The Black Death in England and Germany; Tauler calls on the priests to hold public worship, despite the interdict.
1350. Second Jubilee at Rome; Arrest of Rienzi at Prague, by Charles IV.
1351. Statute against Provisors, or priests recommended for benefices by the pope, passed in England.
1352. Rienzi in prison at Avignon; Death of Clement, Dec. 6.
1353. Statute of Præmunire passed by Parliament to prevent appeals to the pope; Publication of the *Decameron* by Boccaccio.
1356. The Golden Bull, making emperors independent of popes, issued by Charles IV.; The *Last Age of the Church* published in England; University of Heidelberg founded.
1357. Marzia Ordelaffi defends Cesena against Cardinal Albornöz; The seige begins in April; She surrenders, June 21; Fitzralph, archbishop of Armagh, argues against Mendicant Friars, before the pope and cardinals.
1358. Insurrection of French peasants, the Jacquerie.
1360. Greek taught at Florence by Leo Pilatus; Death of Fitzralph under surveillance at Avignon; Wycliffe, master of Baliol, publishes a translation of the *Gospels* in his *Commentary*.
1361. Death of Tauler.
1362. Death of Vidal of Narbonne, the Jewish rationalist; Composition of Langland's *Vision of Piers Plowman* this year or 1363.
1363. Birth of Christine de Pisan and Gerson.
1364. University of Cracow founded.
1365. University of Vienna founded; Urban V. demands tribute of England; Dec. 9, Wycliffe becomes warden of Canterbury Hall; John Ball begins to preach.
1366. Papal Claim rejected by Parliament.
1367. New warden of Canterbury appointed before March 31.
1368. Milicz imprisoned at Rome, where he has preached reform; Wycliffe *On Dominion* published; University of Geneva founded.
1369. Urban V. returns to Rome; Birth of John Huss on July 6, this year or 1373.
1370. Bastile built and *Theologia Germanica* written.
1371. Parliament taxes clergy, and excludes prelates from office; Wycliffe made D.D. at Oxford.
1373. Joan of Aubenton burned.
1374. Wycliffe one of seven

ambassadors to meet papal envoys at Bruges.

1375. Death of Boccaccio; New College founded at Oxford; Florence sends out in December an army, with "Liberty" on its banners, against the pope, from whom 80 towns and cities revolt.

1376. Bishop of London retracts at Paul's Cross his publication of the pope's bull against Florence; The Good Parliament denounces sale of bishoprics, bad appointments, and other extortions by the pope, whose collectors are threatened with death.

1377. Langland publishes the second edition of the *Vision;* Jan. 17, Cesena sacked by the pope's soldiers and 5000 citizens murdered; Thursday, Feb. 19, Wycliffe's trial in St. Paul's Cathedral brings on a riot; May 22, five bulls against him; That fall his advice is asked by Parliament, and given against letting money go to Rome; Nicholas of Basel builds a retreat, between that city and Constance, for the Friends of God.

1378. Wycliffe tried at Lambeth in Feb. or March, for saying that the State may disendow the Church, that the Gospel is a sufficient guide, and that papal censures are not valid unless in harmony with the Bible; Urban VI. chosen, April 9, and Clement VII. Sept. 20, causing the Great Schism.

1379. Urban takes castle of St. Angelo from Clement's officers; Wycliffe sends out his itinerants, the Poor Priests; Unpopular poll tax in England.

1380. Wycliffe translating the New Testament.

1381. Revolt against taxation in Essex in May, also in Kent on June 9, when Walter the Tyler kills a collector; June 13, the rioters reach London; John Ball is freed from prison; and the archbishop of Canterbury beheaded; Walter is killed on Saturday, the 17th; the rioters disperse under promise of pardon, which is broken; John Ball hung, July 15, and many others that summer and fall; Parliament forbids education of the poor; and orders all sheriffs to swear to suppress Lollardism, as was actually done until 1626; Wycliffe's opposition to transubstantiation condemned at Oxford.

1382. Wycliffe's views generally condemned by the Earthquake Council, May 17; Many of his preachers silenced under a pretended Act of Parliament; His New Testament finished in June as well as parts of the Old.

1383. Nicholas of Basel burned.

1384. Death of Wycliffe, Dec. 31; His Bible finished.

1385. Wycliffe's writings known in Bohemia.

1386. University of Heidelberg founded; Battle of Sempach, July 9; Five cardinals murdered by Urban VI., Dec. 15.

1387. Margaret becomes Queen of Denmark.

1388. Wycliffe's Bible published; Margaret conquers Sweden; Battle of Falkioping; Bech burned in Piedmont for asserting the right of Christians to take interest.

1389. Compact of Nuremberg between emperor and princes against the Jews.

1390. Massacre of Jews in Seville; Pope's collector pronounced a public enemy in England; Birth of Pecock; Rights of the people to the Bible in their own tongue asserted by Lancaster in Parliament; Bible as revised by Purvey published.

1392. Statute against Provisors,

or papal nominees, passed by Parliament; University of Erfurt founded.
1393. Gerson chancellor of University of Paris.
1394. The University of Paris tells the king, Jan. 25, that both popes should resign, or a General Council be convoked; Death of Bohemian reformer, Janovius.
1395. Those Mystics and Waldenses, known in common as Winkelers, persecuted at Mainz; Lollards, now at their strongest, petition against the temporal power, auricular confession, etc.
1397. Chrysolaras teaches Greek, and John of Ravenna Latin at Florence; Union of Calmar.
1398. The pope besieged at Avignon.
1399. Christine de Pisan begins to write; Huss defends some of Wycliffe's views at Prague; Richard II. deposed, Sept. 29.
1400. Birth of Gutenberg; Death of Chaucer, Oct. 25; The *Vision of the Orchard* written; Purvey recants and dies in prison soon after; The *Noble Lesson* written by a Waldensian; That sect persecuted at the Christmas of Pragela.
1401. Sautre burned Feb. 24; Statute *de Hæreticis Comburendis* passed in March; *De Ruina Ecclesiæ* written; A bank at Barcelona.
1402. Huss preaches at Bethlehem Chapel.
1403. Wycliffe's views condemned at Prague; Ghiberti begins his gates.
1405. Huss exposes false miracles; Guarino of Verona returns from Constantinople, where he has learned Greek, and brings many manuscripts; Other Italians do the same, and many learned Greeks come to Italy during this century; Many Mss. discovered.
1406. Birth of Valla; Death of Salutato; Wood cuts in use.
1407. Risby, a Lollard, burned in Scotland; Bank of Genoa opened.
1408. Pope's bull torn up by order of the States General of France.
1409. Circulation of Bible in England forbidden by Convocation; Huss deprives his adversaries, the Germans at Prague, of the control of the university; They secede, and found that of Leipsic; Council of Pisa, March 25 to Aug. 7; Its supremacy declared May 29.
1410. Badby burned, Feb. 21; Accession of John XXIII. May 17; July 16, 200 Wycliffite books burned at Prague; On the 18th, Huss is excommunicated, after which he defies the pope; Oil painting invented about this time by Van Eyck.
1411. University of St. Andrews founded.
1412. Birth of Joan of Arc about this time; Death of Queen Margaret; Christine de Pisan writes her *Book of Peace;* Sale of indulgencies to help crusade against Naples opposed by Huss and Jerome on June 7; The pope's bull of indulgencies burned by the students, June 24; Three Hussite mechanics beheaded, July 11.
1413. Huss writes *De Ecclesia* in retirement; Oldcastle on trial, Sept. 25.
1414. Secular courts in England empowered to convict heretics; November 5, Council of Constance opens; Huss arrives on the 3d, and is arrested on the 28th.
1415. The Council declares its superiority to the pope on March 29 and April 6, and de-

poses John XXIII., then under arrest, on May 29; Gregory forced to abdicate, July 4; Huss burned, July 6; Agincourt, Oct. 25.

1416. Jerome of Prague burned May 30.

1417. Utraquism established at Prague, March 7; Benedict VIII. deposed, July 26, at Constance, where a plan for future councils at regular intervals is adopted, Oct. 9; Oldcastle burned, Dec. 14.

1418. Council of Constance closes, April 22.

1419. Zizka a rioter at Prague, Sunday, July 30.

1420. Victories of Zizka over Sigismund; Brunelleschi laboring on Cathedral of Florence; Winkelers banished from Strasburg; Poggio visits England in search of manuscripts; Battle on Zizka's Mountain, July 14; The Four Articles.

1421. Sigismund driven out of Bohemia; Zizka persecutes opponents of transubstantiation and Adamites.

1424. The Bloody Year of Civil War in Bohemia; Waldenses and Mystics burned at Worms.

1425. Scotch law against Lollards; The *Imitation of Christ* written about this time.

1426. Waldenses and Mystics burned at Spire; Victory of Procopius at Aussig, Sunday, June 16.

1427. Death of Purvey.

1428. Hussites invade Austria and Bavaria; Joan of Arc announces her mission.

1429. She relieves Orleans, May 6 and 7, wins battle of Patay, June 18, and has her king crowned at Rheims, Sunday, July 17, but fails in September, at Paris; Death of Gerson, July 12.

1430. May 24, Joan of Arc taken prisoner; Printing with wooden types said to have been invented by Koster at Haarlem.

1431. Feb. 21, first hearing of Joan of Arc by her judges; Recantation, May 24; Execution, Tuesday, May 30; Aug. 27, Council of Basel opens; Hussites invited in October; Jack Sharp's insurrection.

1432. Sunday, Jan. 4, Hussite leaders enter Basel, where the Council declares itself indissoluble, April 29.

1433. The Orphans reach the Baltic; In November, the envoys of the Council announce to the Diet of Prague, that the use of the cup will be permitted to all Christians in Bohemia and Moravia.

1434. Death of Villena, also of Procopius in battle of Lipan, May 30.

1436. Gutenberg makes metal types; Peace of Iglau, July 5, ends Hussite war; Raymond of Sabieude teaching at Toulouse.

1438. Pragmatic Sanction of Bourges; Council at Ferrara and Florence.

1439. June 25, Pope Eugenius deposed at Basel; Felix made anti-pope, Nov. 5.

1443. Valla exposes the *False Donation* about this time.

1444. Pecock becomes bishop of St. Asaph; Nicholas, of Cusa, writes a book asserting the motion of the earth.

1447. Nicholas V. elected; Ghiberti's gates finished.

1448. Council driven from Basel; Poggio writes against hypocrisy.

1449. May 7, the Council dissolves at Lausanne; Nicholas V. persecutes Mystics at Ancona.

1450. Jack Cade's rebellion; Type cast at Mainz; Death of Pletho; Papal jubilee stirs up Wesel to write against indulgencies;

Copper-plate engraving invented.
1451. Isotta, of Verona, argues publicly that Adam was more to blame than Eve.
1452. Tabor captured; Birth of Leonardo da Vinci and Savonarola; Rescue of a heretic at Bologna.
1453. Conspiracy of Porcaro; Fall of Constantinople, May 29.
1455. First battle in Wars of the Roses, May 23; *Mazarin Bible* printed now or earlier; Birth of Reuchlin.
1456. Condemnation of Joan of Arc revoked by pope, July 7.
1457. Death of Valla; Pecock, now bishop of Chichester, recants publicly on Sunday, Dec. 4.
1458. Waldenses and Mystics burned at Strasburg; Pius II. elected, Aug. 19.
1459. Death of Poggio; Birth of Celtes.
1460. Wesel begins to preach.
1461. Heimburg excommunicated and exiled.
1462. Sept. 16, birth of Pomponatius.
1463. King of Bohemia excommunicated.
1464. Felix Hemmerlein dies in prison about this time; Accession of Paul II., first of five peculiarly wicked popes who reigned until 1513; Death of Nicholas of Cusa.
1466. Birth of Erasmus, this year or the next.
1467. Death of Gutenberg.
1468. Pope persecutes Roman Academy.
1469. May 3, birth of Machiavelli; Death of Filippo Lippi.
1470. Boccaccio's *Decameron* printed; Flanders at the height of prosperity; Great activity of printing during rest of century, especially at Venice.
1471. Birth of Albert Dürer; Death of Thomas à Kempis; Vernias begins to preach Averroism at Padua; Bible printed in Italian at Venice; Tolerance in Italy until 1542.
1472. Da Vinci's Medusa; Birth of Cranach and Mutianus; Death of Heimburg.
1473. Feb. 19, birth of Copernicus; Lucretius published; Execution of Lollards.
1474. Isabella begins to reign; Louis XI. tries to suppress University of Paris; First English book, Caxton's *Game of Chess*, printed.
1475. Birth of Angelo, March 6; Platonic Academy founded; Persecution in Piedmont.
1476. Hans Boheim, the peasant prophet and rebel, burned; Swiss conquer at Granson and Morat.
1477. Charles the Bold conquered and slain at Nancy; Marriage of Caterina Sforza; Birth of Titian.
1478. Conspiracy of the Pazzi at Florence; Geiler begins to preach at Strasburg; Maillard protected by women against Louis XI.
1479. Trial of Wesel begins Thursday, Feb. 11.
1480. Birth of Thomas More; Inquisition introduced into Spain; Birth of Gringoire (possibly earlier); Cassandra Fidele defends Averroism; Leonardo da Vinci enters service of Sultan of Egypt, (now or possibly later).
1481. Pulci's *Morgante* published.
1482. Wesel dies in prison; Carniola calls for a council at Basel, July 13; Savonarola begins to preach; Birth of Œcolompadius; Ficino's translation of Plato printed.
1483. Birth of Raphael, April 6; Of Rabelais, soon after, and of Luther, Nov. 10.

1484. Birth of Zwingli; Great independence shown by States General at Tours.
1485. Death of Fra Angelico; End of Wars of the Roses.
1486. Pico's nine hundred theses; Cape of Good Hope discovered; An Encyclopædia published; Birth of Cornelius Agrippa.
1488. Birth of Hutten and Andrea del Sarto; Death of Carniola in prison.
1489. Savonarola begins to preach in Florence; Birth of Vischer and Cranmer; Death of Wesel, Oct. 14.
1490. Birth of Vittoria Colonna and David Lyndsay; A German Bible published; Other versions in this and other languages before 1517.
1491. Birth of Bucer.
1492. Conquest of Granada; A million Arab Mss. burned; America discovered, Friday, Oct. 12; Birth of Vives and Aretin; Accession of Alexander VI., Aug. 11.
1493. Birth of Paracelsus.
1494. Brandt's *Ship of Fools* published; Persecution at Glasgow; Death of Pico di Mirandola; Florence becomes a Republic under the direction of Savonarola; First book on algebra and geometry.
1495. Savonarola invited to Rome, July 25; Birth of Holbein; Pomponatius begins to teach at Padua.
1496. Birth of Berni; Works of Raymond of Sabieude and Lucian published; The *Miller* played at Paris; Jesus College founded at Cambridge in place of a nunnery, suppressed for profligacy.
1497. North America discovered by the Cabots; Birth of Melanchthon, Feb. 16; First bonfire of vanities made by Savonarola, who is excommunicated, May 12; Michael Angelo's Cupid and Bacchus.
1498. Savonarola's ordeal April 7, and execution, May 23; Vasco di Gama reaches India; Louis XII. begins to reign, and favors free speech; Leonardo da Vinci finishes his Last Supper; Dürer illustrates *Revelation*.
1499. Death of Ficino; Recantation of Vernias.
1500. Raphael's first Madonna; The *Adages* of Erasmus published; Peasant victory at Hemmingstadt, Feb. 17; Jubilee and sale of indulgencies in all Catholic lands.
1501. Birth of Cardan; The *Christian Warrior*, by Erasmus, published.
1502. Toleration of Waldenses at Frassinière; Moors banished; University of Wittenberg founded; Caterina Sforza conquered by Cæsar Borgia; Rysswick imprisoned.
1503. Death of Alexander VI., August 18; Accession of Julius II., November 1.
1504. The Mona Lisa and Battle of the Standard finished; Valla's *Annotations* published by Erasmus; More in Parliament; Death of Isabella.
1505. Reuchlin's *Hebrew Grammar* and *Dictionary* published; Birth of Knox; Bebel's *Triumph of Venus* published; Wimpheling attacked for showing that Augustine did not found the Order, which Luther now joins.
1506. Bramante begins to rebuild St. Peters; Birth of Buchanan; Bebel's *Facetiæ* published.
1507. Michael Angelo begins to paint the Sistine Chapel.
1508. Birth of Telesius and Alva; Death of Celtes; The School of Athens.
1509. Birth of Servetus, Calvin, Cæsalpinus and Dolet; Pfeffer-

korn tries to destroy Hebrew literature; Accession, April 22, of Henry VIII., who marries Catherine of Arragon, June 3.

1510. Balboa discovers the Pacific; More translates Pico's *Life of Savonarola;* Gringoire's *Hope of Peace,* and *Chasse du Cerf des Cerfs,* published; Pope's Holy League against France; Council of Tours, afterwards Pisa; Death of Geiler.

1511. Raphael's Parnassus; Council of Pisa; Luther in Rome.

1512. "Perdam Babylonis Nomen;" Papal interdict on France; Colet's sermon on clerical corruption, February 6; Erasmus's *Praise of Folly* published.

1513. Accession of Leo X., March 11; Celtes' *Odes* and the *Julius Exclusus* published; Averroism condemned by Lateran Council, Dec. 19; Reuchlin tried for heresy.

1514. Reuchlin acquitted at Spire.

1515. Birth of Ramus and Castallio; Raphael's cartoons; Wolsey cardinal and chancellor; Lateran Council forbids unlicensed printing; Accession of Francis I.; Cornelius Agrippa writes his *Occult Philosophy* and *Nobility of Woman;* Luther begins to preach.

1516. Luther's edition of the *Theologia Germanica,* those of the Greek Testament and *Jerome* by Erasmus, the latter's *Christian Prince,* Ariosto's *Orlando Furioso,* Pomponatius *On Immortality,* More's *Utopia* and the *Letters of Obscure Men* published; Machiavelli writes the *Prince,* and presents it to Lorenzo dei Medici.

1517. Luther attacks the sale of indulgencies in his *Theses,* Oct. 31; Hutten prints his satire on the Duke of Würtemberg.

1518. Luther appeals from the pope to a general council; Zwingli attacks indulgencies, as does Erasmus in his *Colloquies,* now printed surreptitiously; Sistine Madonna painted.

1519. Zwingli begins to preach at Zurich, Jan. 1; Charles V. elected emperor, June 28; Luther begins, July 4, a dispute with Eck, wherein he gives up the authority of councils as well as popes; *Paraphrase on Corinthians* by Erasmus published; Cortes conquers Mexico; Death of Leonardo da Vinci.

1520. Reuchlin condemned at Rome, Jan. 23; Luther excommunicated, June 16; his *Appeal to the German Nobility* published in August; The bull burned, Nov. 10; He writes and prints one hundred and thirty-three books and pamphlets this year; Magellan enters the Pacific, November 28; Cornelius Agrippa driven from Metz; Pomponatius writes against miracles; Death of Raphael.

1521. April 18, Diet of Worms, after which Luther is carried to the Wartburg; Controversy between him and Henry VIII.; Luther writes on *Christian Liberty;* Erasmus's *Colloquies* published with his consent, also his *Paraphrase of Matthew;* Loyola becomes a monk; Las Casas fails to found a philanthropic colony; Death of Leo X., Dec. 1.

1522. March 7, Luther returns to Wittenberg and puts down the fanatics there; His New Testament published in September, in which month Sickingen attacks Treves; Death of Reuchlin, June 30; Platonic Academy at Florence suppressed.

1523. Jan. 13, Diet of Nuremberg protests against violence to Luther; Death of Sickingen, May 7, and Hutten, Aug. 29; Rabelais imprisoned; Four Lutherans burned at Antwerp, July 1; Luther opposes persecution of Jews; Sweden liberated from Denmark by Gustavus Vasa; New Testament published in French.

1524. Schwenckfeld begins to point out immoral tendencies of Lutheranism; Three of Dürer's pupils banished from Nuremberg for disbelief in transubstantiation and the Bible; *Utopia* translated into German; controversy of Luther and Erasmus on the Will; Carlstadt driven from Orlamünde by Luther, who says: "Reason is the Devil's harlot, and can do nothing but blaspheme;" The *Theologaster* first acted at Paris; Anabaptists burned at Augsburg and Vienna; Peasants rise near Basel, August 24; Birth of Camoens and Palestrina; New Testament translated into Danish.

1525. General rising of peasants, Sunday, April 2; Weinsberg massacre the 17th, after which Luther denounces the rebels; Münzer defeated at Frankenhausen, and Götz at Würzburg, May 15; Death of Pomponatius, May 18; Luther's marriage, June 11; Erasmus attacks the confessional; Paracelsus returns to Germany.

1526. Death of Mutianus Rufus, May 30; Diet of Spire decrees in June, that each state may choose its own religion; Dolet studies at Padua; Paracelsus, professor at Basel, where he burns Galen, Avicenna, etc.; Erasmus places marriage above celibacy; Agrippa writes on the *Uncertainty and Vanity of the Arts and Sciences*; The New Testament published in Swedish and Tyndal's in English, and the whole Bible in Dutch.

1527. Felix Mantz drowned at Zurich for Anabaptist views, Jan. 5; Rome captured by Imperialists, May 6; Denck and other Anti-trinitarians banished from Strasburg; A hundred of their followers beheaded in Baden; Seventy Baptists burned in the Tyrol; University of Marburg founded; sale of 24,000 copies of the *Colloquies* of Erasmus; Death of Machiavelli.

1528. Paracelsus driven from Basel where Denck dies of the plague; Hamilton, first reformer in Scotland, burned; Seventy Anabaptists beheaded in Bavaria; Death of Albert Dürer; Schwenckfeld banished from Silesia.

1529. Hetzer beheaded, Feb. 4, at Constance; Protestants gain their name at Spire, April 25; Marburg conference, Oct. 1; Wolsey's fall, Oct. 18; Basson beheaded at Basel; Agrippa's *Nobility of Woman*, and Bünderlin's books published.

1530. Confession of Augsburg presented June 25; Suppression of German Protestants decreed, Nov. 19; Faber's Bible in French, and Agrippa's *Uncertainty and Vanity of the Arts and Sciences* published; Copernicus finishes his great book; Rabelais studying medicine; Alliance of Hesse and Zurich; Campanus imprisoned in Saxony; Zurich decrees that heresy is a capital crime; Death of Andrea del Sarto, Wolsey, and Sannazaro; Birth of La Boëtie.

1531. Death of Zwingli in battle, Oct. 11; Servetus publishes his *Errors of the Trinity*, as Vives does his *Causes of the Corruption of Learning*, and Franck his *Universal History* for which he has to leave Strasburg; Bainham arrested; Schmalkald League formed.

1532. Bainham burned; Servetus publishes his *Dialogue* and takes refuge in France; Hoffmann imprisoned at Strasburg; Private marriage of Henry VIII. with Anne Boleyn; Publication of Franck's *Proverbs*, Machiavelli's *Prince*, and Bruccioli's Bible in Italian.

1533. Montaigne born; What is now the second book of *Gargantua and Pantagruel* published; Geneva revolts against her bishop.

1534. Franck's *Paradoxes* published; Anabaptists appear at Münster and Libertines in France, where the Jesuits organize; Parliament makes Henry VIII. head of the Church; Claudius banished from Bern; Dolet imprisoned at Toulouse for denouncing persecution; Burning of heretics resumed at Paris, Nov. 10; Luther's Bible published; Protestant conquest of Würtemberg; Las Casas writes against persecution.

1535. Jan. 13, bookselling and publishing made capital crimes in France, by an edict, modified Feb. 24; Sir Thomas More beheaded July 6; Anabaptists burned in England, but tolerated in Moravia until 1547; Their reign at Münster ends June 23; Bucer's book advocating slaying heretics with their wives and children published, also Coverdale's and Olivetan's Bibles, Ludovici's *Triumph of Charlemagne*, Servetus's edition of Ptolemy, and the first book of *Gargantua and Pantagruel;* Death of Cornelius Agrippa; Marot takes refuge in Italy; Geneva becomes Protestant, and Bonnivard is liberated from Chillon.

1536. Deaths of Erasmus, Berni, and Tyndal, last burned Oct. 6; Fourteen Anabaptists burned in England; Three beheaded at Jena, with Melanchthon's approval; Synod of Homburg, Hesse, on Aug. 7, approves of capital punishment for heresy; Three hundred and seventy-six monasteries suppressed in England; Ramus holds a discussion against authority of Aristotle; Menno organizes a peaceable sect of Baptists; Agrippa's *Occult Philosophy*, Calvin's *Institutes*, Dolet's *Studies of Latin Literature*, and Cardan's *Bad Practices of Modern Doctors* published.

1537. Desperrier's *Cymbal*, Manzolli's *Zodiac of Life*, and John Rogers' Bible published; Vesalius becomes professor at Padua.

1538. Franck's *Chronicle of Germany* and *Golden Ark* published as is Lyndsay's *Papingo*. Dolet, bookseller and publisher at Lyons; Luther advises banishing dissenters from Germany.

1539. Birth of Faustus Socinus; Franck banished from Ulm; *Great Bible* printed; Remaining monasteries suppressed in England; Six Articles enacted against Protestants; Freedom of the press established in Poland.

1540. Hoffman dies in prison; Death of Guicciardini; Servetus goes to Vienne; Order of Jesuits sanctioned; Lyndsay's *Three Estates* acted; Bishop Stencho publishes a book showing that all philosophers held the true religion; Osiander writes against persecuting Jews.

1541. Death of Paracelsus and Carlstadt; Calvin returns to Geneva; Berni's *Orlando*, and the Latin version of the Bible with rationalistic notes by Servetus published.

1542. Dolet sentenced to death, Oct. 2; Death of Contarini; Las Casas prevented from publishing his *Ruin of the Indies;* Inquisition revived; Occhino and other Protestants flee from Italy; Joris publishes his *Wonder Book*.

1543. Publication of the attacks of Vesalius on Galen, of Ramus on Aristotle, and of Copernicus on the Ptolemaic system; Death of Copernicus; Dolet released, but rearrested; Luther writes against the Jews.

1544. Deaths of Desperriers, by suicide, Marot, and Margaret of Navarre; Ramus sentenced to silence, March 1; Protestants who call God the author of evil banished from the Grisons; Castalio has to leave Geneva; Calvin writes against the Libertines; Joris comes, under a feigned name, to Basel; Birth of Tasso.

1545. Vaudois persecution, April; Council of Trent opens Dec. 13; Publication of Cardan's *Algebra*, and of the third book of *Gargantua and Pantagruel;* Birth of Andrew Melville; Death of Sebastian Franck.

1546. Calvin writes Farel, Feb. 7, that Servetus shall never quit Geneva alive; Death of Luther, Feb. 18; Protestants defeated at Mühlberg, April 24; Chapius imprisoned, April 27, for calling his son Claude, and not Abraham; Sale of Bible in English forbidden, July 8; Anne Ascue burned, July 16, and Dolet, Aug. 3, when he is thirty-eight; *Index of Prohibited Books* made at Louvain; Society of Unitarians meets at Vicenza, and this view is also taught in Poland.

1547. Knox in penal servitude on a French galley; Conspiracy of Fiesco, Jan. 2; Accession of Edward VI., Jan. 28; Gruet arrested for tolerant views at Geneva, June 28, sentenced Sunday, July 25, and beheaded the 26th; Fourth book of *Gargantua and Pantagruel* published; Rabelais leaves France temporarily; Koran printed at Venice and suppressed by pope; Buchanan imprisoned at Coimbra; Thamer offers to show immoral tendencies of Lutheranism in public discussion, but is forbidden; Death of Francis I.; Birth of Cervantes.

1548. Accession of the tolerant Sigismund II. in Poland, where he reigns until 1572; Trissino's *Italy Liberated* and an Italian version of the *Utopia* published; Tiziano recants rationalism in the Grisons, and Ashton Unitarianism at London; Birth of Giordano Bruno; La Boëtie writes his *Involuntary Servitude*.

1549. Thamer banished from Hesse, Aug. 15; The *Book of Common Prayer* and Gessner's *History of Animals* published.

1550. Joan Bocher burned, May 2, and Gruet's Ms. May 23; Death of Alciati; Unbelief in Christianity discovered in England; Bible published in Danish, and *Utopia* in French.

1551. Van Paris burned; Renato recants, Jan. 19; Bolsec attacks predestination, Friday, Oct. 16, and is banished Dec. 22; His friend, Bourgogne, pleads in vain, on Nov. 9, that "Free speech ought to be permitted to all Christians;" Spifame's *Royal Decisions*, the

Utopia in English, Cardan's *Subtilty of Things*, Castalio' Bible in Latin with a daring preface, and Dumoulin's *Exposure of Papal Abuses*, published.

1552. Feb. 19, Rabelais resigns his benefices; Gryphius beheaded; The forty-two, afterwards thirty-nine Articles published; Castalio professor at Basel; Lutheranism restored to power by Maurice of Saxony.

1553. Death of Rabelais; Accession of Mary, July 6; Birth of Spenser; Vergerio banished from the Grisons for favoring tolerance, and Robert le Moine, on July 27, from Geneva, for disbelief in. hell and in the Bible; Servetus publishes his *Restoration of Christianity*, is betrayed by Calvin to the inquisition, which arrests him, April 4; He escapes, is burned in effigy, June 17, arrested at Geneva, Sunday, Aug. 13, argues with Calvin against capital punishment for heresy, Sept. 1, and is burned on Friday, Oct. 27; Gribaldi remonstrates in vain.

1554. Publication of censures of the murder of Servetus by Occhino, Lyncurt, Renato, Bolsec, and Castalio, the last under the name of Martin Bellius; Minos Celso writes a book to the same effect, published 1584, and Zurkinden of Bern a private letter to Calvin; Similar sentiments are expressed by Lælius Socinus, Cellarius, professor at Basel, Vergerio, and many other Protestants; Birth of Hooker; Many Free-willers and Arians arrested in England; Pereira's *Margarita*, an attack on Aristotle, and Las Casas's *Destruction of the Indies* published.

1555. Accession of Philip II. in the Netherlands and of the intolerant pope, Paul IV.; Gribaldi banished from Geneva, and Foncelet, author of a poem against Calvin, from Bern; Persecution in England begins as Rogers is burned, Feb. 4; Castalio's French Bible published; Death of Lyndsay, and on April 12, of Queen Juana; Peace of Augsburg, Sept. 25.

1556. Pomponatius *On Miracles*, and Poynet's *Political Power* published; Death of Loyola and Joris; Robert King on trial for saying, "It is not lawful to put a man to death for conscience's sake;" Charles V. resigns the crown of Spain to Philip II.

1557. Thamer goes over to Rome about this time; A Frenchman banished from Geneva, Nov. 28, for thinking nothing of the Gospel; Philip II. makes peace with the pope.

1558. Accession of Elizabeth, Nov. 18; Lyndsay's *Dreme*, Queen Margaret's *Heptameron*, and Knox's *Blast against the Monstrous Regiment of Women* published; Blandrata and Gentilis leave Geneva, where four hundred people are punished, this year and the next, for dancing, laughing in church, etc.

1559. Peace of Câteau Cambresis unites France and Spain against Protestantism, April 2; Joris found to have called himself Christ David; His books and bones burned at Basel, May 13; Knox preaches in Edinburgh; Riot in Rome against the inquisition; First Huguenot synod at Paris.

1560. Birth of Sully and Arminius; Reformation established in Scotland by her parliament, Aug. 24; Speech of L'Hôpital to the States General in favor of toleration, Dec. 13.

INDEX.

Abelard, Peter, origin of name, 144; philosophy, 144, 145; marriage, 146, 147; persecutions for rationalism, 147-152; death, 153.
Abubacer, Moslem Mystic, 156.
Academy, Florentine, 276, 279; Plato's, 28; Roman, 279.
Acquasparto, orthodox Franciscan, 219.
Adamites, heretical Mystics, 255.
Adrian IV., Pope, 142.
Ænesidemus, a Skeptic, 37.
Æschylus, represents Jupiter as the oppressor of mankind, 7, 41.
Afer, Domitius, a witty Roman orator, 64.
Agincourt, a peasant victory, 304.
Agnosticism, of Melissus, 5; of Protagoras, 14; of Galen, 91; of Ockham, 234; of Nicholas of Autricuria, 235; misrepresented, 398.
Agobard, Bishop, writes against witchcraft and ordeals, 129.
Agrippa, Cornelius, philosophy, 313; on the Nobility of Women, 314; on errors of his age, 339, 375.
Agrippina, as a politician, 77.
Ailly, d', bishop and afterwards cardinal, inspires Columbus, 182; at council of Pisa, 257; at council of Constance, 259.
Alamanni, skeptical poet, 357.
Albigenses, see Catharists, also 135.
Albornoz, Cardinal, sacks Cesena, 236.
Alcæus, banished for teaching Epicureanism, 49.
Alciati, on astrology and witchcraft, 351.
Alcibiades, persecuted, 9, 10.
Aldine press, 292.
Alençon, Duke of, 263.
Alexander, of Aphrodisias, denier of immortality, 99, 290.

Alexander, of Macedon, pupil of Aristotle, 34.
Alexander Polyhistor, 2.
Alexander VI., Pope, establishes censorship of the press, 279; tolerates satirists, 282; vices of, 297, 309.
Alexander, the false prophet, 89-92.
Alexandrian library, destroyed, 116.
Alexandrianism, or Neo-Platonism, 102.
Alexius Comnenus, a persecutor, 139.
Alfar, Hugo d', assassin of inquisitors, 171.
Alfonso, king of Naples, protector of Valla, 277.
Alfred, of England, pupil of Erigena, 128.
Al Gazali, founder of Sufism, 156.
Allah, Abul, skeptical poet, 131.
Allegorism, of Origen, 101; of the Catharists, 134; of the Waldenses, 158; of Savonarola, 320; its delusive tendencies, 330.
Amafinius, Epicurean poet, 50.
Amalric, pantheistic Mystic, 157, 174.
Ambrose, opponent of persecution, 118; of philosophy, 119, 150.
Amelius, Neo-Platonist, 103.
American Revolution, condemned by the New Testament, 79.
Ammianus, tolerant historian, 113.
Ammonius Saccas, founder of Neo-Platonism, 102.
Amos, against authority of priests, 1.
Anabaptists, Mystics opposing infant baptism and zealous for political liberty, 342-346, 364, 366, 376.
Anastasius, Pope, persecutor, 101; heretic, 217.
Anaxagoras, opinions, 7; persecution, 8, 9.

Anaximander, evolutionism of, 4.
Anaximenes, teacher of the order of nature, 4.
Andrelini, author of a satire against Pope Julius II., 306.
Anniceris, follower of Aristippus of Cyrene, 30.
Anselm, as a theologian, 137, 150.
Anti-Christ, pope called so, 232, 248.
Antinomianism, of German Mystics, 221-223; of Lutherans, 373; of Joris, 376.
Antisthenes, the first Cynic, 30, 100.
Antistius, Roman satirist, 74.
Antonia, deliverer of Tiberius, 77.
Antoninus, Marcus Aurelius; see Aurelius.
Antoninus Pius, liberty-loving emperor, 88.
Antony, of Florence, exposed *False Decretals*, 281.
Antwerp, early heresy at, 140.
Anytus, prosecutor of Socrates, 21.
Apollinaris, defender of Christianity against Porphyry, 103.
Apollonius, of Perga, a mathematician, 57.
Apostolic Brethren, a sect of Mystics, 177.
Apostolic Constitutions, forbid rebelling against the clergy, 83; or reading heathen books, 97.
Apostles' Creed, spurious, 111, 277, 301.
Aquinas, Thomas, on miracles, 180; on immortality, 288, 290.
Arc, see Joan of.
Arcesilaus, a skeptical Platonist, 38.
Archelaus, holds right and wrong merely conventional, 29.
Archimedes, founder of hydrostatics, 57.
Arduino, calls *Divina Commedia* spurious, 214.
Areopagus, banishes Stilpo for impiety, 29.
Arete, daughter and follower of Aristippus of Cyrene, 30.
Aretino, 357.
Ariosto, on monasticism, 283.
Aristarchus, first to declare the sun central, 58.
Aristippus, the Cyrenaic, 17, 29, 230.
Aristophanes, assailant of Eurip-ides, 11; describer of Socrates, 18-20.
Aristotle, opinions, 32-34; honored like Jesus, 85; not to be studied by Christians, 97, 175, 180; medieval influence, 153, 156, 175, 182, 189, 287, 347; authority questioned by Bacon, 182; by Nicholas of Autricuria, 235; by Ramus, Vives, and Cardan, 350; appealed to in attacking Christianity by Pomponatius, 291, and Rysswick, 319.
Arians, origin, 111; intolerance, 112, 115; missionaries, 116; suppression, 116, 117, 126; revival, 364, 365.
Arnold, of Brescia, pupil of Abelard, 141; liberator of Rome, 142; martyrdom, 143, 145.
Arnold, an earlier martyr, 141.
Arria, Platonist, 99.
Arria, wife of Pœtus, 70.
Arria, wife of Thrasea, 74.
Arrian, recorder of discourses of Epictetus, 85.
Art, influence of, 292-295.
Artemonites, primitive Unitarians, 97.
Articles, the Four, 254; the Twelve, 343, 344.
Arulenus Rusticus, friend of Thrasea, 74, 76.
Assassination, of Domitian, 76; of Conrad and other inquisitors, 171-173, 197, 221; of duke of Milan, 279.
Ascue, Anne, martyr for disbelief in transubstantiation, 332, 333, 364.
Asoka, first tolerant monarch, 2.
Aspasia, on trial for unbelief, 8.
Astarotte, forerunner of Mephistopheles, 282.
Astrolabe, son of Abelard and Heloise, 146.
Astrology, opposed by Roman senate, 57; favored by Bacon, 182, and Cecco, 235; opposed by Favorinus, 87, by Pico, 280, and by Rabelais, 353.
Athanasian Creed, when forged, 111, 130.
Athanasius, opinions and persecutions, 111-115.
Atheism, of Hippo, 4; of Diagoras, 11, 12; of Critias, 21; of Theo-

INDEX. 437

dore, 30; of Cotta, 38; of Pacuvius, 51; of Dolet, doubtful, 358.
Athens, persecutes philosophy, 8; to her own ruin, 9; murders Socrates, 23; prohibits teaching of philosophy, 35; allows freedom of thought during seven centuries, 35, 60.
Atomic theory, taught by Leucippus and Democritus, 12; by Epicurus, 44, 45; by Lucretius, 53.
Atonement, doctrine of the, 137; disbelief in the, 375,·376.
Atticus, an Epicurean, 50.
Attius, Epicurean poet, 51.
Augsburg, treaty at, 332.
Augury, exposed by an augur, 59.
Augustinian Averroist, 280.
Augustine, opposes taking interest, 107; extols celibacy, 108; favors persecution, 120–122, 125, 150; criticised by Valla, 277.
Augustus, tries to suppress liberty of thought, 60-64.
Aurelian, conquers Zenobia, 105.
Aurelius, Marcus, Antoninus, his regard for liberty while emperor, 88; his *Meditations*, 88, 89; his superstition, 89, 90; his persecution of Christianity, 90.
Aussig, battle of, 256.
Autier, Pierre, Catharist, 172.
Avempace, Moslem Mystic, 156.
Averroes, the Moslem rationalist, 153, 154; opponent of Mysticism, 156; forbidden to be read, 175, 180; translated, 180; placed highest amongst teachers, except Aristotle, by Rysswick, 319.
Averroism, materialistic disbelief in immortality, 180, 235, 280, 288, 319.
Avicebron, Jewish Mystic, 136, 155.
Avicenna, Moslem philosopher, 189.
Axiochus, translated by Dolet, who is punished capitally for a mistake, 358.
Aylmer, Bishop, against absolute monarchy, 351.
Aylmer, real name of Cade, 304, 305.
Babylonish captivity, of the papacy at Avignon, 207, 244.
Bacchic worship, denounced by Heraclitus, 6; forbidden by Roman senate, 57.
Bacon, Roger, imprisoned for love of science, 181–183; not mentioned by Dante, 217.
Badby, Lollard martyr, 250.
Bainham, burned for belief in superiority of morality to ceremony, 364.
Balboa, discoverer of the Pacific, 296.
Ball, John, preaches insurrection, 246; hung, 247.
Bandello, satirical novelist, 282.
Banking, introduced without ecclesiastical sanction, 296.
Baptism, rejected by the Catharists, 134; by Bünderlin, 376.
Barbadori, appeals from the pope to Christ, 244.
Basel, Council of, struggles against pope, 259, 260; makes peace with Hussites, 256, 257.
Basel, Defense of the Council of, 311.
Basel, a tolerant city, 370, 371, 372.
Basil, a Bulgarian Catharist, 139.
Basilides, Gnostic, 85.
Bassen, Conradin, Unitarian martyr, 380.
Bathing, revived by crusades, 294.
Baunet, anti-Romish moralist, 301.
Bebel, anti-clerical satirist, 312, 313.
Becket, why sainted, 138, 273.
Beghards, and Beguines, charitable societies inclined to Mysticism, 221.
Bellius, see Castalio.
Bembo, protector of Pomponatius, 290.
Benedict XI., Pope, 206.
Benedict XII., tries to reform the Church, 232.
Benedict XIII., anti-pope, deposed by council of Constance, 258.
Berengar, opponent of transubstantiation, 135.
Berlichingen, Götz von, leader and betrayer of the rebel peasants, 344, 345.
Bern, more tolerant than Geneva, 371, 372, 376, 379.
Bernard of Clairvaux, persecutor of Catharists, 135; of Arnold

141; of Abelard, 148, 152; a Mystic, 155.
Bernard Sylvester, Mystic, 155.
Bessarion, a reviver of Platonism, 276.
Bible, as a platform, 241, 330; its authority rejected, 299, 300, 319, 375, 379; versions, 116, 133, 157, 242, 245, 303, 329.
Biblical criticism, by Origen, 101, 396; by Porphyry, 104; by Chivi, 134; by Abelard, 149, 150; by Heloise, 151, 152; by Valla, 277; by Erasmus, 318, 338; by Servetus, 365, 366, 396.
Bilgard, early heretic, 131.
Black Cross Knights, oppose pope, 231.
Black Death, 224, 245.
Blanche, Queen of France, 168, 193, 194.
Blandina, Christian martyr, 90.
Blandrata, Unitarian, 372.
Blasphemy, a capital crime at Geneva, 334.
Boccaccio, 235, 281, 302.
Bocher, Joan, or Joan of Kent, martyr, 342, 364.
Bogomiles, a party among the Catharists, 139.
Boheim, Hans, a rebellious Mystic, 304.
Bohemia, revolts from Rome, 251, 257.
Bohlke, peasant leader of rebellion, 188.
Boiardo, anti-clerical poet, 283.
Bolsec, opponent of Calvinism, 371.
Bonaventura, Mystic and persecutor, 181.
Boniface VIII., Pope, persecutor of Mysticism, 220; claimant of absolute authority, 195, 196, 200, 204; prisoner in the Vatican, 206; prosecuted for vice and unbelief, 207; put in hell by Dante, 215, 216.
Bonivard, Genevan patriot, 334.
Book-men, as servants of liberty and progress, 393, 395.
Books, idolatry of, opposed by Paracelsus, 348; by Galen, 349; by Vives and Cardan, 350; by Rabelais, 353, 354.
Borgias, 279–282, 297.
Bourgogne, Jacques de, first to claim free speech for Christians, 371.

Brandt, Sebastian, satirist, 303.
Brown, John, compared to Dolcino, 177, 212.
Browning, Robert, 103, 348.
Bruni, anti-clerical scholar, 276.
Bruno, Giordano, 259.
Brutus, a skeptic, 38; his memory, 76, 86, 88.
Bucer, advocates massacring heretics, 346.
Buchanan, George, satirist and dramatist, 361, 362.
Buddha, and Buddhism, 2, 3.
Bull, pope's, burned at Paris, 203; Prague, 252; Wittenberg, 328.
Bünderlin, Mystic of advanced views, 375, 376.
Bundschuh, peasant's shoe and standard of revolt, 343.
Burgo, Lucas de, early algebraist, 286.
Cabalistic philosophy, 313.
Cabots, 296, 298.
Cade, Jack, misrepresented in *Henry VI.*, 304, 305.
Cæsar, Julius, an Epicurean, 49, 50; reformer of the calendar, 58; tolerant, 50.
Caligula, 64, 70.
Calixtines, the moderate Hussites, 253–257.
Calvin, Institutes, 334; intolerance, 334, 335, 365–372, 376–379; share in murder of Servetus, 365–370.
Calvinism, defined, 121, 128, 330; opposed by Hoffmann, 342; by Servetus, 367; by Bolsec, 371; by Franck, 374.
Calycles, coins made from chalices, 253.
Cambridge, colleges founded at, 298.
Campanus, persecuted Unitarian, 363, 364.
Canterbury Tales, 249, 250.
Capnio, name assumed by Reuchlin, 311.
Cappel, battle of, 331.
Caputiati, medieval levelers, 144.
Carbeas, heretic general, 127.
Carcassonne, taken by crusaders, 165; revolts against inquisition, 220.
Cardan, tries to introduce scientific methods, 350, 351.
Carlstadt, liberal Protestant, 375.

Carneades, skeptical Platonist, 38.
Carniola, Archbishop of, and his attempts at reform, 297.
Carpocrates, the Gnostic, 85.
Casale, Franciscan Mystic, 218, 220.
Caspi, Jewish rationalist, 235.
Cassius, Caius, conspirator against Julius Cæsar, 50, 73.
Cassius, Avidius, conspirator against Marcus Aurelius, 88.
Cassius Severus, persecuted historian, 63.
Castalio, advocate of tolerance, 370, 371.
Castruccio, an imperialist, 231.
Catharists, origin, 133, 134; views, 132–135, 138, 139; in Southern France, 131, 132, 135, 138–140, 163–172; in England, 138; in Germany, 133, 138, 172; in Italy, 133, 135, 137, 172, 173, 189; their high morality, 135, 202; ruinous error, 174.
Catherine, of Siena, 262.
Catius, Epicurean poet, 50.
Cato, the Censor, opponent of skepticism, 38.
Cato, of Utica, 39, 74, 76, 86, 88, 217.
Catullus, Epicurean poet, 50.
Cauchon, persecutor of Joan of Arc, 263–267.
Caxton, the printer, 298.
Cecco, of Ascoli, martyr for astrology, 285.
Celestine II., Pope, friend to Arnold of Brescia, 141, 142, 145.
Celestine V., Pope, 178, 196, 216, 219.
Celibacy, favored by Paul and the Church Fathers, 108; also by the Manichæans, 118; established in Church of Rome, 118; the result, 137, 225, 244, 249, 254, 258, 273, 278, 281, 282, 297, 305, 313, 332, 336, 337. See also Marriage.
Cellarius, opposes persecution, 372.
Celso, Minos, opposes persecution, 372.
Celsus, early writer against Christianity, 85, 90.
Censorship, of the press, established by Alexander VI., 279.
Cerberus, Trinity compared to, 366.
Cerinthus, Gnostic, 85.

Cesena, defended by Marzia Ordelaffi against crusaders, 236, 237.
Chaldæan astrologers, expelled from Italy, 57.
Champeaux, William of, a Realist conquered by Abelard, 144, 146.
Charlemagne, restoring order, 130.
Charles IV., becomes emperor, 233; imprisons Rienzi, 228.
Charles V., keeps his mother imprisoned, 341.
Charles, of Anjou, sent by pope to conquer Naples and Sicily, 192.
Charles, the Bald, protector of Erigena, 128.
Charles, the Bold, conquered by the Swiss, 304.
Charmides, aristocrat and friend of Socrates, 17, 21.
Chaucer, 184, 249, 250, 388.
Chivi, Jewist rationalist, 131.
Christine de Pisan, earliest professional authoress, 301.
Christopher I. of Denmark, imprisons an archbishop, 194.
Chrysolaras, revives study of Greek in Italy, 276.
Cicero, skeptical Platonist, 38, 59; not to be studied by Christians, 119; influence in favor of liberty, 86, 279.
Cinthio, novelist used by Shakespeare, 282.
Circulation of the Blood, discovered by Servetus, 365, 367.
Claudius, independent bishop, 129.
Claudius, the emperor, 64, 70.
Cleanthes, Stoic poet, 40; opponent of science, 58.
Clement, independent bishop, 128.
Clement, of Alexandria, a liberal Christian, 101, 107, 124; loses his place among the saints, 390; mentions the Buddha, 2.
Clement IV., Pope, patron of Bacon, 181, 182, and Charles of Anjou, 192.
Clement V., Pope, in French service, 206, 207; destroys the Templars, 209, 210; put by Dante in hell, 216.
Clement VI., Pope, lover of Joanna of Naples, 205, 207; enemy to Rienzi, 227, 228.
Cleomenes, patriotic king, 39.
Cleopatra, influence in politics, 61.

Clerical authority, how far favored by Jesus, 69; and by the New Testament, 81–83, 270; fully recognized in the second century, 83. See also Papacy.
Clopinel, nickname of Jean de Meung, 184.
Cobham, Lollard martyr, 250.
Colet, liberal Catholic, 315.
Colonna, Vittoria, calls Italian art irreligious, 294.
Colonna, Sciarra, enemy to Boniface VIII., 205–207, 231.
Columbus, sources of information, 182, 286; importance of his discovery, 206.
Coluccio, champion of study of classic poets, 276.
Come-outers, led by Dolcino, 212.
Communism, charged against Dolcino and the Strasburg Mystics, 221; preached by John Ball, 246; also by Hans Boheim, 304; taught in the *Utopia*, 316, and by Anabaptists, 346.
Commerce, its effects on Christianity, 296, 298.
Conceptualism, 145, 163.
Confession, to be made at least once a year, 167; its result, 241, 282; opposed by Wycliffe, 248; and by Erasmus, 337.
Congregationalism, how far favored by Jesus and the Apostles, 69, 333; established among the Paulicians, 126; and Taborites, 254; favored by Luther, 328; demanded by the insurgent peasants, 343.
Conrad, last Hohenstauffen emperor, 192.
Conrad, inquisitor, 172.
Conradin, son of the emperor, Conrad, 192.
Conservatism, causes of, 397–401.
Constance, Council of, membership, 258; burns Huss, 253; other proceedings, 258, 259.
Constantine, the emperor, establishes Christianity, 110–112, 115; his alleged grant to the pope, 130, 215, 277, 281, 301, 356.
Constantine, the Paulician, 126.
Constantinople, captured with doubtful effect on western scholarship, 276.
Constantius, Arian persecutor, 112.

Contarini, liberal Catholic, 334.
Copernicus, 1, 350, 381.
Cordus, Cremutius, martyr for free speech, 70, 86.
Cornutus, Stoic, 75.
Cornwall, Earl of, 192, 195.
Councils, their authority denied by Frederic II., 191; Ockham, 234; Huss, 252; Wesel, 324. See for single councils, Basel, Constance, Earthquake, Ferrara, Lateran, Lyons, Nicæa, Pisa, Sens, Soissons, Vienne.
Cotta, an atheist, 38.
Courtrai, victory of Flemish artisans over king of France, 304.
Cranmer, Archbishop, 333.
Crates, the Cynic, 31, 32.
Crazy Socrates, nickname of Diogenes, 31.
Creation denied, 180, 319.
Crecy, a peasant victory, 304.
Cremutius Cordus, see Cordus.
Critias, atheist and tyrant, 21.
Crito, friend to Socrates, 16, 17, 23, 24.
Crœsus, enslaver of Ionia, 4.
Crotus Rubianus, author of the *Letters of Obscure Men*, 310, 311.
Crusades, against the tolerant Languedocians, 139, 164–169; against the Stedingers, 188; against the Bohemians, 254–256; against Marzia Ordelaffi, 237; against the Asiatics, 137, 273, 294; these last unnecessary, 187; their failure taken as a judgment from God, 159.
Cusa, Cardinal de, teaches that the earth moves, 259, 286.
Cybele, worship of, forbidden, 64.
Cynics, 30–32, 35, 38, 47, 75.
Cyprian, 83, 107–109.
Cyril, murderer of Hypatia, 114.
Cyrenaics, 29, 30, 35.
Damasus, Pope, a pattern of orthodoxy, 116, 117.
Damis, an atheist in *Lucian*, 93, 94.
Damon, music teacher, exiled, 8.
Danaæ, Epicurean, 45.
Dance of Death, 260.
Daniel, Book of, a forgery, 104.
Dante, an imperialist, 213, 214, 216, 217; antagonist of the papacy, 214–217; admirer of the heretical Mystics, 218, 219.

Dark Ages, 120, 272.
David of Dinanto, Mystic, 175.
Deborah, ruler of Israel, 78.
Decameron, by Boccaccio, 235, 281, 302.
Decius, persecutor of Christianity, 101, 109.
Decretals, ridiculed by Rabelais, 354, 355. See also False Decretals.
Defensor Pacis, its anti-papal views, 230.
Délicieux, Bernard, Mystic, and enemy of the inquisition, 220, 221.
Demetrius, the Cynic, 75.
Democritus, his opinions, 12–14; influence over Epicurus, 42–45.
Demonax, rationalistic philosopher, 95.
Demoniacal possession, 397; questioned by Pomponatius, 290.
Denck, Unitarian and Universalist, 376.
Desperriérs, satirist, 357, 358.
Despotism, necessarily unstable, 106, 108, 109, 124; and immoral, 399.
Diagoras, the atheist, 11, 12.
Dicæarchus, peripatetic materialist, 35.
Diet, of Germany, opposed to pope, 233.
Dignity of Labor, taught by Dion Chrysostom, 76; by Clement of Alexandria, 101; in the *Romance of the Rose*, 184; in *Piers' Plowman*, 242, 295.
Diocletian, persecutor of Christianity, 110.
Diogenes Laertius, 95, 98.
Diogenes, of Apollonia, 12.
Diogenes, the Cynic, 31.
Dion Chrysostom, 76, 85, 96.
Dion, of Syracuse, 9, 28.
Dionysius, a bishop who claimed the right to read heretic books, 101, 102.
Dionysius, the Epicurean, 92, 93.
Dionysius, the tyrant, 28, 30.
Diopeithes, intolerant priest, 8.
Divorce, in imperial Rome, 78.
Docetism, 84.
Dolcino, levies war against the Church, 177, 211–213, 221.
Dolet, skeptic and martyr, 358.

Domenico, Fra, mystic and martyr, 322.
Dominic, opponent of Catharism, 164, 167.
Dominicans, as inquisitors, 169. See also Friars, Inquisition, and Monasticism.
Domitian, 75, 76, 96.
Domitius Afer's jest, 64.
Donatists, fanatical levelers, 110, 122.
Door Opener, nickname of Crates, 31.
Droso, inquisitor, 172.
Dubois, Pierre, anti-clerical statesman, 205.
Dumoulin, liberal Catholic, 340.
Durer, Albert, 302.
Dyer, John the, a rebel peasant, 247.
Earth, motion of. taught by Pythagoras and Aristarchus, 58; by Jean de Meung, 185; by Cardinal de Cusa, 259; by Copernicus, 350, 381.
Earthquake Council, condemns Lollards, 247.
Eccelin, anti-papal prince, 172, 183.
Ecclesiastes, Epicurean, 44.
Eckhart, or Echard, mystic, 222–224.
Eclipses, terrify Athenians and Macedonians ruinously, 9, 59.
Education, neglect of, 272; reform proposed by Rabelais, 353, 354.
Edward I., first foe, then friend to English liberty, 195.
Edward III., opposes pope, 233, 238.
Edward VI., 333.
Eleans, or Eleatics, Italian skeptics, 4–6.
Electoral princes, protest against papal tyranny, 232, 233.
Eleusinian mysteries, treated irreverently by Alcibiades, 9; by Diagoras, 12; by Socrates, 21; by Demonax, 95.
Eliacs, Greek skeptics, 29.
Elias, liberal Franciscan, 190.
Elizabeth, of England, 333.
Elizabeth, of Hungary, 172.
Emerson, forerunners of, 129, 160, 223, 225.
Empedocles, patriot and rationalist, 6, 7, 53.

England, resists an interdict, 185; establishes Magna Charta, 186, 194, 195; makes laws against the pope, 238, 249; persecutes the Catharists, 138, and the Lollards, 250; comes late into the Renaissance, 298, 315; welcomes the Reformation, 332, 333; noted for scholarly women, 391.
English literature, begins, 238.
Ennius, Epicurean poet, 50, 51.
Eon, the Star, mystical heretic, 141, 155.
Epicharmus, one of the first to ridicule the gods, 6, 51.
Epictetus, 39, 64, 75, 77, 85.
Epicurus, authorities about, 44, 86, 98; life and character, 42, 43, 46, 49; teachings, 44–49; disciples, 44, 49–51, 62, 63, 90, 92–95, 99, 217.
Episcopalianism, 69, 252, 333.
Equality, social, advocated by Cynics, 30; by Gracchus, 39; by King Cleomenes, 39; by Seneca, 71, 72; by Dion Chrysostom, 76; by the New Testament, 82, 343, 392; by Juvenal, 87; by the Donatists, 110; by the Caputiati, 144; by Freidank, 179; by Reinmar, 180; by Ruteboeuf, 183; by Jean de Meung, 184; by the Stedingers, 188; by Dolcino, 212, 221; by Rienzi, 226; by John Ball, 246; by the Taborites, 254; by Poggio, 277; by Hans Boheim, 304; by Jack Cade, but very moderately, 304; by More, 316; by Cornelius Agrippa, 339; by the German peasants, 343, 345, 392.
Erasmus, as a reformer, 316–319, 336–339, 363.
Eretrians, skeptical philosophers, 29.
Erigena, Johannes Scotus, mystic and rationalist, 128, 129; books burned, 135.
Esclarmonde, Catharist lady, 165–167, 171.
Eternal Gospel, 155, 176, 177.
Eubulides, skeptical philosopher, 29.
Euclid, the geometrician, 57; not to be studied by Christians, 97.
Euclid, the skeptic, 29.
Eudo, or Eon, 141.

Eudoxus, Platonist astronomer, 26.
Eugenius IV., Pope, at war with Council of Basel, 259, 260.
Eunomians, Arian rationalists, 117.
Euripides, against the gods, 11.
Eusebius, 103, 110.
Evangelical Brotherhood, of rebel peasants, 343.
Evemerus, against the gods, 30, 51.
Evolutionism, of early philosophers, 4, 6; of Lucretius, 55; of Cardan 351.
Faith, due to compulsion, 389.
Faith, not to be kept with heretics, 165, 252.
Falais, Lord of, advocates freedom of speech, 371.
False Decretals, when forged, 130; exposed, 142, 277, 281, 301.
False Donation, see Constantine.
Fannia, Stoic heroine, 74, 76, 77.
Farel, pastor at Geneva, 366, 369.
Farinata, imperialist and skeptic, 183, 217.
Fastolf, 263.
Fate, dark views of, 41, 42.
Fathers, of the Church, their narrowness, 83, 84, 107, 108; see also Ambrose, Augustine, Clement, Cyprian, Cyril, Gregory, Jerome, and Tertullian.
Faust, the printer, 303.
Favorinus, assailant of astrology, 87.
Felix, anti-pope, 260.
Ferrara, Council of, 259, 276.
Ferrara, Duchess of, 359.
Ficino, reviver of Platonism, 279, 280.
Fidele, Cassandra, Averroist lecturer, 280.
Figueira, anti-papal troubadour, 179.
Fitzralph, Archbishop, opposed to the begging friars, 238.
Flagellants, 261.
Florence, full of Catharists, 172; center of Renaissance, 235; makes war on pope, 243, 244; rejects hereditary distinctions, 277; seat of a Council, 259, 276; republic, 320, 321.
Flotte, Pierre, anti-papal lawyer, 203.
Folengo, skeptical poet, 357.

Foncelet, opposes persecution, 372.
Four Articles, of the Hussites, 254, 256.
France, chief seat of Catharism, 132, 138; cradle of Mysticism, 129, 155; center of medieval learning, 144; struggles for political liberty, 143; against the inquisition, 169, 170, 202; against the pope, 200–211, 257, 305.
Francis I., patron of Rabelais, 354, 355.
Franciscans, inclined to Mysticism, 177, 178, 218–221; imprison Bacon, 181, 182, and Rabelais, 352. See Friars and Monasticism.
Franck Sebastian, tolerant Mystic, opposed to Calvinism, 373–375.
Fratricelli, Franciscan Mystics, 178, 218–221.
Frederic I., Barbarossa, 142, 143.
Frederic II., his strife with the popes, 187, 188, 190-192; his government, 188–190; his skepticism, 188–190.
Frederic, of Austria, 230, 231.
Free Spirit, Brothers and Sisters of the, heretical Mystics, 221, 222, 261.
Free-will, 277, 330, 342, 367, 371, 374.
Free-Willers, 364.
Freidank, liberal poet, 179.
French Revolution, aided by Plutarch, 86.
Freron, immoral clergyman at Geneva, 371.
Frezzi, anti-clerical poet, 357.
Friars, attacked by William of St. Amour, 181; by Rutebœuf and Jean de Meung, 183, 184; by Archbishop Fitzralph, 238; by Wycliffe, 248; by Bebel, 313; by Erasmus, 336; by Cornelius Agrippa, 339; by Rabelais, 355; by Lyndsay and Buchanan, 361. See Dominicans, Franciscans, and Monasticism.
Fulk, wicked bishop, 168, 217.
Future, of Liberty of Thought, 402.
Galen, 64, 85; an agnostic, 91; not to be studied by Christians, 97; his authority renounced by Paracelsus, 348, 349 and Vesalius, 349.

Galeottus, believer in morality, 278.
Gallicus, lawyer murdered for defending his client, 64.
Gama, Vasco di, discoverer, 296.
Geiler, popular preacher, 303.
Gemistus Pletho, a reviver of Platonism, 276.
Geneva, casts off her bishop, 333; but comes under Calvin, 334; yet shows occasional independence, 371, 372.
Gentilis, Unitarian martyr, 372.
George, archbishop of Alexandria, and champion of England, 114.
Gerard, Catharist, 133.
Gerard, editor of the *Eternal Gospel*, 176.
Germany, Catharists in, 133, 138, 172; mystics, 175, 176, 221–225, 261, 262, 323–325, 373–376; rationalistic poets, 179, 180, 310, 311; free cities, 193; revolts against the pope under Louis of Bavaria, 230–233, and under Luther, 328, 332.
Gerson, leader at Constance, 258, 259.
Gersonides, Jewish rationalist, 235.
Geyer, Florian, leader in the Peasants' war, 344, 345.
Ghibellines, or imperialists, 143, 183, 213, 214.
Gibbon, unjust to Zenobia, 105.
Gilbert, of Poitiers, mystic, 155.
Gnostics, 84, 85, 124, 127.
Goch, German mystic, 323.
Gods of Greece and Rome, assailed by early philosophers and poets, 4–7, 11; by Epicurus, 42; deserving attack, 41.
Götz, von Berlichingen, leader and traitor in the Peasants' war, 344, 345.
Golden Age, according to the *Romance of the Rose*, 185.
Golden Bull, against papacy, 233.
Gorgias, Sophist, 15.
Gottschalk, forerunner of Calvin, 128.
Gracchus, 39, 86.
Gregory, of Nazianzus, 112.
Gregory IX., Pope, 180, 187, 190, 191.
Gregory XI., 262.
Granson, victory of Swiss at, 304.
Gratian, destroyer of Paganism, 116.

Greek, its study revived, 276; punished in Rabelais, 352.
Gribaldi, follower of Servetus, 369, 372.
Gringoire, anti-papal dramatist, 305, 306, 359.
Grostête, Robert, liberal bishop, 181, 194.
Gruet, beheaded for opposing persecution at Geneva, 377–379.
Gryphius, writer against the inquisition, 357.
Guarino, teacher of Greek in Italy, 276.
Guelfs, or papists, 143, 213.
Guicciardini, skeptical historian, 357.
Gunpowder, made effective by Zizka, 254, 269.
Gutenberg, inventor of printing, 302, 303.
Guy, of Auvergne, Templar and martyr, 211.
Guyot, of Provence, satirist, 178.
Gymnastics, forbidden in *Maccabees*, 293.
Hadrian, the emperor, 76, 86–88.
Hanseatic League, 193.
Hanska, martyr for opposing transubstantiation, 255.
Happiness, not diminished by Skepticism, 400, 401.
Hapsburgs, 193.
Hebrew prophets, 1, 3, 78.
Hebrews, see Judaism.
Hegel, anticipated by Heraclitus, 6.
Hegesias, the Orator of Death, 39.
Heimburg, Gregory, 303.
Helfenstein, Count of, slain by the rebel peasants, 344.
Heloise, 144, 146, 151–153.
Helvia, mother of Seneca, 72, 77.
Helvidius, Stoic martyr, 75, 76, 88, 96.
Hemmerlein, Felix, persecuted scholar, 303.
Hemmingstadt, a peasant victory, 304.
Henricians, followers of Henry of Cluny, 141.
Henry of Cluny, also called Henry the Deacon and Henry of Lausanne, early reformer, 141.
Henry II., of England, as a persecutor, 138.
Henry III., at war with Parliament, 194, 195.

Henry IV., and Henry V. as persecutors, 250.
Henry VIII., prophesied, 242; founds a new church, 332, 333; persecutes, 332.
Henry IV., emperor, 135.
Heraclitus, forerunner of Stoicism and Hegelianism, 5–7.
Hereford, Lollard, 248.
Heresy, condemned in New Testament, 81, and by the Church Fathers, 97, 101, 121; persecuted, 112, 117, and often afterwards; consists mainly in obstinacy, 252.
Heretics French, 176.
Hermits, 108.
Hesus, worship of, forbidden, 64.
Hetzer, Unitarian poet and martyr, 364.
Hildebrand, 135.
Hildegard, tolerant abbess, 155.
Hincmar, intolerant archbishop, 128.
Hipparchia, Cynic, 32.
Hipparchus, the astronomer, 58.
Hippias, Sophist, 15.
Hippler, Wendel, leader in the Peasants' war, 345.
Hippo, atheist, 4.
Hippocrates, founder of medicine, 13, 290, 348.
Hoffmann, Melchior, leading Anabaptist, 342.
Hohenlohe, Counts of, fraternize with the peasants, 344.
Hohenstauffen, fall of the, 192.
Homburg, Synod of, intolerant, 346.
Homer, honored like Jesus, 85.
Homoousianism, orthodox, 111.
Hooper, Protestant martyr, 333.
Horace, Epicurean and time-server, 62.
Hosea, against priests, 1.
Hospitallers, their tolerance, 224, 278.
Humanists, 278–279.
Hungary, the Master of, a rebel, 193.
Huss, 251–253, 259.
Hussites, 253–257, 260, 269.
Hutten, the knight-errant of the Reformation, 306, 310, 362, 363.
Hypatia, 114, 120, 124.
Ibn Badja, or Avempace, Moslem mystic, 150.
Ibn Gebirol, Jewish mystic, also known as Avicebron, 135, 136.

Ibn Roshd, see Averroes.
Ibn Tophail, or Abubacer, Moslem mystic, 156.
Iconoclasm, 127.
Iglau, Peace of, 257.
Ignatius, early Father, 83, 87.
Imitation of Christ, 258, 261.
Immorality, in Italy, how caused, 287, 399, 400.
Immortality, questioned by Democritus, 12 ; by Aristotle, 34, 99, 288 ; by Decæarchus, 35 ; by Cicero, 38 ; by Epicurus, 45 ; by Cæsar, 50 ; by Lucretius, 54 ; by Epictetus, 76 ; by Lucian, 94 ; by Alexander of Aphrodisias, 99, 290 ; by the Averroists, 180, 235, 280, 288, 319 ; by Pomponatius, 287–290 ; by Rysswick, 310 ; by Anaptists, 379 ; by Ludovici, 380.
Imperialism, necessarily unstable, 106, 109 ; and immoral, 399.
Index of Prohibited Books, 336.
Indulgencies, condemned by Huss, 251 ; by Wesel, 323 ; by Wessel, 324 ; by Luther, 328 ; by Erasmus, 336, 337.
Innocent III., Pope, persecutor of Catharism, 135, 140, 163–165, 167 ; called a new Judas, 179 ; conquers King John, 185, 186 ; tries to nullify Magna Charta, 186 ; opposes Hanseatic League, 193.
Innocent IV., tries to depose Frederic II., 191 ; and to sell Naples and Sicily, 192.
Innocent VI., sends Rienzi back to Rome, 228.
Innocent VIII., condemns Pico as a heretic, 279 ; is very vicious, 297.
Ionic philosophers, 3–10, 12.
Inquisition, originated, 140 ; fully established in Southern France, 169–177, where it is checked, 202, 220 ; in Italy and Germany, 172, 173, 214, 277, 336 ; in Spain, 281.
Intelligence, nickname of Anaxagoras, 7.
Interdict, resisted by England, 185 ; by Germany, 224, 231, 233 ; by the Stedingers, 188 ; by Christopher I., of Denmark, 194 ; by the Ordelaffi, 236 ; by Huss, 251 ; laid on Jerusalem, 187, and Rome, 142.
Interest, not to be taken by Christians, 107, 295, 296, 330 ; permitted by Frederic II., 189.
Isabella, of Castile, 281.
Isaiah, against priests, 1.
Isis worship, immoral, 57 ; forbidden at Rome, 64.
Islam, see Moslemism.
Isotta, argues that Adam is more to blame than Eve, 280.
Italy, 4, 133, 135, 137, 143, 162, 172, 173, 183, 189, 212, 275, 298, 336. See also Florence, Milan, Rome, Naples, Papacy, Venice.
Jacob, or Jacobell, of Mies, asserts right of all Christians to sacramental cup, 253.
Jacquerie, or peasant rebellion, 237.
Jäger, or Crotus Rubianus, author of *Letters of Obscure Men*, 311.
Jamblichus, Neo-Platonist, 102.
Jeu du Prince des Sots, anti-papal comedy, 305.
Jehovah, forbidden to be worshiped, 64 ; considered an evil deity, 84, 126, 132–139.
Jeremiah, opposes priests, 1.
Jerome, intolerant, 101, 104, 107 ; zealous for monasticism, 108, 120 ; scourged by angels for reading Cicero, 119.
Jerome of Prague, 251–253.
Jesus, 2, 65–70, 79–81, 84, 101, 104, 107, 122, 123, 151, 218, 295, 312, 318, 319, 393.
Jesuits, 336.
Jews, see Judaism.
Joachim, of Floris, Mystic, 155, 176, 218.
Joan, of Arc, 262–268, 314.
Joan, of Aubenton, Mystic, 261.
Joan, of Kent, martyr, 342, 364, 400.
Joanna, of Naples, 127.
Jodelle, writer of anti-clerical comedy, 359.
John, of England, 185–187.
John, of Parma, Mystic, 176.
John, of Ravenna, scholar, 275.
John, of Strasburg, Waldensian martyr, 175, 176.
John, the Apostle, 84, 85, 89.
John, the Dyer, King of Norwich, 247.

John XXII., made pope, 230; persecutes Fratricelli, 218, 221; tries to dethrone the emperor, 230, 231; is burned in effigy, 232; guilty of heresy and rapacity, 232.
John XXIII., deposed, 258.
Joris, David, Anabaptist come-outer, 376.
Jovinian, opponent of monasticism, 120.
Juana, Queen, imprisoned for tolerance, 281, 341.
Jubilee, Papal, 196, 228, 323.
Judaism, its merits, 1, 2. 78, 83, 131, 153, 154, 163, 235, 272; defects, 66, 87, 107, 114, 122, 293, 313; persecuted, 61, 64, 104, 127, 130, 137, 150, 281, 297, 331; tolerated, 36, 105, 189.
Judas Iscariot, Gospel according to, 84.
Judges, Book of, favors rebellion, 79.
Julian, liberal bishop, 121.
Julian, the emperor, 113–115, 124.
Julius II., Pope, his tolerance, 282; his vices, 297, 305–310, 317, 318; in danger of deposition, 305, 309.
Justification by Faith, 81, 323–329, 338, 373.
Justin Martyr, 84, 90, 368.
Justinian, as a persecutor, 101; his *Pandects,* 142.
Juvenal, 77, 85–87, 96.
Kanus, Stoic Martyr, 70.
Kapila, Hindoo skeptic, 3.
Kempis, Thomas à, 262, 323.
Ketzer, derived from Catharist, 133.
King, Robert, opponent of persecution, 364.
Knox, as a champion of political liberty, 351.
Koster, supposed inventor of printing, 302.
Kraut, communistic tailor, 346.
Labienus, patriotic historian, 63.
La Boëtie, patriotic essayist, 351.
Labor, see Dignity of Labor.
Lancaster, defends Wycliffe, 244, 249.
Land Tenure of, 361.
Landgrave of Hesse, champion of the Reformation, 330–332, 345.
Langland's poems, 242, 249, 295, 301.

Langton, patriotic archbishop, 186.
Las Casas, champion of the natives of the West Indies, 346, 347.
Last Age of the Church not written by Wycliffe, 237.
Lateran Council, Fourth, 167; Fifth, 280.
Latimer, Protestant martyr, 333.
Lawyer, murdered for defending his client, 64.
Lecky, testimony to Epicurus, 43.
Leibnitz, aided by Valla, 277.
Leicester, patriotic nobleman, 195.
Leipsic University founded, 251.
Leo, the iconoclast, 127.
Leo X., Pope, 282, 297.
Leon, Athenian patriot, 17.
Leonardo da Vinci, 283–286, 293, 294.
Leontium, Epicurean authoress, 43.
Leucippus, founder of atomism, 12.
Leutard, a mysterious heretic, 131, 132.
L'Hôpital, tolerant legislator, 340.
Libertines, Mystics or rationalists, 377.
Liege, wicked bishop of, 244.
Lipan, battle of, 257.
Lisoi, Catharist martyr, 132.
Literature, checked by Augustus and his successors, 64; revives under constitutional rulers, 85.
Livia, active in politics, 77.
Livy, 64, 287.
Lollards in Germany, 221; in East of England, 248; petition, 249; share in rebellions, 245–248, 251; persecuted, 250, 260; written against by Pecock, 299–301; welcome the Reformation, 332.
London, chooses her own mayor and helps win Magna Charta, 186.
Longfellow, quoted, 214, 215.
Longinus, a lover of liberty, 104, 105.
Loquis, martyred by the Hussites, 255.
Lorraine, Duke of, traitor to the peasants, 344, 345.
Louis, of Bavaria, chosen emperor, 230; protests against opposition of Pope John XXII., 230;

burns him in effigy and appoints a rival pope, 232 ; summoned to Rome by Rienzi, 227; dies under the ban, 233.
Louis IX., opposes the pope, 192, 194.
Louis XI., 302.
Louis XII., opposes the pope, 305.
Lowell, J. R., indebted to Prodicus for his *Parting of the Ways*, 15.
Lucan, patriotic poet, 73, 74.
Lucian, 64, 85, 90-96, 124, 276, 292.
Lucilius, Seneca's friend, 62.
Lucilius, the satirist, 51.
Lucretius, 42, 44, 50-57, 59, 275-277, 280, 292.
Ludovici, poet who disbelieves in immortality, 380.
Lully, Raymond, his method and martyrdom, 229.
Lutatius, historian, 38.
Luther, his Mysticism, 261, 324, 325 ; reforms, 328 ; conservatism, 329-331 ; controversy with Erasmus, 330, 338 ; conduct towards the rebel peasants, 343, 344 ; position about persecution, 331, 364, 375.
Lyceum, Aristotle's, 35.
Lyncurt, defender of Servetus, 372.
Lyndsay, liberal Scottish poet, 346, 360, 361.
Lyons, Poor Men of, name given to the Waldenses, 157.

Maccabees in favor of rebellion, 79; against gymnastics, 293.
Machiavelli, 279, 286, 287, 356.
Mæcenas, patron of Horace and an Epicurean, 62.
Magellan, the discoverer, 296.
Magna Charta, 186, 194-195.
Maillard, popular preacher, 302.
Maimonides, Hebrew philosopher, 154, 156.
Mainz, seat of invention of printing, 303.
Majella, Monte, retreat of mystics, 228.
Man, origin of, 4, 55.
Manes, and Manichæans, 117, 118, 121, 125, 133.
Manfred, anti-papal prince, 192.
Manilius, tries to answer Lucretius, 56.
Mantz, Anabaptist martyr, 363.
Mantovano, anti-papal satirist, 282.
Manzolli, anti-clerical poet, 357.
Map, Walter, anti-clerical poet, 154.
Marcellina, Gnostic, 85.
Marcellus, augur, who exposes augury, 59.
Marcion, Gnostic, 85, 127.
Marcus Aurelius, see Aurelius.
Margaret of the Pocket-Mouth, an heiress, 233.
Margaret of Trent, martial mystic, 212-213.
Margaret, queen of Denmark, 268, 280.
Margaret, queen of Navarre, her writings and tolerance, 340, 357, 359, 377.
Marguerite, d'Argoulême, see Margaret, queen of Navarre.
Margutte, caricature of unbelieving scholar, 282.
Marietta, faithful servant, 203.
Marot, anti-clerical poet, 359.
Marriage, approved by Clement of Alexandria, 101 ; by the Greek Church, 118 ; by Jovinian and Vigilantius, 120 ; by the Paulicians, 127 ; by Bishop Clement of Ireland, 128 ; by Henry of Cluny, 141 ; by the Waldenses, 157 ; by Jean de Meung, 184 ; by Erasmus, 337.
Marsilius, writer against the papacy, 230.
Marsuppini, poet and unbeliever, 277.
Martial, 64.
Martin V., Pope, 280.
Martin, martyred mystic, 262.
Martin, tolerant bishop, 116, 118.
Martyr Justen, 84, 90, 108
Mary, the Bloody, 333.
Marzia, see Ordelaffi.
Masonic lodges, in 12th century, 229.
Masuccio, novelist, 282.
Materialism, of Anaximander and Anaximenes, 4 ; of Heraclitus and Empedocles, 6 ; of Democritus, 12 ; of Strato and Dicæarchus, Peripatetics, 35 ; of the Stoics, 39 ; of Epicurus, 44, 45 ; of Lucretius, 53 ; of Tertullian, 98 ; of the

Averroists, 180, 280; of Pomponatius, 288; of Rysswick, 319.
Mauclerc, nickname of an anti-papal nobleman, 193.
Maximilla, prophetess, 98.
Mayfred, martyred mystic, 177.
Medici, 276, 279, 286—Lucretia dei, 280.
Megaric skeptics, 29, 35.
Megasthenes, early writer about India, 2.
Melanchthon approves of persecution, 346, 364.
Melchiorists, followers of Melchior Hoffmann, and leaders at Münster, 342, 345, 346.
Melissus, an agnostic, 5.
Menno, peaceable Anabaptist, 346.
Mental Culture, advocated by Socrates, 20; by Seneca, 71; by Epictetus, 75; by Gnostics, 84; by Clement of Alexandria, 100; by Averroes, 153; by Pomponatius, 291; by Rabelais, 353; discouraged by Christianity, 81, 84, 90, 97, 119, 180, 183, 272, 291, 318.
Merswin, *Rudolph*, Mystic, 224.
Messala, skeptical Platonist, 38, 64.
Messalina, as a politician, 77.
Metaphysics, ridiculed by Lucian, 93; by Rabelais, 355.
Meton, early astronomer, 8, 26.
Metrodorus, friend of Epicurus, 43.
Meung, Jean de, poet with advanced ideas, 184.
Micah, prophet opposed to priests, 1.
Michael Angelo, 279, 282, 293, 294.
Middle Ages, 268-274.
Mieulx que Devant, comedy, 302.
Milan, a Catharist center, 135, 137; in strife with Frederic I., 143; under the anti-papal Visconti, 235.
Mill, J. S., quoted, 78.
Millennium, 271-274.
Minnesingers, opposed to Rome, 179, 180.
Miracles, exposed by Huss, 251.
Monasticism, a check on transmission of virtue, 108, 120, 125, 272; proved corrupt in Parliament, 332; condemned by cardinals, 336; unfavorable to scholarship, 272, 316, 395; attributed to the devil by Wycliffe, 245; by Procopius, 256; ridiculed by Ariosto, 283; by Wympheling, 311; by Bebel, 313; by More, 316; by Erasmus, 316, 317, 336, 337; by Agrippa, 339; by Rabelais, 354, 355; by Lyndsay and Buchanan, 361.
Monségur, Catharist castle, 166, 171.
Montaigne, 361.
Montanists, heretics who permit women to prophesy, 97, 98, 127.
Montefeltro, *Battista de*, learned lady, 280.
Montfort, crusader against the Albigenses, 165-168.
Montfort, patriotic earl of Leicester, 195.
Morality, improved by skepticism, 20, 290, 398-400; natural to man according to Pelagius, 120; to Sebastian Franck, 374; placed above ceremony by Hebrew prophets, 1; by Jesus, 66-68; by Paulicians, 126, 127; by Catharists, 133-135; by Waldenses, 157; by Mystics, 221; by Wycliffe, 245; by Hussites, 254; by Galeottus, 278; by Mudt, 312; by Erasmus, 317; by Savonarola, 320; by Anabaptists, 342; by Franck, 374; by Schwenckfeld, 375; shown by Erasmus, 338; Servetus, 365, and Thamer, 373, to be holier than faith.
Morat, Swiss victory, 304.
Moravians, derived from Hussites, 257.
More, Sir Thomas, 315, 332, 339.
Moreale, soldier of fortune, 229.
Morgante Maggiore, quoted, 282, 283.
Morgarten, battle of, 230, 304.
Moses, opposes Pharaoh, 1; is set aside by Jesus, 66; is ridiculed by Rysswick, 319; by Gruet, 377, 378.
Moslemism, more enlightened and tolerant than medieval Christianity, 110, 130, 131, 161, 189, 272; but sometimes guilty of persecution, 153-156, 300.
Motazalites, Moslem rationalists, 130, 131, 158.
Mother-taught, nickname of the younger Aristippus, 30.

Mudt, Muth, or Mutianus Rufus, champion of morality against ceremony, 312.
Mühlberg, Lutheran defeat, 332.
Mühldorf, victory of Louis of Bavaria, 230.
Mühlhausen, Anabaptist defeat, 345.
Münster, Anabaptists at, 345, 346.
Münzer, Anabaptist leader, 345.
Munyer, le, farce, 302.
Muth, see Mudt.
Mutianus, Rufus, see Mudt.
Mysticism, defined, 155; inspires Dante, 217-219; Rienzi, 226-229; and Luther, 324, 325; unfit basis for organization, 240, 241; its medieval origin, 155-157.
Mystics, Neo-Platonists, 102; martyrs, 174-178, 202, 220-225, 261-267, 319-325; persecutors, 148, 181; warriors against the church, 212, 213; revolutionists, 329, 342-346; reformers of Lutheranism and Calvinism, 342, 373-376, 379.

Names, pagan, take the place of Christian, 298.
Nancy, Swiss victory at, 304.
Naples, with Frederic II. against the pope, 188.
Nearchus, tyrant of Elea, 5.
Necessarianism, 330.
Negri, skeptical poet, 357.
Neo-Platonism, as originally held, 102-105; its revival attempted by Gemistus Pletho, 276; its influence on Cornelius Agrippa, 313; on Paracelsus, 348; on Servetus, 366.
Nero, and his victims, 62, 71-75; allusions in the *Apocalypse*, 80, 89.
Nerva, rules constitutionally, 76, 96.
Nicæa, Council of, 111, 112, 118.
Niccolini, his drama on Arnold of Brescia, 143.
Nicene Creed, 111, 216.
Nicholas, of Autricuria, agnostic, 235.
Nicholas, of Basel, martyred mystic, falsely supposed to have instructed Tauler, 225, 262.
Nicholas, of Verona, opponent of transubstantiation, 278.

Nicholas IV, Pope, persecutes Bacon, 183.
Nicholas V., Pope, patron of the Renaissance, 260, 276-278.
Nicias, ruined by his superstition, 9.
Nine Rocks, mystical book, 224.
Nobility, hereditary, assailed by Seneca, 72; by Juvenal, 87; by Freidank, 179; by Reinmar, 180; by Jean de Meung, 184; by Poggio, 277; by Cornelius Agrippa, 339; discarded at Florence, 277.
Nogaret, William de, conqueror of Boniface VIII., 204-207.
Nominalism, exposure of the unreality of abstractions, 103, 136, 137, 145, 234, 257.
Novara, Georgio, Unitarian martyr, 281.
Nude, study of the, 293, 294.

Oath, to suppress Lollardism, 247.
Obscure Men, Letters of, 310, 311.
Occam, see Ockham.
Oceanic discovery, 296.
Ochino, a Unitarian, 371, 372.
Ockham, anti-papal author, 205, 218, 234; his nominalism and agnosticism, 234.
Octavia, patron of Virgil, 77.
Octavius, see Augustus.
Odenathus, husband of Zenobia, 104, 105.
Œdipus, 41.
Oldcastle, Sir John, Lollard martyr and original of Falstaff, 250.
Old Testament, censured by Julian, 114; by Erasmus, 338; rejected by Gnostics, 84; by Paulicians, 126; by Catharists, 134.
Olgiati, assassin of Duke of Milan, 279.
Oliva, Peter John, anti-papal Franciscan, 177.
Ophites, Gnostic serpent worshipers, 84.
Orator of Death, name given to Hegesias the Cyrenaic, 30.
Ordeal, opposed by Bishop Agobard, 129; used to detect heretics, 172, 175; forbidden by Frederick II., 189; appealed to by Savonarola, 322.
Ordelaffi, Francesco, and Marzia,

at war with popes and crusaders, 236, 237.
Order of Nature, taught by Democritus 12; by Cleanthes, 40; by Epicurus, 44, 45: by Lucretius, 53; by Averroists, 180; by Aristotle, 291; by Pomponatius, 291; by Cardan, 351.
Origen, Christian rationalist, 90, 101, 128, 396.
Orphans, party among the Hussites, 255-257.
Ortlieb, mystic heresiarch, 175.
Otho, emperor supported by the senate, 79.
Ovid, why banished, 63.
Oxford, Provisions of, in confirmation of Magna Charta, 195.
Oxford theologians, against Wycliffe, 247.

Pacuvius, Epicurean poet, 51.
Padilla, Spanish patriot, 341.
Padua, center of Averroism, 280, 358.
Pætus, see Pœtus.
Painting, 292-295, 302.
Palingenius, skeptical poet, 357.
Panætius, Stoic who opposed augury, 40.
Pandects, discovered in Italy, 142.
Pandolf, Roman republican, 229.
Pantænus, teacher of Clement of Alexandria, 99, 100.
Pantagruel's prayer, 353.
Pantheism, of Xenophanes, 5; of Erigena, 129; of Amalric, 157, 174, 175; of Eckhart and other German mystics, 221-223; of Servetus, 366.
Papacy, a logical development of Christianity, 68, 69, 83, 270, 271; attacked by Marsilius, 230; by Ockham, 234; by Wycliffe, 248; by Huss, 252; by Luther, 328; censured by medieval satirists, 178-180; by Dante, 214-217; by Tauler, 224, 225; by Langland, 242; by Machiavelli, 287, 356; by Hutten, 310; by Erasmus, 316, 318; by Savonarola, 321; by Cornelius Agrippa, 339; claimed by a woman, 177; claims absolute power, 201, 203, 204, 327; disgraced by immorality, 207, 287, 296, 297, 341; in captivity at Avignon, 207; propped up by fraud, 130, 273; resisted by John of England, 185, 186; by Frederic II., 187, 188, 190, 191; by Louis IX., 194; by Philip the Fair, 203-206; by Louis of Bavaria, 232, 233; by Visconti, 235; by Ordelaffi, 236, 237; by Parliament, 238, 243, 349, 332; by Florence, 243; by Bohemia, 253-257; by Councils, 257-260; by Caterina Sforza, 280, 281; by Louis XII., 305; ridiculed by Andrelini, 306-310; Rabelais, 354.
Paphnutius, saves Eastern Church from sacerdotal celibacy, 118.
Paracelsus, the Luther of medicine, 347-349.
Paris, center of medieval learning, 144.
Paris, George van, Unitarian martyr, 364.
Parker, Theodore, compared to Tauler, 225.
Parliament, admits representatives of cities, 195; at war with Henry III., 195; deposes Richard II., 249; resists papacy, 238, 242-244, 249, 332; the Good Parliament, 243; the Mad Parliament, 194.
Parmenides, skeptic, noted for virtue, 4, 29.
Parson's Tale, not by Chaucer, 249.
Pastoral visits, established at Geneva, 334.
Paterines, Italian Catharists, 135.
Paul II., Pope, 279, 281, 297.
Paul III., Pope, 336.
Paul IV., Pope, 336.
Paul, the Apostle, 67, 78-82, 85, 103, 107, 114, 115, 122, 126, 338, 393.
Paulicians, liberal Christian sect, 126-128.
Payne, English Taborite, 256.
Peasants, as rebels, 110, 122, 144, 163, 188, 212, 213, 230, 237, 245-247, 251, 253-357, 269, 304, 305, 342-345; as warriors otherwise, 304.
Pecock, rationalistic bishop, 299-301.
Pedro II., King of Arragon and protector of Catharism, 164-167.
Pelagius, heretic who teaches that virtue is natural to man, 120, 121.

Pelerin Passant, satire on Louis XII., 305.
Pelopidas, ruined by superstition, 9.
Peregrinus Proteus, hero of Lucian's satire on Christianity, 91.
Peretto, nickname of Pomponatius, 288.
Pericles, persecuted for following Anaxagoras and Protagoras, 7-9, 14.
Peripatetics, see Aristotle, also 35, 38, 44, 90, 99.
Perrin, judge friendly to Servetus at Geneva, 369.
Persecution, fatal to Phidias, 8, 9; to Socrates, 24; to Cremutius Cordus, 70; to Thrasea, 74; to Ignatius, 87; to Polycarp, 90; to Origen, 101, 109; to Hypatia, 114; to Priscillian, 117; to Paulicians, 127; to Catharists, 131-133, 138, 164-166, 169-174; to Mystics, 174-177, 221, 255, 261; to Cecco of Ascoli, 235; to Lollards, 250; to Huss, 253, 259; to Joan of Arc, 267; to Rysswick, 319; to Savonarola, 322; to Anglican Protestants, 332, 333; to Anabaptists, 342, 345, 363, 364; to Dolet, 358; to Servetus, 369; to other Unitarians, 281, 364, 372; to Gruet, 379; ruinous to Athenian liberty, 9, 10; to Roman literature, 64; sanctioned by the Bible, 69, 80, 81, 122, 264, 315, 378.
Persians, tolerant to philosophy, 7.
Peter Martyr, assassinated inquisitor, 172.
Peter of Bruis, reformer and martyr, 140, 141, 160.
Peter, the Apostle, 78-82, 103, 104, 114, 116, 123, 126, 140, 309, 313
Peter, see also Pierre and Pietro.
Petrarch, pioneer of the Renaissance, 207, 235, 275, 276, 280.
Pfefferkorn, persecutor of Judaism, 311.
Phædo, skeptical disciple of Socrates, 29.
Pharisees, 67.
Phidias, persecuted for philosophy, 8, 9.
Philip Augustus, 185, 186.
Philip, of Hesse, champion of the Reformation, 330-332, 345, 346.

Philip, the Fair, conqueror of Pope Boniface VIII., 201-211, 217, 220.
Philip, the Magnanimous, see Philip of Hesse.
Philiscus, banished for teaching Epicureanism, 49.
Philodemus, Epicurean, 50.
Philosophy, compared to one of the plagues of Egypt, 119.
Philpot, persecutor and martyr, 365.
Philumene, learned Gnostic authoress, 85.
Physicians, their services to freedom, 347, 393.
Pico, of Mirandola, rationalist, 279, 280, 315.
Picquigny, Jean de, assailant of the Inquisition, 220.
Pierre, of Saint Cloud, an author of *Reynard the Fox,* 178.
Piers Plowman's Vision, 242.
Piers Plowman's Crede, 249.
Pietro, of Abano, skeptical physician, 202, 235.
Pisa, first Council of, 257, 258; second, 305, 309, 315.
Pius II., 260, 286.
Pius III., 297.
Plato, dialogues, 14, 24-27, 77, 107, 156; influence during Middle Ages, 128, 156; influence at Renaissance, 275, 276, 279, 280; thought inspired, 100, 374; and infallible, 102, 103; honored like Jesus, 85; life, 27, 28.
Platonic Academy, 279.
Platonism, skeptical, 28, 38, 386.
Platonists, 28, 38, 44, 90, 92, 103, 128, 276, 279.
Pletho, reviver of Neo-Platonism, 276.
Pliny, the naturalist, 62-64, 290.
Pliny, the younger, 64, 85-88.
Plotinus, Neo-Platonist, 102, 103.
Plutarch, influence at Renaissance, 275, 276, 279; misrepresents Epicurus, 46; writings otherwise, 77, 85, 86, 96.
Podiebrad, George, tolerant king of Bohemia, 260.
Pœtus, husband of Arria, 70.
Poggio, free-speaking scholar, 277, 278, 298, 335.
Poland, tolerant, 372.
Polybius, 38.

452　　　　　　　　*INDEX.*

Polyhistor, Alexander, 2.
Political liberty, closely connected with religious liberty, 391, 394, 395; defended by Thales, 4; by Zeno the skeptic, 5; by Empedocles, 6, 7; by Stoics, 39, 70–76, 86–89, 96; by Plutarch and Tacitus, 86; by Donatists, 110; by Arnold, 142, 143; by French, German and Italian cities, 143, 162, 193; by Caputiati, 144; by Jean de Meung, 185; by Rienzi, 225–228; by Walter the Tyler, 246, 247; by Hussites, 254; by Humanists, 278–279; by Cade, 304, 305; by More, 316; by Savonarola, 321; by German peasants, 342–345; by La Boëtie, Knox, Poynet, and Aylmer, 351; by Lyndsay, 361; by Hutten and Sickingen, 363; opposed by Plato, 27; in the New Testament, 66, 79.
Pollio, founder of first public library at Rome, 59, 64.
Polycarp, Christian martyr, 83, 90.
Pomponatius, skeptic, 287, 291, 297.
Pontano, anti-papal satirist, 282.
Poor Men of Lyons, or Waldenses, 157.
Poor Priests, Lollard itinerants, 245.
Popular Education, among Waldenses, 158; among Hussites, 254; more common in Moslem than in Christian lands, 272.
Porcaro, Roman Patriot, 278.
Porphyry, rationalist and biblical critic, 103–106, 116, 124.
Porretta, Margaret, martyred mystic, 221.
Portia, the Stoic heroine, 39, 77, 80.
Posidonius, Stoic honoring mechanical invention, 107.
Postel, defender of natural religion, 380.
Poverty of Jesus, considered absolute by Dante and the Franciscan mystics, 218–220.
Poynet, Bishop, advocate of regicide, 351.
Prague, revolts against the pope, 251–255.
Præmunire, Statute of, a check on papal power, 238, 249.

Pragmatic Sanctions, anti-papal measures, 194, 260.
Prick of Conscience, early English book, 237.
Printing, 292, 302, 303.
Priscillian, first martyr under Christian rule, 117, 118, 122, 125.
Procopius, Hussite general, 255–257.
Prodicus, Sophist and moralist, 15, 21.
Promiscuous charity, censured, 71, 120.
Property, incompatible with Golden Age, 185.
Protestants, first called so, 331. See also Reformation.
Protagoras, first Sophist, 14, 15.
Provisions of Oxford, confirm Magna Charta, 194, 195.
Provisors, Statute against, passed to check papal aggression, 238, 249.
Ptolemy Soter, king of Egypt and patron of science, 36, 57.
Ptolemy, the astronomer, criticised by Bacon, 182; by Copernicus, 350.
Pulci, skeptical poet, 280, 282.
Pungiloro, Catharist thought worthy of canonization, 173.
Pyrrho, founder of sect of Skeptics, 36, 37, 57, 114, 123, 398, 400, 401.
Pythagoras, not a free-thinker, 4; his influence over Plato, 25, 27; honored like Jesus, 85; superstition, 313; system of astronomy, 58, 259, 286.

Quarto-decimans, heretics, 117.

Rabelais, imprisoned for studying Greek, 352; real position, 352, 356; ridicule of Lent, metaphysics, monasticism and the papacy, 354, 355; suggestions about education, 353.
Rabirius, an Epicurean poet, 50.
Rambam, name given to Maimonides, 154.
Ramus, critic of Aristotle, 350.
Raphael, 293, 294.
Rationalism, of Greek and Roman philosophers, 4–60, 71, 75, 91–96, 103–106; of Gnostics, 84, 85;

of Clement of Alexandria, 100; of Origen, 101; of Eunomians and Manicheans, 117, 118; of Erigena, 129; of Berengar, 135; of Roscellin, 136; of Abelard, 144, 145, 149, 150; of Averroes, 153; of Maimonides, 154; of Simon of Tournay, 160; of Catharists, 174; of Averroists, 180, 235, 280; of Farinata, 183; of Frederic II., 189, 190; of Ockham and his contemporaries, 234, 235; of Pulci, 282, 283; of Leonardo da Vinci, 283-286; of Pomponatius, 287-291; of Pecock, 299-301; of Raymond, 300; Mudt, 312; Erasmus, 318, 329, 338; of Rysswick, 319; of Agrippa, 339; of Rabelais, 356; of Dolet, 358; of Hutten, 362; of Servetus, 365, 366; of Gruet and other unbelievers, 377-380; favorable to morality, 20, 290, 398-400.

Rationalists in Politics, 391-395.

Raymond, of Sabicude, or Sabunde, rationalist, 300.

Raymond Roger, persecuted viscount of Béziers, 164, 165.

Raymond VI., Count of Toulouse, persecuted for tolerance, 164-168, 187.

Raymond VII., son of Raymond VI., 168, 169.

Ravenna, early heresy at, 131.

Realism, 103, 136, 137, 144.

Red flag of Liberty, 226, 243, 344.

Reformation, causes, 325-328, limitations, 329, 331, 333, 347, 370, 373; progress in Germany, 328-332, 373-376; in England, 332, 333; in Switzerland, 331-335, 372; and in other countries, 335.

Regenbogen, liberal German poet, 183.

Regicide, advocated by Seneca, 73, and by Bishop Poynet, 351.

Reign of the Spirit, 155, 176, 177, 225-229, 261.

Reinmar, singer of new truth, 180.

Relic-worship, opposed by Jovinian and Vigilantius, 120.

Religion, attacked by Epicurus and Lucretius, 142.

Renato, censures the murder of Servetus, 371, 372.

Renouncing, when perjury, 252.

Reuchlin, founder of Christian study of the old Testament, 311, 313.

Revelation, of John, its meaning, 80.

Revival of Letters, 275-283.

Reynard the Fox, the unholy bible, 178, 184, 303.

Riario, tyrant of Forli, 280.

Richard I., of England, dies under the ban, 185.

Richard II., deposed by Parliament, 249.

Ridley, Protestant martyr, 333.

Robin Hood, a real character, 195.

Roger Bernard, early advocate of religious liberty, 168.

Roger, heretical viscount of Béziers, 139, 140.

Rogers, Protestant martyr, 333.

Rohan, Adamite leader, 255.

Rolle, Richard, writer against Rome, 237.

Rome, republican, 38, 49-57, 60; imperial, 61-64, 70-78, 85-91, 106-109, 116; in revolt against the papacy, 141, 143, 187, 231, 232, 278, 336; liberated by Rienzi, 225-229; visited by 2,000,000 pilgrims, 196; fall from power prophesied, 155, 180, 302, 303, 310.

Romans, Epistle to the, censured by Erasmus, 338.

Roscellin, Nominalist, 136, 137, 144, 147.

Rose, Romance of the, 184.

Roses, Wars of the, 298.

Rowe, translator of Lucan, quoted, 73.

Rubianus, Crotus, see Jäger.

Rufus, champion of right of women to study philosophy, 75.

Runnymede, Magna Charta signed there, 186.

Rutebœuf, anti-monastic satirist, 183.

Rysswick, martyred rationalist, 319.

Sabbath, ridiculed by Juvenal, 87. See also Sunday.

Sabellianism, 147, 365, 372.

Saccas, see Ammonius Saccas.

Sachsenhausen, protest at, 230.

Sadducees, 69, 83.

St. John, Knights of, see Hospitallers.

Saladin, 154, 159.
Salinguerra, anti-papal soldier, 183.
Salutato, Coluccio, defender of classic poetry against the monks, 276.
Samos, philosophers of, 4, 42, 58.
Sanitary laws, punishment for proposing, 347.
Sankhya philosophy, 3.
Sannazzaro, anti-papal satirist, 282.
Satirists, English, 242, 249, 316; French, 178, 183–185, 305–310, 352–360; German, 179, 303, 310, 313, 339, 340, 362; Greek, 6, 91–95; Italian, 277, 282, 283, 356, 357; Roman, 74, 77, 87; Scotch, 360–362; Erasmus, 316–318, 336, 337.
Sautre, Lollard martyr, 250.
Savonarola, 315, 319–322.
Schism, the great, 244–5, 258.
Schmidt, Conrad, martyred mystic, 261.
Schwenckfeld, champion of morality against theology and ceremony, 375.
Schwestriones, German mystics, 222.
Schwytz, at war with the Church, 141, 142.
Sciarra Colonna, enemy of the pope, 205–207, 231.
Scientific methods, advocated by Ionic philosophers, 3–9; by Democritus, 12; by Hippocrates, 13; by Aristotle, 32, 33; by Stoics, 40; by Epicurus, 44, 45; by Lucretius, 52; by Lucilius, 62; by Pliny, 62, 63; by Galen, 91; by Roger Bacon, 181–183; in *Romance of the Rose*, 185; by Pietro of Abano, 202; by Nicholas of Autricuria, 235; by Leonardo da Vinci, 284–286; by Paracelsus, 347, 348; by Vesalius, 349; by Copernicus and Vives, 350; by Cardan, 350; 351; summary of the above, 385, 386.
Scott, Michael, an Averroist, 180, 189, 217.
Scotus, see Erigena.
Secret Societies, 95.
Segarelli, martyred mystic, 177, 212.
Sempach, peasant victory, 304.

Senate, a persecutor of philosophy, 38; refuge of Roman liberty, 63, 73–75, 77, 79, 86, 88, 96.
Seneca, 39, 44, 64, 70–75, 107, 123, 182, 275, 290.
Sens, Council of, 152.
Sepulveda, defender of right to conquer the heathen, 347.
Servetus, Unitarian martyr, 365–369.
Servilia, Stoic martyr, 75, 77.
Sextus Empiricus, skeptic, 37, 99.
Sforza, Caterina, 280, 281.
Sforza, Galeazzo, tyrant of Milan, 279.
Sforza, Ippolita, learned lady, 280.
Shakespeare, Italian materials, 282; injustice to Jack Cade, 304, 305.
Sharp, Jack, English rebel, 251.
Sibylline books, destroyed by Augustus, 64; others forged by Christians, 89.
Sic et Non, skeptical treatise by Abelard, 149, 150.
Sicilian philosophy, 6, 7; legislation of Frederic II., 188, 189; vespers, 192, 193.
Sickingen, ally of Hutten, 362, 363.
Sigier, teacher of hated truth, 217.
Sigismund, convokes council of Constance, 258; makes war on Bohemia, 253–257.
Sigismund, tolerant king of Poland, 372.
Simeon, Paulician martyr, 127.
Simon, of Tournay, rationalist, 160.
Siricius, pope, favorable to celibacy, 118.
Sisterers, heretical mystics, 222.
Sixtus IV., pope, tolerant, 278; immoral, 297.
Skepticism, favorable to happiness, 30, 37, 400, 401; productive of virtue, 20, 290, 398–400.
Skeptics, members of the sect, 36, 37, 99, 114; Lucian, 91–96; Abelard, 150; Frederic II., 189, 190; Ockham, 234; Pomponatius, 287–291; Erasmus, 318, 329, 338; Rysswick, 319; Agrippa, 339; Rabelais, 356; Dolet, 358; Gruet, 377–379. See also Rationalism.
Slavery, denounced by Dion Chrysostom, 76; by Donatists, 110;

sanctioned by Aristotle, 33 ; by New Testament, 79; position of Socrates, 18 ; of Seneca, 71–73 ; of Las Casas, 347.
Social equality, see Equality.
Socinus Lælius, Unitarian, 372.
Socrates, 14–29, 84, 122, 386.
Soissons, Council of, 147, 148.
Solo, Doctor da, anti-Christian astrologer, 281.
Song of Solomon, called immoral, 370.
Sophia, the Wisdom, nickname of Protagoras, 14.
Sophists, vindicated against misrepresentation, 14–16.
Soranus, Stoic martyr, 75.
Sorcery, 232.
Speech, freedom of, claimed by Socrates, 19, 20 ; by the Cynics, 30–32, 75 ; by Jesus, 65 ; by Helvidius, 75 ; by Cremutius Cordus, 86 ; by Reinmar, 180 ; by Bishop Pecock, 300 ; by More, 316 ; by Erasmus, 337 ; by Rabelais, 353 ; by Dolet, 358 ; by Servetus, 368 ; by Bourgogne, 371 ; by Renato, 371 ; by Bünderlin, 376 ; by Gruet, 377 ; permitted by Athens, 35 ; by Julius Cæsar, 50, 63 ; by Roman Republic, 59 ; by Stoic emperors, 87 ; by Catharists, 135, 139 ; by Taborites, 257 ; by popes, 281, 282 ; by Louis XII., 305.
Speusippus, a Platonist, 28.
Spifame, practical reformer, 347.
Spirit, age of the, 155, 176, 177, 212, 225–229, 343.
Spirit, Brothers and Sisters of the Free, 221, 222, 261, 377.
Spirituales, Franciscan mystics, 218.
Stabat Mater, 220.
Stafford, tries to kill Joan of Arc, 265.
States General resist the Pope, 203; condemn the Templars, 209.
Staupitz, instructor of Luther, 324.
Stedingers, peasants at war with knights and priests, 163, 188.
Stenckfeld, nickname of Schwenckfeld, 375.
Stephen, Catharist martyr, 132.
Stilpo, skeptic, 29.
Stoics, as teachers, 38–41, 58, 93, 94,
99 ; as martyrs for liberty, 70–76 ; as rulers, 85–90.
Strasburg, opposed to interdict, 231 ; masonic center, 229 ; mystics, 175, 176, 221, 224, 261, 262, 375, 370.
Strato, atheistic Peripatetic, 35.
Stylites, Simeon, hermit, 108.
Suetonius, 85, 86
Sufism, 156.
Suger, liberal abbot, 148.
Sulpicia, satirist, 77.
Sulpicius, philosophic priest, 40.
Summary, of ancient history, 122–125 ; of thirteenth century, 196–199 ; of Middle Ages, 268–274 ; of Reformation, 380–384 ; of scientific positivism, 385, 386 ; of philosophic skepticism, 386, 387 ; of mysticism, 387 ; of growth of tolerance, 387–389 ; of emancipation of women, 389–391 ; of rise of political liberty, 391 ; of biblical criticism, 396, 397.

Tabor, Hussite city, noted for tolerance, 254, 257.
Taborites, 254–257.
Tacitus, 77, 85, 86, 96.
Talbot, conquered by Joan of Arc, 263.
Talmud, not to be studied by Christians, 183, 201, 311.
Tanchelm, heretical enthusiast, 140, 155.
Tauler, independent mystic, 224, 262.
Taxing nobility and clergy proposed in vain, 347.
Tell, William, 230.
Templars, not heretics, but not innocent of crime, 188, 201, 208–211.
Tephrica, the Paulician capital, 127.
Tertullian, as a reactionist, 97, 98, 121, 124.
Thales, founder of Greek philosophy, 3.
Thamer, champion of morality against Lutheranism, 372, 373.
Theano, wife of Pythagoras and writer on philosophy, 4.
Theater, at work for freedom, 6, 11, 51, 282, 302, 305, 359–361.
Thelema, Abbey of, 354.
Theodosius, as a persecutor, 116, 117

Thibaud, tolerant crusader, 179.
Theodore, the Atheist. 30.
Theologaster, farce, 359.
Theologia Germanica, 224, 261, 325.
Theophilus, destroyer of the Alexandrian library, 116.
Theophrast, opposes sacrifices, 35.
Thirty tyrants at Athens, 17, 21.
Thrasea, martyr for liberty, 70, 74–76, 79, 88, 96.
Thrasybulus, liberator of Athens, 16.
Thucydides, 7, 9, 38.
Tiberius, 64, 65, 70, 77, 79, 96.
Tibullus, independent poet, 64.
Timæus, Plato's, 103, 156.
Times, published where Wycliffe was condemned, 247, 248.
Titian, 173.
Tiziano, disbeliever in the Bible, 380.
Todi, Jacopone da, mystic, 220.
Tolerance, practiced by Buddhists, 2; by Persians, 7; by Athenians, 35, 43, 60; by Macedonians, 44; by Julius Cæsar, 50; by Roman republic, 59; by Jews, 83; by Hadrian and Antoninus Pius, 87; by Zenobia, 105; by Constantine, 110; by Julian, 113; by Moslems, 130, 131; by Languedocians, 135, 138, 162, 164, 168; by Frederic II., 188, 189; by Philip the Fair, 202, 203; by Taborites, 257; by Renaissance popes, 281, 282; by Louis XII., 305; by Philip of Hesse, 332; by Bavaria, Austria, Bohemia, Poland, and Venice, 335, 365, 372; by Margaret of Navarre, 340; taught by Stoics, 72; by Tacitus, 86; by Hildegard, 155; by Reinmar, 180; in *Orchard Vision*, 302; by More, 316; by Erasmus, 337; by Rabelais, 353, 355; by Dolet, 358; by Servetus, 368; by many who regretted his death, 369, 372; by Franck, 373, 374; by Bünderlin, 375; its growth corresponds to that of unbelief, 389.
Trajan, 86–88, 108, 216, 217.
Transcendentalism, defined, 102; Neo-Platonic, 102, 103; Christian, 156, 160, 223, 299, 374.
Transubstantiation, attacked by Erigena, 129; by Berengar, 135; by Wycliffe, 247; by Hanska, 255; by Nicholas of Verona, 278; by Zwingli, 363; by Anne Ascue, 332, 333; by other English martyrs, 364.
Trent, Council of, 336.
Triangle, showing where medieval thought was most active, 240.
Trissino, anti-clerical poet, 357.
Troubadours, 154, 162, 178, 179.
Turlupins, heretic mystics, 261.
Twelve Articles, of the peasants, 343.
Tyler, Walter the, 246, 247.
Tyre, Old Man of, see Porphyry.

Ulfilas, translator of the Bible, 116.
Understanding, Men of, heretical mystics, 261.
Unitarianism, of the Artemonites, 97; of Arians, 111; of Catharists, 134; of Georgio Novaro, 281; of Campanus, 363; of Hetzer, Joan Bocher, and George van Paris, 364; of Servetus, 365–370; of Gribaldi, Gentilis, and Blandrata, 372; of Denck, 376.
Universalism, of Carpocrates, 85; of Origen, 101; Erigena, 129; of Catharists, 139; of Pierre Cardinal, 170; of Strasburg Communists, 221; of Men of Understanding, 261; of Anabaptists, 342; of John Denck, 376.
Universities, English, 247, 298; German, 251, 303; Italian, 190, 272, 280, 287, 358; Paris, 160, 162, 174, 257; Prague, 251, 252.
Urban V., Pope, resisted by Parliament, 242.
Utilitarianism, of Democritus, 13; of Protagoras, 14; of Socrates, 18, 19; of Plato, 27; of Aristippus, 29; of Aristotle, 33, 34; of Stoics, 39, 40, 75; of Epicurus, 45–48; of Valla, 276, 277; of Pomponatius, 290; of More, 316.
Utopia, 315, 316.
Utraquism, or right of all Christians to communion cup, 253.

Valens, opponent of Monasticism, 108; persecutor, 115.

Valentine, Gnostic, 85.
Valla, independent scholar, 276, 277.
Varro, defender of religion as expedient to the community, 38, 59.
Vatican, the prison of Boniface VIII., 206, 220; enriched with a library, 276; turned into a harem, 297.
Vaticanus, nom de plume of Bolsec, 371.
Veiento, banished for attacking priests, 62.
Venice, noted for tolerance, 173, 335, 365, 389; for Averroism, 235; for printing, 292.
Venus, displeased at chastity, 41.
Vergerio, too tolerant Protestant, 372.
Vernias, Averroist, 280.
Vesalius, disproves Galen's infallibility, 349.
Vicenza, noted for Unitarianism, 365.
Vidal, troubadour, 154.
Vidal, Jewish rationalist, 235.
Vienne, Council of, 207, 210.
Vigilantius, assails monasticism, sacerdotal celibacy, and indiscriminate charity, 120.
Vilgard, mysterious heretic, 131.
Villena, Averroist, 280.
Villeneuve, see Servetus.
Vinci, Leonardo da, 283–286.
Virgil, liberal bishop, 128.
Virgil, the poet, 56, 63, 77, 131.
Virgins, Champions of the, 172, 173.
Vischer, Peter, 302.
Visconti, oppose pope, 235.
Vision of Piers Plowman, 242.
Vitellius, 79.
Vives, assails Aristotle's infallibility, 350.

Waldenses, founded by Waldo, 157, 158; inclined to mysticism, 158, 175, 229, 261; persecuted, 165, 175, 176, 189, 202, 229, 261.
Wallace, 200.
Walter of the Vogelweide, antipapal poet, 179.
Walter, founder of the Lollard sect of mystics, 221.
Walter, the Tyler, rebel leader, 246, 247.
War, opposed by Jesus, 66; by early Christians, 108; by Dante, 215; by Langland, 242; by Huss, 251; by Christine de Pisan, 301; by author of *Orchard Vision*, 302; by Andrelini, 309; by Las Casas, 346, 347; by Franck, 373.
Weavers, name given to the Albigenses, 135.
Weeping Philosopher, nickname of Heraclitus, 5.
Weinsberg, massacre at, 344.
Wesel, John of, persecuted mystic, 323, 324.
Wessel, John, mystic, 324.
Westminster, Statutes of, confirm Magna Charta, 195.
White Cross, Knight of the, noted for tolerance, 224, 278.
Wilhelmina, mystic Messiah, 177.
William, of Champeaux, Realist, 144, 146.
William, of Hildesheim, mystic, charged with Universalism, 261.
William, of Ockham, see Ockham.
William, of St. Amour, opponent of monasticism, 181.
William Rufus, 136.
William, the Conqueror, 135.
William, the Goldsmith, pantheistic mystic, 175.
Winkelers, Waldensian mystics, 261.
Witchcraft, existence denied by Agobard, 129; by Alciati, 351; often punished in 15th and 16th centuries, 281, 334.
Women, as authors, 4, 43, 77, 151, 155, 301; as heretics, 132, 166, 177, 261; as philosophers, 4, 7, 30, 32, 43, 76, 77, 99, 100, 120, 280; as rulers, 105, 268, 340, 341, 359; as soldiers, 168, 171, 212, 236, 237, 254, 263, 281, 345; completely emancipated in pagan Rome, 77, 78, 87, 96; sent back to subjection by the apostles, 78, 79; permitted to preach by heretics, 97, 98, 157, 254; looked to for a new Messiah, 177, 380; entitled to mental culture according to Seneca, 71, 72; to Plutarch, 77, 86; to Clement of Alexandria, 100; to Averroes, 154; to Pierre Dubois, 205; to Chaucer, 250; to Cornelius Agrippa, 313–315; to Erasmus,

337; furnished with schools, 303, 304; their emancipation closely connected with growth of intellectual liberty, 389–391, 402.
Worms, Diet of, 363.
Worship, forbidden as immoral, 57.
Würtemberg, conquest of, 331, 332.
Wycliffe, founder of Protestantism, 241; tried for heresy, 244, 259; his reforms, 245, 248; his influence in Bohemia, 251.
Wympheling, on monks, 311.

Xanthippe, her ill temper exaggerated, 17.
Xenocrates, Platonist, 28.
Xenophanes, early Pantheist, 4, 5, 7, 29.

Xenophon, account of Socrates, 17–20; own character, 22.

Yellow cross, imposed on heretics, 170.

Zebedee, tolerant Calvinist, 369.
Zeno, the skeptic, 5,
Zeno, the Stoic, 29, 38–40, 46.
Zenobia, 104–106, 124, 388.
Zizka, Hussite general, 253–255, 269.
Zoroaster, honored like Jesus, 85.
Zurkinden, advocate of tolerance, 370.
Zwickau, Prophets of, 343.
Zwingli, 331, 363.

www.ingramcontent.com/pod-product-compliance
Lightning Source LLC
Chambersburg PA
CBHW022113300426
44117CB00007B/690